JOHN CAREW ROLFE

CLASSICAL STUDIES
IN HONOR OF
JOHN C. ROLFE

EDITED BY
GEORGE DEPUE HADZSITS

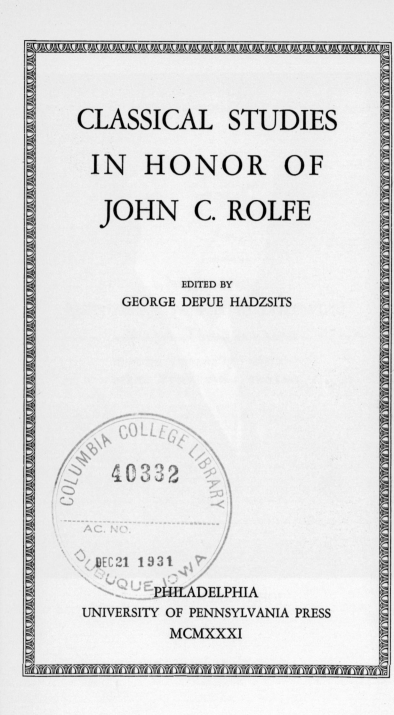
PHILADELPHIA
UNIVERSITY OF PENNSYLVANIA PRESS
MCMXXXI

CONTENTS

v

CLASSICAL STUDIES

ILLUSTRATIONS

PREFACE

It is as a tribute of affection and esteem that we offer this Honor Volume to Professor John Carew Rolfe.

His distinguished services are known to all classical students and friends of classical studies. The bibliographical record that appears on pages 345–352 is an eloquent statement of a life of intellectual interests and of great learning. This record gives no clue, however, to the many ways in which Professor Rolfe has always, most generously, given of his time and experience to sustain the Classical Cause. His closest friends are deeply aware of that generosity, which is a fine expression of a character, notable for its devotion and tolerance.

It is only fitting that we should record, here, a few of the honors that have been bestowed upon Professor Rolfe:

Second year and Final Honors in Classics (Harvard) 1879 and 1881.

A.B. (Harvard) 1881, A.M. (*ibid.*) 1884, Ph.D. (Cornell) 1885.

Φ.B.K. (Harvard), Φ.Κ.Φ. (Cornell).

Member of the American Philosophical Society, 1907.

Annual Professor, American School of Classical Studies in Rome, 1907–8.

Professor in charge, *ibid.,* 1923–24. Trustee, and member of the Executive Committee, American Academy in Rome.

Member of the Executive Committee of the Council of Learned Societies.

President of the American Philological Association, 1910–11.

Visiting Professor, Summer Session, University of Michigan, 1902.

Visiting Professor, Summer Session, Cornell University, 1903.

Visiting Professor, Summer Session, Columbia, 1909.

Visiting Professor, Summer Session, Harvard, 1910.

Visiting Professor, Summer Session, California, 1914.

Litt.D., University of Pennsylvania, 1925.

Commendatore della Corona d'Italia, 1930.

These honors have reflected credit upon the University to which he has given twenty-nine years of his life, and the total of his career is written into the records of the University of Pennsylvania that justly takes pride in all of his achievements.

The members of the Greek and Latin departments of the University of Pennsylvania have collaborated in the making of this book. Pressure of work alone has prevented all from participating in this labor of love. We have also invited other scholars to assist us, who have been intimately associated with Professor Rolfe as colleagues elsewhere. A few of Professor Rolfe's graduate students have likewise added their testimony of affection and have contributed chapters to this volume of Classical Essays.

To those friends who have given to the publication fund we owe a special debt of gratitude, for without their help this testimonial could never have been completed:

Dr. Thomas G. Ashton
William L. Austin
John C. Bell
Miss E. Josephine Brazier
Theodore A. Buenger
Miss Sophia Cadwalader
Hampton L. Carson
Morris L. Clothier
Miss Mary E. Converse
Arthur G. Dickson
Mrs. Joseph M. Dohan
Horace Howard Furness, Jr.
Thomas S. Gates
Judge John Marshall Gest
William P. Gest
Albert M. Greenfield
John Gribbel
David Halstead
Miss Margarette S. Hinchman

S. F. Houston
Archer M. Huntington
Charles E. Ingersoll
Alba B. Johnson
Arthur H. Lea
George McFadden
Judge J. Willis Martin
Mrs. William R. Mercer
J. Vaughan Merrick
F. Corlies Morgan
Effingham B. Morris
Harrison S. Morris
John S. Newbold
George Wharton Pepper
Philadelphia Classical Society
Edward B. Robinette
George W. Wickersham
Joseph E. Widener
Owen Wister

Herbert W. Wolff

QUINTUS OF SMYRNA AND THE SIEGE OF TROY

William Nickerson Bates

AMONG the works of Greek literature which the vagaries of fortune have preserved to modern times is a long epic poem in fourteen books which is comparatively little known today. This is the *Posthomerica* (τὰ μεθ᾽ Ὅμηρον) of Quintus of Smyrna. Very little information has come down to us about the author, and that little is to be found in the poem itself. In the Twelfth Book (lines 308 ff.) the poet tells us that when he was a young man pasturing his sheep in the neighborhood of Smyrna, upon a hill near the temple of Artemis, the Muses inspired him with song. This statement was no doubt suggested by the well-known lines of Hesiod,[1] but we may safely infer from it that Quintus lived at or near Smyrna and that in early life he was a shepherd. This passage justifies the epithet *Smyrnaeus* now regularly applied to him as a distinguishing mark; and it is supported by various references in the poem which show that the author, like the traveler Pausanias before him, was familiar with the region about Smyrna. For example, he knows the Niobe on Mount Sipylus[2] and he knows the Hermus river;[3] also the regions lying to the south. At the same time he shows us that he is acquainted with other parts of Asia Minor such as Caria and Phrygia, for in the Tenth Book[4] there is apparently a reference to the white incrustation from the warm springs of Hierapolis. No further identification of him is possible with our present evidence. In the manuscripts he is called simply ΚΟΙΝΤΟΣ.[5] The appella-

---

[1] *Theog.* 22 ff.   [2] 1.294 ff.
[3] 1.296; 12.311.   [4] Vss. 132 ff.
[5] Various futile attempts have been made to identify him with the late grammarian Corinthus, with Aemilius Macer, with Alcibiades, with Quintus Ennius, with Quintus Cicero. All are impossible for one reason or another. See T. R. Glover, *Life and Letters in the Fourth Century*, p. 79.

1

tion "Calabrian" by which he was known to early scholars is wholly unjustified and due merely to the fact that the first manuscript of his poem discovered in modern times was found at a convent near Otranto in Calabria.

His date, too, is nearly as obscure as his personality, for it is nowhere definitely given. There are, however, two passages in the poem[6] which seem to indicate that he lived in the fourth century A.D. and that date is now generally accepted.

In his poem Quintus undertakes to tell the story of Troy from the place where Homer leaves it at the end of the *Iliad* to the fall of the city and the departure of the Greeks for home. In other words he makes his poem serve as a sort of connecting link between the *Iliad* and the *Odyssey*. A summary of it will not be out of place because it is so little known to modern readers.

BOOK I.

THE poet loses no time, but plunges at once into his narrative. "When godlike Hector was slain by the son of Peleus and the pyre had consumed him and the earth concealed his bones, then the Trojans remained in the city of Priam fearing the mighty force of the bold-hearted descendant of Aeacus," and he goes on to compare them with cattle huddling together in terror in a thicket when they know that a lion is in the neighborhood. But they are suddenly cheered by the arrival of Penthesilea, queen of the Amazons. She had accidentally killed her sister Hippolyte when hurling a spear at a stag. She wishes to purge herself of this terrible deed and, at the same time, to help the Trojans. Her beauty is highly extolled. The Trojans entertain her and the next day follow her forth to battle when she attacks the Greeks. Her glorious exploits are related at length. Supported by the Trojans she sweeps all before her and reaches the ships, when Ajax and Achilles sally out against her. She attacks them furiously and hurls two spears at Ajax. He is

[6] 5.531 ff. and 13.335 ff.

unharmed and turns aside to attack the Trojans, leaving Achilles to deal with the Amazon. Achilles hurls his spear and pierces her breast and then thrusts his second spear through her horse and into her body. Penthesilea dies. Achilles utters scornful words over her and starts to despoil her body; but when he removes the helmet and sees her beautiful face he is stricken with remorse and stands gazing at her. Thersites jeers at him, but Achilles is in no mood to accept rebukes. He strikes Thersites with his fist and kills him. The body of Penthesilea is given to the Trojans who burn it on a great pyre and then bury her bones together with her arms and her horse in the tomb of Laomedon.

BOOK II.

AT the beginning of the Second Book we find the Trojans much depressed and anxious. Priam urges them to remain within the walls and await the arrival of Memnon who had been sent for, long before. Polydamas, however, sees the struggle only prolonged. He advises them to give back Helen and all her belongings, and even to double their value. Paris bitterly assails him, but is quickly silenced. Soon after this Memnon arrives with a great army of Ethiopians. A banquet is held in his honor. He does not long remain present, retiring early so as to be in good condition for fighting on the next day. He is a giant in stature and eager for the fray. Trojans and Ethiopians sally forth under his leadership and fierce fighting follows. Memnon slays Antilochus, the son of Nestor, and many others. He wounds Achilles in the arm. Both draw their swords and a furious duel ensues, ended at length when Achilles thrusts his sword through the breast of his adversary. Memnon's body is quickly borne away by the winds to the river Aesopus, and his men are transformed into birds. Eos, the Dawn, in grief for her son refuses to appear, and only resumes her usual course when frightened by the thunder of Zeus.

BOOK III.

BOOK III begins with an account of the burial of Antilochus near the ships. Achilles is determined to avenge him and he pursues and slays countless Trojans. Apollo at length intervenes, but Achilles defies him and resumes his slaughter. Apollo in anger shoots an arrow and hits Achilles in the ankle. The wounded hero draws out the shaft and continues slaying until forced by weakness to desist. Even then he terrifies the Trojans with his shouts as he stands leaning on his spear. At length he falls, but still the Trojans fear him. Paris urges them to carry off the body, but Ajax protects it, having no more regard for the Trojans than a man who robs a beehive has for the bees. Odysseus is wounded in the knee as the struggle over the body becomes fiercer, but he fights on. Paris aims an arrow at Ajax, who knocks him unconscious with a huge stone. Paris is quickly carried back to Troy. The Trojans are then driven off. Loud wailing fills the Greek camp. Thetis, the Nereids and the Muses mourn for the dead Achilles, as does Briseis. A great pyre is erected and upon it Trojan captives, horses and bulls, sheep and swine, are slaughtered. Then the body of Achilles is placed in the midst and the pyre is lighted. After it is consumed, the bones of the hero are buried under a huge mound. Poseidon now checks the grief of Thetis and promises that her son shall become a divinity and be worshipped on an island in the Euxine Sea.

BOOK IV.

THE Greeks are still grieving and the Trojans exulting when Thetis comes from the sea and offers prizes for the funeral games to be held in honor of her son. Nestor sings of the marriage of Peleus and Thetis, and then of the glorious deeds of Achilles. Thetis gives him as a reward the swift horses which Telephus had once given Achilles. The athletic events then follow. The foot-race is won by Ajax, the Locrian. In wrestling Diomed and Ajax, son of Telamon, are closely matched.

Each has a fall when Nestor stops the bout. Nobody dares to stand up against Idomeneus in the boxing and he is awarded the chariot and horses which constitute the prize. Then two men of lighter weight, Epeus and Acamas, the son of Theseus, box and the bout is declared a draw. A contest in shooting with the bow follows and Ajax, son of Oileus, wins, receiving as his prize the arms of Troilus. Next a huge mass of iron (σόλος) is brought out for the heroes to throw. This had once belonged to Heracles and had been given to Achilles by his father as a means of testing his strength. Ajax alone can hurl it. Then in succession come contests in the broad jump, in javelin throwing, in the chariot race, the last of which Menelaus wins, and in the horse race, won by Agamemnon. In the pancration Ajax, son of Telamon, is unopposed.

BOOK V.

THETIS now brings out the arms of Achilles which are described at length, particularly his wonderful shield. She proposes to award them to the warrior who saved the body of her son, and was the best of the Achaeans. Ajax and Odysseus both claim them. Ajax suggests that a committee consisting of Idomeneus, Nestor, and Agamemnon decide between them. Odysseus is willing, but the three chiefs decline to serve as judges. Nestor then proposes that Trojan captives be required to judge the merits of the two heroes. Ajax is indignant that Odysseus should claim the arms and challenges him to a single combat, but the latter gives his wound as an excuse for not fighting. The Trojan captives are called upon to give judgment, and decide in favor of Odysseus. Ajax is astounded and led to the ships by his friends in a state of bewilderment. He refuses to eat and even thinks of setting the ships on fire, or murdering Odysseus, when Athena afflicts him with a sudden fit of madness. He goes forth in his armor and kills the sheep belonging to the army, thinking he is slaughtering Greeks. One ram he believes to be Odysseus and apostrophizes it when he has slain it. At length Athena frees him from his madness and Ajax, filled with shame at the sight of what he has done, thrusts the sword of Hector into his throat and dies. The Greeks are terribly distressed, but bear the body to the ships, burn it, and heap a great mound over the bones.

BOOK VI.

IN order to test the feelings of the army Menelaus now suggests that they abandon the siege and sail home. Diomed is enraged at the very thought. Calchas tells them that the fall of the city is not far off, and urges that Odysseus and Diomed be sent to the island of Scyros to bring Neoptolemus, the son of Achilles, to their assistance. They depart on this errand; but a mighty hero, Eurypylus, son of Telephus and grandson of Heracles, comes with an army to help the Trojans. His shield is embellished with the exploits of Heracles,—the hero as a baby strangling the serpents, his twelve Labors, the freeing of Prometheus, the slaughter of the Centaurs, the conquest of Antaeus, the rescue of Hesione, and other unnamed exploits. The Trojans under his leadership march out and meet the Greeks in battle. Eurypylus performs mighty feats of valor. In fact a considerable portion of the Sixth Book is devoted to a narration of his exploits, and it ends with the triumph of the Trojans and the discouragement of the Greeks.

BOOK VII.

IN the Seventh Book Eurypylus is still triumphant. The Trojans are masters of the field and the Greeks are on the defensive, cowering within the rampart of their ships. The battle rages furiously. At length a truce is arranged for the burial of the dead.

Here the poet takes up the story of the ship sent to Scyros. Odysseus and Diomed upon their arrival at the island find the young Neoptolemus practising throwing the lance and driving

6

his chariot. Odysseus introduces himself and explains the purpose of their visit. He begs him to come to Troy and promises him his father's armor. Menelaus, too, will give him his daughter Hermione for his bride. Neoptolemus invites the two warriors into his palace where they meet Deidamia. When she learns the object of their errand she is in great distress and makes the house resound with her cries; but Neoptolemus is eager to go. He finally leaves the island with Odysseus and Diomed and accompanied by twenty of his followers. The ship reaches the Greek camp at a critical moment when it seemed as if it would surely be taken. They disembark and hasten to the hut of Odysseus to arm. Neoptolemus is given the armor of Achilles. He puts it on and thus appareled hastens with the others to the place where Eurypylus and the Trojans are mounting the walls. He hurls them back together with their scaling-ladders. The Trojans are frightened and think they see Achilles. Neoptolemus kills many of them from the walls. Eurypylus and his men withdraw as night puts an end to the fighting. Neoptolemus visits his father's hut and inspects the spoil that he had won.

BOOK VIII.

THE Greeks now swarm out like wasps and follow Neoptolemus. The fighting is resumed and many single combats are described. Neoptolemus kills many of his foes and, finally, after a furious battle, Eurypylus. The Trojans are frightened and retreat, but Ares comes to their assistance and rallies them. Neoptolemus is, however, unafraid and ready to engage in battle with the god when Athena intervenes. The two divinities are on the point of fighting, but lightning from Zeus separates them. The Trojans take refuge within their city and fight from the walls. The Greeks attack so fiercely that they are about to take the town when Ganymede appeals to Zeus, who shrouds Troy in a cloud. The Greeks then withdraw to their ships for the night.

BOOK IX.

PRIAM asks a truce for the burial of the dead and it is granted. Neoptolemus mourns at his father's tomb. The fighting is then resumed and the Trojans under the leadership of Deiphobus attack the Greeks. The Trojan hero performs many brilliant exploits and kills many of his enemies, when Neoptolemus drives up in his chariot to attack him. Apollo sends a cloud and rescues Deiphobus. He even prepares to kill Neoptolemus when Poseidon appears and overawes him. The Greeks withdraw to their ships and Calchas informs them that Troy cannot be taken without the aid of Philoctetes. This he had learned through his skill in divination. Diomed and Odysseus are sent to Lemnos to bring back the unfortunate warrior. They find him in a cave clothed in the skins of birds which he had shot for food. He is living in the midst of squalor, haggard and unkempt, suffering like a wild animal which has been caught in a trap, and forced to bite through its paw in order to get free. The ulcer on his foot had increased in size and eaten to the bone. Beside him lie the great bow of Heracles and the quiver full of arrows. When he sees Odysseus and Diomed approaching he seizes his bow to shoot them, but Athena quiets him and he tells them of his sufferings. His wrath melts away when they urge him to return with them and he readily consents. They lead him to the shore, bathe his foot, and feed him. In the morning they set sail. It is interesting to recall how differently this scene is handled by the tragic poets. When the three reach the Greek camp Podalirius, son of Asclepius, heals the sore and, by the help of the gods, Philoctetes recovers his strength. Agamemnon entertains him and makes him valuable presents. All is forgiven and the next day the Greeks march out for another attack on Troy.

BOOK X.

POLYDAMAS advises the Trojans to remain within their walls, but Aeneas opposes the plan. When the fighting begins again,

Aeneas on one side and Neoptolemus on the other perform deeds of valor. The brilliant exploits of Philoctetes are related. At length he meets Paris and shoots an arrow at him. This wounds him on the wrist. He shoots a second arrow which strikes Paris in the groin. The latter is in agony and withdraws to the city. No physician can help him, for it is fated that he can be cured by Oenone alone, if she will consent. Sore against his will Paris goes to Mount Ida and begs the wife whom he had deserted for Helen to save him from death. Oenone with bitter words sends him away, bidding him ask Helen to save him. He starts down the mountain, but does not live to get back to Troy. Hera on Olympus has heard Oenone's reply with pleasure, and she tells her attendants that it is fated that Helen shall, after the death of Paris, marry Deiphobus; that the disappointed Helenus in anger will withdraw to the mountains where he will be captured by the Greeks; that he will reveal to them the secret that Troy cannot be taken as long as the Palladium remains there; and that Diomed and Odysseus will scale the wall, slay the guard Alcathous and steal the statue. A herdsman bears news of the death of Paris to Hecuba, who bewails him. Helen pretends to mourn, but is anxious only for her own safety. Oenone, however, who had loved Paris dearly, is deeply grieved. When night comes on, the body of Paris is burned. Oenone secretly leaves her father's house on Mount Ida and in a wild frenzy rushes down the mountain. She casts herself upon the funeral pyre and dies clasping the body of her faithless husband in her arms. Herdsmen collect the ashes of the two, put them in a golden vase and heap a mound over them.

BOOK XI.

DESPERATE fighting between the two armies now takes place. On the Trojan side Aeneas especially distinguishes himself, and among the Greeks, Neoptolemus and Philoctetes. Apollo encourages Aeneas and Eurymachus, and many Greeks fall before them. Athena comes to the assistance of the Greeks, but Aphrodite quickly saves Aeneas by pouring a mist about him. The Trojans are driven into their city which the Greeks attack. The desperate assault on the gates is successfully withstood by the Trojans under Aeneas, who hurls great stones from the walls. Philoctetes shoots twice at Aeneas but Aphrodite keeps the arrows from penetrating his shield. He challenges Aeneas to come out and fight.

BOOK XII.

CALCHAS now tells the Greeks that they can capture Troy only by guile, and Odysseus suggests the following plan: that they build a great horse in which their bravest men shall hide; that the other Greeks burn their huts and sail away to Tenedos; that one man be left behind to tell the Trojans that the Greeks have set sail for home and left the horse as an offering to Athena; and then, when the horse has been taken into the town, a torch be raised in the night as a signal to the fleet to return. Neoptolemus and Philoctetes prefer to fight face to face with the enemy, but they are overruled. Then the Greeks go to Mount Ida, cut down trees and bring them to the Hellespont. There planks are fashioned and the construction of the Wooden Horse is begun. Epeus makes the feet first, then the paunch, and so on. In three days the work is completed.

Zeus now goes to the streams of the Ocean, and the gods, partisans of Greeks and of Trojans, engage in battle. Ares opposes Athena, but Themis at length parts them.

Sinon, a Greek unknown to the Trojans, volunteers to remain beside the Horse and declares he will stand by his story no matter how much he may be tortured. The poet now calls upon the Muses to tell the names of the heroes who entered the Wooden Horse. Nestor in spite of his age desires to be one of the band, but is told that he is needed with the fleet. The first man to enter is Neoptolemus. He is followed by Menelaus, Odysseus, Sthenelus, Diomed, Philoctetes, Menestheus,

Idomeneus, Ajax, and others. Epeus enters last, draws up the ladder, and closes the door. Nestor and Agamemnon superintend the breaking up of the camp and lead the fleet to Tenedos. The Trojans behold the burning huts with joy. They come down to the shore, discuss the Horse and question Sinon. They torture him. His nose and ears are cut off and he is beaten and burned, but stands by his story. He explains his presence by saying that he was to be sacrificed but had seized the feet of the Horse and the Greeks did not dare to drag him away.

Laocoon declares that the Horse is a trick of the Greeks and that it should be burned; but Athena in anger makes him ill and blinds him and so makes the other Trojans afraid. They place a rope around the neck of the Horse and drag it to the city, having first wreathed it about with flowers and made a breach in the walls so that it might be taken inside. Epeus had made the task easy for them by placing rollers under its feet. Laocoon still urges the Trojans to burn the Horse, and Athena still further afflicts him. She stirs up monstrous serpents which dwell in a cave beneath a great cliff on the island of Calydna. They come swiftly to the city and men and women flee in terror. The monsters seize the two sons of Laocoon in their jaws while the boys stretch out their hands to their father for help in vain. Other unfavorable omens appear. Cassandra sounds her warning but the Trojans only scoff at her and drive her away when she tries to set fire to the Horse. Then they have a great feast.

BOOK XIII.

WHEN the Trojans heavy with wine are all asleep Sinon raises on high the signal torch for the Greeks to set sail from Tenedos. He then goes to the Horse and calls softly to those within. Epeus and Odysseus are the first to venture out. The men from the fleet soon reach the camp and hasten in silence to the city. They quickly enter, and there ensues a terrible slaughter of the inhabitants who fall beneath the Greek swords like sheep attacked by wolves and jackals in the absence of the shepherds.

Neoptolemus slays Trojan after Trojan and finally comes face to face with Priam, who begs for death. The son of Achilles does not hesitate, but with one stroke of his sword cuts off his head. The poet stops for a moment to moralize over the fate of the aged king. Hector's little son Astyanax is torn from the arms of Andromache and hurled from a high tower. She begs for the same fate in vain. Antenor and his house are spared. Aeneas, like the captain of a ship who has matched all his skill against wind and sea, and, when the ship is foundering, leaves it in a small boat, seeing that Troy is lost takes his father on his shoulders and his little boy by the hand and with the help of Aphrodite escapes. Calchas warns the Greeks to keep away from him for he is destined to found a great city by the Tiber, and his descendants are to rule from the rising to the setting sun. Then, too, he should be spared because he preferred his father and son to gold. Menelaus slays Deiphobus in his home, but Helen hides. At length he finds her and fierce as his resentment is he spares her.

The city is now all ablaze, and the poet gives us a vivid description of the horrors which take place, some of the people being killed by their foes, others by the fire. Demophon and Acamas, sons of Theseus, find their grandmother Aethra and learn her identity with joy. She had been carried to Troy with Helen.

BOOK XIV.

THE Greeks loaded with spoil and leading the captive Trojan women return to their ships. They make a thank offering to the gods and celebrate their victory with a feast. A bard sings about the expedition,—the gathering of the forces, the exploits of Achilles, Ajax, Philoctetes, and the other heroes. Helen tells Menelaus that she was carried off by force and that she had tried to kill herself, but had been restrained. Menelaus forgives her. The shade of Achilles appears to Neoptolemus and praises him. It directs the Greeks to sacrifice Polyxena on his

12

tomb. The advice of the dead Achilles to his son is worth quoting in full. "Always be first of the Argives, yielding to no man in valor. In council take the advice of older men, and all will have friendly words to say of you. Honor noble men who are wise, for the good man is dear to the good and the wicked to the bad. If you have good thoughts you will also attain to good deeds, but no man has reached the goal of Virtue who did not have a righteous mind. Her trunk is hard to climb and her branches extend far into the sky. But those who have strength and will to labor, as a result of their toil, climb the glorious tree of fair-crowned Virtue and pluck her delightful fruit. But come, be noble; and with prudent mind do not be too much distressed in heart at sorrow, nor take too great joy in success. Let your mind be gentle towards friends and comrades, to your sons and your wife, remembering that the gates of baneful death and the abode of the dead are near mankind. The race of men is like flowers of grass, spring flowers, some of which fade while others flourish. Therefore be kindly."

Polyxena, with tears streaming down her face is now led to the tomb of Achilles and there slaughtered by Neoptolemus. Hecuba, frantic with grief, is transformed by some god into a dog, and then turned to stone. The Greeks set sail for home. Calchas, who foresees disaster and cannot restrain them, remains behind, as does Amphilochus, and the two eventually reach Pamphylia and Cilicia. Athena, angered at the outrage of Ajax, son of Oileus, on Cassandra, begs a thunderbolt from Zeus. A terrible storm falls on the Greek fleet and the ship of Ajax is struck by lightning and sinks. He swims ashore and clings to a rock, but the cliff falls and crushes him. Many of the Greeks perish. Poseidon sends a flood and washes away the walls of the Greek camp on the Hellespont. Eventually those of the army who escape from the storm reach home.

Such is the story of the poem which, in Zimmermann's edition, amounts to 8,772 lines. There are a few lacunae in it, but for

the most part they are very short. There can be little doubt
that the chief sources from which the poet drew were the old
poems of the Trojan Cycle, particularly the *Aethiopis,* the *Little
Iliad,* and the *Iliupersis.* In fact the early scholars who discussed the *Posthomerica* believed it to be little more than an
elaboration of those poems; but as they no longer exist it is impossible to say how far this may be true. If we are to form an
opinion based upon the poem itself and the manner in which
Quintus uses Homer we should say that although he drew from
the Cyclic Poets as sources he made the material entirely his
own. On the other hand it has been maintained that the poems
of the Epic Cycle were no longer in existence in the fourth century A.D., and that Quintus knew them only at second hand,
through summaries or, perhaps, through books of mythology
based upon them.[7] This is really a gratuitous assumption. The
question cannot be settled with our present evidence. Until
more definite information is at hand I prefer to believe that the
poems of the Epic Cycle were still extant in his day and that he
had access to them.

Another problem which has agitated students of the *Posthomerica* for many years is whether or not Quintus knew Virgil.[8] Here again certainty is impossible, but the probabilities
are that he knew nothing of the *Aeneid.* In spite of his name
Quintus must surely have been a Greek, and, like other Greeks,
would have little reason to make himself familiar with any
other literature than his own. He might well know that the
Romans claimed Aeneas as an ancestor without having read a
line of Virgil. Where there would seem to be agreement between the *Posthomerica* and the *Aeneid* it is not unlikely that
both poets were using the same source.

[7] E.g., F. Kehmptzow, *De Quinti Smyrnaei fontibus ac mythopoeia,* p. 7, *et
passim,* and the long review of this work by Noack, in *Gött. Gel. Anz.* (1892),
pp. 769 ff.; also Baumstark, in *Philol.,* LV (1896), 284 ff., and Wilamowitz-
Moellendorf, *Homer. Untersuchungen,* pp. 335 f.
[8] For a recent discussion, with references to the literature of the subject, see
P. Becker, in *Rh. Mus.,* LXVIII (1913), 68 ff.

When it comes to the question of language and of versification, there can be no hesitation. Quintus had, so to speak, steeped himself in Homer and had made himself a thorough master of Homeric diction. This does not mean that he merely employed the epithets used by Homer, or the tag ends of Homeric lines. He does neither of these things. He had become so familiar with the language and thought of the *Iliad* and the *Odyssey* that he had made them his own. He wrote Homeric hexameters with the greatest facility, and as if he actually lived in the Homeric age. Only very rarely do we find in his poem references to a later time.[9]

If we examine the style of the *Posthomerica* we find that its most striking characteristic is the manner in which its author uses similes. Epic poetry is naturally rich in similes, but Quintus far surpasses other epic poets in the number and variety of those which he employs. What is more, his similes are invariably good. They are often taken from the sea, especially the sea in a storm, from the mountains, from wild animals such as the lion, the boar, the wolf, etc., and from many other sources. Thus Penthesilea[10] pursues the Greeks like a wave following the swift ships when a stiff breeze fills the sails and the breakers roar on the shore. Or, again,[11] Deiphobus slays the Greeks who had rushed into the river Xanthus in flight, like a fisherman harpooning swordfish caught in a net, and the water becomes red with blood. Several times he has similes taken from bees. Thus[12] the Trojans swarm about the corpse of Achilles like bees about their hive; but Ajax heeds them no more than the man who takes their honey heeds the angry bees. A river in flood is a natural source of comparison. The youthful Nireus[13] lies dead on the field of battle like a young olive-tree, uprooted by a stream in flood. The woodsman, too, is called upon. The Greeks fall beneath the hand of Deiphobus[14]

[9] See Glover, *op. cit.*, p. 87.   [10] 1.320 ff.
[11] 9.172 ff.   [12] 3.221 ff.
[13] 6.377 ff.   [14] 9.162 ff.

as trees fall before the woodsman who exults in his work. The eagle is repeatedly used for comparison. Thus shepherds[15] cower in terror of the mad Ajax like hares in the bushes when an eagle is hovering overhead, screaming shrilly.

In a different vein are the following: The Greeks, after driving the Trojans into their city, get a moment's breathing-space like oxen which have dragged a heavy load up a steep hill.[16] The Trojans in their city cannot frighten off the Greeks any more than farmers can frighten away a great flock of starlings or jackdaws which has settled down in an olive orchard[17] to devour the fruit. Troy burns[18] like a forest fire on a mountain when the wild creatures rush in every direction to escape death. Medon,[19] shot by Philoctetes, falls from the tower like a wild goat shot by the hunter. The wife of Laocoon[20] wails for her dead sons as a nightingale laments her young, devoured by a snake.

There are other similes still more striking. Thus the Trojans[21] rejoice at the sight of Eurypylus as tame geese in a pen do when they see the man who feeds them, and they fawn about him. Again, the Trojans cower in fright about Eurypylus like small children about their father's knees when there is a heavy thunder-shower.[22] Neoptolemus kills Trojans just as a boy swings his hand around when flies are swarming about a bowl of milk and kills many of them and takes pleasure in his sport.[23]

These examples will give some idea of the range and character of the similes of Quintus. I have set them down baldly in a few lines for the sake of brevity, but in the text they are elaborated in true epic fashion.

Quintus is often very happy in his narrative and descriptive passages. Thus the few lines in Book IV[24] where Nestor sings of the marriage of Peleus and Thetis as a sort of prelude to his

15 5.433 ff.
16 8.372 ff.
17 8.387 ff.
18 13.487 ff.
19 11.483 ff.
20 12.485 ff.
21 6.125 ff.
22 7.530 ff.
23 8.331 ff.
24 4.128–143.

account of the exploits of Achilles are admirable. Again, we have a vivid description of a battle when the Greeks rally at their ships and engage in fierce combat with the Trojans.[25] Still more effective is his account of the fight between Neoptolemus and Eurypylus,[26] in which the latter loses his life. His description of Troy captured and burning[27] would seem to suggest that the poet had actually been present on some occasion when a town was captured and burned with all the horrors of war.

In his account of the armor of Achilles[28] Quintus is following a well-known epic tradition, and his lines at once invite comparison with Homer[29] and with the poem which has come down to us under the name Hesiod;[30] but they hold their own very well. So, too, his description of the shield of Eurypylus,[31] on which are pictured the various exploits of Heracles, is very well done.

Our poet, too, is not without insight into the impulses which move mankind, and he knows how to tell a story effectively. Perhaps the best examples of this in his poem are the Deidamia episode in the Seventh Book,[32] to which Glover has called attention,[33] and the story of Oenone in Book X,[34] made familiar by Tennyson.[35] But these are not solitary examples, for other excellent narrative passages might be mentioned.

From this account of the *Posthomerica,* brief as it is, some idea may be had of this interesting late epic poem. That any man living in the fourth century of our era could make himself so complete a master of Homeric thought and diction as to produce such a poem is certainly cause for astonishment. It is not a great masterpiece compared with the *Iliad* as a standard; but it is not artificial, and in any other literature less rich than

[25] 6.350–364.
[26] 8.162–209.
[27] 13.430–477.
[28] 5.6–120.
[29] *Iliad,* 18.478 ff.
[30] The Ἀσπίς, or *Scutum Heraclis.*
[31] 6.198–293.
[32] 7.242–343.
[33] *Op. cit.,* pp. 93 ff.
[34] 10.259–489.
[35] *The Death of Oenone.*

Greek, it would be hailed as an important work fit to hold a place of honor. As it is, it deserves to be more widely read. If, therefore, this paper helps to make Quintus and his poem better known, its object will have been accomplished.

UNIVERSITY OF PENNSYLVANIA

A WEAVER'S LIFE IN OXYRHYNCHUS

HIS STATUS IN THE COMMUNITY

Ethel Hampson Brewster

BY a merry caprice of chance the rubbish heaps of Bêhnesâ in the Nile valley have yielded in considerable number the archives of a humble weaver who lived in Egypt in the first century of the Roman Empire. These documents, published in volumes I and II of Grenfell and Hunt's Collection of Oxyrhynchus Papyri,[1] make it possible to follow the fortunes of a mere ordinary "man in the street" at an important period in history, and are therefore extremely interesting to students of social life and economics in the ancient world.

The weaver thus rehabilitated is Tryphon, son of Dionysius, of the "metropolis" of Oxyrhynchus in the Thebaid. His years from birth to apprenticeship have already been traced elsewhere.[2] Born about 9 A.D., he had finished his weaver's apprenticeship about 24 or 25 A.D. at the age of fifteen or sixteen, and was ready to play the part that was open to him in his community. How extensive was the rôle? By accident of birth he found himself settled in a unique province of the Roman Empire at a period of universal reconstruction. What did it mean to him to be living in this vital quarter at the beginning of a new epoch?

It is a familiar story to the student of ancient history that after the death of Cleopatra and the conquest of Alexandria in 30 B.C., Egypt was incorporated into the Roman Empire and garrisoned by legions to keep it quiet. It is customarily con-

---

[1] I (1898), 37, 38, 39, 99; II (1899), 235, 264, 267, 269, 275, 282, 288, descriptions 304-326: *The Oxyrhynchus Papyri*, I–XVI, ed. by B. P. Grenfell and A. S. Hunt, London, 1898–1924; XVII, ed. by Hunt (1927). References will be cited thus: *Oxy*. 37.3–5, col. 1, *Oxy*. 304 desc. G. & H. in footnotes designate the editors.

[2] Cf. E. H. Brewster, "A Weaver of Oxyrhynchus," in *T.A.P.A.*, LVIII (1927), 132–154.

19

sidered that the province became the private property of the Roman emperor. As Mommsen pointed out, however, its "abnormal form of government was applicable" in principle, at the outset, for any non-senatorial province, and "Egypt was private property of the emperor just as much or just as little as Gaul and Syria." But in the case of Egypt Augustus abolished the interest and supervision of the senate beyond all bounds and precedent; the senate was not consulted with regard to the government of the country, senators were cut off from all participation in the administration which was consigned to knights of inferior rank, and persons of the senatorial order and knights of the highest class were prohibited from entering the province without the emperor's special permission.

While Egypt, then, became the emperor's personal concern and a part of the *patrimonium Caesaris,* passing by inheritance from emperor to emperor, it is probably untenable to maintain that it was his personal possession, *res familiaris.* The Memorial of Augustus expressly states: *Aegyptum imperio populi (Ro)mani adieci.* Although this statement is sometimes interpreted as an Augustan innuendo, it is strongly supported by B. A. Van Groningen in a recent study of the relation of Egypt to the Roman Empire. He concludes that it was definitely annexed to the domain of the *Populus Romanus,* and that its government by equestrians indicates a difference in administrative practice, not a difference in principle. That Egypt with its strategic position, its rich revenues, its vast corn supplies, its incentives to revolution should have been set apart for the personal supervision of the emperor was natural. That it should have been treated as the personal domain of the emperor and have been so considered by the inhabitants was almost inevitable, for it was, in a sense, the spoil of the battle of Actium and had constituted the private estate of the Pharaohs or the Ptolemies whom the Roman emperor now represented.[8]

[8] On the status of Egypt, see *Mon. Ancyr.* 5.27; Tac. *Ann.* 2.59, 12.60, *Hist.* 1.11; T. Mommsen, *Provinces of the Roman Empire,* tr. by W. P. Dickson,

A WEAVER IN OXYRHYNCHUS

The Romans found in Egypt an elaborate system of organization and administration which had been developed by the Hellenistic kings. According to their usual policy in the east, they adopted this with few radical changes: Augustus merely reformed or modified the Ptolemaic regimen. The framework of organization consisted of the capital at Alexandria, which was regarded as quite distinct from the rest of Egypt; three grand divisions of the country into Upper Egypt (the Thebaid), Middle Egypt (the Heptanomis, with the Arsinoïte nome, differentiated probably under Vespasian), Lower Egypt (the Delta); and subdivisions into nomes. The wave of urbanization which assumed such vast proportions under Augustus and Claudius did not reach Egypt. Even the influx of Greeks in the Hellenistic period—creators of cities—had had little effect in this direction, a fact which in itself shows how imperfectly Egypt had been Hellenized.[4] The only "cities," in the Graeco-Roman sense, in the early empire were the old Greek foundation Naucratis, and Alexandria in the Delta; Ptolemaïs in Upper Egypt; and in the second century, Antinoöpolis founded by Hadrian on the Greek model; and these were truly neither πόλεις nor *municipia,* so restricted was their self-government. The nomes, still further subdivided into toparchies, were a conglomerate group of landholdings, farmsteads, hamlets, and villages. Civic centers, to be

New York, 1909, Vol. II, pp. 232 ff.; W. T. Arnold, *Roman System of Provincial Administration,* Oxford, 1914, pp. 128 ff.; J. G. Milne, *History of Egypt under Roman Rule*[3], London, 1924, p. 120; B. A. Van Groningen, "L'Egypte et l'Empire," in *Aegyptus,* VII (1926), 189–202; M. Rostovtzeff, *History of the Ancient World: Rome,* Oxford, 1927, pp. 188 f. For a discussion of the *Patrimonium Caesaris* and *Fiscus* and a summary of views, see H. Mattingly, *The Imperial Civil Service of Rome,* Cambridge, England, 1910, pp. 1–26.

[4] On the Hellenization of Egypt, see: H. I. Bell, "Hellenic Culture in Egypt," in *J.E.A.,* VIII (1922), 139–155; W. L. Westermann, "The Greek Exploitation of Egypt," in *Pol. Sc. Qtly.,* XL (1925), 517–539; M. Rostovtzeff, *Social and Economic History of the Roman Empire,* Oxford, 1926, pp. 6, 257–264, 571; J. G. Milne, "Egyptian Nationalism under Greek and Roman Rule," in *J.E.A.,* XIV, 226–234; W. W. Tarn, *Hellenistic Civilization,* London, 1927, ch. 5; P. Jouguet, *Macedonian Imperialism and the Hellenization of the East,* New York, 1928, pp. 322–347.

sure, grew up in each nome, for administrative purposes, supporting the imposing name of "metropoleis," but though the Hellenized quarters became more and more "urban," they remained for the most part scarcely more than overgrown villages or at best country towns. M. Rostovtzeff describes them as "large and dirty Egyptian villages with a more or less Hellenized and civilized town center."[5]

At the head of the administrative hierarchy was the Prefect, the personal representative of the emperor and viceroy for him as heir of the Ptolemies. An equestrian, but invested with proconsular powers, he directed every branch of the government, financial, judicial, and military, going on circuit from Alexandria annually in the administration of his duties. His chief assistants were the *dikaiodotes,* a legal expert for the judiciary; and two financial supervisors, the *dioiketes,* concerned especially with public works, and the *idiologos,* who as supervisor of temple revenues was also titular high priest of Egypt.

Each of the three grand divisions (*epistrategiai*) of the country was administered by an *epistrategos,* appointed by the emperor, whose powers, strictly civil and stripped even of fiscal entanglements, were generally delegated by the Prefect. Like the Prefect, he apparently went on circuit from Alexandria. One of his important functions was the selection of men by lot from lists prepared by local authorities for the unremunerated State agencies known as liturgic offices. He also nominated for appointment by the Prefect the officials next below him in rank, the *strategoi,* who were at the head of the nomes and were the chief civil administrators in the local government of the country. Financial matters were transacted directly with Alexandria. In other cases the strategi regularly received orders through the epistrategus. Among other things they directed the police,

[5] *Soc. & Ec. Hist.,* p. 255, cf. pp. 81–83, 262, 271–273; *Hist. of Anc. World: Rome,* pp. 247, 256. On urbanization in Egypt, see also U. Wilcken in *Grundzüge und Chrestomathie der Papyruskunde* by L. Mitteis and U. Wilcken, Leipzig, 1912, Vol. I.1, pp. 38–39, 43–53; J. G. Milne, *Hist.,* 132–135; W. L. Westermann, "Greek Culture," in *Encyclopaedia of the Social Sciences,* I, 32.

made preliminary investigations in legal cases, and supervised for their districts the machinery of taxes, census returns, the letting of state lands, and the corvée for the maintenance of dikes and canals.

In close relation to the strategus was the "royal scribe," βασιλικὸς γραμματεύς; he was mainly interested in the financial end of local administration, but acted as deputy for the strategus in his absence. Copies of all official records of the nome were filed in a Record Office, in two departments, one for land registry, βιβλιοθήκη ἐγκτήσεων, the other for financial documents, δημοσία βιβλιοθήκη; each department was regularly under the care of two *bibliophylakes* who were subordinate in rank to the royal scribe and subject to the strategus.

The units of the nome were its villages and the "metropolis." In the villages, a village scribe κωμογραμματεύς furnished the central government with the requisite lists for census, taxes, and liturgies. In the metropoleis two γραμματεῖς μητροπόλεως functioned similarly; they also acted as intermediaries between the strategi and the town magistrates. These "magistrates" performed special duties for the public welfare which in the early empire they probably assumed voluntarily as well-to-do metropolites; they seem not to have had collective authority until the reform of Severus in 200 A.D., when they were organized into councils as ἄρχοντες or τὸ κοινὸν τῶν ἀρχόντων. Certainly until the third century the metropoleis were entirely without autonomy. By that time the liturgies were no longer voluntary but were required from nominations ratified by the strategus. Among the more important town "magistracies," as they developed, were the offices of the gymnasiarch, exegetes, cosmetes, archiereus, agoranomus, and eutheniarch, concerned respectively with the upkeep of the gymnasium, the status of inhabitants, the training of ephebes, the function of high priest, the function of notary, and the local food supplies.

In addition to these officials, of course, there were temporary appointments and staffs of subordinates; it is to be noticed that all offices were carefully balanced, checked, and counter-checked and that each was successively responsible to a head higher up. The higher officials were supported from revenues, special imposts, and exactions; their subordinates, beginning presumably with the *bibliophylakes,* were liturgists.[6]

With all this officialdom the weaver Tryphon had no concern objectively. He dwelt in the Hippodrome Quarter, later in the Temenouthis Quarter of the metropolis of Oxyrhynchus.[7] Oxyrhynchus was the administrative center of the Oxyrhynchite nome, one of the most important towns in the Thebaid and probably one of the best Hellenized cities in Egypt. A. Calderini's topographical investigations from papyri attest the size and importance of the nome. But the inhabitants of Oxyrhynchus, as of Egypt in general, had no voice in their government. Directly or indirectly all state appointments in Egypt were held from Rome.

The highest officials resided at Alexandria. The Prefect, his chief assistants, and the epistrategi were Roman citizens, drawn

[6] On the general organization and administration of Egypt, see: P. Jouguet, *La Vie Municipale dans l'Egypte Romaine,* Paris, 1911, chs. 3 and 4, *Mac. Imp.,* pp. 286–321 (Ptolemaic); U. Wilcken, *Grundzüge,* Vol. I.1, pp. 34–43; S. H. Ballou, "The Carrière of the Higher Roman Officials in Egypt in the Second Century," in *T.A.P.A.,* LII (1921), 96–110; J. G. Milne, *Hist.,* pp. 120–150, 289–291; W. M. Flinders Petrie, *Social Life in Ancient Egypt,* London, 1924, pp. 31–64; V. Chapot, *The Roman World,* New York, 1928, pp. 243–267; P. M. Meyer, *Das Heerwesen der Ptolemäer und Römer,* Leipzig, 1900, for list of Prefects; V. Martin, *Les Epistratèges dans l'Egypte Grèco-Romaine,* Geneva, 1911, "Stratèges et basilocogrammates du nome Arsinoïte à l'époque romaine," in *Archiv für Papyrusforschung,* VI (1920), 137–175, 216–218; J. G. Tait, "The Strategi and Royal Scribes in the Roman Period," in *J.E.A.,* VIII (1922), 166–173. On liturgies, see F. Oertel, *Die Liturgie,* Leipzig, 1917; U. Wilcken, *Grundzüge,* Vol. I.1, pp. 339–355; M. Rostovtzeff, *Soc. & Ec. Hist.,* pp. 265, 269, 333–338; G. Flore, "Sulla βιβλιοθηκη των εγκτησεων," in *Aegyptus,* VIII (1927), 43–88; B. A. Van Groningen, *Le Gymnasiarque des Métropoles de l'Egypte Romaine,* Groningen, 1924, reviewed in *J.R.S.,* XVI (1926), 132 ff. *P. Flor.* 3.312 indicates that the system was established considerably before 91 A.D.; *Oxy.* 3.473 shows the principle of compulsion under way in the time of the Antonines.

[7] *Oxy.* 99, 288, 311 desc.; 308 desc., cf. 251.9, 310 desc. On Oxyrhynchite localities, see P. Jouguet, *Vie Municipale,* pp. 282–292; U. Wilcken, *Grundzüge,* Vol. I.1, pp. 40–41; H. Rink, *Strassen u. Viertelnamen Oxyrhynchos,* Giessen, 1924; A. Calderini, "Località dell' Ossirinchite," in *Rend. Ist. Lomb.,* LVIII,

from not the highest class of equestrians. The rest of the administration, from the office of strategus down, was in the hands mainly of Egypto-Greeks and men of the class of Hellenes who resided in the community, though the strategi in the Roman period, as J. A. Tait argues, seem not, as a rule, to have been appointed from the nome in which they were normally residents. The lower liturgic offices were probably consigned to local "natives" who could afford to support them. These would be Hellenized Egyptians with possibly a slight admixture of Greeks and foreigners of the same status, who constituted a sort of upper middle class in the social order: landowners, traders, and merchants whom M. Rostovtzeff terms the bourgeoisie.[8]

Tryphon belonged to none of these orders. In the mixed population of Romans (few in number in Oxyrhynchus in his day, and probably veterans and their descendants), Alexandrians, Greeks, Egyptians, Jews, and other foreigners who resided in Oxyrhynchus, he seems to have fallen into a lower middle class of little-Hellenized Egyptians, including apparently a considerable foreign element—craftsmen, artisans, and laborers, but somewhat above the lowest class of native Egyptian peasant serfs and drudges, the oppressed fellahîn who drifted into the towns. Tryphon certainly did not rank with the lowest stratum, for he was registered in selective lists, *epikriseis,* of the forty-first and forty-second years of Caesar (11/12 and 12/13 A.D.), and as a privileged metropolite paid a reduced poll tax.[9] He is termed in some documents a Persian of the Epigone.

529–536, "Ricerche topografiche sopra il nomo Ossirinchite" in *Aegyptus,* VI (1925), 79–92.

[8] On social organization in Egypt, see H. I. Bell, "The Byzantine Servile State in Egypt" in *J.E.A.,* IV (1917), 86 ff.; L. C. West, "Phases of Commercial Life in Roman Egypt," in *J.R.S.,* VII (1917), 56–57; M. Rostovtzeff, "The Foundations of Social and Economic Life in Egypt in Hellenistic Times," in *J.E.A.,* VI (1920), 161–178, *Soc. & Ec. Hist.,* pp. 255–259, 261–271; W. M. Flinders Petrie, *Social Life,* pp. 1–30; W. W. Tarn, *Hellenistic Civilization,* pp. 157–164; P. Jouguet, *Mac. Imp.,* pp. 268–271, 341–342.

[9] For the privileges of Tryphon and his "family," see *Oxy.* 288.7, 16, 25, 35–

CLASSICAL STUDIES

Tryphon's "privileges" have already been considered by the present writer in a chapter on *A Weaver of Oxyrhynchus*. As was there recorded, it was necessary, in order to be listed in an epikrisis, to give evidence that one's father and maternal grandfather had previously been "selected" in the class for which application was made, that is among κάτοικοι, οἱ ἀπὸ γυμνασίου, or μητροπολῖται δωδεκάδραχμοι. That Tryphon's family belonged to the μητροπολῖται who enjoyed the privilege of reduced poll tax is assumed from their tax receipts. Why this class originally acquired the privilege is not clear. There is evidence[10] that at Oxyrhynchus in the second century the "twelve drachmae citizens" might also be included, under proper conditions, among "those belonging to the gymnasium," who seem to have enjoyed certain municipal advantages and may have contributed to the ranks of the lower local officials. Tryphon, very obviously from his records, did not belong to this latter class which would be made up largely from the Greek and highest Graeco-Egyptian elements of the population.

With the problem of the "Persians of the Epigone," papyrologists are still wrestling. P. Jouguet in his volume on *Macedonian Imperialism* concisely summarizes the various opinions —and their sponsors—for the Ptolemaic period: that οἱ τῆς ἐπιγονῆς were non-Egyptian sons of "kleruchs," that they were sons of soldiers even without κλῆρος, that they were new immigrants, that they were descendants of immigrants. P. Jouguet himself inclines to the belief that in the third century B.C., they were the first descendants of immigrants. This is in line with the view of F. Von Woess that by the Roman period they were remote descendants of immigrants. The present writer sees no

42; 289, 311 desc., 314 desc.—compare with *Oxy.* 313, 389; see also E. H. Brewster in *T.A.P.A.*, LVIII, 132–137, 145, 147, 151.

[10] *Oxy.* 1452 (cf. introd.) ; cf. also *P. Brit.* 1600 and H. I. Bell in *Archiv,* VI (1920), 107–109. On epikrisis and classes at Oxy. in the first two centuries, see further *Oxy.* 257 (& introd.), 258, 478, 714, 1028, 1109, 1266, 1306, 1451; cf. P. Meyer, *Heerwesen,* pp. 109 ff.; U. Wilcken, *Grundzüge,* Vol. I.1, pp. 40, 138–145, 196–202; A. E. R. Boak, "The Epikrisis Record of an Ephebe of Antinoöpolis Found at Karanis," in *J.E.A.,* XIII (1927), 151–154.

reason to modify radically the conclusion reached in *A Weaver of Oxyrhynchus,* following F. Pringsheim, that "Persians of the Epigone" originally designated descendants of Persian soldiers who had served in the Ptolemaic army. First applied probably in the third century B.C., the term continued to be used for the descendants of Persian immigrants, even when descent was remote and much diluted, but in the Roman period it acquired juridical significance and was apparently applied only in transactions where the contracting party was answerable to an obligation before the law. Tryphon, for instance, accepting liability for the return of a dowry in *P. Oxy.* 267.1, is recorded as Πέρσης τῆς ἐπιγονῆς; he is not so described in *P. Oxy.* 269.1.1, where he himself makes a loan, but the term is applied to his debtor Dioscorus, son of Zenodorus, and the father is included in the appellation.[11]

J. G. Tait, followed by W. W. Tarn, goes a step farther and maintains that since in the Roman period the title was employed solely to enforce liability to personal execution, it became a mere "legal fiction" to designate debtors in contracts, whether they were "Persians" or not. While it is logical to agree with Mr. Tait's reasoning that the Persian ranks had become so diluted as to form a class of "Egyptian pseudo-Persians," it is not so tenable to hold that it would be impossible to ascertain who were and who were not descended from Persian settlers of the Ptolemaic period. With the intricate registration which was required by the government for every detail, there can be little doubt that the status of every inhabitant of Egypt was carefully recorded. The epikrisis of 11/12 A.D., in which Tryphon was registered at the age of three, contains the name of his father Dionysius, his grandfather Tryphon, aged sixty-four, and his great-grandfather Didymus. This document alone, therefore, traces his ancestry back into the late Ptolemaic period. Grandfather Tryphon, the head of the house, doubtless had possessed

---

[11] Cf. *P.S.I.* 8.908 and see P. Meyer in *Zeitschrift der Savigny-Stiftung für Rechtsgeschichte, Romanistische Abteilung,* XLVIII (1928), 601.

records of his own to prove his claim to an epikrisis, and great-grandfather Didymus would have carried the family annals still farther back. Little can be argued, either for or against nationality, from names, because of the common interchange of Greek and Egyptian appellatives and the adoption of Greek names by Egyptians and foreigners. P. Jouguet thinks that there must have been official lists in which persons were classified according to their racial designation.

The indications are, then, that Tryphon's family was of Persian descent. This nationality had become numerous in Upper Egypt. As a Persian, Tryphon would rank, while Hellenistic tradition persisted, above the mass of Egyptians, but in the eyes of Greeks and high-class Graeco-Egyptians, Persians were low in the rating of foreigners, and Persians of the Epigone were liable, in case of debt, to personal execution. What this entailed is not clear. H. Lewald's theory that in the Ptolemaic period the penalty was enslavement is offset by W. L. Westermann's study *Upon Slavery in Ptolemaic Egypt* (Columbia Univ. Press, 1930) which shows that anybody might be made a slave for debt under the Ptolemies. W. W. Tarn accepts the view of F. Von Woess that the penalty prohibited the right of asylum both in Ptolemaic times and later. But even with a legal guarantee, whereby settlement was promised "without delay," the "execution" apparently did not go into effect automatically upon non-payment. *P. Oxy.* 259 records the case of Sarapion, son of Sarapion, who had been imprisoned for debt incurred, possibly, on behalf of a relative of Tryphon. He had been bailed out by Theon in September or October, 22 A.D.; seven months later Theon signed an agreement with the superintendent of the prison to produce Sarapion within thirty days or pay the debt himself, without power to obtain a further period of time or transfer himself to another prison. Tryphon himself, according to *P. Oxy.* 269, in attempting to secure payment from Dioscorus in 57 A.D. at the end of a three months' loan, did not claim the right nominated in the bond, but wrote a letter to his friend

Ammonas, inclosing a copy of the agreement and urging him to dun Dioscorus for the amount.[12]

Though Tryphon's status did not permit him to be "of the officials," he was very much within their jurisdiction and circumscribed by them. An endless roll of red tape is revealed in his archives, and yet these are but a chance remnant of many documents that were left, in copy, in his possession, duplicated in the Record Office of the *bibliophylakes* at Oxyrhynchus, and forwarded to Alexandria. His relations with officials have thus been docketed. We discover that in 55 A.D., transacting through the agoranomi, Andromachus and Diogenes, he purchased from his mother's cousin for 32 copper talents half of a three-storied house; in 59 A.D. he contracted a loan of 160 drachmae in connection with the purchase of a house through the μνημονεῖον, an office which appears to have been associated at Oxyrhynchus with the *agoranomeion;* about the same time, perhaps in connection with the purchase of the same house, he, with his wife and brother, negotiated a loan of 314 drachmae from his maternal grandmother, Tryphaena, through an agent of the associate agoranomi.

In the year 12/13 A.D., preliminary registration of Tryphon's infant brother Thoönis for an epikrisis had been made by the komogrammateis; about 44 A.D. this same brother evidently—now without trade and without means—moved away from the Temenouthis Quarter, and these facts, significant for tax returns, were carefully registered by his mother, under oath, with

---

[12] For Persians of the Epigone at Oxy., in the first century A.D., see *Oxy.* 259.2, 267.1, 269 (cf. *supra,* pp. 18–19), 271.11, 278.2, 280.4, 320 desc.; cf. 270.3, 319 desc. On the whole problem discussed on pp. 26–29 above, see H. Lewald, *Zur Personalexekution im Rechte der Papyri,* Leipzig, 1910; U. Wilcken in *Archiv,* VI (1913–20), 367–369; VII (1923–24), 96; F. Pringsheim, "Die Rechtsstellung der Πέρσαι τῆς ἐπιγονῆς," in *Zeitschrift der Sav.-St.,* XLIV (1924), 396–526; F. Von Woess in *Zeitschrift der Sav.-St.,* XLII (1921), 139 ff., 641–643; XLVI (1926), 38 ff., 42 ff., 50 ff.; also *Das Asylwesen Aegyptens in der Ptolemaërzeit,* Munich, 1923, pp. 66 ff.; J. G. Tait in *Archiv,* VII (1923–24), 175–183, in *J.H.S.,* XLVI (1926), 143–144; W. W. Tarn, *Hellenistic Civilization,* pp. 158 f.; P. Jouguet, *Mac. Imp.,* pp. 331–333, 341–343.

the topogrammateis and komogrammateis who seem to have been filling at this time in Oxyrhynchus a joint office regularly covered later by the γραμματεῖς μητροπόλεως. Epikrisis records, together with complete tax accounts, were in all probability kept in the financial branch of the Record Office, δημοσία βιβλιοθήκη, under the supervision of the *bibliophylakes* who issued and certified abstracts.

In the early 30's Tryphon petitioned the strategus Alexandrus for redress in the matter of desertion by his first wife Demetrous who had gone off with some of his property. A few years later, in 37 A.D., he petitioned the strategus Sotas in a case of assault, presumably by this same Demetrous and her mother, upon his second wife Saraeus. In 49 A.D. Saraeus was a defendant in court over the identity of her infant son and a foundling whom she had nursed for a certain Pesouris. The full minutes of the strategus, Tiberius Claudius Pasion, are preserved. The strategus made a compromise judgment in the name of the Prefect, demanding from Saraeus a refund of wages which she had received as nurse, but rejecting the claim of the plaintiff Pesouris. A year and a half later, in 50 A.D., Pasion the strategus was petitioned to act against an assault upon Tryphon and his wife by a woman and other persons unnamed. Whether this was an outgrowth of Saraeus' trial or whether it harked back to the previous assault of Demetrous thirteen years before, or was a totally new aggression is not clear. At all events Pesouris—or Syrus, as he is also called—had not been willing to abide by the decision and hindered Tryphon in his trade, whereupon Tryphon appealed by letter to the Prefect Gnaeus Vergilius Capito to sustain the judgment and secure to Tryphon his rights. A couple of years later, in 52 A.D., this same Prefect granted Tryphon release from military service because of failing eyesight. Two copies of the release have reappeared in Tryphon's archives.[13]

[13] For Tryphon's contact with officials, see *Oxy.* 99, 306 desc. (cf. 318 desc. and 238.2–4 and note), 320 desc. (cf. *supra*, p. 39); 288, esp. lines 41 f. and

A WEAVER IN OXYRHYNCHUS

The most persistent and exacting relations which Tryphon had with officialdom were with the office of tax collectors and with the banks. It has been seen that the administrative system of Egypt was a bureaucracy focused on securing for the State the greatest possible amount of revenues in money or in grain. To this end the economic organization instituted by the Pharaohs, developed by the Ptolemies, and exploited by the Romans had been built upon the principle of centralization with rigid governmental control. H. I. Bell holds taxes and liturgies mainly responsible for the later degraded condition of the Byzantine Servile State. And V. Martin's researches upon the Roman fiscal policy, its principles, methods, and results, draws even for the first two centuries a somber picture of a ruthlessly grinding machine.[14] Tryphon's taxes which were regularly 36 drachmae on his trade, 12 drachmae poll tax, 2 drachmae 1½ obols pig tax, 6 drachmae 4 obols dike tax—an annual total of 56 drachmae 5½ obols without incidentals—have already been considered in detail.[15] It now remains to note his dealings with the banks for the payment of these taxes and for other negotiations.

The story of banking in Ptolemaic and Roman Egypt which is being steadily unfolded from papyri is most illuminating. The Egyptians had long avoided the use of coins, clinging to barter or payment in kind or in metals measured by weight; their traditions in currency, as in so many other respects, thus stood apart from the rest of the world. The Ptolemies, at the end of the fourth century B.C., curtailed natural economy, to some ex-

note (cf. A. E. R. Boak in *J.E.A.*, XIII, 151–154), 251 (cf. 252, 254, 255 and U. Wilcken, *Grundzüge*, Vol. I.1.11 f.) ; 282, 315 desc.; 37, 38, 316 desc. which is presumably the introd. to 324 desc.; 39, 317 desc.

[14] H. I. Bell in *J.E.A.*, IV (1917), 86 ff.; V. Martin, *La Fiscalité romaine en Egypte aux trois premiers siècles de l'Empire*, Geneva, 1926; cf. M. Rostovtzeff, "The Foundations of Social and Economic Life in Egypt in Hellenistic Times," in *J.E.A.*, VI (1920), 161–178; J. G. Milne, "The Ruin of Egypt by Roman Mismanagement," in *J.R.S.*, XVII (1927), 1–13; W. L. Westermann, "New Historical Documents in Greek and Roman History," in *Am. Hist. Rev.*, XXXV (1929), 30–32.

[15] In *T.A.P.A.*, LVIII, 142, 143, 144–153.

tent, by introducing a national coinage which took hold gradually. Money payments became regular for trade, industry, and taxes, though the tax on corn, land, and certain commodities was always paid in kind. When currency was instituted, copper played a larger part than was usual elsewhere, and became the unit of account, probably not in token in the Ptolemaic issues, from the end of the third century B.C. Gold was current to the middle of the second century, silver until the Roman occupation, but it had become greatly debased.[16]

With the introduction of coinage and the impetus of Greek business efficiency, a banking business developed on Greek models. Under the Ptolemies it was a State monopoly: banks had been established mainly for tax payments, but they received private deposits, carried accounts, and negotiated money orders and the transfer of goods. Papyri and ostraka show how strictly the business was controlled. The central treasury into which the revenues of the State flowed was the *Basilikon,* maintaining the Great Royal Bank at Alexandria. This had branches, *trapezai,* licensed to official bankers, *trapezitai,* in the nome capitals and even in small towns and villages. Side by side with the *trapezai* were the public granaries, *thesauroi,* managed by *sitologoi.* These were genuine banks with a capital of natural wealth, for in Egypt natural economy, money economy, and credit economy flourished together. G. Glotz claims that "never, in any other country in the world, was credit more universally practiced than in Ptolemaic Egypt." While this statement is unduly extravagant, it is apparently true that by a highly centralized and carefully controlled system of finance the State grew tremendously enriched beyond any of the other Hellenistic kingdoms and the Ptolemies became the bankers of their world.[17]

[16] On Egyptian currency, see *Annals of Arch. and Anthrop.,* VII, 51–66: "The Currency of Egypt under the Romans to the Time of Diocletian"; A. R. Burns, *Money and Monetary Policy in Early Times,* New York, 1927, pp. 79–83, 147 f., 334 f., 406–418, 443, 474, 476; J. G. Milne, "The Currency Reform of Ptolemy II," in *Ancient Egypt* (1928), pp. 37–39; H. Mattingly, *Roman Coins from the Earliest Times to the Fall of the Western Empire,* London, 1928, cf. index.

[17] On banking in Egypt, see H. Maspero, *Les Finances de l'Egypte sous les*

A WEAVER IN OXYRHYNCHUS

Sources for the principate of Augustus give evidence of the effect produced at Rome when the treasure of Egypt poured into Roman coffers after the Alexandrian triumph of Augustus in 29 B.C. The Treasury was replenished and ready money was so plentiful that the price of goods rose, the value of real estate was increased, interest was reduced for a time from 12 per cent to 4 per cent, State loans were made free of interest to property owners who had the designated security, and old debts were cancelled.[18]

Imperial policy in turn had its effect upon the fiscal regimen of Egypt. According to Augustan regulations, the emperor had the sole right to issue gold and silver for the whole empire. Authority to issue bronze was granted as a local right, but Egyptian currency, minted at Alexandria, continued almost independent of Rome. Until the third century A.D. apparently neither denarii nor bronze coins of the common imperial mintage were circulated there. In 19 A.D. Tiberius revived the tetradrachm which had not been struck since the death of Cleopatra. Now coined with a mixture of silver and copper, it became the unit of exchange until it was utterly debased in the third century. It was considered equivalent to a denarius, though with only 24 obols against 28 or 25 to the denarius. In the first two centuries bronze drachmae, mainly modelled on the Roman sestertius, were also in circulation.

For some reason the Roman government abandoned the Ptolemaic system of the State banking monopoly and opened the business to private enterprise—or perhaps it would be more

---

Lagides, Paris, 1905; Fr. Preisigke, *Girowesen im Griechischen Aegypten,* Strassburg, 1910; U. Wilcken, *Griechische Ostraka aus Aegypten und Nubien,* Leipzig, 1899, Vol. I, pp. 630 ff., *Grundzüge,* Vol. I.1, pp. 152 ff.; G. Glotz, *Ancient Greece at Work,* New York, 1920, pp. 363–367; J. Hasebroek, "Zum Griechischen Bankwesen," in *Hermes,* LV (1920), 113–173; Kiessling, "Giroverkehr," in Pauly-Wissowa: *Real-Encyclopädie, Supplement-Band,* IV (1924), 700–709; E. R. Bevan, *A History of Egypt under the Ptolemaic Dynasty,* London, 1927, pp. 150–152; P. Jouguet, *Mac. Imp.,* pp. 316–321, 326 f.; J. Desvernos, "Banques et Banquiers dans l'ancienne Egypte sous les Ptolémés et la domination romaine," in *Bull. Soc. Arch. d'Alex.,* XXIII (1928), 303–348.

[18] See Suet. *Aug.* 4; Dio 51.21.5, 53.2.1, 55.12.3a; cf. *Mon. Ancyr.* 17.

accurate to say "pseudo-private," because all banks were still operating in large measure on behalf of the State, though some seem to have been less official than others. The management was responsible to the State to make good any deficiency in assessment; by the second century the office had become a liturgy and managers were nominated for a given period.

Tryphon's financial documents richly illustrate certain bank practices in Oxyrhynchus in his time. The charts appended here have been compiled from these papyri. Charts A, B, and C, representing tax receipts for annual payments and payments covering a period of years, afford an interesting study in bank bookkeeping.[19] Obviously tax collectors, who as liturgists drew the costs of their employment from private means, had personal accounts at various banks. It would seem that regularly, as *P. Oxy.* 288 and 289 expressly state, taxpayers paid their installments at the bank, apparently to the account of the collector. Total assessments were periodically transferred to the State Bank. The evidence indicates that separate cash daybooks were carefully kept by local banks for various receipts, and at the end of the year statements of extracts of accounts were drawn up. Confusion in bookkeeping or inaccuracy in copying is evidenced in the chronology at the end of Tryphon's long tax account (Chart A), where several entries are made out of their natural order. The chronological arrangement in the columns of the document of Thoönis also (Chart C) is noticeable. Column I runs from 66 to 68 A.D.; Column II continues to 76 A.D.; at this point the account is incomplete or missing for several years; for the years 81 A.D. and following, it returns to Column I, and the last lines, 17 to 20, are written parallel to lines 11 to 16—Grenfell and Hunt specify that entries were made at different times, but apparently in the same hand. All of this signifies that accounts were brought up to date by a central hand from various receipts. Interesting in connection with bank bookkeeping,

19 Charts A and B are reprinted with modifications from *T.A.P.A.*, LVIII (1927), 145, 147.

Chart A—Tax Document of Tryphon, Son of Dionysius: 22-25 A.D.

Oxy. 288 Line	Egyptian Year	Egyptian Month, day	Roman Year A.D.	Roman Month, day	γερδιακὸν Dr.	γερδιακὸν Ob.	Ἱππο-δρόμου	ἐπικεφάλ(αιον) Dr.	ἐπικεφάλ(αιον) Ob.	ὑική Dr.	ὑική Ob.	χωματικ(όν) Dr.	χωματικ(όν) Ob.	Bank	Miscellanea
1	9th Tib.	Hathyr 16	22	Nov. 12	7	3								Paapis	Cf. p. 44
3		Choiach 25		Dec. 21	3	4½									
		Tybi 5		Dec. 31	7	4½									
4		Mecheir 19	23	Feb. 13	3	4½									
5		Pharmuthi 30		Apr. 25	3	4½									
		Pachon 4		Apr. 29	3	4½									
		Payni Seb. ?		June ?	2	1½									
6															Total: 36 dr.
7	9th	Payni 2	23	May 27			Ἱππο-δρόμου	12		2	1½	6	4	Diogenes	σὺν καταγωγίωι Cf. Oxy. 311 desc., Chart B
9		Payni 29		June 23											
10		Mesore 4		July 28											
11	10th	Choiach 17	23	Dec. 13	7	3	Ἱππ[ο]-δρόμου							Paapis	Total: 32½ dr. + 7½ infra
14		Mecheir 16	24	Feb. 10	7	3									
		Pharmuthi 22		Apr. 17	7	3									
15		Payni 8		July 2	3	4½									
		Mesore 3		July 27	6										
16	10th	Mecheir 13	24	Feb. 7			Ἱππο-δρόμου	8	4	2	1½	6	–	Diogenes	σὺν κα(ταγωγίωι)
19		Pharmuthi 24		Apr. 19											
		Payni 21?		June 15?											
20		Epeiph 16		July 10											
22	11th	Thoth 13	24	Sept. 10	7	3	Ἱππο-δρόμ[ο]ν							Dionysius	Cf. p. 44 and note 24
23		Tybi 19	25	Jan. 14	7	3									
		Phamenoth ?		Feb. 25-Mar. 26	7	3									
24		Payni 17		June 1	7										Total: 36 dr.
		Epeiph 15		July 9	6										
25	11th	Mecheir 15	25	Feb. 9	7	3	Ἱππο-δ[ρόμου]	8	4	2	1½	6	4*	Diogenes	σὺν κα(ταγωγίωι)
27		Pachon 13		May 8	3										
		Epeiph 13		July 7											
28		Epeiph 28		July 22											
29	8th	Mecheir 18	22	Feb. 12	7	3	['I]ππο-δρόμου							Paapis	Total, 23-24 A.D.: 7½ dr. + 32¼ supra
32	10th	Phaophi Seb. 3	23	Oct. ?	3	4½									
34		Hathyr 3		Oct. 30	3	4½	Ἱππο-δ[ρόμου]								

*Listed in text as ὑκῆς, probably mistake for χωματικοῦ, for amount ὑκῆς is stated at beginning of line; cp. *supra* and Chart B.

Chart B—Tax Documents of Tryphon and Documents Found with Them with the Addition of Oxy. 389: 17/18-56 A.D.

Oxy.	Desc.	Egyptian Year	Egyptian Month, day	Roman Year A.D.	Roman Month, day	Name	γερδιακόν Dr.	γερδιακόν Ob.	ἐπικεφάλαιον Dr.	ἐπικεφάλαιον Ob.	ὑική Dr.	ὑική Ob.	χωματικόν Dr.	χωματικόν Ob.	Bank
309 desc.	23 ll. col. i col. iv col. iii	4th Tib. 5th Tib. 5th Tib.		17/18 18/19 18/19		Thoönius ἀπελ(εύθερος) Πτολε(μαίου)	? 36 total						6 6	4 4	
311 desc. Cp. 288, ll. 7-11	6 ll.	9th Tib.		22/23		Tryphon Ἱπποδ(ρόμου)			12		2	1½	6	4	
312 desc.	3 ll.	For 22d Tib. Dated 1st Gaius	Mesore	35/36 37	July 25-Aug. 23	Included by G. & H. in Tryphon documents							3 incomplete?	4½	Dorion & Ptolemaeus
308 desc. Cp. 288 & 289	17 ll. 2 cols.	6th/10th Claud.		45/50		Tryphon Τε(μενούθεως)	incomplete?		λαογραφία incomplete?		1	4	6	4	
313 desc. Cp. G. & H. introd. 289	5 ll.	For 7th Claud. Dated 8th Claud.	Phaophi	46/47 47	Sept. 28-Oct. 27	Paësis, son of Paësis Λ(αύρας) Π(ομμενκῆς)?			λαογρ..... (αφία) 12 4		1	4½	6	4	
310 desc.	6 ll.	2d Nero	Payni 20	56	June 14	Apion, son of Tryphon, Τευμε(νούθεως)?	36 total								
389 desc.	Col. i; ends of lines. Col. ii, 1-5, connected with building. 32 ll. "Only entries concerning Horthoönis and Dionysius seem to be indicated."		Neo-Sebastos 25 (Hathyr)	Early 1st century	Nov. 21	Theo.			λα(ογραφία) 80		5	[5½]	14	1	Total Dr. Ob. 100 ½
						Amoetus			40		14		136	1½	190 1½ (G. & H., "194—1½")
						Xenon			20		12	½	67	5½	100 1½
						Heraclidus					26	4½	12	3	39 1½ (G. & H., "39½—1½")
						Horthoönis			16		13	3	[3]13	4	36 ½
						Atrion			24		6	4½	6	2	64 ½
						Dionysius			12		5	5½	6	4	24 3½
						Par—			20				9	3½	

Chart C—Tax Document of Thoönis, Relative of Tryphon: 66-83 A.D.

Oxy. 289 Line	Egyptian Year	Egyptian Month, day	Roman Year A.D.	Roman Month, day	Name Thoönis	φ...?	λαογ(ραφία) Dr.	λαογ(ραφία) Ob.	υἱκή Dr.	υἱκή Ob.	χωματ(ικόν) Dr.	χωματ(ικόν) Ob.	Bank	Miscellanea
col. i. 1	12th Nero	Phamenoth 29	66	Mar. 25	λΠ=λ(αυρας) Π(οιμενικης)?		8		3	3			Dorion & Chaeremon	"Grandson of Chaeremon," probably error from name of banker written above, cp. col. i.5, col. ii.2 υἱκη, l.4, includes payment of brother, Eudaemon
3		Pachon 2		Apr. 27				4			6	4		
4		Pachon 29		May 22	Grandson of Chaeremon?				1					
5		Epeiph ?		June 25-July 24	Grandson of Onnophris									
6														
6	13th Nero	Pachon 29	67	May 22			8		1					
7		Epeiph 5		June 29		1	4				6	4		
8		Mesore 5		July 29										
9	14th Nero	Payni (?) 3	68	May 28			8		1	4½				
9		Payni (?) 4		May 29		1	4				6	4		
10														
10														
col. ii. 1	2d Galba	Phaophi 5	68	Oct. 2	λΠ Grandson of Onnophris		8		1				Dorion & Chaeremon	
2							4				6	4		
3	1st Otho	Phamenoth 21	69	Mar. 17			8		1	4½			Dorion & Chaeremon	Otho died Apr.16(?), cf. Wilcken, Ostraka, vol. 1.801. G. & H. accept Apr. 12. Didymus is probably an agent.
5		Pachon 5		Apr. 30				4			6	4		
6	2d Vesp.	Thoth 5	69	Sept. 2	λΠ	?1							Didymus?	
7														
7	2d Vesp.	Phamenoth 3	70	Feb. 27			8		1	4½				
8		Pharmuthi 26		Apr. 21				4			6	4		
9		Mesore 28		Aug. 21										

Chart C—Tax Document of Thoönis, Relative of Tryphon: 66-83 A.D.—(Continued)

Oxy. 289 Line	Year	Egyptian Month, day	Roman Year A.D.	Roman Month, day	Name Thoönis	φ..?	λαογ(ραφία) Dr	Ob	νική Dr	Ob	χωματ(ικόν) Dr	Ob	Bank	Miscellanea
10	3d Vesp.	Phamenoth 3 / Pachon 5	71	Feb. 27 / Apr. 30	λII		8	4						
11 / 11		Mesore 3		July 27	λII				1	4½	6	4	Chaeremon & Apollonius	
12	4th Vesp.	Mecheir 29	72	Feb. 23			8	4						
13 / 13		Pachon 5		Apr. 30					1	4½	6	4	Chaeremon & Sons of Apollonius	
13	5th Vesp.	Phaophi 5		Oct. 2										
14 / 15 / 16	5th Vesp.	Pharmuthi 27 / Payni 2	73	Apr. 22 / May 27			8	4						
16	6th Vesp.	Phaophi 4		Oct. 1										
16 / 17 / 17	6th Vesp.	Pachon 2 / Payni 3	74	Apr. 27 / May 28	λII		8	4	1	4½	6	4		
17	7th Vesp.	Thoth 5?		Sept. 2?	λII				1	4½	6	4		
	7th Vesp.		75											Missing
18	8th Vesp.	Pharmuthi 5	76	Mar. 31	λII		8							Incomplete
col. i 11	3d Titus	Mecheir 28	81	Feb. 22	λII		8	4						
13 / 13 / 14		Pachon 5 / Epeiph 5		Apr. 30 / June 29					1	4½	6	4	Chaeremon & Associates	
14 / 15 / 15	1st Domit.	Pachon 13 / Epagomeni 3	82	May 9 / Aug. 26	λII		4		1	4	6			
17	2d Domit.	Mecheir 1	83	Jan. 26	λII		8						Chaeremon & Associates	

though it does not concern Tryphon, is *P. Oxy.* 513 (184 A.D.) which demonstrates the method of transferring payment from one account to another.

The financial business of Tryphon and his family, apart from tax payments, chiefly concerns loans. Chart D lists eight papyri in this connection, two of which appear not to relate to Tryphon himself. The normal formula includes the acknowledgment of the loan, the signature of the payee, with sometimes the signature of the lender, the docket of the bank at which payment was made, receipt for repayment, and the date. When a loan has been settled, the document bears lines of cancellation. Occasionally the receipt for repayment is on a separate sheet. In some cases contracts, guarantees, and penalties are included in the formulae. The debtor is regularly termed Πέρσης τῆς ἐπιγονῆς; if a woman, Περσίνη. One transaction was made at a so-called "private bank," ἰδιωτικὴ τράπεζα. Important contracts, such as those concerned with the sale of property, were regularly registered in a notarial office, as has already been noted under Tryphon's contacts with officials; Apollonius of *P. Oxy.* 320 is not specified to have been a "banker,"—he was probably a financial agent of the agoranomi.[20]

Tryphon's loan transactions, as Chart D indicates, were normally with family connections. He had loaned his mother 16 drachmae in 37 A.D., about the time that his wife presented him with a dowry! He borrowed 104 drachmae from a relative, Thoönis, in 55 A.D., the year that he bought part of a house in the Temgenouthis (*sic*) Quarter "to the west of the lane leading to Shepherds' Quarter." About three years and a half later, in May or June (Payni) 59 A.D., he appears to have participated in the purchase of another house in the same vicinity,[21] probably in conjunction with his brother Onnophris, together with whom on June 25 he and his wife borrowed 314 drachmae

---

[20] Cf. *Oxy.* 268.20.
[21] Cf. *Oxy.* 306 desc. and 318 desc. with 99 and 320 desc.

Chart D—Documents for Miscellaneous Financial Transactions of Tryphon and Documents Found with Them: 20-59 A.D.

Oxy.	One Party	Transaction	Second Party	Date Egyptian Roman	Sum	Bank or Agency	Miscellanea
305 desc.	Heracleus, son of Soterichus and wife, Thermoutharion, ἀλευθέρα Σωτάδου	Loan Acknowledgement	Thoönis Πατ Βέως Lender	6th Tib. 20 A.D.	104 dr.	Harpocration ἰδιωτικὴ τράπεζα	Signature—Docket Receipt—Cancellation Same formula as Oxy. 269
323 desc.	Member of Althean deme	Repayment Acknowledgement		22d Tib. Choiach 35 A.D. Nov.-Dec.		Pamphilus	Signatures—Docket (περιλέλυνται ἡ διαγρα- φή) Receipt—Cancellation
267	Tryphon, son of Dionysius, Πέρσης τῆς ἐπι[γ]ονῆς	Dowry Acknowledgement Repayment Acknowledgement	Saraeus, daughter of Apion, ward of Onnophris	1st Gaius Pachon 27 37 A.D. May 22 3rd Claud. Payni 15 43 A.D. June 3	Silver 40 dr. Earrings = 20 dr. Chiton = 12 dr. Total 72 dr. 72 dr.	Sarapion, son of Kleandrus, at the Serapeum	Signatures by proxy Receipt for repayment dated June 9, 43 A.D. instead of Oct. 27, 37 A.D. (2d Gaius, Phaophi 30) as per agreement
319 desc.	Thamounis, daughter of Onnophris, Πέρσινη	Loan Acknowledgement	Tryphon, son of Thamounis Lender	2d Gaius 37-38 A.D.	16 dr.		Same formula as Oxy. 269
264	Tryphon, son of Dionysius	Sale of loom Contract	Ammonius, son of Ammonius Vendor	14th Claud. Mesore 15 54 A.D. Aug. 8	20 dr.	Sarapion, son of Lochus, at the Serapeum	Signature of vendor by proxy—Receipt and guarantee Docket
304 desc.	Tryphon	Loan Acknowledgement	Thoönis, son of Thoönis Lender	2d Nero 55 A.D.	104 dr.	Ammonius and Epimachus	Signatures—Docket Receipt—Cancellation Same formula as Oxy. 269

Chart D—Documents for Miscellaneous Financial Transactions of Tryphon and Documents Found with Them: 20-59 A.D.—(Continued)

Oxy.	One Party	Transaction	Second Party	Date Egyptian Roman	Sum	Bank or Agency	Miscellanea
99	Tryphon, son of Dionysius	Sale of House Contract Tax Payment	Pnepheros, son of Papontos, cousin of Thamounis Vendor	2d Nero Hathyr 6 55 A.D. Nov. 2	3 talents (copper) 1200 dr. = 10% tax on sale (32 copper talents) additional fee	Sarapion καί μέτοχοι, at the Serapeum (?)	Contract with guarantee negotiated before agoranomi—Docket resembles those on Ptolemaic contracts
269	Dioscorus, son of Zenodorus, [Πέρ]σαι τῆς ἐπιγονῆς	Loan Acknowledgement	Tryphon, son of Dionysius Lender	3rd Nero Pachon 18 57 A.D. May 13	52 dr.	Archibius, son of Archibius, at the Serapeum—through agent Theon, son of Syrus	Promise to pay on Aug. 23 (Mesore 30). with guarantee. Signature of borrower by proxy Docket—No cancellation—No receipt—Letter about dun follows
318 desc.	Tryphon	Loan Contract	Antiphanes, son of Heraclas Lender	5th Nero Payni 59 A.D. May-June	160 dr.		διὰ τοῦ μνημονείου Cancellation—Guarantee includes stipulations for lender.
306 desc.	Tryphon	Repayment Acknowledgement	Antiphanes, son of Heraclas Lender	5th Nero Epeiph 59 A.D. June-July	160 dr.		Same formula as Oxy. 269.
320 desc.	Tryphon, Saraeus and Onnophris, brother of Tryphon	Loan Contract	Tryphaena acting with son-in-law Dionysius	5th Nero Payni 25 59 A.D. June 19	314 dr.		Contract negotiated with associate agoranomi through agent Apollonius (formerly Secundus?)—Docket in second hand—Endorsement on verso. Cancellation. Same formula as Oxy. 269.

from their grandmother. The next month Tryphon himself borrowed 160 drachmae from the seller, apparently as a sort of short-term mortgage, the repayment of which was contingent upon dislodging the seller's son from the premises.

Within the period of these two deals in real estate, Tryphon loaned to Dioscorus 52 drachmae which he presumably failed to get back, for the document is not cancelled. Partly because it presents the typical formula for a loan, partly because it possesses a widely human interest, *P. Oxy.* 269, which records the transaction, is herewith translated in full.

Col. I.

Copy. Dioscorus, son of Zenodorus, Persians of the Epigone, to Tryphon, son of Dionysius: Greeting. I acknowledge the receipt from you at the Serapeum at Oxyrhynchus through the bank of Archibius, son of Archibius, of the sum of 52 drachmae of silver of Imperial coinage, which is the total amount of my debt. I will pay this back to you on the 30th of the month Caesareus of the present third year of Nero Claudius Caesar Augustus Germanicus Imperator, without any postponement. If I do not pay you back according as has been written, I will hand out to you the stipulated sum plus one half and proper interest for overtime, and you have the right of execution on me and all my property as if in accordance with legal decision. This hand is valid wherever produced, by whomever produced. The third year of Nero Claudius Caesar Augustus Germanicus Imperator, on the 18th day, Augustus, of the month Germanicus.

Copy of signature. I, Dioscorus, son of Zenodorus, have received the 52 silver drachmae in full and will pay them back as stipulated. I, Zoilus, son of Orus, have written for him since he is illiterate. The third year of Nero Claudius Caesar Augustus Germanicus Imperator, on the 18th day, Augustus, of the month Germanicus.

Copy of docket. The third year of Nero Claudius Caesar Augustus Germanicus Imperator, on the 18th day, Augustus, of the month Germanicus. Through Theon, son of Syrus, agent of the banker Archibius, registration has been recorded.

In spite of all strictures Dioscorus did not keep to his agreement. Tryphon thereupon dunned him through a friend, enclosing a copy of the contract in a letter which read as follows:

A WEAVER IN OXYRHYNCHUS

Col. II. Second Hand.

Tryphon to his dear friend Ammonas, the Tall:[22] Greeting. If you can, I entreat you, worry Dioscorus and make him pay what he has set his hand to, and if he gives you the money, give him a receipt, and if you find a safe person, give him the money to bring to me. Greetings to all your family. Farewell.

To continue the analysis of Chart D,—the transaction in *P. Oxy.* 267 might be termed a pseudo-loan. Tryphon's wife, Saraeus, brought him a dowry of 40 drachmae in cash in addition to jewelry and garments amounting to 32 drachmae, a total of 72 drachmae. He promised to pay her back in five months. He actually made restitution in seven years. The provisional arrangement, and the final repayment of the dowry, which usually signifies a separation or the death of the husband, raise interesting questions which will be considered in a subsequent chapter on Tryphon's domestic life.

The two remaining financial documents in Tryphon's archives give details on special purchases. According to *P. Oxy.* 99, to which a passing allusion was made in discussing loans, Tryphon paid for half of a three-storied house in the "Temgenouthis Quarter" thirty-two copper talents; his own appearance and the location of the house are minutely described in the contract. The sale was executed through the office of the agoranomi, but a 10 per cent purchase tax and some other charge were paid at a bank. Grenfell and Hunt compare the bank docket to the dockets of the Royal Bank on Ptolemaic contracts. The lesser purchase, recorded in *P. Oxy.* 264, was a weaver's loom. The contract includes a careful description of the loom; the guarantee and penalty specified are typical—they read:

I will guarantee the sale with every guarantee, or pay back to you the price which I have received from you plus half as much again and damages.

This purchase, too, was negotiated at a bank.

---

[22] This is the interpretation of Bror Olsson (*Papyrusbriefe aus der frühesten Römerzeit,* Uppsal, 1925, p. 106) for Ἀμμωνᾶτι τῷ [μ]ακρῷ on the analogy of *Mark* 15.40, Ἰάκωβος ὁ μικρός.

From the foregoing survey, the importance of banking in Roman Egypt is obvious.[23] Arsinoë, the capital of the Fayûm, is said to have had seven different banks at the same time. Tryphon's archives indicate considerable variety at Oxyrhynchus for the period of his lifetime. There were—as Chart D indicates—the Bank of Harpocration in 20 A.D., the Bank of Pamphilus in 35 A.D., of Ammonius and Epimachus in 55 A.D., of Archibius in 57 A.D.; at all of these, loans were negotiated by Tryphon or members of his circle. Tryphon's poll tax, detailed in Chart A, was paid in the years 22 to 24 A.D. to Paapis who was presumably a banker, as Fr. Preisigke concludes, although it may be argued that he was a πράκτωρ ἀργυρικῶν or other agent. In 24/25 A.D. Dionysius may have been his successor, but the name in this instance seems rather to be a substitution indicating inaccuracy in copying.[24] Tryphon's other taxes for the years 22 to 25 A.D. were paid at the Bank of Diogenes. A dike tax in 37 A.D. (Chart B) is recorded for the Bank of Dorion and Ptolemaeus. All taxes of Thoönis, presumably, (Chart C) were paid at the same bank, except for the doubtful φ with which the name Didymus, probably an agent, occurs once. Thoönis' documents, covering the period 66 to 83 A.D., show what is evidently a succession in bank partnerships: Dorion and Chaeremon, Chaeremon and Apollonius, Chaeremon and the sons of Apollonius, Chaeremon and associates. Another succession in the years 37 to 57 A.D. may be represented in Chart D by Sarapion the son of Kleandrus, Sarapion the son of Lochus, Sarapion and associates. The following Chart E, compiled from Charts A, B, C, D, summarizes the

[23] On Egyptian banking in the Roman period, in addition to notes 16 and 17, see L. Mitteis, "Trapezitica," in *Zeitschrift der Sav.-St.,* XIX (1898), 198 ff.; Fr. Preisigke, "Buchführung der Banken," in *Archiv,* IV (1908), 110–114; F. Oertel, *Liturgie,* pp. 247–257; G. & H., XIV (1920), 57 ff.; W. L. Westermann, "Papyri as Historical Material," in *C. W.,* XIX (1925–26), 53 f.; J. G. Milne, *Hist.,* pp. 138, 261–264; M. Rostovtzeff, *Soc. & Ec. Hist.,* pp. 170 f., 541 f.

[24] See the writer's note 55 in *T.A.P.A.,* LVIII, 144.

banking represented in Tryphon's documents and those found with them.

Chart E—Banking Represented in Documents of Tryphon
and Documents Found with Them: 20-83 A.D.

Oxy.	Date Roman	Bank	Payment on
305 desc.	20 A.D.	Harpocration	Loan
288	22-24 A.D.	Paapis (?)	Poll tax
	22-25 A.D.	Diogenes	General taxes
323 desc.	35 A.D.	Pamphilus	Loan
312 desc.	37 A.D.	Dorion and Ptolemaeus	Dyke tax *et al.*
267		Sarapion, son of Kleandrus	Dowry
264	54 A.D.	Sarapion, son of Lochus	Minor sale
99	55 A.D.	Sarapion and Associates	Tax on sale of house
304 desc.		Ammonius and Epimachus	Loan
269	57 A.D.	Archibius	Loan
289	66-71 A.D.	Dorion and Chaeremon	Poll and general taxes
	72-76 A.D.	Chaeremon and Apollonius	Poll and general taxes
	81-83 A.D.	Chaeremon and Associates	Poll and general taxes

The bank of Sarapion appears to have been an establishment of some importance. Its location is designated "at the Serapeum." The Bank of Archibius also was "at the Serapeum." To maintain banks in temple precincts was an old established custom in the East and in Greece and Rome. The Serapeum was the center of the worship of Serapis, the collective soul of the dead Apis bulls, whose cult, adapted by the Greeks from the ancient Egyptian cult of Apis and Osiris, had spread throughout Egypt since the Ptolemaic period. Apparently the Serapeum was the important banking district at Oxyrhynchus.

This account of infinite registration by a myriad of officials, including an occasional lawsuit and frequent negotiations with banks mainly in connection with taxes and loans, covers the record of what may be called Tryphon's public life. Simple indeed was the rôle which he played in a thrilling period. He appeared upon the stage, that was about all, a lay figure, paying his taxes and plying his trade—but his trade must be reserved for another chapter.

SWARTHMORE COLLEGE

SOME ANCIENT ANALOGUES OF "CONSIDERATION"

Joseph H. Drake

The Prehistoric Contract

FROM the time that men began to have commercial relations with each other we find that there has been a desire to draw a distinction between an informal agreement, a *nudum pactum,* and such an agreement as would result in a binding obligation, a *contractus* in the modern sense. A need has been felt for some specific mark that would distinguish an agreement of the former type from one of the latter. This mark in all early systems is definite and concrete, so that its presence or absence is readily cognizable by the senses when presented to them and easily proved when brought before the primitive tribunal. We may therefore start with this conception: A contract is an agreement plus some stamp of the law that will turn the informal consensus into an enforceable obligation.[1] It should be noted that the above proposition is not an *a priori* definition to which all contracts must conform, but is rather an enumeration of the basic elements which every contract must contain, if it is to conform to the idea of justice, determined by the standard of the reasonable expectation of the parties to the contract as to the nature of the obligation assumed by them through their agreement.

Any such generalization is however quite beyond the power of the mind of primitive peoples. Indeed we find in the codifi-

---

[1] The validating marks of the contract in English law are the seal and consideration. The one is a concrete mark, appealing to the senses, that makes the agreement to which it is affixed enforceable at law; the other is a psychological mark the character of which the jurists have difficulty in defining, although all agree that, if it is present, the agreement is binding and the courts will enforce it. The purpose of this paper is to discuss the elements in the Roman contract having an analogous function.

47

cation of the Roman law by Justinian, more than a thousand years after the dawn of Roman juristic history, simply a list of fourteen different contracts brought together in a very loose classification with but little attempt at finding a unifying principle.[2] It is this so-called system of Roman contracts supplemented by a string of pacts and natural obligations trailing after it like the tail of a comet that Pothier criticises as "not being founded on the law of nature, and being indeed very remote from simplicity." It is submitted that this elaborate and in some respects unsystematic classification may be presented in a scientific, uniform system by recognizing that every contractual obligation has two and only two essential elements; namely, the consensus of the parties and the stamp of the law that makes the consensus enforceable by the tribunal. It is of course assumed that here as in all bilateral transactions there must be competent persons as subjects, and an object to be attained of which the law approves.

We find in the first book of Livy[3] a contract between states, sanctioned by an appeal to the gods—the *jusjurandum*—that presents clearly these two basic elements of contract. The Romans and the Albans at the conclusion of their fighting have

[2] A. Formal Contracts
   1. Nominate Real Contracts
     (a) *Mutuum*
     (b) *Commodatum*
     (c) *Depositum*
     (d) *Pignus*
   2. Innominate Real Contracts
     (a) *Do ut des*
     (b) *Do ut facias*
     (c) *Facio ut des*
     (d) *Facio ut facias*
   3. Contracts *verbis*
   4. Contracts *litteris*
B. Informal Contracts
     (a) *Emptio-venditio*
     (b) *Locatio-conductio*
     (c) *Societas*
     (d) *Mandatum*
[3] Cf. 1.24.4–9.

met to conclude an armistice. The two armies stand facing each other. The fetial priest, Marcus Valerius, appoints Spurius Fusius as *pater patratus* to ratify the treaty. This official first announces the terms of the contemplated agreement. The recital of the concord between the parties is found on tablets of wax, the purport of which is clearly understood by each party, but the recital alone has no binding force. It is simply the expression of the proposed consensus. The Divine Power is still to be invoked to make the agreement effective. The priest then says: "If we fail to perform our agreement, 'do you, Father of Light [*Diespiter*], strike down the Roman people as I here strike this pig today.'" Then comes the dramatic climax. "He struck (*percussit*) the pig with a flint rock." Here is the "essence" of the contract. The something that makes the agreement binding. Simultaneously with the striking of the blow there is, in the sacrifice, the other impressive phenomenon of the spurting of the blood, and it seems natural that these two dramatic incidents should be preserved as the ratifying marks of a valid contract in historic times. "The Albans likewise recited their formulae and their oath through their dictator and their priests," says Livy. We have then here two separate agreements, each ratified by the "blow" and the attendant "pouring out of blood," two unilateral conventions sanctioned by the ratifying mark that makes of each an inviolate contract.

The word used in describing the blow seems significant: "may you, Father of Light strike down (*ferito*) the Roman people, as I here strike (*feriam*) this pig today, and do you strike (*ferito*) with the greater force as you are stronger and more powerful." Thus far we have some form of the simple word *ferio* to describe the stroke. When however we come to the significant part of the ceremony Livy uses a word of peculiar implication. After the priest had solemnly invoked the vengeance of the God, if the Romans should violate their agreement, he struck (*percussit*) the pig with a flint rock. Livy here uses a form of the verb *percutio*, which, derived from *per* and *quatio*, has the connotation of a shattering, riving blow, like that with a weapon or that of a thunder-bolt. It is this type of blow which appears later as the validating mark of the classical contract.

This account shows on its face that it belongs to a very early time, antedating the period of authentic history. Livy himself says that it is very ancient. The King Tullus mentioned in this connection is the successor of Numa Pompilius, the second of the seven semi-mythical Kings of primitive Rome. The *Diespiter,* Father Jupiter as God of Light, invoked carries us back to the period of worship of the forces of nature, here the lightning stroke. The flint rock used as an instrument in the sacrifice is possibly reminiscent even of the stone age. The description of the ceremony is apparently that of an eyewitness and, although we can hardly suppose Livy is using an original source, it is not an impossible surmise that the annalist whom he has copied did take it from some record of the fetial priests. In the ceremony itself we find the elements of a perfect contract. The formula recited by the parties embodies their solemn agreement. The blow with the flint rock makes this consensus a binding contract.

Contract in the XII Tables

OUR earliest strictly juristic source for the history of contract is found in the Twelve Tables, published in the middle of the fifth century B.C. We have in Table VI of this earliest Roman code the following statement:[4] "When one shall make a *nexum* and (or) a *mancipium,* as he has announced by word of mouth, so let the law be." This conforms to the type of contract set forth above and, as might be expected in this primitive document, the description of the validating mark of the contract, *cum nexum faciet mancipiumque (ve),* occupies a more prominent position than does the recital of the agreement, *uti lingua nuncupassit.* If one shall go through the ceremony de-

---

[4] *Cum nexum faciet mancipiumque, (ve) uti lingua nuncupassit, ita jus esto,* XII, Tab. VI, 1. Cf. Bruns, *Fontes Juris Romani Antiqui,* Pars Prima, p. 25.

scribed as the making of a *nexum* and (or) a *mancipium,* then the agreement expressed by word of mouth is to be *jus* (law).

The discussion of the meaning of the two words, *nexum* and *mancipium,* and of their relation to each other has given rise to much controversy.[5] A statement by the lexicographer Festus, of the early imperial period,[6] leaves no doubt as to the original meaning of *nexum.* He says:[7] "*Nectere* means '*ligare*' (to bind fast) and it is frequently found in very many writers." A *nexum* is then a tie or a bond or a link, and *nexus* is a 'tying.'[8] The *nexi,* whose distress as prisoners for debt Livy so graphically describes in his earlier books, are 'the bound.' Dionysius calls them δουλωθέντες, 'the enslaved.' We may be certain then that the *nexum* of the Twelve Tables is the binding ceremonial that makes effective the agreement mentioned in the clause following the one describing the *nexum* ceremony.

It is however the relation between *nexum* and *mancipium* and the reason for their juxtaposition that present the greatest difficulties. The question arises, is the one of these institutions identical with or derived from the other or are they antithetical concepts? Varro, a contemporary of Cicero, is one of the earliest of the literary sources of information as to the character of these institutions. He says:[9] "Manilius writes that *nexum* is everything that is done with the scale and bronze, in which are *mancipia;* Mucius, what things are done with the bronze and balance that (the parties) may be bound, except those things

---

[5] F. D. Zulueta, "The Recent Controversy about Nexum," in *Law Quart. Rev.,* XXIX (1913), 137 ff. This is an able presentation of the various theories as to the nature of the institutions of *nexum* and *mancipium,* with full citations of the sources and literature. It practically ignores however the question as to the possible connection of the classical contract with the ancient ceremonial.

[6] Festus wrote in the second or third century of the Christian era. His work was abstracted from that of the Augustan, Verrius Flaccus, who in turn depended upon Varro, of the late republican period.

[7] *Nectere 'ligare' significat et est apud plurimos auctores frequens.* Bruns, *op. cit.,* Pars Post., p. 16; Festus, 165M.

[8] Cf. Roby, *Roman Private Law,* II, 296 ff.

[9] *Nexum Manilius scribit omne quod per libram et aes geritur, in quo sunt mancipia, Mucius, quae per aes et libram fiant ut obligentur, praeter quae mancipio dentur.* Bruns, *op. cit.,* p. 60.

which are given in *mancipio.*" Manilius lived in the middle of the second century B.C., Mucius a half century later. It will be seen that the former identifies *nexum* with *mancipium,* while the latter apparently put them in antithesis. Furthermore there has always been a question as to whether in the passage cited above from the Twelve Tables[10] the enclitic of *mancipium* should be the conjunctive *que* or the disjunctive *ve.*

"At the earliest dawn of jurisprudence, the term in use for Contract was . . . *nexum,*"[11] says Maine. On the other hand mancipation was a conveyance, and the definition of Manilius seems to confound contract and conveyance, which in juristic discussion are not only kept apart but are even opposed to each other. Maine's ingenious explanation of this is that at first there was a solemn ceremonial for every solemn transaction and its name was *nexum* because the ceremonial itself created the bond between the parties to the ceremony. When however the transaction with 'copper and balance' had for its function the transfer of property, it received the new and special name of *mancipium* or *mancipatio.*

This identification of *nexum* with *mancipium* which is supported by the use of the *que* with *mancipium*—the received reading—is in accord with the theory of Niebuhr[12] that "the borrower sold himself by a mancipation in the usual form to the lender." "We start with a sale as an ultimate conception and we derive from it a transaction whose operation is *in personam* only because the person is treated as a thing; an intelligible transition from conveyance to contract." Furthermore "if *nexum* was a modified mancipation, we can understand why later speech made *nexum* synonymous with mancipation." Savigny and others have argued against this, that "self mancipation was entirely unknown to Roman law; that a conditional mancipation is against all principle"; and, furthermore, Mucius seems to say that *nexum* is not to be identified with *mancipium.*

[10] Cf. n. 4.
[11] Maine, *Ancient Law,* with Notes by Sir Frederick Pollock, pp. 328, 331.
[12] Cf. *Law Quart. Rev.,* XXIX (1913), 141.

The opposing view of Huschke would identify *nexum* with *judicatum* and not with *mancipium*. According to his argument "*nexum* covers every debt arising *per aes et libram*, including a loan so contracted. This loan took the form of a weighing of the metal to be lent, before *libripens* and witnesses, accompanied by a formula spoken by the creditor in which he declared the debtor *damnas* to repay him. These *nexum* debts were precisely equivalent, so far as they were liquidated, to a judgment debt (*judicatum*) and were therefore enforceable by the creditor without judgment on the person of the debtor by *manus injectio*. They stood to *judicatum* as *mancipatio* to *in jure cessio*."

Without entering into the discussion of the institutional analogy or lack of analogy between *nexum* and *mancipium*, which has developed quite a literature of its own,[13] it may be said that the identification of the one with the other finds some justification in the argument that the mancipatory ceremony as the validating mark of the agreement has in it a survival of the prehistoric, sacrificial validation by the blow with a flint described in the ceremonial of ratification of the treaty between the Romans and the Albans, in Livy's account. We may thus turn from the discussion of the character of *nexum* and *mancipium* and of their interrelation, and may fix our attention on the *cum nexum faciet mancipiumque* as the validating mark of the agreement which is described in the *uti lingua nuncupassit*.

The derivation of the word *mancipium*, 'a taking with the hand' or 'a stroke by the hand,' seems to furnish a clew, though perhaps a somewhat tenuous one, to the relation between the prehistoric contract described by Livy and the earliest mention of a classical contract in the Twelve Tables. Out on the edge of *bona fide* contracts—those depending on consensus alone—there is found a contract, the so-called *mandatum*, which seems to be identical with or closely analogous to this most ancient *stricti juris* contract, the *mancipium*. This *mandatum*,

---

[13] Cf. n. 5.

'a giving of the hand' is a recognized form of contract in the latter part of the third century B.C. Plautus, the writer of Roman comedy who lived during this period, gives us a dramatic account of the making of such a contract. Tyndarus and Philocrates, two of his characters, are described as discussing the terms of a certain agreement as follows:[14]

Tyndarus

This I beg of you by your right hand holding you with my right hand, that you may not be less faithful to me than I am to you. Shake on it. [*Hoc age tu*]. You are now my master, my patron, my father. I commend to you my hopes and my fortunes.

Philocrates

You have given your hand in due form. Are you satisfied, if I perform the mandates given me?

Tyndarus

Perfectly.

The slangy translation of *Hoc age tu* of the Latin text merits especial attention. This rendering makes intelligible what would otherwise be difficult to explain. Tyndarus entreats Philocrates to enter into an agreement of reciprocal fidelity. As the stamp that will make this mutual agreement binding he joins hands with Philocrates saying, 'shake' or 'put 'er

[14] Plautus *Captivi* 442–446.

Tyndarus

Haec per dexteram tuam te dextera retinens manu
Opsecro, infidelior mihi ne fuas quam ego sum tibi.
Hoc age tu: tu mihi erus nunc es, tu patronus, tu pater:
Tibi commendo spes opesque meas.

Philocrates
Mandavisti satis.

Satin habes mandata quae sunt facta si refero?

Tyndarus
Satis.

In a note on the meaning of *hoc age* Professor John C. Rolfe says: "Although *hoc age* (*agite*) evidently acquired two distinct meanings, it is probable, as has been said, that their origin was the same, and that *hoc age* in the formula

there,' just as does the boy today when he wishes to make his agreement binding, so that, in case of failure to perform, the delinquent may be subject to all the pains and penalties of boy-law. Every boy knows that when you 'shake on it' the simple agreement becomes a binding obligation. This phraseology is used in describing the lethal blow given the animal in a sacrifice. Ovid[15] tells us that in the performance of the sacrificial rite, the attendant at the altar said to the priest, *Agone?* 'Shall I strike?' and the latter answered, *Age*, 'Strike.' The blow with the weapon of the assistant in the sacrifice is described by exactly the same phrase as is the blow with the palms of the contracting parties, in the *Hoc age tu* of Plautus. The *stricti juris mancipium* is therefore etymologically identical with the *bona fide mandatum*.

The jurists have always had difficulty in fitting the *mandatum* into any scheme of classification of contracts.[16] The fact that this contract was well known in the time of Plautus, when Roman thought was beginning to be influenced so much by the

---

alluded to by Varro, Ovid, and Seneca gave rise to that mentioned by Plutarch, the former meaning attaching to the words when a victim was offered up; the latter, when the worshippers were exhorted to look and listen. The meaning 'pay attention' is by far the more common of the two." See *Trans. Am. Phil. Assoc.*, XLV (1914), 39.

But inasmuch as Plautus is describing the making of a *mandatum*, the *hoc age* would seem to refer to the validating mark of that contract rather than to be simply an exhortation to 'Keep at it,' i.e. 'to attend to the business.' Furthermore the description of the *mandatum* by Plautus comes at the point in the history of Roman law when the old formal contract of the *jus civile*, validated by the 'stroke,' was passing over into the *bona fide* contract of the *jus gentium*. The *mandatum* in this transition period harks back to its source in the XII Tables, in the *mancipium*, but it already has the character of *bona fides* as is shown by the exhortation to good faith in the passage just preceding the *Hoc age tu*.

[15] Cf. Ovid *Fasti* 1.321.
> *Qui calido strictos tincturus sanguine cultros,*
> *Semper agatne, rogat, nec nisi jussus agit.*

[16] Cf. Hunter, *Roman Law*, p. 533. "The circumstance that mandate alone of the consensual contracts presents an *actio contraria*, excites a suspicion that it is not in its right place." In his scheme of classification Hunter puts the *mandatum* in the category of contracts *re*, though the Roman jurists classify it among the contracts *consensu*. Cf. n. 2 and n. 14.

legal practices of the *jus gentium*, brought in by the commercial contact of Rome with the Greek cities of Magna Graecia, and by the philosophic theories of the Greek *jus naturale*, might seem to indicate an easy transition from the *manu capere* of the *jus civile* to the *manum dare* of the *jus gentium*. The old affiliation indicated by the name and the new connotations brought in by the influence of the foreign ideas would thus explain the confusion of the concepts and the consequent difficulty of classification.

The probable connection of this stroke of the hand with the blow given by a weapon is treated at greater length in another place.[17] The blow with a weapon of the sacrificial ceremony as described by Livy survives in the mancipatory transaction of early Roman law and probably also in the *stipulatio*, as we shall see later. In the feudal period a sale is made binding when the "buyer strikes with the right hand the palm of the right hand of the seller." Blackstone says that "anciently among all the northern nations, shaking of the hands was held necessary to bind the bargain." Vinogradoff describes a contract of Indian marriage as follows: "The bride and bridegroom concluded the agreement as to common life and perpetual union by giving the hand (Handfasting), described in Rome as *dextrarum prehensio*." In Scotch-Irish customary law a sale is perfected when "the vendee places a penny in the palm of his hand and strikes with it the palm of the hand of the vendor, the penny being transferred to the vendor in the process." "The Century Dictionary says that 'swat' is perhaps a variant of 'swap.' The Oxford Dictionary says that swap 'signifies a smart resounding blow.' Swat is defined in identical terms as 'a smart or violent blow.' If this is true, it would appear that the *festucam imponebat* of the *legis actio sacramento* (Gaius 4.16) and the

---

[17] Cf. *Mich. L. Rev.*, XXI (1922–23), 83 ff. The various instances of this usage were collected for the seminary in comparative law by Dr. George Sellett, now Dean of the School of Comparative Law in Shanghai, China, and the brothers Dr. Shih C. Ho and Dr. Shih H. Ho of Shanghai, China. Cf. Brissaud, *History of French Private Law*, p. 374. See also Tac. *Ann.* 12.47.

percutit libram of the transfer *per aes et libram* (Gaius 3.174) may be related to the 'swap' that affects a conveyance and depends for its validity on the Anglo-Saxon 'swat' or the Teutonic '*Handschlag,*' which accompanies it."

The Formal Contracts of the Classical Period

1. *Mancipatio*

IT seems like a far cry from the fifth century before Christ to the second century of our era, but we make this jump of nearly seven centuries in passing from a consideration of the institution *mancipium,* as presented in the Twelve Tables, to the mancipatory process as described by Gaius,[18] who flourished about 180 A.D. In his account of the process of *mancipatio,* the sale of a man, he says: "Mancipation is then, as we have said above, a symbolic form of sale, which is, too, within the competence of Roman citizens alone. The transaction is conducted as follows: in the presence of not less than five citizens who have attained the age of puberty, and with another person of the same status, who holds a bronze balance and who is called the balance holder, he who takes under his control (the vendee), holding a piece of bronze in his hand, says, *this man, I say, is mine by Quiritary right and he has been bought by me by this piece of bronze and bronze balance;* then he strikes (*percutit*) the balance with the piece of bronze and gives the bronze piece to him from whom he receives *in mancipio* by way of a price."

Although the form in which this has come down to us dates from the latter part of the second century of our era, it shows on its face evidences of very much greater antiquity. In the first place it describes in minute detail, under the name of *mancipatio,* the same process of validating an agreement that is described in the passage from the Twelve Tables, above cited,[19] under the name of *mancipium.* The ceremony is a public one,

---

[18] Cf. *Inst.* 1.119. [19] Cf. n. 4.

in the presence of five Roman citizens as witnesses. These are ordinarily understood to be representatives of the five classes into which Servius Tullius divided the people, during the time of the early kings. The balance is of bronze. The balance holder and witnesses must not be deaf,[20] that they may be able to hear the blow struck by the piece of bronze[21] which is afterward transferred as symbolic payment instead of the actual pieces of bronze which were originally weighed out. We have in short the ceremony for validating a transaction, dating from a time probably prior to the Twelve Tables.

In this ceremony we find the word *percutit* used by Gaius to describe the 'blow' struck by the vendee which is to ratify the transaction.[22] It seems even more significant here than it does in the ceremony for ratification of the treaty described by Livy. In the passage from Livy some form of the word *ferio* has been used several times just preceding the *percussit,* which describes the fatal stroke, and it may well be argued that the use of a form of *percutio* by Livy is simply a stylistic variation to avoid repetition of the same word, but in the Gaius passage there is no reason for using the stronger word. The vendee simply 'touches' the scale with the piece of bronze. It seems very likely then that Gaius must have derived the word *percutit* from some very early record and that it is an indication of the survival of the 'blow' of the primitive sacrifice.

There is found at the end of the account of the mancipatory contract as given by Gaius a description of the last step in the ceremonial which seems to indicate that the later contract *re* may have been derived from the same parent stem. "The vendee touches the balance with the piece of bronze and gives that bronze to the vendor as if in lieu of a price." There is in this

---

[20] *Mutus surdus, furiosus, pupillus, femina neque familiae emptor esse, neque testis libripensve fieri potest.* Ulpian, *Fragmenta,* 20.7. Cf. Huschke, *Jurisprudentiae Antejustinianae,* p. 556.

[21] . . . *in mancipando, cum dicitur "rudusculo libram ferito," asse tangitur libra.* Bruns, *op. cit.* Festus 265M, cf. n. 6, n. 7. Pars Post., p. 33.

[22] *Deinde aere percutit libram. Inst.,* 1.119. Cf. n. 18.

ceremonial then the delivery of a thing which becomes the essence of the contract *re*. It is given as a 'price,' an essential element of the consensual contract of sale. It is a *quid pro quo* in which is found the germ of the modern *causa,* the analogue of our much discussed consideration.

2. *Stipulatio* and *Sponsio*

THE relation of the terms *stipulatio* and *sponsio* has been as much of an enigma as that of *nexum* and *mancipium*. According to the theory formerly prevailing, the *nexum* was the parent stem from which sprang the other formal contracts, *stipulatio* and *expensilatio,* though this theory has been vigorously combated.[23] An examination of the somewhat scanty sources of information on this point would seem to indicate that the one is not derived from the other but that both go back to an earlier source. The classical writers themselves were about as much in the dark as to the origin of *stipulatio* and its relation to *sponsio* as we ourselves are. One of our earliest bits of information is found in Festus[24] (second or third century of our era). He quotes Verrius, a writer of the Augustan period, who probably used Varro, a contemporary of Cicero. Festus says: "Verrius thinks that *spondere* is used because the thing is promised *'sua sponte,'* of one's own accord, i.e., voluntarily; and then forgetting this, at a later point he says that *sponsum* and *sponsam* are derived from the Greek, because they (the Greeks) make σπονδάς in the performance of sacred rites." It is quite evident that the second thought of Verrius or of his source, Varro, is better than the first, and we may well see in the σπονδαί, the libations of wine, oil, or milk poured out by way of sacrifice, a survival of the pouring out of blood in the slaying of the animal. It seems reasonably certain that the *sponsio* was the primitive form of the *stipulatio* and that the latter "was a secularization of a religious undertaking, perhaps by oath." *Sponsio*

---

[23] Cf. Hunter, *op. cit.,* 4th ed., p. 537.
[24] Bruns, *op. cit.,* Pars Post., p. 40.

was the name originally given to a contract concluded by a libation, i.e., by a formal denunciation, to the following effect; "Even as the wine now flows, so may the punishing Gods cause the blood of him to flow who shall be the first to break this engagement."[25]

Our principal juristic sources[26] of information as to these two terms confirm this conjecture. Gaius says: "A verbal contract is formed by question and answer, thus: *dari spondes? spondeo; dabis? dabo; promittis? promitto;* etc. . . . This formula, *dari spondes? spondeo,* is peculiar to Roman citizens. The other formulae belong to the *jus gentium* and are binding on all men whether they be Roman citizens or foreigners. . . . Furthermore this obligation *verbis; dari spondes? spondeo,* is so peculiar to Roman citizens that it cannot properly be carried over into the Greek language by translation, although it is said to be derived from a Greek word." It is plain that the conjectural derivation by Gaius is well founded. *Spondeo* is derived from the Greek, σπένδω, 'pour out,' equivalent to the Latin *libo.* The formula *dare spondes? spondeo,* peculiar to Roman citizens, could not in the time of Gaius be "carried over into the Greek language by translation." It could only be transliterated. This would seem to indicate that the use of these words, as the only sacred validation of the contract, goes back to the early Italic period when only the old *Quirites,* the aristocratic conquering spearmen, had full rights under the *jus civile,* including this right of ratifying a contract with the words that were symbolic of the pouring out of blood or other libation; namely, *spondesne? spondeo.*[27]

[25] Buckland, *A Manual of Roman Private Law,* p. 262. Also Sohm, *Inst.,* 64, n. 16. Cf. Leist, *Graeco-italische Rechtsgeschichte,* 1884, pp. 457 ff.

[26] Gaius *Inst.* 3.92.93; Justinian *Inst.* 3.15.1. The account of Justinian is almost identical with that of Gaius.

[27] It was not until the latter part of the fifth century of the Christian era that the use of the old form was specifically remitted, so that any words expressing the agreement of the parties might be used. This was of course centuries after all distinctions between the primitive *Quirites* and the plebeians or the *peregrini* were wiped out. Cf. *Cod.* 8.37.10.

In the next section from Gaius,[28] the following statement appears: "It is said that in one case only can a foreigner also be bound by this word; namely if our imperator, in concluding a treaty of peace, should thus interrogate the leader of some foreign people: 'do you promise there shall be peace?'[29] and the Roman himself should be interrogated in the same language." This case, that seems anomalous to Gaius, may readily be explained if we recognize that the transaction is here between leaders of sovereign states, who in making the treaty must use the words reminiscent of the pouring out of blood in the sacrifice; and this carries us back again to the agreement ratified by the sacrificial ceremony as described by Livy.

The word *stipulatio* is constantly used in juxtaposition with the word *sponsio*. Under a discussion of the "meaning of words" Paul says:[30] "Not only is that called *sponsio* which is concluded by question in the betrothal but every stipulation and promise"; and Ulpian[31] tells us that the word "*sponsalia* is derived from *spondere;* for it was the custom with the ancients to make a stipulation and promise to those who were to be their wives." It is therefore quite plain that the institution *stipulatio* is identical with the institution *sponsio*. They are used indifferently to describe the ceremonial contract that has been bequeathed to our marriage ceremony in the "Do you take this woman to be your wedded wife?" Answer: "I do." The modern contract, like the old one, is, too, a unilateral convention whose essence is found in the interrogatory form of the ceremony. The woman must make a like response to a similar question.

The *nexum*, the *stipulatio*, and the *expensilatio* (to be mentioned later) are the three formal contracts of the primitive law and it has been a favorite theory that the last two are derived from the first and therefore came into existence at a later time. Maine says:[32] "the question and answer of the stipulation were

---

[28] *Inst.* 3.94.   [29] *Pacem futuram spondes?*   [30] *Dig.* 50.16.7.
[31] *Dig.* 23.1.2.   [32] *Ancient Law*, p. 339.

61

unquestionably the Nexum in a simplified form." But Hunter[33] thinks that this hypothesis, though an attractive one, is not supported by the evidence. He says that we must recognize that the stipulation is of equal antiquity with the *nexum*. It would seem from the etymological evidence, presented above, that they both go back to the more ancient contract between states, solemnized by the blow and the pouring out of blood.

Justinian[34] tells us that "the obligation *verbis* is contracted by means of a question and answer, when we stipulate that anything be given to or done for us. . . . The name (he says) is used for the reason that *stipulum* meant 'firm' with the ancients, derived possibly from *stipes*." Now Festus[35] defines *stipes* as *fustis terrae defixus*. Here *fustis* seems to mean 'stake.' In a passage of Plautus[36] it means 'staff' or 'cane.' As used by Horace[37] it apparently means, in the plural, 'sticks' of wood. It is frequently used by the writers of slap-stick comedy to describe a rod used for cudgeling.[38] The derivation from *stipes* is preferred by the best authorities, instead of the fanciful one from *stips*, 'coined money,'[39] or *stipula*, 'a straw,' given by the late writer, Isidor.[40] So far as this evidence goes, then, it would seem to indicate that *stipulatio* is etymologically connected with the word that means the *instrument* with which a blow is struck, and this is used by metonymy instead of the word 'blow' itself. If this is so, we have in the word 'stipulation' a survival of the blow or stroke of the ancient contract, ratified by the sacrificial ceremony. The *stipulatio* is then not derived from the *nexum* but both are derived from the same source. The contract *verbis*, therefore, made by the question and answer, retains both the

[33] *Roman Law*, p. 525.
[34] *Inst.* 3.15, *pr.*
[35] Cf. Bruns, *op. cit.*, Pars Post., p. 41.
[36] *Asinaria* 2.4.21, *tamquam si claudus sim, cum fusti est ambulandum.*
[37] *Od.* 3.6.41, *severae Matris ad arbitrium recisos Portare fustis.*
[38] Cf. Plautus *Amphitruo* 1.1.202, *Auferere, non abibis, si ego fustem sumpsero.*
[39] Cf. Bruns, *op. cit.*, Pars Post., p. 41; Festus 313M.
[40] Cf. *Origines* 5.24.30.

symbolism of the 'blow' in the name *stipulatio* and the symbolism of the 'pouring out' in the correlative term *sponsio*.[41]

It should be observed that this argument is pertinent only to the question as to the possible survival of the old validating marks of the sacrificial contract in the later contracts, *nexum* and *stipulatio*. It does not attempt to explain why the contract *verbis* has assumed the interrogative form while, as Hunter says,[42] "every formula handed down to us as belonging to the transaction *per aes et libram* is direct and categorical not interrogative." Perhaps Maine's explanation[43] of the interrogatory form is as good a guess as can be made.

3. *Expensilatio*

As regards this contract, of which mention was made above,[44] it need only be said that our sources of information are so scanty—even in the time of Justinian little was known as to its real character—that nothing can be said as to the affiliations of this contract with other ancient contracts of its type. The essence of this contract was formal written words just as the essence of the contract *verbis* was formal spoken words. Of the character of the formal entry or entries nothing can be said with any degree of certainty.

Contracts Re. *The Transitional Type*

It has often been remarked that there is no field of knowledge

---

[41] Cf. n. 24.   [42] *Op. cit.,* p. 540.

[43] "I think we must admit," says Maine, "that this Question and Answer, had it been expressly devised to answer the purpose which it served, would have been justly designated a highly ingenious expedient. It was the *promisee* who, in the character of the stipulator, put all the terms of the contract into the form of the question, and the answer was given by the *promisor*. 'Do you promise that you will deliver me such and such a slave at such and such a place, on such and such a day?' 'I do promise.' Now if we reflect for a moment, we shall see that this obligation to put the promise interrogatively inverts the natural position of the parties, and by effectually breaking the tenor of the conversation, prevents the attention from gliding over a dangerous pledge." *Ancient Law,* p. 340.

[44] Cf. p. 61. For the scanty information in regard to the character of this institution reference may be made to the standard works of Buckland, Hunter, Muirhead, and Salkowski.

in which men are so uninventive[45] as in that of political and legal institutions, and we may well expect that this will be true in the subject of contract which is so conservative in its character. In the newer type, therefore, we may expect to find survivals of the old formalities. What relation is there then between the older formal contracts, *nexum, stipulatio,* and *expensilatio,* and the later contracts *re* and contracts *consensu?* The differences between the two show on their face. The 'essence' of the old contract is the formal mark that makes of the agreement a binding obligation, and it has been shown above that this formal mark is probably descended from the prehistoric sacrificial contract ratified by the 'blow' or the 'pouring out' of blood or by both. But with the introduction of the contract *re* we get over into an entirely different field, psychologically. Here delivery of the thing by the vendee to the vendor imposes a legal duty of redelivery of the same or another thing and this, "evidently on ethical grounds."[46] For the first time, then, moral considerations appear as an ingredient of Contract-Law.[47]

While the old formal contracts were a creature of the *jus civile,* the contracts *re* were developed by the praetor in his administration of the *jus gentium.* After the incorporation of Sicily and the Greek colonies of Magna Graecia into the Roman state, at the conclusion of the Second Punic War, there was a large influx of foreigners into Rome. The *praetor peregrinus,* as an officer hearing cases in which non-Romans were involved, had his attention directed to rules of law of foreign communities. The incorporation of such rules into the Roman law broadened and liberalized it. The old *jus civile* laid down a particular rule; the *jus gentium,* introduced by the praetor,

---

[45] Cf. Muirhead, *Roman Law,* p. 137.

[46] Cf. Maine, *op. cit.,* p. 343.

[47] Cf. Hunter, *op. cit.,* p. 471. In the contracts *re* "an obligation arises not from the observance of an ancient form but from some act or fact. This fact or *res* consisted in the delivery by one person to another of some property with the intention of imposing duties on the receiver."

through the extension of the old rule developed a general principle; the *jus naturale*, which was at this time borrowed from Greek philosophic thinking, expanded the principle of law into a standard of justice. The contract *re*, developed by the praetors, is the connecting link between the ancient formal contracts belonging to the *jus civile* and the contracts *consensu* which were the creature of the *jus naturale*. As an intermediate type it preserves a bit of the old form and at the same time has the ethical germ of the new contract within it.

In his account of the old *mancipatio*, Gaius[48] points out the road probably traversed in passing from the old contract to the new. After describing the touching of the scale with the piece of bronze in the mancipatory ceremony, he continues: "and he gives the piece of bronze to the one from whom he receives in *mancipio* as if by way of a price." The delivery of the piece of bronze is the 'essence' of the new contract. This giving of a thing is in itself a pure formality, as formal as is the touching of the scale with the bronze. Here the contract *re* harks back to the old formal contract. But by the transfer of the bronze to the vendor by the vendee, there arises on the part of the former a moral obligation to give something or to do something in return. Otherwise the vendor would be unjustly enriched at the expense of the vendee. The old requirement of form is retained but the real significance of the contract is found in the moral obligation. The delivery of a thing—anything—with the implied agreement that something shall be returned, is of much more general application than is that of a simple 'touching' or 'pouring out.' We have advanced from the realm of a particular concrete mark as the essence of the contract to a much broader generality. The old *jus civile* is behind us, we are in the current of the newer *jus gentium*. The particular concrete mark is superseded by a more general and more abstract one.

The 'essence' of the so-called 'real' contracts of the Roman law, namely, *mutuum, commodatum, depositum,* and *pignus,* is

[48] *Inst.* 1.119.

65

then to be found not in the *res* itself but in the delivery of the thing. This transfer of the thing is either for consumption, for use, for safe keeping, or as security for a loan. It is this group of contracts that was adopted by Lord Holt in *Coggs* v. *Bernard*[49] as the basis of his classification of bailment contracts, which are defined as "contracts whose essence is a delivery of the possession of personal property in trust, with an agreement express or implied that the trust will be faithfully performed and the property redelivered." The bailment like every other contract of English law must have as an essential mark an actual consideration. But the concept of consideration was never hit upon by the Romans as a necessary element of a contract. During the republican period only those contracts were classified as 'real' in which the *res* delivered, or some equivalent of it, as a bushel of wheat or a gallon of wine, could be redelivered to the owner; but from the beginning of imperial times the conception was extended to include the so-called innominate real contracts, in which a something different from the thing delivered might be redelivered, and this something might be the giving of a thing (*dare*) or the performance of a service (*facere*). The essence of the contract however continued to be the formal mark of the delivery of some thing.[50]

The validating mark of the formal contract is one that appeals to the senses, the blow can be seen. It also must be audible. If one of the parties is deaf, it is not valid.[51] The validating mark of the contract *re* has also in itself a like appeal. But the delivery of the *res* has besides an appeal to the fairness and justice of the agreement. At this point, therefore, the Romans might well have turned to our doctrine of consideration as a

[49] 1 *Lord Raymonds Reports*, 909 (1703).

[50] These innominate real contracts were divided by the Romans into four categories: *do ut des, do ut facias, facio ut des, facio ut facias*. These categories of the innominate real contracts bring us so close to the modern doctrine of consideration, as a *quid pro quo*, that Blackstone classifies them as the four species of consideration recognized by the civilians. *Commentaries*, II, 444. Cf. *Dig.* 19.5.5, *pr.*

[51] Cf. n. 20.

66

general mark validating the agreement. Instead of doing so they developed, in the consensual contract, the universal standard of reasonableness as a test of the validity of the agreement. They jumped over the general principle of the real contract—later to play so important a rôle in our doctrine of consideration—and passed directly to the universal standard of the reasonable man who determines in the light of all the facts what the intention of the parties was in making the contract.

The Consensual Contracts

We started with the proposition that a contract consists of two elements: (1) the agreement, (2) the stamp of the law that makes the agreement legally binding, i.e., enforceable at law. The consensual contract of the Romans has been defined[52] as a transaction "in which the mere agreement was a binding contract." But we have seen in the study of the law of Rome up to this point that "through the whole of its history, though in course of time subject to an increasing number of exceptions, (the) mere agreement between two persons did not give him in whose favour it was conceived a right to demand its enforcement."[53] If we accept this definition of the consensual contract, we seem to have eliminated one of the two essential elements of a contract. If we endorse the argument quoted above, we are met by the difficulty that in our most important class of contracts the agreement itself is the validating mark of the *consensus,* and the only one. The two elements of the contract by coalescing are reduced to one. This most important class of contracts can thus be explained only as an exception to the general course of development. The truth seems to be that when the Romans reached the stage of development at which the consensual contract came into existence, the particular formal marks of the blow and the pouring out of blood were lost sight of. The general principle of the *jus gentium* used as the stamp

[52] Cf. Buckland, *A Text Book of Roman Law,* p. 478.
[53] Cf. Muirhead, *Roman Law,* p. 137.

of enforceability in the contracts *re,* which embodies also the general principle of consideration in our law and *cause* in French law, was passed over and the universal standard of the *jus naturale,* the standard of what a reasonable man would assume was the intention of the parties, became the test of distinction between the enforceable and the non-enforceable agreements.

Whatever may have been the actual course of development— as to which the Roman jurists were quite as much in the dark as we are—it seems certain that the 'essence' of the consensual contract was the *consensus* itself. We thus leave behind us the mechanical test of the existence of the contract, determined by some mark easily recognized by the senses. The more general and abstract test called in modern English law 'consideration' and in French law *cause* apparently escaped the notice of the Romans. There is no such concept as consideration in classical Roman law. Instead of a particular rule or a general principle used as a test of the existence of a contract they passed immediately to the universal standard, endeavoring thus to determine the intention of the parties by an investigation of all the facts.

When it was recognized that in the consensual contracts there was a new principle involved, they were grouped together as the formless contracts and as such were contrasted with the formal contracts which had preceded them. "Obligations are created by *consensus* in sale, hire, partnership and agency," says Gaius. This is copied verbatim by Justinian who however elaborates on this statement as follows: "Now an obligation is said to be created in these cases because there is no need at all of writing nor of the presence of the parties, and it is not necessary that anything be given that the obligation may take effect, but it is enough that those who enter into the transaction should agree."[54]

In each of the four types of consensual contracts enumerated

[54] See Gaius *Inst.* 3.135.136; Cf. Justinian *Inst.* 3.22. This may be compared with the statement of the *German Civil Code,* Art. 145: "One who pro-

by Gaius, the validity of the agreement depends upon the *consensus*. For example, "sale is a contract whereby one party (the vendor) agrees to deliver a thing, and the other party (the purchaser) agrees to pay a sum of money called the 'price.' "[55] There is no formal mark and nothing corresponding to consideration, of the English system. Why then is it valid? The answer of the commentators is that "the contract is valid the moment the parties are agreed in regard to the thing to be made over and the price to be paid." The same principle is enunciated in the *German Civil Code* quoted above.[56] Because of the completion[57] of the solemn agreement, the reasonable man—the observer of the transaction—would say that the parties intended to be bound. The essence of the contract is the consensus fully expressed, thus perfecting the agreement.[58]

The last of the consensual contracts, specifically so called, is the *mandatum*. Coming as it does out on the edge of the *bona fide* contracts, it presents the final attenuation of the consensual concept as such. There is in the name an apparent survival of the old mark of the formal contract;[59] namely, the striking together of the hands. This together with the fact that it alone

poses to another the conclusion of a contract, is bound by the proposition"; and the correlative statement in Art. 151: "The contract is completed by acceptance." In both systems the contract is perfected by consensus alone. There is nothing in either corresponding to the 'consideration' of English law nor to the *cause* of modern French law.

[55] Cf. Sohm, *Institutes of Roman Law*, 3d ed., p. 396.

[56] Cf. Art. 145, 151.

[57] It has often been said that the mere perfecting of a gratuitous trust makes the trust enforceable, but this seems to be rather on the theory that the completing of the trust takes the place of *delivery* of the gift in trust, not that it becomes effective by the proffer of the agreement and the acceptance of such proffer. Cf. Ex parte Pye, 18 Veysey 140 (1811).

[58] The doctrine of Seavy v. Drake that any "expenditure after a promise and on the faith thereof will make the promise enforceable in equity" seems rather to rest upon the theory that something done *after* the proffer is made on the faith of the promise contained therein, is consideration given for the promise, thus making an enforceable contract. "In civil law the *causa civilis* can come after the pact." Cf. 62 N. H. 393 (1882). Cf. also Crosbie v. M'Doual, 13 Veysey 148 (1806).

[59] Cf. n. 14.

of the consensual contracts has an *actio contraria* has suggested the theory[60] "that it is not in its right place, and that it should rather go along with the contracts *re*," and Hunter so classifies it.

This contract has also been found difficult of explanation on any doctrine of consideration. In an early New York case[61] the defendant had made a gratuitous promise that he would effect insurance on an outgoing vessel; he failed to do it. After the wreck of the vessel an action on the case for damages was brought. It was held there could be no recovery because nonfeasance was not detriment in the technical sense of that word as used in the definition of consideration. Recovery would have been allowed in this case in Roman law in an action *ex mandato,* and Sir William Jones argued[62] that "this species of undertaking (should) be as extensively binding in the English law" as it is in Roman law, but Ch. J. Kent answered this by saying that non-feasance was not detriment, though mis-feasance would have been so considered. The New York Court in *Thorne* v. *Deas* came close to adopting the standard of justice as the essential mark of a contract, thus bringing the theory of the English law of contract into harmony with that of the *bona fide* contract of the Roman law and that of the *German Civil Code.*[63] The American court, however, apparently did not see its opportunity to arrive at a universal standard, but fell back on the general principle of 'consideration' just as the Roman

[60] Cf. n. 16. See also n. 2.

[61] Thorne v. Deas, 4 Johns. (N. Y.) 84 (1809).

[62] Jones, *An Essay on the Law of Bailments,* as quoted by Ch. J. Kent, in Thorne v. Deas, at p. 96. Cf. Siegel v. Spear & Co. 234 N. Y. 479 (1923). See also *The American Law Institute. Commentaries on Contracts. Restatement No. 2,* Sec. 88, p. 18. Here Williston says: "There is no element of consideration in this case, Siegel v. Spear, the bailment being gratuitous. There is simply reliance." On the basis of this case and others involving a similar question Williston says in Sec. 90 of the *Restatement of the Law of Contracts. Proposed Final Draft. No. 1:* "A promise which the promisor should reasonably expect to induce action or forbearance of a definite and substantial character on the part of the promisee and which does induce such action or forbearance is binding, if injustice can be avoided only by enforcement of the promise."

[63] Cf. Art. 145, 151.

praetor had failed to see that there was the general psychological principle of consideration in the innominate real contract and had classified the innominate with the nominate real contracts on the basis of the formal mark of delivery of a thing.

In the English law we stop with the general principle of consideration whereas we should rather seek a universal standard of the reasonable expectation of the parties. Would a reasonable man who stood on the outside of the transaction say that, considering all the facts, the plaintiff was justified in depending upon the promise? The Roman law seems on the whole to have reached the more rational solution. Although there is in the contract *mandatum:* (1) A survival of the old formal mark of the striking of the hands, indicated by the name itself; (2) The survival of the contract *re,* in the delivery of a thing, here an abstract thing, a service; (3) The consideration of detriment or equivalency, it rejects all three and rests on consensus alone. If we had accepted Sir William Jones's suggestion that "this species of undertaking should be as extensively binding in the English law" as it is in the Roman, we should have avoided all the difficulties of properly delimiting consideration and should have, instead of a general principle used as a stamp of enforceability, the universal standard of reasonableness to differentiate our non-legal from our legal agreement.[64]

Pacts

After the Romans had closed their system of contracts, they found there were many agreements that in equity and good conscience ought to be enforced but that did not fall within any of the contractual categories. Even in the time of the old civil law equitable extensions of these categories were made, and under the influence of the praetor's court, the reasoning of the jurists and the later enactments of the emperors, there was an extension of legal obligations out into the field of moral obliga-

[64] Cf. Roscoe Pound, *An Introduction to the Philosophy of Law,* New Haven, Yale University Press, p. 282.

tions. They were enforced because they ought to be enforced. Like the consensual *bona fide* contracts they depended for their validity upon a standard of justice determined by a reasonable interpretation of the intent of the parties. Justinian even went beyond the moral out into the religious realm, to get a sanction for legally enforcing a promise to give a gift to the Holy Church. The unconscientious and impious breaker of such an agreement was thus subjected to the penalties of the law and also to the vengeance of Heaven.[65] We have thus completed the cycle and returned to the religious sanction of the sacrificial contract with which we started.

If the foregoing arguments are valid, it is plain that the complicated system of contracts described in the *Corpus Juris Civilis* may be reduced to a few very simple forms. The three formal contracts, *mancipatio, verbis, litteris,* analogous to our contracts under seal, are derivatives of the prehistoric sacrificial contract in which the validating mark is either the 'blow' or the 'pouring out' of blood, wine, oil or milk, or both. The eight 'real' contracts, which mark a transition stage from the old formal contract to the new formless contract, retain 'form' —here the act of delivery—but contain also the equitable mark of enrichment of the vendee. In other words, this contract contains beside the 'form,' the old concrete validating mark, also the psychological mark of equivalency, which might have ripened into the conception of 'consideration,' but did not. For that we have to wait more than a thousand years. The four formless contracts, sale, hire, partnership, and agency, reach at one bound the modern type of contract, adopted in the *German Code* but not yet recognized in English law, in which the validating mark of the contract is the equitable standard of the reasonable man, who determines whether, on taking into account all the facts, the parties intended to be bound. We here leave behind us all mechanical or psychological tests of the existence of a contract and inquire simply as to the intention of

[65] *Cod.* 8.53.35.5(d).

the parties. The stamp of the law then that makes an agreement enforceable with the Romans, is either a concrete rule of law or a standard of justice. The intermediate psychological principle of 'consideration' or *cause* is not yet born.

LAW SCHOOL,
UNIVERSITY OF MICHIGAN

THE SOURCES OF ARISTOTLE'S *POETICS*

Alfred Gudeman

I.

FOR well-nigh four centuries, ever since the appearance of Robortelli's elaborate commentary on the *Poetics* (1548), this collection of lecture-notes, for it is nothing more than that,[1] though lamentably incomplete, has attracted the attention of philologians, literary and aesthetic critics, philosophers and poets to an incomparably greater degree than any other treatise of its size ever penned.[2]

Under these circumstances it might, indeed, seem a work of supererogation to devote any time or labor to the subject under notice. But incredible as it may appear, this is so far from being a case of *acta agere,* that no one has hitherto even so much as attempted to give anything like a comprehensive survey of Aristotle's presumable predecessors and the extent of his indebtedness to them, so far as this may still be determinable.

The reasons for this neglect of an investigation of such intrinsic importance and interest are not far to seek. In the first place, "source-researches" were up to the nineteenth century virtually an untilled field of philological study.

But even at a later period, the irreparable loss of most, if not all, the literary works which might have furnished a later writer with copious information and influenced him profoundly often acted as a deterrent to enquiries of this nature. This applies with special force to the *Poetics,* for with one notable exception, namely Plato, the pre-Aristotelian literature on the subject has

---

[1] For proof see my forthcoming edition to which I must also refer the reader for all textual and exegetical comment, necessarily excluded here, owing to the spatial limits to which this paper is confined.

[2] Cf. L. Cooper and A. Gudeman. "A Bibliography of the Poetics of Aristotle" in *Cornell Studies in English,* XI (1928), 179.

wholly perished, beyond a few names, titles, and citations or allusions. This latter phenomenon is largely due to the deplorable practice of ancient authors, always barring mere compilers, lexicographers, scholiasts, and their kin, to suppress their sources of information. Occasional departures from this rule are generally due to polemical motives, but even in these cases, the adversary is often alluded to but vaguely and, to make matters still worse, such phrases as τινές (ἔνιοι) φάσι, οἴονται, λέγουσι, *quidam tradunt, arbitrantur, memorant, dicunt,* etc.—for other examples in the *Poetics,* see below—do not even necessarily imply a plurality of sources.[3]

In view of this paucity of direct quotations from earlier writers, it was perhaps but natural, that Plato should loom up large as one of the possibly primary and paramount 'Quellen' of the *Poetics,* dealing, as he did, profusely with the content, character, and effect of poetical productions, it being overlooked, however, that the Platonic utterances concerning the art of the poet and the technique of poetry which constitute the very essence, the "pith and moment" of Aristotle's treatise, are by comparison but few and sporadic. This belief[4] now seems to hold undisputed sway (v. Wilamowitz, Christ-Schmid, Bywater, Ueberweg-Praechter, and Rostagni, to mention only these), having reached a grotesque culmination in *Finsler,* to whom Aristotle, though assuredly one of the world's greatest intellects, is nothing more than a minor planet revolving about the Platonic

---

[3] I have space here for only one, but a quite irrefutable illustration furnished by Aristotle himself. In *Poet.* 25.1461ᵃ22 two λύσεις of Homeric ζητήματα are attributed to one *Hippias* of Thasos. Now these identical instances are again recorded by Arist. *Soph. Elench.* 4.166ᵇ1 as follows: οἶον καὶ τὸν ᵘΟμηρον ἔνιοι διορθοῦνται . . . λύουσι γάρ, etc., where the scholiast, referring directly to our *Poetics,* tells us that Hippias of Thasos was the λυτικός alluded to, under the guise of the plural!

[4] Cf. C. Belger, *De Aristotele etiam in Arte Poetica componenda Platonis discipulo* (Berlin Diss., 1872), p. 89. Long before him P. Beni added to his commentary (1613) an appendix "Platonis Poetica ex eius dialogis collecta" and J. B. Keiser published in 1829 a *Comparatio placitorum Platonis et Aristotelis de ratione et principiis artis poeticae,* pp. 19–84. Both these collections were unknown to Belger and to G. Finsler, *Platon und die Aristotelische Poetik,* 1900, pp. 263 ff.

sun, the *Poetics* shining throughout with borrowed light. We shall see, in what I may call the negative part of this paper, that the *communis opinio* regarding Aristotle's profound indebtedness to Plato rests on no foundations.

Omitting for the present the direct evidence of sources supplied by the *Poetics* themselves, it can be asserted with entire confidence, that a very extensive literature on one or the other aspect of the art and theory of poetry was accessible to Aristotle, which in his case is tantamount to saying, that he made use of it, so far as it suited his purpose.[5] Among these, the *Sophists* must have occupied a very prominent place, for they took all literary and cultural studies for their province. And, if we recall the intimate relation that always existed between music and poetry among the Greeks, it would follow as a matter of course, that they also devoted considerable attention to the art of poetry, even if all positive evidence to that effect were now lacking. For all the fine arts, poetry, music, painting, sculpture, and dancing, are they not in the last analysis only so many manifestations or species of the genus, *rhythm,* to wit the rhythm of language and meter, of tunes, of color, of form, and of movement? If any further proof of the above statement were needed, it would be furnished by the *Frogs* of Aristophanes, for this comedy, as is well known, deals extensively with minute details of dramatic composition, metrical niceties, choral music, etc., which imply an astounding acquaintance with such technical topics on the part of his vast audience, a knowledge which can only have been disseminated by the Sophists, the great public educators of their time.

These general inferences are amply confirmed by a *number of names and titles of the works of pre-Aristotelian or contem-*

---

[5] In this connection a characteristic utterance in *Polit.* VIII. 7 is well worth quoting. Speaking of the educational value of music, harmony, and rhythm, he says: νομίσαντες οὖν πολλὰ καλῶς λέγειν περὶ τούτων τῶν τε νῦν μουσικῶν ἐνίους καὶ τῶν ἐκ φιλοσοφίας ὅσοι τυγχάνουσιν ἐμπειρίας ἔχοντες τῆς περὶ τὴν μουσικὴν παιδείας, τὴν μεθ' ἕκαστον ἀκριβολογίαν ἀποδώσομεν ζητεῖν τοῖς βουλομένοις παρ' ἐκείνων, νῦν δὲ νομικῶς διέλωμεν τοὺς τύπους μόνον εἰπόντες περὶ αὐτῶν.

porary scholars of whom the following represents a tolerably complete list: Theagenes of Rhegion, Περὶ Ὁμήρου, Demokritos, Περὶ ῥυθμῶν καὶ ἁρμονίης, Περὶ ποιήσιος, Περὶ καλλοσύνης ἐπέων, Περὶ εὐφώνων καὶ δυσφήμων γραμμάτων, probably subtitles of a larger work, Περὶ Ὁμήρου ἢ Ὀρθοεπείης καὶ Γλωσσῶν, Περὶ ἀοιδῆς, Περὶ ῥημάτων which implies a treatise Περὶ ὀνομάτων perhaps concealed under the title Ὀνομαστικά, Gorgias,[6] Protagoras' Ἀλήθεια, of which Περὶ ὀρθοεπείας formed a part, Glaukos[7] of Rhegion, Περὶ Ὁμήρου, probably a subtitle of Περὶ τῶν ἀρχαίων ποιητῶν καὶ μουσικῶν, Metrodoros of Lampsakos, Stesimbrotos of Thasos, Hippias of Elis, Περὶ μουσικῆς, Περὶ ῥυθμῶν καὶ ἁρμονιῶν (cf. Plat. *Hipp. Mai.* 285[b] περί τε γραμμάτων δυνάμεως καὶ συλλαβῶν καὶ ῥυθμῶν καὶ ἁρμονιῶν), Περὶ Ὁμήρου, Damastes of Sikyon, Περὶ τῶν ποιητῶν καὶ σοφιστῶν, Kritias, Περὶ Ἀρχιλόχου καὶ Ἀνακρέοντος, Dieuchidas of Megara, Hereas of Megara, Alkidamas Περὶ Ὁμήρου,[8] Herakleides Pontikos Περὶ ποιητικῆς καὶ ποιητῶν, περὶ λύσεων Ὁμηρικῶν.[9] Finally, there would be no chronological difficulty in the assumption, that the famous works of Dikaiarchos, perhaps the most brilliant of Aristotle's pupils, entitled Περὶ μουσικῶν ἀγώνων[10] and the Ὑποθέσεις τῶν Εὐριπίδου καὶ Σοφοκλέους μύθων, may also have been at Aristotle's disposal.

[6] Cf. W. Süss, in *Ethos* (1910), 82–98, and M. Pohlenz, "Die Anfänge der griech. Poetik," in *Nachr. Goetting. Gesell. der Wiss.*, (1920), 142–178, on Gorgias esp. pp. 158 ff.

[7] W. Kranz, in *Jahrb. f. Klass. Altert.*, XLIII (1919), 149, identifies this Glaukos with the critic Glaukon, cited *Poet.* 25.1461[b]1, but this surmise lacks all evidence.

[8] According to a papyrus II/III cent., A.D. Cf. J. G. Winter, in *Trans. Amer. Phil. Assoc.*, LVI (1925), 120 ff.

[9] The ζήτημα referring to the landing of Odysseus in Ithaca, alluded to by Aristotle (24.1460.35 ff.), was dealt with at length by Herakleides, as we learn from Schol. Hom. *Od.* 13.119 ff. and Eustathios *loc. cit.* (pp. 563–565, Dind.).

[10] Whether this was only a portion of his most famous book, the Βίος Ἑλλάδος, or an independent treatise can no longer be determined. In a brief notice which happens to have been preserved he attributed, in agreement with the *Poetics* (c. 4), the introduction of the third actor to Sophokles. It stands to reason that such an item was not an isolated statement, but must have been found in a larger context, such as a history of the Greek drama.

SOURCES OF ARISTOTLE'S POETICS

II.

BEFORE entering upon a more detailed enquiry into the demonstrable indebtedness of Aristotle to his predecessors, the strongest emphasis must be laid upon one source of supreme importance, it being nothing less than the *condicio sine qua non* of a technical treatise on poetry, although, strange to say, attention has never been drawn to it except incidentally by the poet Schiller,[11] and in more recent days by R. C. Flickinger, *Greek Drama*[2], p. 5, commentators presumably regarding it as too self-evident to be dwelt upon. I refer to the *vast storehouse of Greek poetry,* in particular the epic, the dithyramb, tragedy, the old and so-called middle comedy, still accessible to Aristotle in all its glorious entirety, from Homer down to his own day.[12] The phenomenal reading which this implies is perhaps not surprising in the author of the Διδασκαλίαι, but it acquires a special significance in view of our lamentably poor inheritance, for, to take only the famous tragic triad by way of comparison, we can pit but thirty-one plays against nearly three hundred tragedies of Aischylos, Sophokles, and Euripides familiar to Aristotle! This fact calls for extreme caution on the part of the modern investigator in estimating the validity of Aristotelian doctrines, so far as they were directly based upon his incomparably superior knowledge. Convincing evidence of the wide range of the author's reading is furnished by the *Poetics* themselves in spite of their small compass. In the field of *epic* poets besides Homer, including the *Margites,* which Aristotle regards as Homeric, we meet with the *Kypria,* the *Little Iliad,* a *Herakleis* and *Theseid,* Chairemon's *Centaur,* Empedokles, Hegemon the Parodist, the *Deliad* of Nikochares and Kleophon. The tragedies quoted are: Aischylos' *Choephoroi, Prometheus, Phorkides, Philoktetes, Niobe,* and by allusion Sophokles' *Mysoi,*

---

[11] "Man kann des Aristoteles' Poetik nie ganz verstehen und würdigen, weil seine Ansicht von der Tragödie auf der Empirie einer Menge für uns verlorener Stücke beruhte."

[12] The so-called new comedy of the great triumvirate Menander, Diphilos, and Philemon, is posterior to Aristotle.

79

Antigone, Elektra, Oidipos (Tyrannos), *Odysseus Akantho-plex, Peleus, Phthiotides, Tereus, Thyestes;* Euripides' *Elektra,* the two *Iphigeneias, Kresphontes* (Merope), *Medea, Mela-nippe* ἡ σοφή, *Orestes, Philoktetes;* Agathon's "Ανθη; Karkinos' *Amphiaros* (?), *Thyestes;* Astydamas' *Alkmaion;* Dikaiogenes' Κύπριοι; Theodektes' *Lynkeus, Tydeus.* To these must be added the *Aiax* dramas (c. 18), *Meleagros, Telephos* (c. 13), and the tragic stories in the "Little Iliad" which according to Aristotle (c. 23) could be or rather were dramatized, namely the ʽΟπλων κρίσις, the *Philoktetes* (already mentioned), *Neoptolemos* or Eurypylos, the Πτωχεία or Λάκαιναι, the ᾽Ιλίου πέρσις, *Sinon* and *Troades,* for almost all these titles coincide with plays actually composed by well-known dramatists. Of comedians only a few are referred to, incidentally, namely Epicharmos, Phormis (?), Chionides, Magnes, Krates, and Aristophanes, but without the title of a single play, a fact easily accounted for by the loss of the chapter on Comedy. Finally a num-ber of dithyrambs are mentioned, the *Cyclops* by Timo-theos and Philoxenos, the *Skylla* perhaps by Timotheos, the *Iphigeneia among the Taurians* by Polyeides, and a nomos or dithyramb by Argas, if the corrupted text is thus prop-erly emended. Of *prosewriters* only the mimes of Sophron and Xenarchos, Herodotos, and the Socratic dialogues (Plato) are alluded to. These direct citations are further augmented by a number of general statements which would be inexpli-cable except on the assumption of an exhaustive acquaintance with epic and especially tragic literature, to wit: c. 3. ὅτε μὲν ἀπαγγέλλοντα ἢ ἕτερόν τι γενόμενον . . . ἢ ὡς τὸν αὐτὸν καὶ μὴ μεταβάλλοντα. c. 4. πολλὰς μεταβολὰς μεταβαλοῦσα ἡ τραγῳδία ἐπαύσατο . . . ἐκ μικρῶν μύθων (sc. ἡ τραγῳδία ἐγέ-νετο) . . . λέξεως γελοίας etc. . . . ὡς ἕκαστα κοσμηθῆναι λέγεται. c. 5. αἱ μὲν οὖν τῆς τραγῳδίας μεταβάσεις καὶ δι' ὦν ἐγέ-νοντο οὐ λελήθασιν, ἡ δὲ κωμῳδία . . . ἐξ ἀρχῆς ἔλαθεν . . . ἤδη δὲ σχήματά τινα αὐτῆς ἐχούσης οἱ λεγόμενοι (doubtless recorded in the official didascalic archives) αὐτῆς ποιηταὶ μνημονεύονται . . . ἔτι δὲ τῷ μήκει ἡ μὲν (sc. τραγῳδία) μάλιστα πειρᾶται ὑπὸ μίαν περίοδον ἡλίου εἶναι . . . ἡ δέ ἐποποιία ἀόριστος τῷ χρόνῳ . . . τὸ πρῶτον ὁμοίως ἐν ταῖς τραγῳδίαις τοῦτο ἐποίουν καὶ ἐν τοῖς ἔπεσιν. c. 6. αἱ γὰρ τῶν νέων τῶν πλείστων ἄηθεις τραγῳδίαι εἰσὶν καὶ ὅλως ποιηταὶ πολλοὶ τοιοῦτοι . . . οἱ ἐγχείροντες ποιεῖν πρότερον δύνανται τῇ λέξει καὶ τοῖς ἤθεσιν ἀκριβοῦν ἢ τὰ πράγματα συνίστασθαι οἷον καὶ οἱ πρῶτοι ποιηταὶ σχέδον ἅπαντες . . . οἱ μὲν γὰρ ἀρχαῖοι πολιτικῶς ἐποίουν λέγοντες, οἱ δὲ νῦν ῥητορικῶς. c. 9. τὰ τυχόντα ὀνόματα ὑποτιθέασιν . . . ἐν ἐνίαις (sc. τραγῳδίαις) μὲν ἐν ἢ δύο τῶν γνωρίμων ἐστὶν ὀνομάτων, τὰ δὲ ἄλλα πεποιημένα, ἐν ἐνίαις δὲ οὐθ' ἕν, etc. . . . περὶ οὓς (sc. παραδιδομένους μύθους) αἱ τραγῳδίαι εἰσίν. c. 11. αἱ μὲν (sc. ἀναγνωρίσεις) θατέρου πρὸς τὸν ἕτερον μόνον, ὅταν ᾖ δῆλος ἕτερος τίς ἐστιν etc. . . . (of πάθη) οἵ τε ἐν τῷ φανερῷ θάνατοι καὶ οἱ περιωδυνίαι καὶ τρώσεις. c. 12. the entire chapter on the μέρη τραγῳδίας κατὰ τὸ πόσον. c. 13. πρῶτον μὲν γὰρ οἱ ποιηταὶ τοὺς τυχόντας μύθους ἀπηρίθμουν, νῦν δὲ περὶ ὀλίγας οἰκίας αἱ κάλλισται τραγῳδίαι συντίθενται, οἷον περὶ 'Ἀλκμαίονα καὶ Οἰδίπουν καὶ 'Ὀρέστην καὶ Μελέαγρον καὶ Θυέστην καὶ Τήλεφον. c. 14, on the plays that excite pity and fear, ὥσπερ οἱ παλαιοὶ ἐποίουν etc. . . . οὐδεὶς ποιεῖ ὁμοίως, εἰ μὴ ὀλιγάκις, οἷον ἐν 'Ἀντιγόνῃ τὸν Κρέοντα ὁ Αἵμων, and on the various cases of homicide among blood relations in Greek tragedies, with or without ἀναγνώρισις, illustrated by a few characteristic examples. c. 18, regarding the relevancy of choral odes in Sophokles and Euripides and the innovation of the ἐμβόλιμα by Agathon. c. 23. "Ὅμηρος . . . οἱ δ' ἄλλοι περὶ ἕνα ποιοῦσι . . . οἷον ὁ τὰ Κύπρια ποιήσας καὶ ὁ τὴν μικρὰν 'Ἰλιάδα. c. 24. εἰ τῶν ἀρχαίων ἐλάττους καὶ αἱ συστάσεις εἶεν . . . "Ὅμηρος . . . μόνος τῶν ποιητῶν . . . οἱ μὲν οὖν ἄλλοι αὐτοὶ μὲν δι' ὅλου ἀγωνίζονται, μιμοῦνται δὲ ὀλίγα καὶ ὀλιγάκις, etc.[13]

[13] It was Aristotle's custom to delegate to gifted pupils, e.g., Theodektes, Eudemos, Menon, Kallisthenes, and perhaps Theophrastos and Dikaiarchos the task of collecting under his advice and supervision the requisite material which subsequently served as a basis for his own systematic superstructure. It is, therefore, highly probable, that he pursued the same method in the case of the Art

This consummate knowledge of the documentary material of his subject on the part of Aristotle, raises a question of prime importance, but I can give to it but a passing glance here for obvious reasons. Briefly stated the problem is this: did the author arrive at his conclusions, tenets, and rules by a deductive process or, were they, if not primarily, yet largely, the result of an induction, to be subsequently tested by an appeal to poetic practice? A careful sifting of the contents of the *Poetics* warrants me in stating that its author employed now one, now the other method, the various strata, so to speak, being clearly distinguishable.[14]

III.

TURNING now to the determination of the sources of Aristotle in detail, it will be conducive to clearness, if I treat the subject under the following heads:

(1) predecessors mentioned directly by name or by allusion;
(2) passages which for one reason or another imply the existence of an earlier source, dealing with a similar topic;
(3) the question of Aristotle's indebtedness to Plato.

(1) In c. 3.1448ª25 ff. we are informed, that τίνες derived the term δρᾶμα from δρῶντες and that the Dorians, more particularly the Megarians in the Peloponnesus and in Sicily, laid claim (ἀντιποιοῦνται) to the invention of both comedy and tragedy, ποιούμενοι τὰ ὀνόματα σημεῖον. αὐτοὶ μὲν γὰρ κώμας περιοικίδας καλεῖν φασιν, Ἀθηναῖοι δὲ δήμους, ὡς κωμῳδοὺς οὐκ ἀπὸ τοῦ κωμάζειν λεχθέντας, ἀλλὰ τῇ κατὰ κώμας πλάνῃ . . . [καὶ τὸ ποιεῖν αὐτοὶ μὲν δρᾶν, Ἀθηναίους δὲ πράττειν προσαγορεύειν].

The reasons for the Megarian provenience of tragedy are omitted in our *Poetics,* the words καὶ τῆς τραγῳδίας ἔνιοι τῶν ἐν

of Poetry and that, at least, some of the categorical assertions and observations enumerated above were founded upon the evidence furnished by these συναγωγαί of his pupils.

[14] Further details will be given in my commentary.

Πελοποννήσῳ (i.e., the Sicyonians) being inserted in the midst of the Megarian argumentation, thus seriously interrupting the context. But we are here not concerned with the textual difficulties of the passage nor with the validity of the arguments advanced but solely with the fact, that some Dorian critic[15] claimed the priority of the drama, for the plural cannot, of course, designate the public opinion of the Megarians nor need it imply several independent sources (see above). Now, ἀντιποιεῖσθαι always presupposes an adversary or some kind of opposition. This being so, it follows that some earlier Athenian scholar had written an account of the origin and development of the drama, in which he gave the credit of its invention to an Attic playwright. Against this contention the patriotic Megarian vigorously protested. That this probably unexpected attack was not left unanswered might have been conjectured, even if passages like the following did not confirm it: *Schol. Arist. Eth. Nic.* p. 186, 9 H. διασύρονται[16] γὰρ οἱ Μεγαρεῖς ἐν κωμῳδίᾳ ἐπεὶ ἀντιποιοῦνται αὐτῆς, ὡς παρ' αὐτοῖς πρῶτον εὑρεθείσης, etc., and Ps. Plat. *Minos* 321[b] ἡ δὲ τραγῳδία ἐστὶ παλαῖον ἐνθάδε (sc. Athens) οὐχ' ὡς οἴονται ἀπὸ Θέσπιδος ἀρξαμένη οὐδ' ἀπὸ Φρυνίχου ἀλλ', εἰ ἐθέλεις ἐννοῆσαι, πάνυ παλαιὸν αὐτὸ εὑρήσεις ὂν τῆς δὲ τῆς πόλεως εὕρημα. This latter passage looks suspiciously like a rebuttal which by way of a compromise abandoned the Attic Thespis[17] as the εὑρετὴς τῆς τραγῳδίας, but substituted a number of alleged predecessors—we hear of sixteen—the earliest of whom might thus well have antedated Epigenes of Sikyon, put up as the Dorian claimant. We cannot name this predecessor of Aristotle, but, whoever he was, it is a very reason-

---

[15] There is considerable plausibility in the supposition of Wilamowitz, that it was *Dieuchidas* of Megara, an older contemporary of Aristotle.

[16] This proves that the scholiast did not derive his information from our chapter.

[17] Thespis is not mentioned in our *Poetics,* but it is probable that Aristotle discussed the rival claims in his dialogue Περὶ ποιητῶν (cf. Themist. *Orat.* XXVI). His name first occurs in Charon of Lampsakos (V cent.), for on the well-known passage in Arist. *Vesp.* 1478 f. the scholiast remarks: ὁ κιθαρῳδός, οὐ γὰρ δὴ ὁ τραγικός.

able supposition that the *Poetics* contain other items of historical information culled from this or some other similar source,[18] as e.g., in c. 4. τῶν ὑποκριτῶν πλῆθος ἐξ ἑνὸς εἰς δύο πρῶτος Αἰσχύλος ἤγαγε καὶ τὰ τοῦ χοροῦ ἠλάττωσε καὶ τὸν λόγον πρωταγωνιστὴν παρεσκεύασεν, τρεῖς δὲ καὶ σκηνογραφίαν Σοφοκλῆς . . . ἔτι δὲ ἐπεισοδίων πλήθη καὶ τὰ ἄλλα ὡς ἕκαστα κοσμηθῆναι λέγεται[19] ἔστω ἡμῖν εἰρημένα and again c. 5. αἱ μὲν οὖν τῆς τραγῳδίας μεταβάσεις καὶ δι᾿ ὧν ἐγένοντο οὐ λελήθασιν (because preserved in *literary* tradition), ἡ δὲ κωμῳδία διὰ τὸ μὴ σπουδάζεσθαι ἐξ ἀρχῆς ἔλαθεν καὶ γὰρ χορὸν κωμῳδῷ (or κωμῳδοῖς) ὀψέ ποτε ὁ ἄρχων ἔδωκεν (the didascalic archives left no doubt on this point), ἀλλ᾿ ἐθελονταὶ ἦσαν (Aristotle may have found this statement in his 'Quelle' or it may have been a very natural inference of his own); ἤδη δὲ σχήματά τινα αὐτῆς ἐχούσης οἱ λεγόμενοι αὐτῆς ποιηταὶ μνημονεύονται. τίς δὲ πρόσωπα ἀπέδωκεν ἢ πρόλογον ἢ πλήθη ὑποκριτῶν (see above) καὶ ὅσα τοιαῦτα ἠγνόηται, which implies that the εὑρεταί of *tragic* masks, etc., had been handed down in literary records accessible to Aristotle; c. 8. 1451ª15 ff. μῦθος δ᾿ ἐστὶν εἷς οὐχ᾿ ὥσπερ τινὲς οἴονται, ἐὰν περὶ ἕνα ᾖ . . . διὸ πάντες ἐοίκασιν ἁμαρτάνειν, ὅσοι τῶν ποιητῶν Ἡρακληΐδα καὶ τὴν Θησηΐδα . . . πεποιήκασιν. οἴονται γὰρ ἐπεὶ εἷς ἦν ὁ Ἡρακλῆς, ἕνα καὶ τὸν μῦθον εἶναι προσήκειν. Here the subject of the second οἴονται must, of course, be the same critic whom Aristotle refutes, not the epic poets, as might appear at first glance, for nothing can be more certain than that the difference between unity of plot and unity of hero never disturbed their reflections, for even in the case of the incomparable Homer, who, we are told, avoided the serious error in question, Aristotle is not sure, whether he did so διὰ τέχνην ἢ διὰ φύσιν. The discussion under notice justifies one other conclusion which applies with equally telling force to a large number of passages

[18] It is intrinsically not improbable, though a mere surmise, that the chief authority consulted here was Dikaiarchos.

[19] This is a clear source reference; πολύ, etc., on the other hand indicates the copiousness of the work utilized, for otherwise the reason given for omitting these details in his lecture would have been somewhat pointless.

still to be treated. It seems to me next to impossible that Aristotle's elaborate argumentation was directed against a brief, *incidental* and *isolated utterance,* which he happened to come across, to speak anachronistically, in some "Brief Mention," contributed by an earlier critic to the columns of a philological periodical published in Athens! It cannot but have constituted an integral part of the context of a larger treatise dealing with kindred topics. This scholar may, like so many literary critics of later times, have laid special stress on ἦθος (character drawing), a view which did not meet with Aristotle's approval, who never tires of inculcating the paramount importance of μῦθος (plot) in a perfectly constructed epic or tragedy.

In c. 13 the following explicit references to an earlier source occur: ἀνάγκη ἄρα τὸν καλῶς ἔχοντα μῦθον ἁπλοῦν εἶναι μᾶλλον ἢ διπλοῦν, ὥσπερ τινές φασι καὶ μεταβάλλειν οὐκ εἰς εὐτυχίαν ἐκ δυστυχίας, ἀλλὰ τοὐναντίον, the same critic or critics being doubtless mentioned later on, δευτέρα δ' ἡ πρώτη λεγομένη ὑπό τινῶν ἔστιν σύστασις ἡ διπλῆν τε τὴν σύστασιν ἔχουσα . . . δοκεῖ δὲ εἶναι πρώτη διὰ τὴν τῶν θεάτρων ἀσθένειαν etc.[20] These τίνες I am strongly inclined to identify with the οἱ Εὐριπίδῃ ἐγκαλοῦντες who unjustly censured the poet, because so many of his plays ended unhappily, it being possible that Aristotle in this one chapter consulted no fewer than three predecessors dealing with the same subject. In any case these three allusions testify to the existence of a kind of pre-Aristotelian τέχνη ποιητική or δραματική and of *obtrectatores* (or an *obtrectator*) *Euripidis* whose work may possibly have been utilized even by Aristophanes, the Εὐριπιδομάστιξ par excellence.

In c. 17 Aristotle lays down the rule, that the tragic poet must in the process of composition vividly visualize the doings and movements of his *dramatis personae,* if he desires to avoid scenic incongruities. The neglect of this prerequisite on the part

[20] This still popular view, known as poetic justice, according to which the virtuous are invariably rewarded and the wicked punished at the end, was feelingly espoused, among many others, by Dr. Samuel Johnson, but ridiculed by Goethe.

85

of Karkinos, a contemporary of Aristotle, once led, we are told, to the failure of one of his plays on the stage, the audience resenting a serious oversight (ὁ ἐπιτιμᾶτο Καρκίνῳ . . . ἐπὶ δὲ τῆς σκηνῆς ἐξέπεσεν δυσχερανάντων τοῦτο τῶν θεατῶν). Now ἐπιτιμᾶτο—note also the present tense—cannot, of course, refer to the audience, for their displeasure is sufficiently emphasized by δυσχερανάντων, nor can Aristotle himself have been the ἐπιτιμητής; the incident must, therefore, have been recorded by some writer as an historical example of the fatal effect which the violation of the above-mentioned canon may bring about.

In c. 18 four species of tragedy are enumerated and some dramas are cited by way of illustration. Aristotle thereupon continues: μάλιστα μὲν οὖν ἅπαντα δεῖ πειρᾶσθαι ἔχειν, εἰ δὲ μή, τὰ μέγιστα καὶ πλεῖστα, ἄλλως τε καὶ ὡς νῦν συκοφάντουσιν τοὺς ποιητάς· γεγονότων γὰρ ἕκαστον μέρος ἀγαθῶν ποιητῶν, ἑκάστου τοῦ ἰδίου ἀγαθοῦ ἀξιοῦσι τὸν ἕνα ὑπερβάλλειν. In the first place, it is self-evident that if these detractors of the poets made the inexorable, but in Aristotle's opinion quite unreasonable, demand, that every dramatist worthy of the name must attain perfection in each of the four species, these εἴδη τῆς τραγῳδίας must already have been well known to them. But while this is, of course, admitted in passing, e.g. by Bywater, no commentator has recognized the prime significance of the fact itself. For here again we must insist that these hypercensorious critics cannot possibly have restricted themselves to the one item under notice, as this would under no conceivable circumstances have warranted so severe an expression, as συκοφάντουσιν,[21] it being applied, moreover, to poets in general. I, therefore, have no hesitation in again drawing the conclusion that Aristotle was able to utilize literary sources which dealt more fully with technical features of dramatic composition than the brief statement in the *Poetics,* when taken by itself, might at first sight seem to justify.

[21] It is, as a matter of fact, the strongest ever employed by Aristotle when dealing with an opponent, and it is so used only in the above passage. Was νῦν perhaps added to prevent his hearers from understanding also Plato, to whom the word would have been preëminently applicable?

C's. 19–22²² are devoted to *Diction* (λέξις) in its various aspects, such as moods and tenses, grammatical gender, the parts of speech, which had not yet crystallized into the canonic eight, prosody, the physiology of sounds, ordinary and loan words (γλῶσσαι), metaphors, neologisms and solecisms, the use of prosaic and poetic expressions, etc. We have trustworthy evidence that investigations on the subjects mentioned existed in large numbers (see above). Among their authors *Protagoras* was probably the most eminent. He was the first human being, so far as we know, who became scientifically conscious of grammatical gender,²³ moods and tenses. That Aristotle was acquainted with his work would go without saying, even if he had not cited him in *Poet.* c. 19²⁴ and in his *Rhet.* III. 5, as the scholar, who τὰ γένη τῶν ὀνομάτων διῄρει, ἄρρενα καὶ θήλεα καὶ σκεύη (neuters),—the very subject discussed in c. 21.1458ᵃ8 ff. We cannot, of course, distribute the information given in these grammatical and stylistic sections among the sources directly consulted, but this fact, however deplorable, in no way vitiates the validity of the inference to be drawn, namely that Aristotle was to a considerable extent indebted to the results of numerous investigations relating to the topics with which these chapters are concerned.

Among these predecessors we meet with some who owe their immortality to a solitary mention in the *Poetics*. Thus in c. 22, in treating of words and phrases that give a poetical tinge to language and are also conducive to clearness of style, Aristotle

²² The relevancy of these chapters in an Art of Poetry has often been denied, but unjustly, as appears from Arist. himself in *De Interpret.* 4.17a. ῥητορικῆς γὰρ ἢ ποιητικῆς οἰκειοτέρα ἡ σκέψις.
²³ The sensation which his discovery created is reflected in the witty jibes in Arist. *Clouds* 659–692. For further particulars see my article "Grammatik" in the *Realenzyklopädie*, VIII, 8.1781 ff.
²⁴ τί γὰρ ἄν τις ὑπολάβοι ἡμαρτῆσθαι ἃ Πρωταγόρας ἐπιτιμᾷ ὅτι εὔχεσθαι οἰόμενος ἐπιτάττει εἰπὼν "μῆνιν ἄειδε θεά" τὸ γὰρ κελεῦσαι φησὶν ποιεῖν τι ἢ μὴ ἐπίταξίς ἐστιν. We doubtless owe this quotation solely to the fact, that Aristotle took issue with this censure (see above). He was certainly right in rejecting it, but the observation implied the conscious distinction of the functions of the imperative and optative, here made for the first time!

CLASSICAL STUDIES

adds: ὥστε οὐκ ὀρθῶς ψέγουσιν οἱ ἐπιτιμῶντες τῷ τοιούτῳ τρόπῳ τῆς διαλέκτου καὶ διακωμῳδοῦντες τὸν ποιητὴν (i.e. Homer), οἷον Εὐκλείδης ὁ ἀρχαῖος ὡς ῥᾴδιον ποιεῖν, εἴ τις δώσει ἐκτείνειν ἐφ' ὁπόσον βούλεται ἰαμβοποιήσας (i.e. ridiculing) ἐν αὐτῇ τῇ λέξει etc. Now the very context in which this satirical criticism appears can again leave no possible doubt that it was not an isolated *jeu d'esprit,* but was culled by Aristotle from a more or less extensive treatise on metrics and prosody by Eukleides, for that such existed is well attested and further confirmed by Aristotle himself in c. 20 περὶ ὧν καθ' ἕκαστον τοῖς μετρικοῖς προσήκειν θεωρεῖν etc. From the same chapter we learn that one *Ariphrades* τοὺς τραγῳδοὺς[25] ἐκωμῳδεῖ ὅτι ἃ οὐδεὶς ἂν εἴποι ἐν τῇ διαλέκτῳ τούτοις χρῶνται, such as the anastrophe of the preposition (δωμάτων ἄπο),[26] σέθεν (i.e. σοῦ) and νιν (=αὐτόν–ἥν–ὅ, αὐτούς–ἅς–ἅ). Aristotle curtly dismisses this objection to perfectly appropriate locutions, attributing it to the ignorance of the critic (ἐκεῖνος τοῦτο ἠγνόει). In our present enquiry, however, this is not the point at issue, but rather the recognition that the examples cited were selected from a book or treatise[27] of Ariphrades, as οἷον is alone sufficient to show. On what grounds Bywater and others deny the validity of this inference we are unfortunately not informed and I am at a loss to divine any, for it seems on the contrary all but absurd to assume that Aristotle would have dignified by quotation and refutation a few blundering statements of an ignorant criticaster that happened to come within his ken.

C. 25, by far the longest in the *Poetics,* is wholly taken up with the subject of critical προβλήματα and their λύσεις. This is the most favored method of philological exegesis throughout

[25] Bywater's interpretation, "i.e., the tragic actors who are made responsible for what the poet puts into their mouth" is an inexplicable aberration. What *literary* or *stylistic* critic, ancient or modern, ever did this?

[26] It occurs quite frequently also in prose, e.g., in Plato, and is extremely common in our extant tragedies, σέθεν and νιν being also not rare. See my notes *ad loc.*

[27] It may have been entitled περὶ τραγικῆς λέξεως like the famous work of Didymos.

88

antiquity.[28] Aristotle himself published a voluminous work, entitled Ἀπορήματα (Προβλήματα) in six or ten books, of which we still possess some fragments scattered up and down our Homeric Scholia and in Eustathios' Homeric Commentary. We are here in no way concerned with the analysis of the problems themselves and their solutions enumerated in the *Poetics,* but solely with the question, to what extent the 17 illustrations, all taken from Homer, with one exception (Empedokles), had already been discussed by previous λυτικοί.[29] But for this ἀπορία I can offer no satisfactory λύσις, as we must always reckon with the contingency that Aristotle may often enough not have propounded the πρόβλημα himself, merely suggesting a λύσις of his own to one already existing, for he was not the inventor of this method. Long before him sophists and rhetoricians had vied with one another in detecting flaws and incongruities, especially in Homer, which they solved as best they could, but there were also some, who exercised their ingenuity in a less scientific manner, being actuated by a malicious desire to detract from the glory of the idolized poet. The most famous of these *obtrectatores Homeri* was a close contemporary of Aristotle, *Zoilos* of Amphipolis, surnamed Ὁμηρομάστιξ, who wrote 9 books κατὰ τῆς Ὁμήρου ποιήσεως. Now it is interesting to note that two of the προβλήματα cited in the *Poetics* (1461ª10 = *Il.* 1.50, 1461ª-14 = *Il.* 9.202) and in the Scholia, without a clue to their provenience, are expressly assigned to Zoilos by Ps. Herakl. *Alleg. Hom.* 14 and Plut. *Quaest. Conv.* 5.4.2, which proves, if such proof were needed, that Aristotle was well acquainted with this work. It is, therefore, certainly within the range of probability, that some of the Aristotelian λύσεις in this chapter, designed to explain away rather censorious or captious objections, were directly called forth by this detractor of Homer. Among these I am disposed to reckon 1461ª2 (= *Il.* 10.152, attributed to Aris-

[28] Cp. my article Λύσεις in the *Realenzyklopädie,* 13.2511–2529.

[29] In our Scholia nine of these examples re-occur, but only two are expressly attributed to Aristotle.

totle by Porphyry in Schol. *ad loc.*), 1461ª12 (= *Il.* 10.316), 1461ª16 ff. (= *Il.* 2.1), 1461ª18 (= *Il.* 10.11), 1461ª26 (*Il.* 10.251 expressly assigned to Aristotle in Schol. *ad loc.*), 1461ª28 (*Il.* 21.592), 1461ª30 (= *Il.* 20.234), 1461ª33 (= *Il.* 20.272). Finally, it is quite possible that the sound piece of criticism, which in 1461ᵇ1 f. is quoted from one *Glaukon* regarding the unmethodical procedure of some of these "problem" hunters, may have been, in part at least, directed against the same Zoilos. In the case of only two ζητήματα, Aristotle directly cites or alludes to their authors, namely *Hippias* of Thasos (see above) and an "anonymous" solver in 1461ᵇ2 ff.: τοῦτο δὲ πέπονθε τὰ περὶ Ἰκάριον. οἴονται γὰρ ὥσπερ οἱ Κεφαλλῆνές φασι . . . λέγουσι.[30]

The final chapter (26) is chiefly concerned with the elaborate proof that tragedy is a higher form of art than epic poetry. In spite of διαπορήσειεν ἄν τις,[31] Aristotle was not the first to suggest this enquiry, as is sufficiently evident from 1462ª1: τὴν μὲν (sc. ἐποποιίαν) οὖν πρὸς θεατὰς ἐπιεικεῖς φασιν εἶναι . . . τὴν δὲ τραγικὴν (sc. τέχνην) πρὸς φαύλους. εἰ οὖν φορτική, χείρων δῆλον ὅτι ἂν εἴη, with which the arguments advanced by those who favored the epic end. In rebuttal, Aristotle advances seven reasons. It is perfectly clear, throughout, that the author is here taking a decided stand in a controversy against opponents. That Plato was among these, as has been asserted, is, however, an unwarranted assumption (see below).

(2) We have been thus far occupied with the determination of Aristotelian indebtedness to earlier sources, which were indicated by direct citations or allusions. We now turn to passages, which on closer scrutiny reveal a like indebtedness, although all external evidence is lacking.

I begin with some minor observations. Aristotle throughout the *Poetics* is careful to define technical terms, either because

---

[30] This, like οἴονται, refers to the authority quoted, for the Cephallenians were certainly not antiquarians!

[31] On this and other technical formulae for propounding ἀπορήματα, see the article Λύσεις, referred to above.

they were new, unfamiliar, or invested by him with new meaning. It is, therefore, a reasonable hypothesis, that in all or most cases, where this practice is not observed, he is dealing with matters, which are supposed not to be a *terra incognita* to his hearers, the expressions having long been incorporated in the technical vocabulary of literary criticism.[32] Among these terms may be mentioned, μῦθος, ἦθος, διάνοια, μελοποιία, λέξις, ὄψις (the six parts of tragedy), μίμησις, πάθος, ῥῆσις, εἰκὸς, and ἀναγκαῖον, ἐπεισοδιώδης, μῦθος, ἐπεισόδιον, ἁπλοῦς and διπλοῦς μῦθος, τραγῳδία ἁπλῆ—πεπλεγμένη—παθητική—ἠθική, the terminology of grammar, phonetics φωνῆεν (earliest extant example in Eur. *frg.* 578), ὀξύτης, βραχύτης, etc., στοιχεῖον, συλλαβή, σύνδεσμος, ἄρθρον, ὄνομα, ῥῆμα, λόγος "sentence," βαρβαρισμός, etc. Indebtedness to earlier sources must also be assumed, as we have seen, for the account of the development of the drama, beginning with c. 4, 9 πολλὰς μεταβολὰς μεταβαλοῦσα ἡ τραγῳδία ἐπαύσατο down to c. 5, 2.

C. 9 οὐ πάντως εἶναι ζητητέον τῶν παραδεδομένων μύθων περὶ οὓς αἱ τραγῳδίαι εἰσὶν ἀντέχεσθαι, etc. This celebrated plea to abandon the time-honored but all too hackneyed subjects of tragedy would lack all force and point, unless we regard it as directed against an actual defence of the traditional practice by some conservative critic, for it is not likely that Aristotle would have conjured up an imaginary adversary simply for the purpose of ridiculing his literary convictions.

C. 12, enumerating the quantitative parts of tragedy with brief definitions of each (πρόλογος, πάροδος, ἐπεισόδιον, στάσιμον, τὰ ἀπὸ σκηνῆς, κομμοί and ἔξοδος), was certainly based upon earlier sources. See the notes *ad loc.* in my commentary.

In c. 15 Aristotle inculcates the rule ἄλογον δὲ μηδὲν <δεῖ> εἶναι ἐν τοῖς πράγμασιν, εἰ δὲ μή, ἔξω τῆς τραγῳδίας οἷον ἐν τῷ Οἰδίποδι τῷ Σοφοκλέους and again, but more fully, in c. 24 προαι-

---

[32] Occasionally terms are used as if familiar, but subsequently defined. But in all these cases (ἁπλοῦς and πεπλεγμένος μῦθος, λύσις and δέσις, περιπέτεια and ἀναγνώρισις) it is done to bring out the antithesis clearly at the place, where these topics are discussed more fully.

ρεῖσθαι τε δεῖ ἀδύνατα εἰκότα μᾶλλον ἢ δυνατὰ ἀπίθανα· τούς τε λόγους μὴ συνίστασθαι ἐκ μερῶν ἀλόγων, ἀλλὰ μάλιστα μὲν μηδὲν ἔχειν ἄλογον, εἰ δὲ μή, ἔξω τοῦ μυθεύματος, ὥσπερ Οἰδίπους τὸ μὴ εἰδέναι πῶς ὁ Λάιος ἀπέθανεν. The author is evidently at pains to explain away a palpable incongruity in his ideal tragedy, the *Oedipus Rex* of Sophokles. Modern scholars, so far as I am aware, have not been convinced by his somewhat specious apology and rightly so. Now, it does not seem plausible that Aristotle laid down an inexorable precept for tragical and epic composition while at the same time being conscious that an otherwise perfect tragedy seriously violated it. I have, therefore, always felt that the unsatisfactory excuse here offered was not of his own volition, but was forced upon him by some critic who had severely censured the flaw in question in some treatise, that dealt with the technique of dramatic composition. Abundant evidence pointing to the existence of some such work has been given in this paper and more of a like nature is furnished particularly by Euripidean scholia.[33]

C. 18 extr. The rule, also inculcated by Hor. *Ars* 193, is here laid down, that the chorus should assume the part of an actor, thus participating in the development of the plot, in the manner of Sophokles, not in that of Euripides, who frequently violates this precept, while other tragedians went so far as to substitute wholly irrelevant intermezzi or interludes (ἐμβόλιμα), an innovation introduced by Agathon. The severe arraignment of this neoteric practice—it has all the appearance of a tag or digression—was in my judgment occasioned by some critic who ven-

[33] Another inference confirmatory of this view I am inclined to draw from an admirable paper by Lane Cooper, in *Amer. Journ. of Philol.*, L (1929), 171–181, in which he ingeniously solves an old 'crux interpretum' in Arist. *Rhet.* 3.16. 1417ᵇ16–20 and deals at length with the rôle of Jokasta in Karkinos' Oidipos. In this play Jokasta repeatedly allayed or brushed aside the constant doubts and fears of Oidipos as to the circumstances that led to the death of Laios etc. by tales that were δύνατα, but in reality ἀπίθανα. This being so, is would seem to follow that Karkinos also was acquainted with the pre-Aristotelian censure passed upon the ἄλογον in the Oidipos of Sophokles and recognizing the validity of the criticism endeavored to avoid the same fault by the dramatic device mentioned.

tured to defend so abnormal a departure from time-honored tradition.

In c's. 21 and 25 Aristotle cites examples of Cyprian and Cretan glosses. It does not seem probable that he was conversant with these dialects. Now, we happen to know of one critic, *Glaukon,* who wrote on Cyprian Γλῶσσαι. This very collection and a similar Cretan glossary may, therefore, for aught we know to the contrary, have been directly consulted by Aristotle.

Finally, attention may be drawn to a paragraph in c. 22 which, as has been pointed out above, contains a number of polemical discussions, occasioned by hypercritical observations of previous scholars, mentioned by name or alluded to. This is, however, not the case in the following passage. Aristotle there maintains, confirming his opinion by apt illustrations, that the substitution of a poetic expression for one more prosaic conduces to stylistic elevation and he adds that anyone disposed to make the experiment κατίδοι ὅτι ἀληθῆ λέγομεν. The form here given to his conviction conveys to my mind an unmistakable touch of emotion, not elsewhere found in Aristotle, when dealing with an adversary, unless it be the famous statement uttered by him, when compelled to refute opinions of his teacher. ἀμφοῖν γὰρ ὄντοιν φίλοιν ὅσιον προτιμᾶν τὴν ἀλήθειαν (*Nic. Eth.* I 4.1096ᵃ16), crystallized in later times in the proverb *amicus Plato, magis amica veritas!* I have, therefore, no hesitation in assuming that Aristotle here too, as in so many other passages discussed previously, took issue with some dilettant critic whose views he regarded as utterly erroneous.

(3) In turning to *Plato,* the only extant author whose contributions to the subject of poetry might on *a priori* grounds be supposed to shed light on Aristotle's indebtedness to earlier writers, it may be well to state at the very outset that there can be no doubt whatever that his pupil was intimately acquainted not only with the dialogues, but also with the views of Plato expressed in his lectures in the Academy. But this indisputable fact by no means involves the assumption that the *Poetics* are a

mere echo of Platonic thought. The extreme advocate of this opinion was, as remarked above, G. Finsler, who without compunctions of conscience thus expresses himself:[34] "wenn das Wesentliche darin (i.e., in the *Poetics*) als platonisches Gut erkannt ist, so lässt sich von einer Kunstlehre des Aristoteles nicht mehr im Sinne einer durchaus ihm eigentümlichen Theorie sprechen. Seine Poetik ist der Abglanz eines grösseren Gestirns und hat ihre Herrschaft durch die Jahrhunderte nur darum ausüben können, weil ihre systematische Zusammenfassung mehr Eindruck machte als die zerstreuten Lichter in den platonischen Dialogen" (p. ix). "Die Poetik (ist) mit den Gedanken Platons ganz durchtränkt und in ihren Ausführungen durch jene fast völlig beherrscht" (p. 5). "Bis zu dieser Stelle enthält das 1. Kap. nicht ein einziges Wort, das nicht aus Platon zu belegen wäre. Mit Ausnahme des Gegensatzes von Kunst und Routine steht alles, was wir bei Aristoteles lesen, auf wenigen Seiten des platonischen Staates beisammen" (p. 32). "Der Anfang der Poetik baut sich ganz auf platonischer Grundlage auf. Aristoteles erblickt in Plato's Aeusserungen eine vollständige Theorie der Dichtkunst" (p. 33). "Seine ganze Poetik ist bis ins Einzelne von Platon abhängig" (p. 147), etc. The absurdity of these wild asseverations is enhanced by the astounding fact that Finsler, as well as Belger, finds himself *restricted to a few utterances in the first six chapters of the Poetics,* fully *three-fifths* of the entire treatise thus offering no material whatsoever on which to base their assertion of Aristotle's colossal dependance upon Plato. But quite apart from this palpable *reductio ad absurdum,* the very arguments advanced by these scholars in defence of their paradoxical statements, upon which they must needs rely to prove their thesis, are one and all quite unconvincing, often casuistical, and generally demonstrably false. To refute them in detail is as easy as it is unfortunately impossible within the narrow limits of this paper. I must, therefore, confine myself here to a few illustrations symptomatic of the

[34] I quote the original German for obvious reasons.

arbitrary methods employed.[35] The πρῶτον ψεῦδος of their argumentation is the unwarranted, *a priori* assumption, that in all cases of genuine or alleged coincidence between Plato and Aristotle, the former is the originator, whereas we can still prove in many instances that the ideas in question were matters of current knowledge or discussion, the most notable case in point being perhaps the famous doctrine of poetic μίμησις πράξεων (or πραττόντων). It constitutes the very cornerstone and foundation of the Aristotelian fabric and yet we are told, over and over again, "that this is to all appearance another reminiscence of Plato,"[36] in spite of the fact that the metaphorical connotation of the term can be clearly shown to have been pre-Platonic. It crops out but rarely for all that in Plato and is nowhere defined, doubtless because the interlocutors are supposed to be familiar with its technical signification. There is, however, another μίμησις theory original with Plato and closely associated with his theories of ideas, the imitation of the artist being three degrees removed from the ideal truth. This conception has, of course, found no place in the *Poetics,* which do not even recognize a false and a true μίμησις πράξεων. Plato's vacillatory use of the term is reluctantly admitted even by Finsler, but the obsession of Aristotelian indebtedness to his teacher everywhere prevents him from drawing logically necessary conclusions.

To what dire straits these scholars, seconded by Bywater, are reduced by their frantic efforts to bolster up an untenable position may be illustrated by a few more specimens arbitrarily selected from a large assortment collected in their pages.

The penetrating analysis, so characteristic of Aristotle, of the three modes of μίμησις, the *means,* the *objects,* and the *manner*

[35] For a fuller discussion see the *Introduction* to my edition.
[36] *Rep.* 3.396ᶜ μιμούμενος τὸν ἀγαθὸν ἀσφαλῶς τε καὶ ἐμφρόνως πράττοντα, 10.603ᶜ πράττοντας, φαμέν, ἀνθρώπους μιμεῖται ἡ μιμητικὴ βιαίους ἢ ἑκουσίας πράξεις. The long discussions from which these statements are extracted by Belger, Finsler, and Bywater, pursue a trend of thought and subserve a purpose wholly different from the mimetic theory in the *Poetics,* so that the alleged reminiscence simmers down to Aristotle's use of a simple phrase (μιμεῖσθαι πράξεις)!

of imitation (c. 1), which are equally applicable to the six constituent parts of tragedy, λέξις and μελοποιία representing the means (οἷς), ὄψις the manner (ὡς), μῦθος, ἦθος and διάνοια the objects (ἅ), we are seriously asked to believe had been anticipated by Plat. *Rep.* 3.392. Now, even a superficial glance at this passage, which is far too long to quote here, will, I am certain, convince every unprejudiced reader that the train of Plato's thought bears no resemblance whatever to the Aristotelian. But this quite fatal objection is complacently set aside as a negligible quantity in view of a locution which occurs no fewer than three times,[37] to wit: 3.392ᶜ τὸ μὲν δὴ λόγων πέρι ἐχέτω τέλος· τὸ δὲ λέξεως . . . μετὰ τοῦτο σκεπτέον καὶ ἡμῖν ἃ λεκτέον καὶ ὡς λεκτέον παντελῶς σκέψεται. 394ᶜ ἔφαμεν ἃ μὲν λεκτέον ἤδη εἰρῆσθαι, ὡς δὲ λεκτέον ἔτι σκεπτέον εἶναι. 398ᵇ κινδυνεύει ἡμῖν τῆς μουσικῆς τὸ περὶ λόγους τε καὶ μύθους παντελῶς διαπεπεράνθαι. ἅ τε γὰρ λεκτέον καὶ ὡς λεκτέον εἴρηται. It is, of course, just a bit disconcerting that Plato unfortunately quite omitted to mention the absolutely essential third element, the *means* (οἷς λεκτέον), for the alleged Aristotelian reminiscence now actually dwindles down to ὡς and ἅ and one is at a loss to explain, why Aristotle did not also, while about it, appropriate from Plato so rare a word as λεκτέον! But he apparently made up for this serious oversight in *Rhet.* 3.9 ἀρχὴ δὲ διότι ἃ ὑπέσχετο, ἀποδέδωκεν (sc. ὁ ῥήτωρ) ὥστε ἅ τε καὶ δι' ὃ λεκτέον, a parallelism which unhappily escaped Belger, Bywater, and Finsler, as did another passage equally evidential in the Platonic Plutarch, namely *Praec. reip. gerendae* 8: 'Αλκιβιάδην . . . μὴ μόνον ἃ δεῖ λέγειν ἀλλὰ καὶ ὡς δεῖ! But there are still other instances which "prove" that Aristotle's command of Greek vocabulary was singularly limited, for we are told that his statement that tragedy imitates σπουδαῖα (c. 3) is clearly borrowed from Plat. *Leg.* 7.817ᵃ τῶν δὲ σπουδαίων, ὡς φασι (!) τῶν περὶ τραγῳδίαν ποιητῶν, that βλαβερά (c. 25) was taken from *Rep.* 3.391ᵈ, while ἡδυσμένος λόγος (c. 6) was pilfered from *Rep.* 10.607

[37] Finsler and Bywater cite but one of these passages.

τὴν ἡδυσμένην μοῦσαν ἐν μέλεσιν ἢ ἔπεσιν, although the term is here used *in malam partem!* The comparison of an artistic entity with a living organism (Plat. *Gorg.* 503ᵈ) so tickled the fancy of Aristotle that he employed it twice in the *Poetics*. Such lack of originality on the part of this author prepares us for the demonstrably false assertion that the famous distinction between history and poetry (c. 9) is based on *Rep.* 5.472. To cap the climax, even the κάθαρσις τῶν παθημάτων is also said to be of Platonic origin, because we read in the *Phaedon* 69ᵃ τὸ δ' ἀληθὲς τῷ ὄντι ἢ κάθαρσίς τις τῶν τοιούτων πάντων καὶ ἡ σωφροσύνη καὶ ἡ δικαιοσύνη καὶ ἡ ἀνδρία καὶ αὐτὴ ἡ φρόνησις μὴ καθαρμός τις ἦ. Not only is the context here as widely different as possible from the Aristotelian, but κάθαρσις, as a medical term, connoting "purgation," was demonstrably familiar, long before, to the Pythagoreans and to Hippokrates! No less convincing is Aristotle's slavish indebtedness to Plato, when it is alleged that the phrase τὸ δὲ τέλος μέγιστον ἁπάντων (c. 6) is modelled upon, *Rep.* 3.377ᵃ οὐκοῦν οἶσθ' ὅτι ἀρχὴ (!) παντὸς ἔργου μέγιστον, which Plato himself and Arist. *Soph. Elench.* 33.183ᵇ 22 μέγιστον . . . ἴσως ἀρχὴ παντός, ὥσπερ λέγεται designate as proverbial! But it is quite useless to multiply examples of this nature. They all but imply that Aristotle had access to a "Platonic concordance," which he utilized much as a schoolboy does a Dictionary. They certainly vanish into thin air, the moment they are put under closer scrutiny. Unfortunately this fixed idea of Plato's profound influence upon the *Poetics* is by no means confined to Belger and Finsler. Even an interpreter usually so sane as Bywater succumbed, as we have seen, to the spell, in proof of which one other illustration, which he does not owe to his predecessors, may still be added. In c. 3, in which the "manner" of imitation is discussed, this scholar declares in an unusually long note (pp. 118 f.), that it would be a "mere enigma to us, if we had not the key to it in Plat. *Rep.* 3.392ᵇ–394ᵈ." It were extremely easy to refute this statement, but as the author is finally forced to admit the existence of very essential differences, he himself removes the very basis upon which his entire argumentation rests.

Finally, I return to the closing chapter of the *Poetics*, in which, as was pointed out above, Aristotle takes direct issue with some adversary or adversaries who contended that the artistic merits of the epos were superior to those of the drama. Many have assumed that this unnamed opponent was no other than Plato, their conviction being based upon a solitary passage of the *Laws* 2.658ᵈ. The Athenian there argues that old men are the only fit judges of poetic excellence, by virtue of their education, experience, and objectivity. Now in this discussion there occurs the following passage: ἐὰν δὲ γ' οἱ μείζους παῖδες (sc. κρινῶσι), τὸν τὰς κωμῳδίας. τραγῳδίαν δὲ αἵ τε πεπαιδευμέναι τῶν γυναικῶν καὶ τὰ νέα μειράκια[38] καὶ σχεδὸν ἴσως τὸ πλῆθος πάντων. (Klinias) ἴσως δῆτα. (Athenian) Ῥαψῳδὸν δέ, καλῶς Ἰλιάδα καὶ Ὀδύσσειαν ἤ τι τῶν Ἡσιοδείων διατιθέντα, τάχ' ἂν ἡμεῖς οἱ γέροντες ἥδιστα ἀκούσαντες νικᾶν ἂν φαῖμεν πάμπολυ. It will be seen at once that there is here no trace of the arguments *pro et contra* enumerated by Aristotle, and that the preference expressed by "old men" for Homer and Hesiod is a purely subjective predilection, in no way influenced or determined by artistic considerations or critical reflections. The question of Aristotle's indebtedness to Plato here must, therefore, again be very firmly answered in the negative.

An unprejudiced survey of Plato's utterances on poetry, particularly in the *Republic* and the *Laws* (others in the *Phaidros*, *Philebos*, and *Protagoras* are of a more incidental nature), cannot but lead to the conclusion that the *Poetics* of Aristotle in their essence constitute a *tacit* protest against the iconoclastic views of his teacher. But they represent at the same time an

---

[38] These statements are palpably false, for surely no one will seriously contend that the *Clouds*, *Birds*, and *Frogs* of Aristophanes, not to mention the *Lysistrata*, were written for μείζους παῖδες and that only educated women, νέα μειράκια, and the groundlings applauded the consummate masterpieces of tragedy, while the γέροντες reserved their vociferous admiration for some *Ion*, or other rhapsodist reciting Homer or—save the mark!—Hesiod's *Works and Days*!

elaborate and successful attempt to rehabilitate the art of poetry by vindicating its right to existence against the anathema of Plato. The views of master and of pupil are as wide apart as the poles, Plato passionately emphasizing the ethical content, while Aristotle, disregarding the moral issue, as vigorously insists that the sole aim and purpose of poetry is to give aesthetic pleasure.[39] We may without hesitation concede, as remarked above, that the views of Plato were very carefully examined by the author of the *Poetics*. Aristotle's indebtedness was, however, all but wholly of a *negative* nature, Plato either arousing his opposition[40] or giving his thoughts occasionally an entirely new direction. Substantial agreement in cases of real import is, indeed, extremely rare, being virtually confined, at that, to matters which had been the subject of wide discussion among scholars of the fifth and fourth centuries.

Originality is at best a relative term. It is not always or necessarily synonymous with creative productivity or inventiveness, for every writer or thinker is unconsciously, to some extent, the inheritor of the past and so, while we may readily concede that the *Poetics* of Aristotle did not like Athena spring full-armed from the head of Jove, it is no less clear that its author consulted and utilized all relevant material that had accumulated about his subject. The ascertainable evidence, confirmatory of this assumption, I have endeavored to collect in the preceding pages; and even if Aristotle's indebtedness to earlier scholars be yet more extensive than we may still be able to determine, owing to the loss of these sources, there can be no reasonable doubt, that he has nevertheless succeeded in breathing

[39] That Aristotle was not the first to advocate this doctrine is clear from Plat. *Leg.* 2.655ᵈ λέγουσί γε οἱ πλεῖστοι μουσικῆς ὀρθότητα εἶναι τὴν ἡδονὴν ταῖς ψυχαῖς πορίζουσαν δύναμιν, who, however, repudiates it, ἀλλὰ τοῦτο μὲν οὔτε ἀνεκτὸν οὔτε ὅσιόν τε παράπαν φθέγγεσθαι.

[40] Cp. Proklos in Plat. *Rep.* I, 42 Kr. τοῦτο (sc. τὸ τὴν τραγῳδίαν καὶ τὴν κωμῳδίαν ἐκβάλλεσθαι), δ' οὖν πολλὴν καὶ τῷ Ἀριστοτέλει παρασχὸν αἰτιάσεως ἀφορμήν i.e. doubtless in the πραγματεία τῆς τεχνικῆς ποιητικῆς and probably in the dialogue περὶ ποιητῶν, for the *Poetics* contain no such attack; they cannot, therefore, have been the source of Proklos' statement.

a new originality even into this borrowed material. For the *Poetics* conspicuously exhibit in their analytic power, their systematic exposition, their thoughtfulness and penetrative insight all of the marks of true Aristotelian genius; and, in consequence, though they may never again also wield the same potent influence, they will continue to enlist the same widespread and intense interest which they have excited for so many generations in the past.

MUNICH, GERMANY

HISTORY OF THE NAME OF THE TEMPLE
OF CASTOR IN THE FORUM

George Depue Hadzsits

In his account of the battle of Lake Regillus, Livy says:

ibi nihil nec divinae nec humanae opis dictator praetermittens, aedem Castoris vovisse fertur (2.20.12).

The dictator Postumius could not afford to neglect divine help and at the final crisis of the battle invoked the aid of Castor to whom he vowed a temple. In fulfillment of the vow, the temple to Castor was, in due time, built in Rome:

Castoris aedes eodem anno idibus Quinctilibus dedicata est. Vota erat Latino bello a Postumio dictatore; filius eius duumvir ad id ipsum creatus dedicavit (2.42.5).

The shrine of Castor was dedicated in 484 B.C. and Livy has no false illusions that Pollux was associated with Castor in the name or, for that matter, in the worship at this temple at that time. It was a temple of Castor, at the beginning, and Livy knew of this shrine only as the temple of Castor. He calls it by no other name. The Campanian knights received Roman citizenship in 340 B.C. and to commemorate the occasion a bronze tablet was fastened up:

in aede Castoris Romae (8.11.16).

Later (307/6 B.C.) Marcius triumphed over the Hernici and an equestrian statue was erected in his honor in the Forum,

ante templum Castoris (9.43.22).

It is no accident, I think, that Livy calls the temple consistently, by this one name only. He is clearly giving, it would seem, the designation that he thought was the official one from the beginning. Just as he does not lend the weight of his authority to a

101

legend of the participation of Castor and Pollux in the battle of Lake Regillus (a legend that we now know was not current at the time of the reputed battle of Lake Regillus, but of much later origin), so he does not employ another (popular) designation of this temple (i.e. of Castor and Pollux), which was primarily derived from the legend. Livy's testimony is of fundamental importance, but it does not stand alone.

This temple was one of great religious and political significance in the first century B.C., as all students of its history know. Under these circumstances, Cicero's frequent references to the temple, as the temple of Castor, becomes doubly significant. Of course, there was nothing to prevent Cicero's calling the temple by another, popular designation, if he so chose, but twenty-four references to the temple by name would seem to indicate pretty clearly what he thought of this temple when he looked upon it or when he spoke of it. It was, to his mind,

aedes (or, templum) Castoris.[1]

Cicero's very many references to this temple by this name, suggest, besides, what name, above all others, was lodged in the mind of the Romans. It might be argued that brevity was responsible for the use of this name. But such an argument could not possibly explain the consistent use of this name in all these cases, under a variety of circumstances, without exception. Moreover, when Cicero speaks of the cult at Tusculum, he says:

Tusculi aedes Castoris et Pollucis (De Div. 1.43.98).[2]

The one exception to Cicero's practice, and the only one as far as I know, is susceptible of a very interesting interpretation which will follow. We have no real reason for believing that

---

[1] In Verr., Act. II Lib. 1.49.129, 50.130, 50.131,132, 51.133, 59.154, 3.16.41; De domo sua, 21.54; Pro Quinctio, 4.17; Pro Milone, 33.91; Philipp., 3.11.27, 6.5.13; Pro Sest., 39.85, 15.34, 37.79; In Pis., 5.11, 10.23; De domo sua, 42.110; In Vat., 13.31, 13.32; De har. resp., 13.28, 23.49; Pro Mil., 7.18; Pro Scaur., 23.46 (temple not mentioned by name) ; Ad. Q. fr., 2.3.6.

[2] Tusculan inscriptions, referring to the cult at Tusculum, always give either the two names or Castores.

the name of Pollux was associated with Castor's in the official designation of the temple. It may well be true that Pollux was associated with Castor, in worship, in this temple during the Republic (the second cen. B.C.); if so, this was in spite of the name; but I cannot believe that such worship was original. We have no evidence and therefore we have no sound reason for believing that there were two statues of two divinities here, at the beginning.

In Plautus' *Curculio* it is

pone aedem Castoris (481),

in the famous passage in which Plautus describes life in the Forum (for the year *ca.* 180 B.C.), and in discussing the use of the word *pro,* as exhibited in early writers, Aulus Gellius uses the phrase

pro aede Castoris (*Noct. Att.* 11.3.2),

which he may be quoting from the *Origines* of Cato. In two inscriptions of comparatively early date, Castor and Castor only is mentioned in references to this temple:

   (1) DE · CASTORUS · PALAM
      C.I.L. I². 582.17 = I. 197 lex incerta reperta Bantiae, rogata inter 133–118 B.C. Time and place are specified for taking oaths, and the phrase stands for *pro aede Castoris;*
   (2) SUB · AEDE · KASTORUS
      C.I.L. I². 586.1 = I. 201. Epistula praetoris ad Tiburtes, of the end of the third century or middle of the second century B.C. L. Cornelius, praetor, has consulted the senate *sub aede Castoris.*

In addition to these passages, one might cite the *Monumentum Ancyranum* which, presumably, ought to give official titles and does. In the well-known list of monuments given in this record, as built or restored by Augustus, we find the phrase

INTER · AEDEM · CASTORIS (4.13).

The Greek version of this phrase I shall mention later. But all of our evidence (so far) is absolutely uniform, to the effect that this great temple was regarded as the "temple of Castor" which was its official designation and proper title (in Latin).[3] The famous story in Suetonius would lose all point, if the temple had either officially or commonly been recognized as, or called, the "temple of Castor and Pollux" in the days of Julius Caesar. Bibulus, colleague of Caesar in the aedileship, complained:

ut . . . nec dissimularet collega eius Marcus Bibulus, evenisse sibi quod Polluci; ut enim geminis fratribus aedes in Foro constituta *tantum Castoris vocaretur,* ita suam Caesarisque munificentiam unius Caesaris dici (*Div. Jul.* 10.1).

Now, part of this statement, viz. that the temple had been erected in the Forum to the twin brothers, may not be true, but the second part that the temple was officially called the *temple of Castor,* alone, is, emphatically, correct. The story requires the assumption that Castor *and* Pollux were associated in people's minds as joint possessors, in one sense or another, of this temple. And it was, without a doubt, a fact in the first century B.C. that the two gods were worshipped here. Important to remember at this point, is the evidence this passage gives us that the official name of the temple was that of Castor.

The next question would seem to be—how did Castor *and Pollux* happen to be associated with the name of this temple which, on the basis of all of our testimony, was, originally and for long, a temple of Castor alone? It was, I believe, the marvellous tale of annunciation and of epiphany that represented Castor and Pollux as taking part in the battle of Lake Regillus and as announcing the victory in the Forum, that was, primarily, responsible for the incorrect notion that this temple had, at the beginning, been dedicated to the two gods, that they were, from the beginning, joint possessors of it, and that they were both equally worshipped here from the beginning. It is important to

---

[3] To these passages should be added Festus *Fr.* 246 = 290 (Lindsay) where we find *pro aede Castoris,* and *Fr.* 286 = 362 (Lindsay) where the same phrase is repeated. Festus *Fr.* 229 = 256 (Lindsay) cannot be cited with any assurance, although Tenney Frank accepts <stor> for *Castoris* (*Mem.,* Am. Acad., V, 79).

recall that neither Livy nor Cicero fell into this error. We have no reason for believing that the tale was in circulation in Rome in the 5th century B.C. (the time of the battle); there is every reason to think that the story was of much later origin (hardly current in Rome before the 4th or 3d centuries B.C.). The story is contrary to all that we know of the status of Roman religion at the beginning of the Republic; the story is of Greek origin, similar to the legends of the battle of Sagra (580/560 B.C.), similar to the stories told of the battle of Pydna (168 B.C.). The legend is not native, not original, but derivative, and it was only after the Greek idea of Castor and Pollux, as twin-gods, had come into Roman life, after Greek mythologies had become familiar to the Roman mind that this charming tale could become a Roman tradition. Once this had taken place, it would follow as a natural consequence that some, perhaps many, would think of this temple and would speak of this temple as the temple of Castor *and* Pollux—in spite of its official designation. We observe once more that Livy did not repeat the tale and calls the temple, only, the temple of Castor.

Dionysius of Halicarnassus, the Greek, on the other hand does give the version of the story in its double aspect, including the epiphany and the annunciation (6.13). And in describing the parade of the cavalry, which took place on the Ides of July (as corresponding to the date of the battle of Lake Regillus), he says the procession moved from the temple of Mars to its objective, the temple of the *Dioscuri*. In Greek religion and mythology, Castor and Pollux were so closely associated that the Greek historian does not hesitate to tell the legend and quite naturally calls the shrine ὁ νεὼς τῶν Διοσκούρων. We cannot tell whether Dionysius knew the correct name of this temple or not, but to him, as a Greek, this was a natural designation and his use of the term, without further comment, may well mean that the term, in popular parlance, was perfectly well known in his day (i.e. vs. the official and correct designation).

The legend does not cause Plutarch any more dismay than it

did Dionysius and in his Life of *Aemilius Paulus* (25.1–2) Plutarch gives his version of the appearance of the Dioscuri in the Forum. In his *Coriolanus* (3.4), Plutarch says that

the day on which this victory was won, viz. the Ides of July, was consecrated to the Dioscuri,

which certainly ought to mean that Plutarch carelessly believed that the temple was originally dedicated to the two gods. Certain it is that Plutarch never calls the temple, the temple of Castor, but only the temple of the *Dioscuri* or of *Castor and Pollux* (*Sulla* 8.3, 33.4; *Pomp.* 2.4; *Cato Min.* 27.4; 28.3). Perhaps the temple was officially called the temple of Castor *and* Pollux in Plutarch's day—which I think was the case; but Plutarch gives us no reason for thinking that he thought the name of the temple was ever anything but "the temple of the Dioscuri." Again, it is a Greek source with which we are dealing.

In Cicero's *De Natura Deorum,* the legend of the horsemen, Castor and Pollux, in battle at Lake Regillus is discussed by the Stoic Balbus (*De Nat. Deor.* 2.2.5–6) as part of his argument to prove the existence of gods; and as proof of the legend Balbus triumphantly exclaims:

But do these seem to you mere fables? Don't you see that a shrine was dedicated by Aulus Postumius to Castor and Pollux in the forum? (3.5.13).

It is extraordinary that Cicero who knew perfectly well what the official name of this temple was (as is witnessed by the twenty-four instances where he in person, with complete familiarity, refers to the temple as the "temple of Castor") should here make this statement. The only reasonable and, I think, the only possible way to interpret the statement is not as a statement of belief of Cicero himself but as the logical statement of Balbus, exponent of Greek Stoicism. To a Stoic, the theory of divine epiphanies was entirely sound; to a Greek the phenomenon was entirely familiar; a Greek could conceive only of the dual worship of Castor and Pollux in the shrine and a Stoic would accept the conclusion, unless his critical examination discovered the truth in this particular case. As with Dionysius, and Plutarch, so here, we are again in the midst of *Greek* psychology, and again find the Greek legend of the two horsemen associated with the name, "the temple of Castor *and* Pollux," as though that had been the name from the start. We know, certainly enough, that it was not. In the case of all three, Dionysius, Plutarch, and the Stoic Balbus the legend, which stands for Greek worship, led the speakers astray into the belief that joint worship had been original and that the name of the temple was the familiar Greek name.[4] Suetonius' comment (*Div. Jul.* 10) that the temple had been erected to the two brothers also becomes clear in the light of these passages that show the Greek conception. Suetonius also knew the legend (cf. *Nero* 1.1). As a Roman he knew that in Caesar's day the temple was still called Castor's, but in the first century after Christ it was much easier, even for a Roman, to think that the dual cult which was a fact, then, had been one always.

But Cicero knew still better. He not only knew the correct name of the temple, but in the *Pro Scauro* (23.46) he seems to give a date for the addition of the Pollux worship to that of Castor in "the temple of Castor": (i.e. the second cen. B.C.)

L. ipse Metellus, avus huius, sanctissimos deos illo constituisse in templo videtur in vestro conspectu, iudices, ut salutem a vobis nepotis sui deprecarentur.

Greek legend and Greek worship were responsible for the ultimate joint worship of the two gods here. Castor arrived alone. Castor did not, as is well known, come to Rome, originally, as a Greek or foreign god at all. But Greek influence added the cult of Pollux to that of Castor, although we may not know the *exact* date of this. Greek influence, likewise, was responsible

---

[4] We find the same result in Valerius Maximus, *Fact. et Dicta Mem.*, 1.8.1: acceptance of legend and assumption that the shrine was *aedis eorum* from the beginning.

for an unofficial designation of the temple. There can, I think, be no doubt of that at least,—what the origin of this designation was. When the legend first appeared, no one can say; but in the first century B.C., legend and unofficial name were, of course, *both known,* perfectly well, and widely known.

Was the name of the temple ever officially changed? The language of Suetonius seems to me to indicate such a change pretty clearly. As we have seen, Suetonius knew perfectly well that in the time of Bibulus and Caesar, that temple bore the name of "the temple of Castor." As is well known, the temple was reconstructed by Tiberius. In speaking of the new dedication by Tiberius, Suetonius makes this remarkable statement:

Dedicavit et Concordiae aedem, item Pollucis et Castoris suo fratrisque nomine de manubiis (*Tib.* 20).

With the proceeds of the spoils from the Germanic campaign, Tiberius restored and dedicated the temple of Concord and, likewise, that of *Pollux and Castor* in his own name and that of his brother. Suetonius clearly distinguishes between the titles "temple of Castor" for the earlier period and temple of "Castor and Pollux" for this time. Nor is this a careless and accidental use of the new title, as we see from the subsequent reference to the temple in the life of *Caligula* (22):

Atque aede Castoris et Pollucis in vestibulum transfigurata,

where Suetonius speaks of Caligula's extension of his palace on the hill and adds that the mad emperor took his place between the *two* gods, awaiting adoration:

consistens saepe inter fratres deos.

While Suetonius does not specifically mention an official change in the name of the title, the marked distinction that he makes in the name points decidedly to the fact of such a change. The known presence of statues of *two* gods here at this time further confirms belief in the change for which I am arguing. It would be comforting if Ovid had said in so many words that the name of the temple was changed at the time of its rededication, but in *Fasti,* as in the Suetonian passages, the implication is, I think, clear and the conclusion inescapable:

> at quae venturas praecedit sexta Kalendas,
>   hac sunt Ledaeis templa dicata deis:
> fratribus illa deis fratres de gente deorum
>   circa Iuturnae composuere lacus *(Fasti* 1.705–708).

> On the sixth day that precedes the coming Kalends
>   To the Ledaean gods a temple was dedicated:
> Brothers of a race of gods to brother gods
>   Have founded the shrine near Juturna's pool.

On the twenty-seventh of January, in 6 A.D., Tiberius restored and rededicated this temple in his own name and that of his deceased brother Drusus, to the *two* gods, Castor *and* Pollux. Participation in the honor of rededication—whether in the form of an inscription on the front of the temple—or otherwise —by the two, Tiberius and Drusus, gave special point to the belated *recognition* of Pollux in the new name of this temple-structure which was, thereafter, officially called either *aedes Castoris et Pollucis* or *aedes Castorum.*

The note in the *Fasti Praenestini*[5] for the twenty-seventh of January cannot be taken as certain evidence for the new name of the temple but, as it stands, it strongly suggests that new name, and only one restoration seems plausible:

> 27 **C** VI **C** AEDiS castoris et poLLVCIS DEDICATa est

Under the circumstances, we are not surprised to find Pliny the Elder referring to the temple, as *Castorum aedem,* least of all as he is telling of a portent that occurred *Tiberio principe* (*N.H.* 10.43.60.121). For him to have called the temple "the temple of Castor" would have been the striking thing, calling for explanation. To maintain that Pliny was guilty of carelessness, that he was employing, simply, a popular or vulgar

---

[5] The date of the additional note in these *Fasti* in all probability follows 6 A.D. (cf. *C.I.L.*).

designation is going contrary to the valid conclusions suggested by Suetonius, Ovid, and the *Fasti Praenestini*. If Pliny were careless, he might use one designation at one time and the other, another time, but he does not (cf. *N.H.* 34.6.11.23, *ante aedem Castorum*).

Cassius Dio knew the story of Caesar and Bibulus which we found in Suetonius. Quite like Suetonius, the Greek historian wrote that Bibulus complained that his fate was the same as that of Pollux, because although that hero possessed a temple in common with his brother Castor, the temple was named only for the latter:

ἐπ' ἐκείνου μόνου ἡ ἐπωνυμία αὐτοῦ γίγνεται (37.8.2).

Cassius Dio knew, therefore, that the original name of the temple was that of *Castor*. Although Dio knew that the earlier name of the temple was that of Castor, none the less he calls the temple the temple of the Dioscuri,

πρὸς μὲν τὸ Διοσκόρειον (38.6.2),

even when speaking of bitter conflicts that took place before the temple in 59 B.C., between Caesar and Bibulus. Such a designation of the temple, for that period, was certainly incorrect. Perhaps Dio hesitated to coin a new term, such as Καστόρειον. Cassius Dio's statement, like that of Suetonius, means that at the time of Caesar, in the first century B.C., Castor and Pollux were commonly associated in people's minds, as common joint owners of the temple. We have already seen to what extent this was true.

In his use of the term Διοσκόρειον, Dio is like Dionysius of Halicarnassus and Plutarch, both of whom called the temple by this very name (or an equivalent), even for the earlier period. In this respect, these Greeks are like Strabo who also called this temple the temple of the Dioscuri (Διοσκούρων ἱερόν) when he ironically takes the Romans to task for building a shrine in honor of the Dioscuri and yet, at the same time, sending plunderers (in the days of Demetrius Poliorcetes) into Greece, the homeland of these gods (5.3.5. = C.232). Similarly Appian uses the phrase

ἐν τῷ νεῷ τῶν Διοσκούρων,

as he tells of the tragic death of Gracchus (*B.C.* 1.3.25). These Greeks simply could not think of the temple otherwise,—because of Greek religious traditions and mythologies that associated the two gods so very closely together. Plutarch, in the first century after Christ, and Appian and Dio, in the second, were justified in calling the temple by this name, in their time; but Dionysius and Strabo should have known better.[6]

Cassius Dio, like Suetonius, knew of Tiberius' rededication of the temple, and Dio's designation of the temple, as τὸ Διοσκόρειον, for the year 6 A.D. and the years after, is not only the natural one for a Greek historian but, as it happens, the correct one:

(55.27.4) Tiberius dedicated τὸ Διοσκόρειον and inscribed not only his own name but also that of Drusus upon it (6 A.D.);

(59.28.5) Gaius Caligula used τὸ Διοσκόρειον as an approach to his palace, whereby he made τοὺς Διοσκόρους (whose statues were in the temple) his gate-keepers (40 A.D.);

(60.6.8) Claudius, he says, restored

τοῖς Διοσκόροις τὸν νεών (41 A.D.).

All correct references to the temple, after 6 A.D., ought (if my theory is valid) to read: (in Greek) τὸ Διοσκόρειον; (in Latin) *aedes* (or *templum*) *Castoris et Pollucis* (or *Castorum*). Such designations, in the first century A.D. and after, ought to signify this title as the accepted one for the later period. Asconius comments on Cicero, *In Pisonem* (10.23), where Cicero had used the phrase, *in templum Castoris,* and Asconius copies from his Cicero, saying *de Castoris templo;* but in commenting on Cicero, *Pro Scauro* (23.46), where Cicero refers to changes

---

[6] Even in the *Mon. Ancyr.* (Greek version) we find (4.13) τ]οῦ τε ναοῦ τῶν Διοσκό[ρων.

in the temple, without mentioning the name of the temple, Asconius' words are:

Castoris et Pollucis templum Metellus quem nominat refecerat (i.e., 117 B.C.).

Florus had derived the story of the divine epiphany from earlier sources and he supposed that the temple was dedicated to Castor and Pollux as associates, because they had been companions in arms of the Romans (*Ep*. 1.11.4 = c. v. *Bell. Lat.*). For this reason, if for no other, he called the temple

aede Pollucis et Castoris,

when, later, he speaks of the miraculous appearance of young men in the Forum, following the Cimbric victory (*Ep*. 3.3.20 = 1. c. 38. *Bell. Cimbr. Teut. Tig.*). But the fact remains, whatever the reason, that Florus uses this title. Lactantius calls it *aedes eorum,* when he writes of the Castor and Pollux legend, of their appearance in the Forum at the time of the Latin war (*Inst*. 2.7.9). Like Florus, he simply took it for granted that the temple had been one for Castor and Pollux from the beginning. Whether Florus and Lactantius knew that the temple was long called *templum Castoris* I do not know, but we do know that in the second and third centuries after Christ they thought the title was: aedes Castoris *et* Pollucis.

In the *Scriptores Hist. Aug.*, Capitol., *Max.* (16.1) we read:

Senatus consultum autem hoc fuit: cum ventum esset in aedem Castorum etc.;

in Trebell, *Valer.* (5.4.) it is:

cum . . . in aede Castorum senatus haberetur;

and in the *Curiosum* and the *Notitia* (Reg. VIII) we find:

Templum Castorum,

from all of which it would appear that this new name had become quite fixed.

I do not believe that I have put my evidence into a straightjacket. On the contrary, a careful interpretation of all of these passages seems to me to lead to this as the logical conclusion: that the temple was at first and for long, Castor's; that, once Greek mythologies were widely diffused, it was possible in popular parlance to think of it and speak of it as the shrine of Castor and Pollux; that Pollux did become associated with Castor in worship,—to what extent, exactly, we cannot tell, nor precisely when, though it would seem that this was an established fact in the second century B.C.; that the Greeks inevitably called it the shrine of Castor *and* Pollux, regardless of dates; that it was officially rechristened by Tiberius (before he became emperor) as "the temple of Castor and Pollux," or as the "temple of the Castors." Pollux then finally came into his own, into full partnership with Castor in worship at this temple, even though poor Bibulus never did win his crown. The name, "the temple of Castor and Pollux," became the correct designation.

Designation of the temple after 6 A.D. by the old title, as the temple of Castor, is witness to the force of tradition, to the hold the old name had in spite of Greek legends and in spite of the official change of title, and it is convincing evidence for the skeptical that such was the original name. Inscriptions[7] of the Empire period continue the use of the older designation:

POST · AEDEM · CASTORIS,

and it appeared, also, upon the Marble Plan.[8] Can it be that these designations prove that the name was never altered? Only on condition that all of our evidence for a change of title is worthless. That is hardly the case. The only alternative, then, is that the old name survived in these documents. In the same way, I should interpret references to the temple in the poets, Martial and Juvenal. The former says:

. . . vicinum *Castora* canae transibis Vestae . . . (1.70.3)

[7] *C.I.L.* VI.363, 9177, 9393, 9872, 10024; (cf. also) VI.8688, 8689, and 2202–3 (with notes).
[8] Cf., e.g., *N. d. S.* 1882, p. 233; Jordan, *Forma Urbis Romae;* and Lanciani, *Ruins and Exc's.,* p. 269.

as he gives directions to his book for reaching the Palatine, and the latter:

. . . ad vigilem ponendi *Castora* nummi (14.260).

Everybody knew, in any case, what was meant, and neither poet was under any necessity of using a newer and fuller title that, besides, might have caused metrical difficulties.

There have been so many conflicting and untrue statements[9] published about the name of this temple that it has seemed worth while to try to bring order out of the seeming chaos of ancient testimony which has caused subsequent uncertainty and confusion. The ancient testimony can be explained, I think, and the truth emerges quite clearly.

[9] E.g., Ashby-Platner, *Top. Dic. of Anc. Rome,* 1929, pp. 102 *seq.;* Bethe, "Dioskuren," in *Pauly-Wissowa,* 1903, IX, 1104; Frazer, Ed. of Ovid *Fasti,* 1929, II, 263 *seq.;* Huelsen-Carter, *The Roman Forum,* 1909, pp. 161 *seq.;* Jordan, *Top. der Stadt Rom,* 1885, I, 2, p. 369; Lanciani, *Ruins and Exc's. of Anc. Rome,* 1897, p. 271; Albert, *Étude sur le Culte de Castor et Pollux,* 1883; Platner, *Top. and Mon's. of Anc. Rome,* 1911, p. 180; Wissowa, *Rel. u. Kult. der Römer,* 1912, p. 268.

UNIVERSITY OF PENNSYLVANIA

SOPHOCLES' PLACE IN GREEK TRAGEDY

Walter Woodburn Hyde

RECENTLY I saw the *Electra* of Sophocles revived by Margaret Anglin in the stately translation of Plumptre. It was an impressive illustration of the living presence of old Greece in the twentieth century that a Greek tragedy, and that by no means the most finished, should still attract many cultivated people. It must have appealed to that audience, as it did to me, how timeless the drama is, and how essentially unchanged its outer form, with a few necessary modifications, has remained from the time of Sophocles to that of Ibsen, Hauptmann, and Shaw. And it must have been apparent how, in one respect at least, Greek drama still surpasses our own—in the rapid development of the plot to the catastrophe, nothing retarding its consummation, a union of simplicity and complexity.

There are few more compelling themes than this of the *Electra,* the grim tale of retribution wreaked on a guilty parent by her son abetted by his sister, "the darkest of all Greek tragedies," as it is also "one of the noblest."[1] As the climax is reached, Electra stands without the palace door with no qualms of conscience, the embodiment of vengeance, triumphing in the murder of Clytemnestra within, now that justice has been done for the slaying of Agamemnon, her father. Before, a normal woman, she is now metamorphosed into one of the Erinyes, who can shout to her brother as she hears her mother's cries (1415):

> Smite her yet again,
> If thou hast strength for it.

No scene of murder, such as is often enacted on our stage, but which religion excluded from the Greek, could produce the effect of the piteous cries for mercy uttered by the unseen victim.

---

[1] So J. T. Sheppard, *Aeschylus and Sophocles: Their Work and Influence,* New York, 1927, p. 68 (in "Our Debt to Greece and Rome Series").

We now know that the theme of the *Electra* is centuries older than the poet found it in a saga of the *Odyssey*.[2] In 1915 there was found in a sepulchral treasure of bead-seals in a Mycenaean rock-tomb near ancient Thisbe in Boeotia an intaglio dating from the early fifteenth century B.C., which represents a hero wreaking vengeance on a guilty pair.[3] To the left a man, clad in armor, is falling mortally stricken; in the center is the slayer who, with uplifted dagger in his right hand, is now turning to the right to attack a fleeing woman, while his left is raised to seize her by the hair. This is evidently the scene of Orestes slaying Aegisthus and Clytemnestra. Moreover, the saga must have had a historical basis in a crime committed in Crete or early Greece, since Aegisthus, in the form *Akashau*, appears among Keftiu or Cretan names on the "London Wood-tablet" from Egypt, which dates from the Eighteenth Dynasty. Its presence there amid a list of names for the use of Egyptian school-boys shows that Aegisthus was a prominent Minoan in some way connected with a tragedy.

Not only Sophocles, but Aeschylus and Euripides employed the saga as they found it in the Epos, each using it in his own way, just as Shakespeare used Plutarch. Thus, in the *Choephori* Aeschylus, who seems to have followed in the main the plot of the earlier *Oresteia* of Stesichorus, places the recognition scene between brother and sister near the beginning, and gives the leading rôle to Aegisthus. The climax is the murder and subsequent madness of Orestes, the latter caused, despite his protestations that he had done a deed of justice, by the Erinyes, and the play ends in the Chorus' expression of doubt:

> Full accomplished, when shall Fate
> Lulled to rest, her stormy ire abate?[4]

[2] 3.193 ff.; the murder, 306 ff.

[3] Sir Arthur Evans, "The Ring of Nestor: A Glimpse into the Minoan After-World, etc.": in *J.H.S.*, XLV (1925), 1, 1–75, fig. 38 and Pl. III, 3; also figs. 31–32 and Pl. III, 1 and 33 and Pl. III, 2, for two other scenes from the Cadmean house. Cf. M. P. Nilsson, *The Minoan-Mycenaean Religion*, Oxford, 1927, p. 44.

[4] Tr. by Anna Swanwick, *The Dramas of Aeschylus*[4], London, 1901 (in "Bohn's Classical Library").

Sophocles places the recognition scene near the end,[5] thus developing Electra's suspense through hope, despair, and final joy, and has Electra play the main rôle. Here the climax is the murder of Aegisthus, which is not described, and the play ends without any hint of Orestes' madness. Euripides, influenced by both his predecessors, gives us a less ideal picture of remorse and reproach among the murderers, and to that extent is false to the Epos, where they show no conscience about the deed. The revival of any of these versions would, as in the performance by Miss Anglin's company, show the truth of Goethe's characterization of Greek tragedy as "grandeur, fitness, soundness, human perfection, elevated wisdom, sublime thought, pure, strong intuition, and whatever other qualities one might enumerate."[6]

When we reflect how near the fifth-century Greeks were to the morning of their world, it is not difficult to understand the simplicity and moderation which appear in their tragedies as in all their literary forms. The dramatist could concentrate the action on one essential theme, unconfused by any minor issues or by-plots, which are so common in modern plays.[7] Thus Sophocles tells the story of the *Electra* in a little over 1,500 verses, which would carry us not quite through two acts of *Hamlet*. But to understand the rapidity with which Greek tragedy reached perfection so soon after it was evolved as a literary *genre* is more difficult. When we remember that the three great tragedians were all in part contemporary, it is amazing that while Aeschylus, who stands at the portal of Greek tragedy as its real creator, shows crudities of style and structure in his earlier work, within his lifetime Sophocles "reached the highest level of dramatic and literary technique."[8] It has often

---

[5] 1097–1321.
[6] *Conversations of Goethe with Eckermann and Soret*[2], Tr. by John Oxenford, London, 1883, p. 254.
[7] See Aristotle on the economy of length and the concentration of tragedy: *Poet.* 26.12.1462b.
[8] Quoting R. W. Livingstone, *The Legacy of Greece*, Oxford, 1922, p. 260.

been pointed out that they had no models, but created almost out of nothing. How much easier it was for the Roman writers, who had Greek prototypes in every field to follow and whose national literature began with translations from the Greek! Instead of feeling ashamed of their debt, they gloried in it. Thus Cicero admits that "in learning Greece surpassed us and in all branches of literature,"[9] and, in the next century, Quintilian, the greatest of ancient schoolmasters, advises boys to begin their studies with Greek, since "Latin learning is derived from the Greek."[10] It is a fact often repeated that all forms of Latin letters—epic, lyric, elegiac, dramatic, epigrammatic, and didactic poetry, and history, biography, rhetoric, oratory, the essay, novel, sermon, letter-writing, and literary criticism in prose—were Greek in origin, as the names of most of them show. And even the Roman claim to have originated satire is more than dubious, as the Old Comedy shows.

If we narrow our attention to tragedy, we shall find that the Athenian tragedians had no dramatic models beyond rustic choruses of fifty men dressed as satyrs who danced and sang around an altar. But out of such crude beginnings there was to evolve in one generation Greek tragedy, which Swinburne has called "probably, on the whole, the greatest spiritual work of man."[11] For ever since Demodocus in the *Odyssey* sang at the court of the Phaeacians, minstrels and chorus-leaders had retold with variations the heroic tales of the Epic in lyric meters. In the seventh century B.C., the Spartan Alcman, "the swan-singer of wedding hymns," had a chorus of girls recite how the Phaeacian maidens surprised by Odysseus on the shore "cowered helplessly like birds when a hawk flies near," and how Nausicaa became conscious of her love for the stranger. A little later,

9 *Tusc. Disput.* 1.1.2, Tr. J. E. King, in "The Loeb Class. Lib.," London and New York, 1927.
10 *Inst. Orat.* 1.1.12, Tr. H. E. Butler, in "The Loeb Class. Lib.," 1921.
11 Quoted by R. W. Livingstone, *op. cit.*, p. 263; J. T. Sheppard, *op. cit.*, p. 16 and n. 10, narrows the poet's statement to the *Oresteia*, quoting from Swinburne's acceptance of the dedication of W. G. Headlam's *Agamemnon*.

Stesichorus, the contemporary of Alcaeus and Sappho, at whose birth a nightingale is fabled to have sat on his lips and sang, retold in choral form the stories of Medea, Helen and the Sack of Troy, and composed an *Oresteia*—the latter the prototype of Aeschylus' supreme achievement—wherein Clytemnestra murders her husband, and in turn is slain with her paramour by her son, thus transferring a heroic saga to lyric form. It is in such choral songs that is to be sought the immediate background of Phrynichus and Aeschylus.

One such lyric type, the *dithyramb,* an improvised accompaniment of the dance and probably brought from Phrygia to Greece along with the cult of the wine-god, seems gradually to have become more serious than at its first appearance in a fragment of Archilochus dating from the first half of the seventh century B.C., in which the Parian poet boasts he "knows how, when his wits are crazed with wine, to lead the dithyramb, the fair strain of Lord Dionysus."[12] But whatever the spirit of the dithyramb as a form of religious celebration in the classical period, whether convivial or serious[13]—since the only complete specimens surviving are the graceful creations of Bacchylides, which are quite different from the fragmentary ones of Pindar—it was first made into a literary composition by the Lesbian Arion, who lived at the court of Periander in Corinth (625–585 B.C.), the poet who "introduced the first drama of tragedy."[14] Finally, soon after the middle of the sixth century B.C., it attained its full development in Athens when Peisistratus instituted the *City Dionysia* in honor of Dionysus Eleutherieus, and added to its sacrifices and ceremonies a tragic contest—perhaps a ritual drama, as the early use of masks and men only in the

[12] Fragm. 77: Th. Bergk, *Poet. lyr. Gr.*⁴, Lipsiae, 1878–82, II, 404.

[13] Sir Wm. Ridgeway, *Origin of Tragedy,* Cambridge, 1910, p. 38, believes the original was grave and solemn; A. W. Pickard-Cambridge, *Dithyramb, Tragedy, and Comedy,* Oxford, 1929, ch. 1, pp. 80–81, believes there is no evidence for this view.

[14] So the recently discovered notice from Solon: H. Rabe, in *Rhein. Mus. f. Philol.,* LXIII (1908), 150. Cf. Herodotus, 1.23, who wrongly regarded Arion as the inventor of the dithyramb.

chorus seem to show. The tyrant also offered a prize for the
"goat-song," which was first won by Thespis of Icaria, who
introduced an actor from his chorus of fifty to reply or "answer"
to its *coryphaeus*,[15] the greatest step toward the completed
drama.

Why the singers of Thespis called their song a "goat-
song" is not clear, whether because they wore goat-skins like
the members of the older Corinthian satyr-choruses, or because
a goat was the prize for the victorious poet, or, perhaps, because
a goat was sacrificed at the performance.[16] But it is out of such
a background that Greek tragedy arose, though in just what
manner is in dispute. For nearly a century from the time of
F. G. Welcker[17] it was accepted as a dogma that the satyr-play
formed a step midway between the dithyramb and tragedy, a
view now yielding to the belief that tragedy did not grow out
of the satyr-play, despite Aristotle's statement to the contrary,[18]
but rather that the two developed separately from the same
literary *genre,* the dramatic dithyramb. Thus the satyr-play,
only brought into connection with tragedy on the reorganization
of the *City Dionysia* by Peisistratus, when each poet had to add
one at the close of his three tragedies, was brought to Athens
from Phlius by Pratinas about 515 B.C., and tragedy was
brought there from Corinth and Sicyon by way of Icaria. This
view is in harmony with another statement of Aristotle,[19] and
one of Plato,[20] who agree in deriving tragedy from the primitive dithyramb, the song in honor of Dionysus' birth. Whatever, then, be the ultimate origin of tragedy, whether this be
sought with Dietrich in funeral dirges, Eleusinian mysteries, and

[15] Diog. Laert. 3.56.

[16] The last two, not in conflict, accepted by Pickard-Cambridge, in *Cl. Rev.,*
XXVI (1912), 59, and R. C. Flickinger, *The Greek Theater and Its Drama,*
Chicago, 1918, p. 13.

[17] *Nachtrag zu der Schrift ueber die Aeschylische Trilogie nebst einer Abhand-
lung ueber das Satyrspiel,* Frankfurt am Main, 1826.

[18] *Poet.* 4.17.1449a; "a development of the satyr-play."

[19] *Ibid.* 4.14.1449a.   [20] *Leg.* 700B.

various aetiological sources, with Ridgeway in ceremonies at
the tombs of heroes, or with Miss Harrison in the "year-spirit"
and sympathetic magic,[21] Aristotle is right in deriving it from
the universal instinct to imitate,[22] and it took the form of a
choral performance, which only gradually became dramatic.
All that was coarse in the half-literary drama of the obscure
period of Thespis and Phrynichus disappeared, and finally, in
the words of Aristotle tragedy "after going through many
changes, stopped when it had found its natural form,"[23] *i.e.,* in
Aeschylus, who introduced a second actor, curtailed the chorus,
and gave the leading rôle to the dialogue. For it was Aeschylus who first, probably, abandoned the satyr-chorus, and assuredly the first who lifted tragedy into a literary form. If,
then, Aeschylus was the real creator of Attic tragedy, it is only
a step further to its perfection under Sophocles, his younger
contemporary.

The greatest of all centuries was nearly spanned by the life
of Sophocles (495–405). Of that long life, apart from legends
handed down by his biographers,[24] we know little. He was
born at "White Colonus,"[25] northwest of Athens, which he has
immortalized as the spot beloved of Dionysus, Aphrodite,
and the Muses, where the nightingale haunts the Cephisus'
glades with their gray-green olives, wine-dark ivy, crocus and
narcissus. He was a splendid example of ὁ εὐφυής—for in him
all the elements of prosperous fortune were blended, health,
beauty, love of pleasure, serenity of temper, and charm of conversation, and withal he received victories in the tragic contests
for over sixty years.

[21] For discussion of theories, see Flickinger, *op. cit.,* pp. 3 ff.
[22] *Poet.* 1.2.1447a: 4.1.1448b.
[23] *Ibid.* 4.14–16.1449a.
[24] Σοφοκλέους γένος καὶ βίος (coll. by Aristoxenus, Satyrus, and Istrus, and
showing marks of Alexandrian origin), published by O. Jahn, in his *Sophoclis
Electra*[3], by A. Michaelis, Bonn, 1882, pp. 1–22. Cf. also W. von Christ
und W. Schmidt, *Geschichte d. Gr. Litt.*[6], Muenchen, 1912, Pt. I, pp. 309–345,
and references.
[25] So-called in *Oed. Col.* 670.

Born too late to take part in the Persian struggle as Aeschylus had done we first hear of him as a beautiful boy of fifteen, chosen to lead naked and with ivory lyre in hand the chorus which danced and sang a paean around the trophy in honor of Salamis. Twelve years later he won his first tragic prize with his *Triptolemus* over Aeschylus. Plutarch repeats an old legend that amid the factions in the theater, the *archon eponymus* as director of plays set aside the usual judges, and left the decision to Cimon and his fellow-generals, who were present.[26] But the story that the older poet left Athens in chagrin is contradicted by the fact that he continued to compete with his rival for ten years more, winning over him with his *Septem* in 467, and *Oresteia* in 458. In all, Sophocles gained between twenty and twenty-four first prizes,[27] and never fell below second choice among the competing poets. At first, till deterred by the weakness of his voice, he followed the Athenian custom by acting in his own plays, for he took the rôle of Nausicaa in the lost play of that name, and in the *Thamyris* he represented the blind bard of Thrace with his harp so successfully that Polygnotus painted him in that pose for the *Stoa Poikile.* Aristotle credits him with introducing a third actor[28]—the last important addition to the external drama, effected probably in 468—and with increasing the chorus from twelve to fifteen.

We have a further glimpse of him in 440, the traditional date of the *Antigone,*[29] on Chios when on his way with Pericles to reduce the Samian revolt. Ion, a contemporary poet, who met him here, describes him as "very agreeable and witty over his cups."[30] His further statement that in political affairs he "behaved as any other virtuous Athenian might have done" is probably a good estimate, even if he did perform his share of civic duties, and only shows that his ambition was artistic, and that it

---

[26] *Cimon* 8.   [27] Diod. 13.103.4; Suidas; etc.

[28] *Poet.* 4.14.1449a; Diog. Laert. 3.56.

[29] But 442, according to U. von Wilamowitz-Moellendorff, *Aristoteles und Athen,* Berlin, 1893, II, 298.

[30] *Ap.* Athen. *Deipnosophistae* 13.81.603e; cf. Cicero *De Officiis* 1.40.

was only in his transcendent poetic genius that he towered over his fellow-citizens. His old age seems to have been unruffled, even if legend tells of domestic trouble ending in a legal process. Thus the story, repeated long after by Cicero[31] and Plutarch,[32] and immortalized in our time by Browning in his *Aristophanes' Apology,* purports to give us a glimpse into his last public appearance. Then, after long "standing on the hateful road of old age," the poet was tried by his son for incompetency, only to be acquitted by his judges when they heard his defence—the reading of the "parodos" ode on the beauties of Colonus already mentioned.[33] This story, an echo of the comic stage and vitiated by the fact that the play in question was produced by his grandson after his death, at least illustrates the popularity of Sophocles, who in extreme old age suffered no decline.

He had seen Athens victorious over the Persians and build up her empire, and had had a share in her glory. But the merciful gods spared him from witnessing his city's final catastrophe. He died in Athens a few months after Euripides died in Macedonia, in whose honor his last chorus appeared in the introductory pageant without the usual garlands. We could believe the story that the Spartans allowed his funeral cortège to leave the beleaguered city for his final resting-place on the road to Decelea, if we could replace Lysander's name with that of Agis, since the former had not yet taken the starving city. As priest of a healing hero who had a chapel on the western slope of the Acropolis, and as the founder of a private *thiasos* of musicians, he was honored after death with offerings, as were Plato and Epicurus later. Aristophanes, whose badinage followed Euripides to the grave, has Dionysus say of Sophocles in Hades that he is "gentle here as he was gentle there,"[34] praise suited to the "singer of sweet Colonus." A contemporary tragedian, Phry-

---

[31] *De Senect.* 22.   [32] *Moralia* 775B.
[33] *Oed. Col.* 668–719.
[34] *Frogs* 82 (which appeared in 405, just after Sophocles' death). For the diatribe against Euripides, *ibid.,* 80, 770 f., 840 f.

nichus, paid him this honor, beautiful enough to have been preserved in the *Greek Anthology:*

> Thrice happy Sophocles! in good old age,
> Blessed as a man, and as a craftsman blessed,
> He died; his many tragedies were fair,
> And fair his end, nor knew he any sorrow.[35]

Often in his plays the poet had cited the Greek proverb, "call no man happy till he dies," as in the closing lines of the *Oedipus Rex:*

> We must call no one happy who is of mortal race,
> Until he hath crossed life's border, free from pain.[36]

Fortune thus had granted him her supreme favor. The late grammarian-poet Simmias of Rhodes thus dwelt on his wisdom and sweetness:

> Gently over the tomb of Sophocles, gently creep, O ivy, flinging forth thy green tresses, and all about let the rose-petal blow, and the clustered vine shed her soft tendrils round, for the sake of the wise-hearted eloquence mingled of the Muses and Graces that lived on his honeyed tongue.[37]

To Aristophanes and Aristotle, Sophocles was the greatest of the tragic poets of Athens, the latter, as is well known, using the *Oedipus Rex,* because of its concentration of plot and tragic intensity, as the model drama, even though it had received only second prize. This shows an interesting difference in taste wrought by the intervening century, since the *Antigone* was the favorite in the poet's day. Similarly, to Virgil the *cothurnus* of Sophocles meant dramatic perfection.[38] In modern days Racine and Lessing have praised him as highly. And we must remember it was a volume of the *Ajax* which Shelley clasped in his

[35] Fragm. 31K: Tr. J. A. Symonds, *Studies of the Gk. Poets,* 2d Ser., London, 1876, p. 220.

[36] Tr. R. C. Jebb, *The Tragedies of Sophocles,* Cambridge, 1905.

[37] Tr. by J. W. Mackail, *Select Epigrams from the Greek Anthology*[2], London, 1906, IV, xii, 179.

[38] *Ecl.* 8.10.

hand when his body was washed ashore.[38a]   Matthew Arnold, whose *Merope* recalls the spirit of the *Electra,* thus expresses his gratitude to the "even-balanced" poet

> who saw life steadily, and saw it whole;
> The mellow glory of the Attic stage,
> Singer of sweet Colonus, and its child.[39]

Of his hundred or more plays, only seven have come down to us along with fragments and a large part of a Satyr-play, the *Ichneutae,*[40] recently discovered. This is only one of the melancholy illustrations of the loss of Greek literature suffered by us. Out of some three hundred and nine poets, and eighteen hundred and seventy plays known to us by name from Greek antiquity only four poets and forty-four plays—including thirty-two tragedies and twelve comedies—have survived from the fifth century.[41] But these four poets have shed an inextinguishable glory on their city.

Although he lived through most of the fifth century, Sophocles belongs neither to its beginning with Aeschylus, nor to its end with Euripides, but rather to the middle period of Pericles and Phidias. By then the gods were not so real to the Athenians as they had been to the victors in the Persian struggle, whose spirit Aeschylus expresses by vindicating the law of righteousness in accordance with which the gods rule. Sophocles rather reflects the ideal heights of the succeeding period, the golden age of "shining Athens, the stay of Hellas," while Euripides, though his contemporary for three-quarters of a century, represents so different a tone of thought that he might have lived in another age. For he best expresses the restless

---

[38a] It is now in the Bodleian Library, Oxford, with other Shelley relics.

[39] *Sonnet to a Friend,* vss. 3–4.

[40] A. S. Hunt, *The Oxyrhynchus Papyri,* London, 1912, IX, No. 1174, 30–86, and Pl. II (cols. IV–V) ; etc.

[41] Thus Aug. Nauck, *Tragicorum Graecorum fragmenta,* Lipsiae, 1856, lists 141 writers and 386 titles; and Th. Kock, *Comicorum Atticorum fragmenta,* Lipsiae, 1880–84, I–III, names 168 writers and 1484 titles; cf. W. von Christ, *op. cit.,* I⁶, 396 and 409.

spirit engendered by the Peloponnesian War, and the succeeding "Age of Enlightenment" whose prophet he was, a period when traditional views of politics, religion, and ethics were undergoing the acid test of experience and reason. Thus in a real sense Sophocles "is a kind of golden mean betwixt the older Aeschylus and the more modern Euripides."[42] If he lacks the "gigantesque" elements of the former, he lacks also the naturalism of the more speculative Euripides. And yet, like Aeschylus, he keeps with modifications the traditional view of religion, which Euripides renounces. He has the same general idea of the divine rule of the world, similar views of retributive justice and destiny, and a similar concept of the drama. Thus, to a large extent, Sophocles continues the older poet's work, the difference between them being one of degree rather than of kind, while an entirely different outlook separates Sophocles from Euripides. We shall now carry a little further the differences between the three poets in religious background and dramatic technique.

The religious background of the drama, ever prominent because of its origin, finds a natural exponent in the nature of Aeschylus. The outstanding characteristic of his dramas is found in the fact that he, like Isaiah, is ever probing to the bottom the great problems of religion and their bearing on life, especially the origin and effect of evil. Born in Eleusis in the awesome atmosphere of the mysteries, which made it after Delphi the most venerated of shrines, he must have pondered from early youth on the contradictions in the moral law which prospered the wicked as well as the virtuous. The mystery of the gods, their wrath, jealousy, and punishment of human transgression, is constantly uppermost in his dramas. His effort to find a harmony between an imperfect world and just rulers leads him to assume a unity behind the contradictions. Now

[42] Lane Cooper, *An Aristotelian Theory of Comedy*, New York, 1922, p. 27. For the same idea of compromise between two ideals, see also W. Y. Tyrrell, *Essays on Greek Literature*, London, 1909, p. 43.

126

and then, despite his general adherence to a primitive theology, he gives us lofty glimpses of the gods which even dimly adumbrate monotheism. Thus, a doubtful fragment, which runs

Zeus is aether, Zeus is earth, Zeus is heaven,[43]

has been assigned to him, but rather belongs to some Orphic source. However, in the chorus of the *Suppliants* he calls Zeus

King of Kings, most blessed among the blessed, of perfect powers most perfect,[44]

and again in the *Eumenides,* "the all-powerful."[45]

He vindicates all that the gods do by assuming an all-pervading law of justice whereby sooner or later the guilty are punished, since evil brings only suffering. Just as Plato, he even anticipates the Christian doctrine of learning through suffering, as when the chorus in the *Eumenides* says:

well-earned is wisdom at the cost of pain.[46]

Many of his religious ideas come from a primitive condition of society in which the family played a greater rôle than in his day.[47] Thus, his idea of hereditary curse—the counterpart of the modern biological law of heredity—whereby the sins of the fathers are visited on the children, who are led into infatuation (which is personified as *Ate,* an evil daemon),[48] first appears in Greek literature in a poem of Solon a century earlier.[49] If we cannot see why one suffers, or suffers overmuch, we must look into his past or that of his family, where a commensurate offence is sure to be disclosed, through which the moral equilibrium has been disturbed and can only be restored through

---

[43] E. A. Ahrens, *Aeschyli et Sophoclis tragoediae et fragmenta,* I, Parisiis, 1846, *fragm.* 345 (from Clement of Alexandria, *Stromata,* V. 603). Aug. Nauck, *De tragicorum Graecorum fragmentis observationes criticae,* Berolini, 1855, is against its Sophoclean origin.

[44] 524–526.   [45] 918.

[46] 520; cf. *Agamemnon* 176–178; etc.

[47] Cf. R. W. Livingstone, *The Pageant of Greece,* Oxford, 1923, pp. 108 ff.

[48] E.g., *Agamemnon* 396 f.   [49] 13.29–32.

Nemesis.[50] This notion is coupled with another primitive concept, that of the *lex talionis,* whereby a son must avenge a parent, a view which aroused the opposition of Euripides. Thus, Orestes must slay his mother or be haunted by his father's spirit, and in any case he will be followed by the avenging Furies. This law of revenge or Nemesis, against which mortals fight in vain, is more important than Destiny in both Aeschylus and Sophocles. It is nowhere better affirmed in Greek literature than in a song of the chorus in the *Choephori:*

> "Let tongue of Hatred pay back tongue of Hate";
> Thus with her mighty utt'rance Justice cries,
> Due penalty exacting for each deed.
> "Let murder on the murderous stroke await!"
> "Do'er of wrong must suffer."—This sage lore
> Tradition utters, trebly hoar.[51]

And Aeschylus' notion of the origin of evil is found in still another primitive idea, that of *Hybris,* or insolent pride—the nearest approach to the Christian idea of sin—which is bred by prosperity, and arouses the jealousy of the gods, who retaliate. This jealousy, already known to Homer, can only be avoided by moderation (*sophrosyne*), which is the central idea of Greek morality.

Aeschylus' characters, like the scepter-bearing kings of the *Iliad,* are essentially supermen caught in the toils of fate and fulfilling their dooms, another idea inseparable from all Greek tragedy. Superhuman action, a blend of the human and divine, is everywhere prominent in his plays.[52] In the *Prometheus,* the grandest of all, the action is altogether on the superhuman plane, every character except Io—and even she is set apart from ordinary humans through her fate—being a god or a demigod. The final scene of cataclysm on the Scythian crag amid thunder,

[50] See R. C. Jebb, *Growth and Influence of Classical Greek Poetry,* Boston and New York, 1893, pp. 181–182; *id., Primer of Greek Literature,* New York, 1888, pp. 81–82; etc.

[51] 309–314 (Swanwick); cf. in same play, 400–404.

[52] Cf. Livingstone, *Pageant,* p. 110.

lightning, and earthquake, which combine to hurl the chained Titan into the abyss, is unearthly in its grandeur, one of the greatest of poetic flights, but the poet's art, supplemented only by the few bits of stage apparatus then known, such as the *bronteion* or thunder mill, is equal to the task.

With Sophocles, despite his deeply religious nature, the gods and Destiny play a less prominent rôle. He also recognizes the moral contradictions here, the conflict between divine law and human duty, but retains his orthodox faith, accepting, while mitigating, the legends about the supernal powers. Thus, the outstanding feature of his plays is the attempt to harmonize and reconcile, the poet following the Heracleitan "harmony of the whole." That at times, however, he regarded the ways of the gods as inscrutable is shown by this fragment:

> But thou couldst not learn the divine acts, if the gods concealed them, not even if thou shouldst go all lengths in examining all.[53]

But Zeus is the upholder of righteousness, which must be vindicated here below. The poet keeps with Aeschylus the primitive notions of hereditary curse and Nemesis to explain apparent injustice, sometimes even in an exaggerated form. Thus, in the *Electra,* the chorus, encouraged by Clytemnestra's dream which seems to foretell speedy retribution on Agamemnon's slayers, sings:

> Not forgetful is the two-edged axe of bronze that struck the blow of old and slew him with foul cruelty,[54]

where, in the fulfilment of the law of retribution, even the axe, the agent of human anger, is regarded as harboring a grudge, and crying out for justice against those who have basely used it. But retribution in general is of secondary importance in his plays, and his view that suffering is never in vain is milder than that of his predecessor, since he shows more sympathy for hu-

[53] Jebb and Pearson, *Fragments of Sophocles,* I–III, Cambridge, 1917; III, fragm. 919.
[54] 484–486 (Jebb).

man weakness. Suffering at last brought wisdom to the unfortunate Oedipus, and the performance of duty meant more than life to Antigone. To quote James Adam: "Sophocles seems to invite us to lift our eyes from the suffering of the individual to a consideration of the ulterior purpose which Providence is thereby seeking to fulfil."[55]

While, then, Aeschylus makes his characters puppets of Fate, whose lots were already determined by the Epic rhapsodists, Sophocles, with his more sympathetic nature and search for moral motives, peoples his stage with πρόσωπα only a little less heroic and a little more human. His plays, while thereby losing in ideality, gain as pictures of life, his men and women acting and speaking as we might ourselves if in their places. He presents most human types except the downright ugly; among the men these culminate in Theseus, "the one perfect character," "the ideal for all time of the perfect gentleman,"[56] and among the women in Antigone, whose devotion to duty is bounded only by death. Aeschylus, true to his more primitive instincts, derives the action of his plays from the pressure of Fate, while Sophocles finds his rather in human passion. In the *Agamemnon* the Queen slays her husband because she is a tool of Fate, even if she deceives herself by trying to find human reasons for her act. She commits the crime not as the result of her imperious nature and will, which indeed place her beyond the pale of womanly decency, and which are her predominant characteristics in Sophocles' *Electra,* but because she is driven on by her Destiny. In the *Choephori,* Orestes is the human agent of Apollo in avenging his father's murder, but in the *Electra* of Sophocles his crime is the outgrowth of his character. Oedipus, horrified at the disclosure of his crimes, in despair puts out his eyes, but later, in the mystic *Oedipus at Colonus,* he gets peace from within, while with the older poet Orestes finds his from

[55] *The Religious Teachers of Greece,* Edinburgh, 1909, p. 173.
[56] So John Churton Collins, *Studies in Shakespeare,* Westminster, 1904, p. 167.

outside, in the reconciliation between Apollo and the Furies. Ajax in his disgrace goes mad, and, as Don Quixote assaults the windmills, he attacks the sheep and cattle, thinking that they are his enemies, the Atridae. But his madness and suicide are not the result of ancestral taint, but more immediate, because he has despised Athena. In the romantic *Philoctetes* the reason for the hero's suffering is not stated, whether because of his own fault or that of his line. Neither he nor Ajax would fit the spirit of the Aeschylean drama. Oedipus and Creon would fit it better, since they are the blind puppets of Destiny, examples of "tragic irony," one of the prominent features of the Sophoclean drama, in accordance with which his characters are often placed in ambiguous situations, in which, while believing that they are acting rightly, they are being impelled to their doom by unseen powers.[57]

Aeschylus, with his colossal forms, well merits the epithets usually given him—heroic, sublime, elemental, gigantic, Hebraic—epithets merited again, perhaps, only by the *Eroica Symphony* of Beethoven, which, with its implication of grand, tragic issues, similarly achieves the same Promethean qualities. Sophocles, with his ideal humans, captivates us by his simple teaching that men must acquiesce in the decrees of Fate, and thereby build up character. As Socrates brought the older Ionian nature philosophy from the skies to earth in the study of man, just so Sophocles may be said to have brought the tragic drama from the Aeschylean heights to the plane of noble mortals. His sympathy led him to dwell on human suffering, a sympathy tinged with melancholy, and at times even reaching the level of pessimism, which we are wont to associate rather with Buddhistic literature or certain books of the Old Testament, but which hovered over Greek thought as it does over that of modern Germany. While this melancholy is deeper in Sophocles than in Aeschylus, it is less prominent than in Euripi-

---

[57] See R. C. Jebb, *Essays and Addresses,* Cambridge, 1907 ("The Genius of Sophocles"), pp. 29–33; von Christ und Schmidt, *op. cit.,* I. 322, and n. 1.

des, in whom it sometimes reaches utter despair. Thus, for the most part it is in harmony with the more moderate sentiment which one meets so often in Greek and Roman writers from Homer to Marcus Aurelius. James Adam has compared it rather with Virgil's gentle pathos, as expressed in the well-known line:

sunt lacrimae rerum et mentem mortalia tangunt.[58]

But there are passages which are downright pessimistic. Thus, in harmony with the thought expressed in the *Iliad* by Zeus—

For in sooth there is naught, I ween, more miserable than man among all things that breathe and move upon earth,[59]

Sophocles regarded man as only a "phantom and vain shadow,"[60] a sentiment coming to a climax in a choral ode of the *Oedipus at Colonus:*

Not to be born is, past all prizing, best; but when a man hath seen the light, this is next best by far, that with all speed he should go thither whence he hath come.[61]

Only the gods are free from sorrow, as Oedipus says to Theseus:

Kind son of Aegeus, to the gods alone comes never old age or death, but all else is confounded by all-mastering time. Earth's strength decays, and the strength of the body; faith dies, distrust is born; and the same spirit is never steadfast among friends, or betwixt city and city.[62]

But just as the general background of Homer and the Old Testament is optimistic, Sophocles' melancholy and moments of pessimism are relieved by brighter pictures. Thus the choral "Hymn to Man" in the *Antigone* is a song of man's triumph over Nature—how he invented ships and ploughs, and ways to

[58] *Aen.* 1.462; Adam, *op. cit.,* p. 179.
[59] 17.446–447; Tr. A. T. Murray, in "The Loeb Class. Lib.," II, 1925; cf. the same sentiment in the *Odyssey* 18.130–131.
[60] *Ajax* 126.
[61] 1225–1227 (Jebb). Here the poet follows almost verbally the thought expressed in the preceding century by Theognis: 425–428.
[62] *Oedipus at Colonus* 607 ff. (Jebb); for the same thought cf. *Iliad* 24.526, and Sophocles, *Fragm.* 860.

capture birds, beasts, and fishes and to tame the creatures of the wild, and has taught himself speech and "wind-swift" thought and how to dwell in houses:

> yea, he hath resource for all; without resource he meets nothing that must come: only against Death shall he call for aid in vain; but from baffling maladies he hath devised escapes.[63]

In artistic structure the two poets are quite as markedly contrasted. Aeschylus, the sublimest of ancient poets, conceives his characters on a colossal scale. To quote Professor Livingstone:

> Milton at his grandest, Marlowe at moments, Shakespeare when he shows us the mad Lear in the storm on the moor, or Macbeth with the witches on the "blasted heath," Victor Hugo in certain passages of *La Légende des Siècles,* come nearest to him.[64]

He is a veritable Michelangelo, though the idea that "he could rough-hew like a Cyclops, but that he could not finish like a Praxiteles" is a misconception.[65] Sophocles, at least after passing his Aeschylean period, which is represented by fragments, was more concerned with the details of his plots and language; his plays, with their fine adjustments of episodes, are well nigh faultless, the embodiment of symmetry of form and rhythm. His clear-cut characters have been likened to statues in the round, and to the calm warriors of Aegina, who, in Oscar Wilde's phrase, "die smiling." They are quite as much works of art as the creations of his contemporaries Phidias and Ictinus in allied fields of art.

Sophocles' diction is as clear as his character-drawing, and surpasses that of Aeschylus, whose exalted language of demigods delights in metaphors and epithets. For Sophocles' language follows the Greek rule of moderation. It is never bombastic as that of the older poet sometimes is, as when the latter

---

[63] 360–362 (Jebb). [64] *Pageant,* p. 113.
[65] As pointed out by J. A. Symonds, *op. cit.,* p. 158.

says of the drowning Persians at Salamis that they are gnawed by

the voiceless children of the unsullied deep,[66]

nor does it delight in the use of long compounds, a tendency of Aeschylus reproved by Aristophanes, who in one place characterizes him by an epithet seventeen letters long,[67] nor is it ever commonplace as that of Euripides so often is. In describing the verities of natural law it sometimes reaches lofty heights, as in Antigone's appeal to the unwritten laws against the earthly ones of Creon:

Nor deemed I that thy decrees were of such force, that a mortal could override the unwritten and unfailing statutes of heaven. For their life is not of today nor yesterday, but from all time, and no man knows when they were first put forth.[68]

When we read so exalted a sentiment, and realize that it was uttered nearly twenty-four centuries ago, it may, in the words of Professor Tyrrell, "encourage us to indulge, not without hope, the thought that after all men may not be descended from apes."[69]

A comparison, finally, between Sophocles and Euripides will show differences in outlook far greater, since the latter was the opposite of the former in everything—genius, character, and fortune. Suidas calls Euripides "gloomy, unsmiling, and unsociable,"[70] and he received few of the gifts which Fortune showered on Sophocles. This unpopularity is shown by the fact that after his first prize, received in 441–440 when the poet was thirty-nine years old,[71] he won only four more with the ninety-two or more plays ascribed to him, and one of these posthumously.[72] Moreover, the *Medea*, which we regard as one of the best, received only the third prize. Like Plato, his younger

---

[66] *Persians* 578 (quoted by Tyrrell, *op. cit.*, p. 46).
[67] *Frogs* 838 ("pomp-bundle-worded").
[68] *Antigone* 453–457 (Jebb).   [69] *Op. cit.* 47.
[70] *s.v.* Εὐριπίδης.   [71] *Parian Chronicle*, l. 75.
[72] Wilamowitz-Moellendorff, in his *Analecta Euripidea*, Berolini, 1875, pp. 145 ff., has argued that 74 of the 92 plays ascribed to the poet by Suidas and the

contemporary, he was not attracted to a life of action, his belief
that the Assembly was the bane of Athens making it impossible
for him to take part in public life. He became, therefore, a recluse, the "first study-poet"[73] of Greece, and was ridiculed as
such by Aristophanes, who, in the *Acharnians* (406–409), has
Dicaeopolis find great difficulty in dragging him away from his
labor of writing tragedies, the poet answering ἀλλ᾿ οὐ σχολή.
To the end he was the butt of the comic stage and finally, in
408 B.C. when over seventy, weary with his fight against conservative views of politics and religion, and vexed by his fellow-
citizens' lack of understanding, and, like Hamlet, feeling

> How weary, stale, flat and unprofitable
> Seem to me all the uses of this world!

he went into voluntary exile to the court of Archelaus in Macedonia. But that exile bore priceless fruit, especially in the *Bacchanals,* a play "born of an ecstatic sense of man's affinity with
nature,"[74] and suited to the freer atmosphere of the rugged land
to the north, the home of the cult of Dionysus, in whose mystic
worship the aged poet finally found peace.

Euripides, finding the outer form of tragedy a completed
entity—his introduction of prologue and epilogue, and fondness
for the *deus ex machina,* which Aeschylus had used before him,
being of doubtful advantage—could only modify its spirit by
further curtailing the lyric element, complicating the plot, and
adding the "Love" motive. His skeptical mind drew him to the
intellectuals of the day, to Socrates, Protagoras, and Anaxagoras,[75] to the latter of whom one of his fragments pays a fine

---

Vita, l. 33, were extant in Alexandrian times. Since then 55 have been lost.
For the reconstruction of their plots see the recent work of W. N. Bates,
Euripides, a Student of Human Nature, Philadelphia, 1930, pp. 200–303.

[73] So called by Livingstone, *The Greek Genius,* p. 172.

[74] Adam, *op. cit.,* p. 312; cf. p. 317. See W. W. Hyde, "The Religious
Views of Euripides as Shown in the Bacchanals," in *The Monist,* XXV (1915),
No. 4, 556–578.

[75] In the *Vita,* l. 9, he is called the pupil of Anaxagoras, Prodicus, and Protagoras, and the companion of Socrates. But there is no indication of the latter's
influence in the extant plays, though much of Anaxagoras.

tribute. Like them he was misunderstood by the many, his speculative nature making him especially impatient of the traditional theology, since he could not accept it without question as Aeschylus had done, nor follow Sophocles' effort to reconcile what to him was irreconcilable. He was not even content to seek the more spiritual values of Olympianism, for to him

if the gods do aught base, they are not gods,[76]

a verse which W. Nestle has characterized as *der Grundgedanke seiner Kritik des Polytheismus.*[77] By contrasting this sentiment alone with the one of Sophocles' which says

nothing to which the gods lead is base,[78]

we can see the gulf between the religious background of the two poets.

In short, Euripides was an intellectual rebel, the spirit of his dramas showing little in common with the past; it is rather in harmony with the newer thought of his day, which he reflects better than any other. The management of the world, the cross-purposes of the gods, and their meddling in the affairs of men as told in so many myths from Homer on, only evoke his doubts. Among the gods only Athena, Dionysus, and Eros are spared by his sacrilegious hand. While Aristophanes ridiculed the popular views of the gods, Euripides made them seem despicable. Nevertheless, a study of his plays convinces us that he never denies the essential truth of religion. Though by nature a "destroyer of illusions,"[79] he never questions Deity itself, even if certain passages from his works have been adduced to prove the contrary. Aristophanes certainly regarded him as a free-

[76] *Fragm.* 300.4 (from the *Bellerophon*) ; F. Wagner, *Fragmenta Euripidis,* Paris, 1846.

[77] *Euripides, der Dichter der griech. Aufklaerung,* Stuttgart, 1901, p. 126; cf. also Th. Gomperz, *Greek Thinkers,* I–IV, New York, 1905–1912, II (Tr. G. G. Berry), p. 13.

[78] *Fragm.* 247 (Jebb and Pearson) ; 226 (Nauck).

[79] So A. and M. Croiset, *Hist. de la Littérature grecque*[2], I, Paris, 1890, p. 113.

thinker, as when in the *Thesmophoriazusae* (446 f.) a poor widow with five children accuses the poet of depriving her of her livelihood, the plaiting of sacrificial wreaths, by his teaching that "there are no gods." The more famous fragment from the lost *Bellerophon*

> Doth any say that there are gods in heaven?
> Nay, there are none[80]

comes from an unknown context and so proves nothing. But it is ever doubt rather than disbelief which is the burden of many another passage, as of the one from the *Nightingale Ode* of the *Helena,* where the chorus complains that none can say

> What is God, or what is not God, or that which lies between.[81]

He seems perplexed by the obscurity of everything connected with religion, and the remark of Orestes that

> In things divine great confusion reigns,[82]

is a fair summary of his doubts. But his polemic against anthropomorphism is real enough.[83]

In one way Greek tragedy was the gainer by Euripides' iconoclasm, for the ideal which he could not find in the gods, he sought in humanity. In this respect he excelled even Sophocles in the portrayal of emotion, for our sympathies are quickened by his delineation of human suffering. It is because of his exploitation of the emotional side of life that he is rightly regarded as the most human and most modern of ancient poets. And for this very reason modern critics have frequently erred in quoting passages from his dramas which they believe contain messages for almost any modern spiritual or social reform. It would be as reasonable, as a recent writer has said, to prove

---

[80] 293.1–2; (F. Wagner); preserved by Justin Martyr, *De Monarchia* 5.
[81] 1137.　　　　　　　　[82] *Iphigenia in Tauris* 572.
[83] For his diatribe, see P. Decharme, *Euripide et l'esprit de son théâtre,* Paris, 1893, ch. 2 (Engl. tr. by James Loeb, New York, 1906); cf. A. W. Verrall, *Euripides the Rationalist,* Cambridge, 1895, pp. 79–81; Hyde, *op. cit.,* pp. 559 ff.; etc.

Shakespeare favorable to Volsteadism because of Sir Toby's behavior in *Much Ado About Nothing*. The way to arouse interest in Greek drama is not to exaggerate such possible bearings on modern problems, but to let it stand by its own beauty and meaning without the help of alien values.

While Aeschylus filled his world with heroes of the epic, and Sophocles his with idealized humans, Euripides peoples his stage with well-bred Athenians, characters who, though similarly taken from the epic legends, are actuated by the motives and use the diction of contemporary life. A new world of ideas was in process of birth of which Socrates and Euripides, each in his own way, were the prophets as well as midwives, and the latter, at least, also belonged to the subsequent period. Aristotle repeats a saying of Sophocles that "he portrayed people as they ought to be and Euripides portrayed them as they are"[84]— meaning thereby that Euripides was a realist while Sophocles, in accordance with the rules of dramatic art, represented men, not as morally perfect, but as they should be represented on the stage, in conformity with the philosopher's view that tragedy should represent "good men."[85] While Sophocles, then, produced ideal pictures, Euripides "produced photographs,"[86] for he painted things as they were.

But Athens, while ready for his rationalism to some degree, could not accept his realism nor emotionalism, for she still preferred the ideal characters and lofty language of Sophocles. Aristophanes treats the latter with exceptional gentleness,[87] and the younger Xenophon gives him the palm of tragedy, as he does that of the epic to Homer.[88] So Euripides' reward came only in the following century, and he continued the supreme tragic poet of Greece to the end of antiquity,[89] despite Aristophanes' fatuous pronouncement that his poetry died with

---

[84] *Poet.* 25.11.1460b. [85] *Ibid.* 3.3.1448a; cf. 15.11.1454b.
[86] Tyrrell, *op. cit.,* p. 43. [87] *Frogs* 785 f. [88] *Mem.* 1.4.3.
[89] In this connection I quote from F. L. Lucas' recent work *Euripides and His Influence,* New York, 1923 (in "Our Debt to Greece and Rome Series"), p. 45, to the effect that there "are said to be more quotations in later literature

him.[90] The survival of eighteen of his plays—exclusive of the disputed *Rhesus*—in comparison with seven each of Aeschylus and Sophocles, and the many commentaries written about him in Alexandrian times shows his later popularity. He became a pattern for the New Comedy, to one of whose poets, Philemon (361–263 B.C.), is attributed the saying:

> if the dead retain their senses, as some say, I would hang myself to see Euripides.

An inscription from Tegea tells us that some of his plays were still successful at Athens, Delphi, and Dodona in the third century B.C.[91] Plutarch says that the *Bacchanals* were being performed before the Parthian court of Orodes in 53 B.C., when the actor who represented Agave gave a horrible reality to the scene by holding up the bloody head of Crassus just slain by the king's general, Surenas.[92] In Rome his plays were early translated or adapted by Ennius, Pacuvius, and Accius, and in the early Empire were used by Seneca and Statius. In the eleventh or twelfth century the cento *Christus Patiens,* containing 2,610 verses, was largely culled from his plays. In the late Middle Ages Dante mentions him to the exclusion of both Aeschylus and Sophocles. From the sixteenth century his popularity has grown. Racine imitated him in his *Athalie* and *Phédre,* and Milton's *Samson* was influenced by "sad Electra's poet." Today Euripides is the most popular of Athens' "tragic triad of immortal fames," as Browning, in his *Balaustion's Adventure,* a poem inspired by the *Alcestis,* calls them.

Nor is it difficult to understand his present-day vogue. While the more perfect creations of Sophocles are embedded in Athens

from his *Orestes* than from all the extant works of Aeschylus and Sophocles; and more quotations from Euripides as a whole than from any other poets except Homer and Menander."

[90] *Fragm.* 130; Kock, *op. cit.,* II. 519.

[91] V. Bérard, in *B.C.H.,* XVII (1893), 14–16 (No. 20). An earlier inscription, dating from 342/1 to 340/39 B.C., shows that plays of Euripides were also reproduced in Athens in those years: *C.I.A.* II, 2 (Berolini, 1883), No. 973.

[92] *Crassus* 33.2.

of the fifth century B.C., and those of Aeschylus in larger Hellenism, "Our Euripides the human," as an English poetess has called him, belongs neither to Athens nor Greece, but to all times and places. His are the first *Tendenz* dramas, quite as universal and timeless as any of Ibsen. Inferior to Sophocles in the construction of plots, he surpassed him both in his humanity and romantic imagination. Jebb has somewhere said that he "is the only Greek except Aristophanes who set foot in the charmed woodlands of fancy." Again, like Ibsen, he disclosed a subtle knowledge of women and the family affections bound up with their lives. Eight of his extant plays are named from them, while four more have choruses made up of women, and most of his great characters are heroines, for we are attracted by only a few of his heroes—the chivalrous Theseus, Hippolytus of Sir Galahad purity, the open-hearted boy Ion, and the peasant husband of Electra. He understood women's natures more than any other Greek—their gentleness, sorrows, courage, and loyalty, and pictured them with such sympathy that it is difficult to account for the ludicrous tradition that he was a woman-hater; happily Athenaeus preserves a different tradition.[93]

Though he paints no such noble woman as Antigone, still his art is so subtle that we admire even his worst women, those turned into demons by circumstances or the resentment of the gods—Medea, Phaedra, Agave, Electra, Clytemnestra. Who can withhold his sympathy from Medea whose passion turns to hatred when her lover, who owed his success to her help and whose children she bore, casts her off? Or who can fail to find excuse for Hecuba who, on finding the body of her son Polydorus washed up on the strand, with the help of fellow-citizens slays the sons of his murderer, Polymnestor, and blinds the king himself? Or again, can we find no compassion for the weakness of Phaedra who, driven on by Aphrodite's resentment, causes her son's death through misrepresentation? But when

[93] *Deipnos.* 13.81.603e (φιλογύνης).

Euripides paints his women at their best—Alcestis, Iphigenia at Aulis and at Balaklava, Andromache, the virgin-martyr Macaria—we are carried away by his power, for he was truly what Aristotle called him, "the most tragic of poets."[94] And so he has remained to our time, unique in his ability to arouse compassion.

These three, then, the grand Aeschylus, the serene Sophocles, and the rational and realistic Euripides, make up the flower of Attic tragic drama. And not the least of them is Sophocles, known in antiquity as the "Attic bee," because of his power of selection and extraction of sweetness from all he touched, and in our day as "the mellow glory of the Attic stage."

[94] *Poet.* 13.10.

UNIVERSITY OF PENNSYLVANIA

"NO TRESPASS" IN LATIN LINGUISTICS

Roland G. Kent

§1: INTRODUCTORY.

"Unhand me, gentlemen. By Heaven, I'll make a ghost of him that lets me!" Thus spoke Hamlet, as he broke loose from his friends Horatio and Marcellus and followed his father's ghost into the blackness of the night.[1]

Countless thousands of schoolboys have been amused—or puzzled—that Hamlet has, to their understanding, said the direct opposite of that which he meant. His friends were not *letting* him, they were trying to hold him back.

But the trouble lies in that there existed two homonymous words of opposite meanings: *let* "to permit", and *let* "to make late, to hinder". The continued existence of two such words, usable in such fashion that even context would in many instances not make clear the meaning, is impossible or well nigh impossible in any language. The one or the other is a trespasser, and must yield; and in this instance it is *let* "to hinder" which has given way, surviving only in the legal phrase *let or hindrance,* and in the tennis term.[2] Still I hazard the guess that many a non-legal person understands *let or hindrance* as antitheses rather than as equivalents, and I know that a *let* in tennis is familiarly felt to be a term of permission to replay the serve, rather than to mean a "hindered" ball—not seldom it is remodeled *net,* to indicate a served ball which has tipped the edge of the net before falling fair. *Let* "to permit" has possession of the ground, having driven off the alternative claimant as a trespasser.

On the other hand, it is not always so. There is probably no

---

[1] Shakespeare, *Ham.* I.4.85–86.
[2] And rarely as a verb in poetry; cf. any English dictionary, s.v.

language in which there are not some homonyms; but it is essential that their meanings should differ in such manner that the context in which they are used will make clear the sense. English *sound* represents at least four words distinct by origin: "noise", "a body of water", "healthy", "to test the depth of water". French *sans* "without", *sang* "blood", *cent* "hundred", *sens* "feels" are pronounced alike.[3] Latin *īs* means "(thou) goest" and is also the dative-ablative plural of a pronominal adjective.

Languages differ in their tolerance of homonyms. As compared with French and with English, Latin suffers but few of them. It is my purpose to study a few of the opportunities for homonymy which the Latin language has avoided, and to note the means utilized to secure this avoidance.

It is of true homonymity, identity of sound, that I speak. I am not discussing synonymity, identity of meaning of different words, which often ousts the one word from its meaning: French *demander* "ask" and *commander* "order" are trespassers which have wrested ownership from the older proprietors. Nor is it of syntactic competition that I speak: *quod* and *ut* clauses displaced the accusative and infinitive, prepositions assumed the functions of the vanishing case-endings, periphrastic verb-phrases replaced the synthetic perfect tenses of the active—all these, and others, as we come down in time from classical Latin toward and into the Romanic languages. In these we see the principle of "no trespass", but here the trespasser normally wins. In matters of identity of sound the two competitors are competing with equal inherent rights: for the normal process of phonetic development has made the competitors identical to the ear, the only human sense to which they have a right to appeal.[4]

---

[3] Except where liaison permits the sounding of the final consonant.

[4] The appeal to the eye is secondary; the written or printed word is not language, but a graphic representation of spoken utterance which must be translated by the eye, for understanding through the ear. That we normally shortcut the process does not refute this formulation of the facts.

§2: SOME HOMONYMOUS ROOTS.

Four groups of words may first come under our attention, the roots of which are at least seemingly independent:

I. *leuk-* "shine", as in *lūx* "light", *lūmen* "light", *lūna* "moon", *lūcēre* "to shine", *il-lūstris* "lighted up".[5]

II. *lou-* "wash", as in *lavere lavāre* "to wash", and many compounds (*ab-*, *al-*, *dī-*, *ē-*, etc.) and derivatives, notably *lūstrum* "purification".[6]

III. *lu-* "loose", as in *luere* "to loose, pay for, expiate", *luēs* "plague" (originally "method of expiation"), *Lua* a personification of the same, *so-lvere* "to loose," etc.[7]

IV. *lu-* as in *lutum* "mud, filth, (potter's) clay", *lŭstrum* "morass; forest; haunt (of wild beasts); brothel, debauchery", *pol-luere* "to pollute".[8]

It must be admitted that the meanings of the four groups admit of a certain amount of crossing. That which has been purified by washing (II) may seem to shine (I), or it may achieve atonement (III); or even the washing-water (II) may be so filthy as to suggest mud (IV)[9]; a means of atonement, as method of expiation, becomes a plague (III), a meaning which seems at first sight to be more naturally associated with mud or filth (IV). This feature must be borne in mind; but a consideration of the words and their derivatives reveals that in general they avoid trespassing on each other's territory, so far as form is concerned, except where meanings run into one another.

Take the form *luō luere*, for example. As an independent verb, this is normally the verb meaning "to loose, pay, atone for" (III), and nothing else: in but a few instances, and these of very obvious meaning, it means "to wash" (II), as the de-

---

[5] A. Walde, *Lat. etym. Wrtb.*[2] s.vv. *lūceo, lūmen, lūna;* F. Muller, *Altital. Wrtb.* 242–244.

[6] Walde, op. cit. s.vv. *lavo, lūstrum;* Muller, op. cit. 244–245.

[7] Walde, op. cit. s.v. *luo;* Muller, op. cit. 247.

[8] Walde, op. cit. s.vv. *lustrum, lutum, polluo;* Muller, op. cit. 247–248.

[9] Cf. especially Muller, op. cit. 247 fin.

composition form of *lavere*.[10] In composition, *lavere* becomes, by the regular process of vowel weakening, *-luere;* and as the commonest verb of this form, it has virtually crowded out its homonyms. There is a single occurrence[11] of *re-luere* "to take out of pawn" (III) ; there is *pol-luere* "to pollute" (IV) and its compound *pro-polluere,* of which there is a single occurrence in Tacitus[12], and that a dubious reading. The verb *-luere* "wash" in composition is found with *ab-, super-ab-, al-* (for *ad-*), *super-al-, col-* (for *com-*), *dē-, dī-* (for *dis-*), *ē-, inter-, per-, praeter-, prō-, re-, sub-, subter-*[13]; but it is not found with *re-* nor with *pol-.* Of course, as *re-luere* (III) is found but once, there was no likelihood of serious interference if **re-luere* "wash again" had been used; but it is worth noting that **luere* "to defile" is restricted to use in *polluere,* with the rare prefix *por-,* found only in this word and in *pollicērī, pollingere, pollūcēre, porricere, porrigere porgere, possidēre,* and their derivatives. The common verb, although not by origin having the form *-luere* but only after the process of vowel weakening had taken place, has ousted two verbs which had *-luere* as their earliest form, leaving to one of them an unusual prefix which was hardly used in formation of new compounds, and was therefore not valuable to the interloper.

But even the prefix *por-* does unite with one derivative of *lavere,* which argues an old verb **pol-luere* "to wash": *pollūbrum* "hand-basin".[14] Yet *polluere* "to pollute" drove out its

---

[10] On the distinction between *lavĕre* and *lavāre,* cf. data and reff. in Walde[2], s.v. *luo.*

[11] Caecil. ap. Fest. 281 M = 388.28 ThdP.

[12] *Ann.* 3.66.

[13] A complete list; some of these are very rare or are of late imperial times only.

[14] Paul. ex Fest. 247 M = 321 ThdP; Non. Marcell. 544.22 M = 873.20 L. Walde[2] s.v. *pollūbrum* takes the word as with prefix *po-,* cf. *po-liō,* remade to *pollūbrum* after *polluō* and other forms with *poll-.* But this, because of the opposed meaning of *polluō,* seems to me less likely than the reverse; and a doubled consonant before the Latin accent was subject to simplification, cf. *mamma* and *mamilla* (Sommer[2] 206). I therefore regard the spelling *pol-* in this word as a phonetic variant for *poll-* before the Latin accent.

homonym, and *pollūbrum* itself is barely recorded—it disappeared because it seems to mean an *instrumentum polluendi* "a means of polluting" and not a "means of washing". Its place was taken by *pelvis* and *trulleum*[15], and the uncompounded word followed *lavāre* and became *lavābrum,* usually shortened to *lābrum.* The only survival of *-lūbrum* is in *dēlūbrum* "temple, shrine", as place of expiation, to be taken as derivative of *luere* "expiate" (III).

Another derivative of these roots is *lūstrum.* The word *lūstrum* means "purificatory sacrifice or ceremony", especially that performed by the censors at the conclusion of the census; and therefore "period of five years", since the census was taken every five years. As the *lūstrum* consisted in a symbolic washing of the people with water and sulphur fumes, by the priests who passed around the gathered populace, it is safer to derive *lūstrum* from *lou-* "wash" than from *lu-* "loose", though absolute certainty cannot be reached.[16] From *lūstrum* there is a denominative verb *lūstrāre* "to purify; to go around, wander; to go around with the eyes, survey; to review (an army); to consider". The derivation of these meanings is quite clear; but there is also another meaning, "to illuminate, make bright", quoted from Lucretius and Virgil.[17] In this meaning we must associate the verb with the root *leuk* "shine".

Lūstrāre "to illuminate" is a shortening of *illūstrare,* denominative to *illūstris* "lighted up", a derivative of our first root.[18] The shortening is of the type by which in poetry we have *pōnere* for *dēpōnere, vertere* for *ēvertere, ruere* for *eruere,* etc.[19]; such shortenings make the word more easily handled within the limits of the hexameter verse. They are also in harmony with

---

[15] Found in various forms: *trulleus, trullium, trullio.*
[16] Cf. literature in Muller, op. cit. 244.16–20.
[17] Lucr. 5.79, 693, 1437; 6.737; Virg. *Aen.* 4.6, 607; 7.148.
[18] Muller, op. cit., 243, posits a **louk[e]s-trom* "Beleuchtung" as basis for this verb and for *il-lūstris;* but this intermediate word seems unnecessary. At any rate, *lūstrāre* "to illuminate" is not an old word, and can hardly be formed to an unrecorded old word which had perished.
[19] E.g., *ponunt* Virg. *Aen.* 1.302; *verteret Aen.* 1.20; *ruunt Aen.* 1.85.

the general principle of shortening long compounds when context makes clear the special application.

When we examine the compounds of *lūstrāre*, we find that *in-* is limited to the denominative to *illūstris,* and we should not call this a compound verb, for it is a denominative to an adjective formed upon the compound verb *illūcēre:* it is adequate, however, to avert a compound of *in* + *lūstrāre* "to purify". But from this last we find *dē-lūstrāre* "to disenchant"; *per-lūstrāre* "to purify, traverse, survey thoroughly"; and *col-lūs-trāre* in the meaning "to survey". On the other hand we have not only *il-lūstrāre* "to illuminate", but *col-lūstrāre* in the same meaning, and *circum-lūstrāre* "to light up around".[20] The latter do not in any way impair the interpretation already given, of *lūstrāre* "to illuminate" as a mere shortening of *illūstrāre;* for *collūstrāre* "to illuminate" is a rare word, found chiefly in Cicero, and *circum-lūstrāre* is found but once in this meaning, Lucr. 5.1437:

> 1436 at vigiles mundi magnum versatile templum
> 1437 sol et luna suo *lustrantes* lumine *circum*
> 1438 perdocuere homines annorum tempora verti

The violent tmesis makes one hesitate actually to list this as a compound word. But the examples of apparent compounds of *lūstrāre* "to illuminate" are all late enough to come from the *lūstrāre* which has been loosed from *illūstrāre*—we do not have to assume a lost **lūstrum* "light, illumination", from which the verbs can be made.[21]

As for *lŭstrum* "morass", the short vowel in the first syllable distinguishes it from the *lūstrum* which we have been discussing; and when it is used in the meanings "brothel, debauchery", the context regularly has synonyms or other phrases which remove any possibility of confusion with *lūstrum* "purification": thus Plaut. *Bac.* 743, (aurum) quod dem scortis quodque in lus-

---

[20] And a single instance "to travel through", in the *Cod. Theodos.* 4.8.5, an obvious etymologizing at a late date, from *lūstrāre* "to travel".

[21] Cf. n. 18.

148

tris comedim; *Asin.* 867, is apud scortum corruptelae est liberis, lustris studet; Cic. *Phil.* 13.11.24, in lustris, popinis, alea, vino tempus aetatis omne consumpsisses; etc.

There are also in Latin homonymous roots *pu-* "cleanse" and *pu-* "stink".[22] From the former come *pŭtus* "cleansed", *pŭtāre* "to cleanse, prune, reckon, think", *pŭteus* "(cleared place), well", *pūrus* "pure", *pūr(i)gāre* "to cleanse", *pius* "dutiful", etc. From the latter come *pŭter* and *pŭtris* "stinking", *pŭtrēre* "to be rotten", *pŭtrēscere* "to become rotten", *pŭtridus* "rotten", *pŭtēre* "to stink", *pūtēscere* "to rot", *pūtidus* "stinking", *pūs pūr-is* "pus". Despite ample opportunity to develop ambiguous homonyms, the two sets of words held themselves distinct, and did not trespass on the same territory.

§3: HOMONYMOUS PARTICIPLES.

Another set of examples of "no trespass" may be found in the perfect passive participles. The reason for interference is the regular phonetic development of the consonantal combinations and the vowel weakening. Thus the suffix of the participle is *-to-*, which, when attached to a root ending in a dental, gives an Italic *-so-*, irrespective of whether the original dental of the root was voiceless or voiced, aspirate or non-aspirate; and similarly the combination of *-k-*, *-g-*, and the corresponding spirant (from Indo-European palatals, velars, and labio-velars) with the participial suffix *-to-*, results in a uniform *-cto-*. Add to this the change of *-a-* to *-e-* in medial syllables, and the opportunities for homonyms are numerous. The theory that homonyms were avoided, motivates a considerable number of analogically lengthened vowels in the participles, as well as some other changes.[23]

(1) *Fatīscere* (also deponent, *fatīscī*) should have a partici-

---

[22] Walde, s.vv.; Muller 356, 366–369. It is immaterial here, whether "trim" or "cleanse" is the primary meaning of *putāre*.

[23] Cf. my article, "Lachmann's Law of Vowel Lengthening," in *Language*, IV (1928), 181–190.

ple *fassus;* but this is transformed to *fessus,* used only as an adjective, "weary". *Fessus* is obviously the decompounded form from *dē-fessus,* with weakened vowel, participle of *dē-fetīscī.* Now *fassus* from *fatīscere* would be identical with *fassus,* participle of *fatērī;* avoidance of this homonymity explains the use of the decompounded *fassus.* But *fassus* from *fatērī* also becomes -*fessus* in compounds: there is no collision, because the only combinations used were *cōn-fessus* and *prō-fessus* from *fatērī,* and *dē-fessus* from the other verb.[24]

(2) From *cadere* there was an original participle *cassus,* used in historic Latin only as an adjective, meaning "empty, valueless".[25] In its place, there was developed a new participle *cāssus*[26], giving *cāsus*[27] in classical Latin. There is also the verb *cēdere,* with the participle *cessus; cassus* in compounds would suffer vowel weakening and become identical with it. To avert such identity, the uncompounded form assumed a lengthened vowel, which did not change in medial syllables. Naturally *cāsus* and its similar derivatives are not very frequent; but we are hardly prepared for its infrequency in compounds. *Cadere* and *cēdere* have, in common, compounds in *ac- con- dē- ex- in- oc- prō- re- suc-;* but the "supine" stem is, in compounds of *cadere,* found only in the rare *recāsūrus* and the familiar *occāsūrus occāsus occāsiō* and derivatives, while it is very common in the compounds of *cēdere,* notably in the fifth declension nouns *accessus con- de-* etc. Quite curiously, in the one instance of frequent formation from *cadere,* namely *occāsus,* there are no derivatives from *cēdere, occēdere* being a very rare word. The avoidance of trespass in the *cadere—cēdere* combination is therefore absolute.[28]

(3) *Pandere* and the deponent *patī* form the participle

---

[24] *Lang.* IV, 183. [25] *Lang.* IV, 189–190.

[26] Cf. Quint. 1.7.20, for -*ss*-.

[27] For convenience, I use the masculine form with the classical -*us* instead of the older -*os;* and -*tus* is to be taken as representing all the similar formations: the nouns in -*tus* -*sus* (Decl. V), -*tiō* -*siō,* -*tūra* -*sūra,* future participles, etc.

[28] *Lang.* IV, 186.

passus. But the inconvenience of this became evident, and *passus* "outspread" became virtually an adjective applied chiefly to loosened hair, to ships' sails, and to grapes spread out for drying into raisins.[29] A new participle *pānsus* was formed, with the *-n-* from the present stem, which automatically caused lengthening of the vowel before *-ns-,* and thus prevented weakening to *-e-* in compounds and confusion with the participle of *pendere* "to suspend, weigh".[30] Derivatives of *pandere* and *patī* divided the field: *passio* and derivatives from *patī; passus* "stretch, step" and *passim* from *pandere; passīvus* from both, but more commonly from *patī* in a grammatical meaning.

(4) *Findere* has the participle *fissus. Fīdere* also should make the same, as is shown by Greek πιστóς, but has lengthened the vowel, giving *fīsus,* by analogy of the rest of the paradigm, and has thus avoided homonymity.[31]

(5) *Scindere* has *scissus* and *caedere* has *caesus.* The retention of the short vowel and of the *-ss-* in *scissus*—in the face of other verbs which lengthen the vowel in the participle—is assured by the existence of the compounds *ab-scissus ex-scissus* and of the similar compounds of *caesus, abs-cīsus ex-cīsus,* which it is linguistically worth while to hold distinct.[32]

(6) *Manēre* "to remain" and *mandere* "to chew" have identical participles, *mānsus;* but as *manēre* is intransitive and the "supine" stem was little used, this probably caused no trouble. We note however an older participle **mantus,* attested by the frequentative *mantāre,* and wonder if *mantus has not given way to *mānsus,* with *s* from the perfect active *mānsī,* because of the possibility of confusion with the participle *mentus* in *commentus* (to *comminīscī*), when the weakening in compounds had taken place. But there seem to be no old compounds of *manēre* except *per-manēre* and *re-mānere;* neither one meets a rival "supine" form or derivative from *re-minīscī,* etc. Perhaps the avoidance is old and thus very complete.

---

[29] Cf. Gell. 15.15, and the lexica.   [30] *Lang.* IV, 185, with n. 23.
[31] *Lang.* IV, 187, n. 32.   [32] *Lang.* IV, 185.

(7) The participle of *cūdere* would properly be **cussus;* but *quatere* has the participle *quassus* which in compounds became -*cussus: con-cussus dis- ex- in- per- reper- prae- re- suc-cussus*. In the presence of these interlopers, the old *cussus of *cūdere* took the long vowel of the other tenses, and became *cūsus,* very rare, uncompounded, but found in *ex-cūsus in-cūsus prō-cūsus*.[33]

(8) The deponent *sequī* had an old participle **sectus,* seen in the denominative *sectārī*. But when the earlier **secitus,* to *secāre,* lost its medial vowel by syncope and became identical with the already existing **sectus,* the newcomer held its ground and forced the old occupant out of the way[34]: for *sectus* was obviously closer to *secāre* than to *sequī,* and thus the latter verb made a new analogical *secūtus,* for which *volvere volūtus, solvere solūtus* gave the model.[35]

(9) *Tegere* once had a participle *tĕctus and *tangere* had *tăctus. The latter would in compounds become *-*tectus,* and thus become identical with the participle of *tegere;* it therefore followed the model of certain other verbs and took a long vowel, *tāctus,* which was immune to vowel weakening. Later, *tectus from *tegere* took an analogical long vowel from the perfect *tēxī*.[36] We might note that *con-tegere* and *con-tingere* are both old verbs found in Plautus, and that *ob-tegere* and *ob-tingere* are also both old, though *ob-tingere* seems to have no participle in use. The other compounds either are not common to the two verbs or are late; Caelius Auratus (fifth century) used both *praetēctus* and *praetāctus*.

(10) A similar relation existed between *lactus from *laciō *lacere and *lectus from *legere*. The participle *lactus is attested in the compounds *al-lectus il-lectus pel-lectus,* and in the derivative verbs *al-lectāre dē- ē- il- ob- prō- sub-lectāre*.[37] In this instance, *lectus from *legere* yielded, and took a long vowel

---

[33] *Lang.* IV, 185, n. 21.   [34] *Lang.* IV, 182–183.
[35] F. Sommer, *Hdb. d. lat. Laut- u. Formenl.*[2] 609.
[36] *Lang.* IV, 186.
[37] There are also the verbs *dēlicere* and *prōlicere,* used in the present stem, but without any perfect participle; and *ēlicere,* with a new participle *ēlicitus*.

from the perfect *lēgī*.[38] The most nearly ambiguous form is the verb *ēlectāre*, which means either "to worm out" or "to select" —but there is no real ambiguity, for in the latter meaning the word has *ē*. Curiously, with this exception no *-lectāre* compound comes from *legere*.

(11) Another such pair is *frīctus* from *frīgere* "to roast" and *frĭctus* from *fricāre* "to rub". The length in *frĭctus* comes of course by analogy from the other forms, but it is promoted by the desire to avoid homonymity.[39]

(12) Finally, a group of three: *vĭctus* from *vincere*, *vīnctus* from *vincīre*, *vīctus* from *vīvere*. The first and third are regular forms; the second has taken its *-n-* from the present stem to distinguish it from the participle of *vincere*, and this has caused the lengthening of the vowel, since all vowels become long in Latin before *-nct-*.[40]

Let me here emphasize that I do not regard the avoidance of homonymity as the sole cause operating to produce these changes in the participles. One and the same linguistic change may have several causes operating jointly to effect it, as here, where the analogy of long vowels in other parts of the verb is normally in evidence.

§4: Homonymous compound verbs.

Another opportunity for trespass is in the present stem of compound verbs: through regular phonetic process, *pangere* here becomes identical with *pingere*, *tangere* with *tingere*, *pandere* with *pendĕre*.

The opportunity for homonymity is of course limited to the present tense system: *pēgī pāctus*[41] cannot become confused with *pīnxī pictus*, nor *tetigī tāctus* with *tīnxī tīnctus*; nor does even the perfect *pandī* suffer weakening of the vowel in com-

---

[38] *Lang.* IV, 184, 186.   [39] *Lang.* IV, 185, n. 21.

[40] *Lang.* IV, 185, nn. 19, 21.

[41] *Pāctus* and *păctus*, the apportioning of which to *pangere* and *pacīscī* (and to the obsolete *pacere pagere*) cannot be regarded as definite. Cf. *Lang.* IV, 184.

pounds, where the weakened vowel would make it identical with -*pendī*, the form which *pependī* assumes in compounds.

Let us take in order the compounds of *pangere—pingere:*

AD: *appingere,* to *pangere,* occurs but once, where it is used in a definition, and is itself glossed by a more familiar word[42]: *Antipagmenta* valvarum ornamenta, quae antis *appinguntur,* id est affiguntur; the word looks as though made up for the occasion, to emphasize the etymology. *Appingere,* to *pingere,* occurs in the present stem from Cicero onward.

COM: *compingere,* to *pangere,* is a reasonably common word[43], found in all forms from Plautus onward; *compingere,* to *pingere,* is quoted in the perfect stem only, from Seneca. The late *re-compingere* is used in the present stem, and is from *pangere.*

DĒ: *dēpingere,* to *pingere,* is found from Plautus onward, in all tense stems. The compound of *pangere* is *dē-pangere,* with unweakened vowel, therefore distinct in the present tense; it is quite infrequent except in the participle *dē-pāctus.*

EX: *expingere,* to *pingere* only, is found in the present tense stem in Pliny and Martial, though the participle in Cicero shows that it is an older verb. The combination of *ex* with *pangere* does not occur.

IN: *impingere,* to *pangere* only, is found in all forms, from Plautus on; but the combination of *in* with *pingere* does not occur.

OB: *oppanguntur* is found in an etymologizing definition, which accounts for the unweakened vowel: *Repagula* sunt, ut Verrius ait, quae patefaciundi gratia [qua] ita figuntur, ut ex contrario quae *oppanguntur.*[44] There is no *oppingere* to *pingere.*

RE: *re-pangere,* to *pangere,* and *re-pingere,* to *pingere,* both occur, in the present tense system only. Both are new formations in imperial times.

SUB: *sup-pingere,* to *pangere,* is found in Plautus in the present stem and in the participle; *sup-pingere,* to *pingere,* is late, and is quoted only in the perfect stem.

SUPER: *super-pingere,* to *pingere* only, is a late formation, without a similar compound of *pangere.*

[42] Paul. ex Fest. 8 M = 6 ThdP.
[43] For citations of passages in which this and the following words are used, reference is here made to the lexica.
[44] Fest. 281 M = 388 ThdP; the text is corrupt.

The avoidance of collision between the two verbs is complete. If both are used with the same prefix, then either *pangere* keeps the radical vowel unweakened, or the ambiguous present tense-system is used in but one of the two verbs.

In the second pair of verbs, *tangere—tingere,* we find but three old compounds of the more common verb, *tangere: at-tingere, con-tingere, ob-tingere,* all occurring in Plautus. At a later date we meet the recompounded verbs without vowel weakening: *per-tangere, re-tangere.* From *tingere,* there are three compounds: *in-tingere* "to dip in", used from Plautus onward; *prae-tingere* "to moisten beforehand", used first by Ovid, and quoted only in the participle; *con-tingere* "to moisten", which seems to be a Lucretian coinage, used also by Virgil, but not accepted into general use.[45] The only conflict here is the limited conflict in the Lucretian word *contingere,* to *tingere.*

In our third pair, *pandere—pendere,* we are confronted by the difficulty of discriminating between *penděre* and *penděre;* but if we accept the listing of the lexicographers, we find the following, all quotable in the present tense-system not later than the Ciceronian period: *ap- com- dē- dis- ex- im- per- re-sus-pendere,* to *pendere,* and *dis- ex- prae-pandere,* to *pandere.* There are also the late *op- re-pandere,* and (in the participle only) *prō-pānsus prō-passus,* as well as some compounds of *pendere* with double prefix (*super-im-,* etc.). Thus conflict is entirely avoided, except in the one form *dispennite,* used by Plautus.[46]

§5: HOMONYMOUS PREFIXES.

Let us next take a striking example of differentiation in the field of prefixes. Latin *ab* and *ad* had virtually opposite mean-

[45] Lucr. 1.934, 938, 947; 2.755; 4.9, 22; Virg. *Georg.* 3.403, 488. [I am not quite satisfied that *contingere* means "moisten" in all these passages, though it does in some of them. G. D. H.]

[46] *Mil.* 1407, with Umbrian *-nn-* for *-nd-.* Cf. also *dispessis manibus, Mil.* 360, on which see Gell. 15.15.4.

ings; but before certain consonants both *b* and *d* suffer complete assimilation, so that the groups are indistinguishable. Thus *b-c* and *d-c* became *cc; b-p* and *d-p* became *pp; b-g* and *d-g* became *gg; b-b* and *d-b* became *bb; b-m* and *d-m* became *mm; b-f* and *d-f* became *ff*.

In this situation the variant forms of *ab* were utilized. For there was not merely the form *ab,* but also *abs,* which had got its *-s* in imitation of *ex* (*eks*)[47]; and *abs* in combination gave groups of consonants different from those which resulted from *ad* plus those same consonants. Let us start with those combinations in which the *b* was unchanged, namely, when it stood before a vowel or before *d h j l n r s*. In these combinations, *ad* was distinct, though it normally—unless remade by analogy—was assimilated to the following *l n r s*. Examples:

abigō abēgī abāctus	*adigō adēgī adāctus*
abiciō abjēcī abjectus	*adiciō adjēcī adjectus*
abeō abīre abitus	*adeō adīre aditus*
abjūdicō abjungō abjūrō	*adjūdicō adjungō adjūrō*
abdīcō abdō abdūcō	*addīcō addō addūcō*
abhinc abhorreō	*adhūc adhaereō*
ablēgō abluō	*allēgō alluō* (or *adl-*)
abnuō abnegō[48]	*annuō annumerō* (or *adn-*)
abripiō abrogō	*arripiō arrogō* (or *adr-*)
absistō absūmō	*assistō assūmō* (or *ads-*)

Before certain consonants, however, the prefix *ab* assumed the form *abs*. By regular phonetic development, a stop was lost in Latin, or in a pre-Latin stage of the language, before an *s* followed by another consonant. This stage is represented by

---

[47] Possibly *abs* is an inherited doublet of *ab,* cf. Greek ἄψ. I use the spellings *ab* and *abs* for convenience, though *ab* is by origin **apo* (Greek ἀπό, Sanskrit *apa*), and *abs* was pronounced *aps*. The old compound *aperiō* from **apweryō* is not included here, since its retention of the original voiceless stop in the prefix definitely differentiated it for all time, and even left it apart from the other compounds in the minds of its users. On *ab* and *ad* as prefixes, cf. Sommer, *Hdb.*[2] 263–264; as prepositions, Sommer[2] 275, 298–299.

[48] Occasionally *amn-;* cf. Sommer[2] 264 sup.

aspellō and *asportō,* the corresponding verbs with *ad* being *appellō* and *apportō.* This development of *aps* is found only before *p;* before *c* and *t* the form *abs* is restored by analogy of the separate word. Thus there are *abs-cēdō abs-cīdō abs-condō,* over against *ac-cēdō accīdō ac-commodō,* etc.; *abs-tēmius abs-tergeō abs-terreō abs-tineō abs-trahō abs-trūdō abs-tulī,* over against *at-tineō at-trahō at-tulī* and many others with *at-t-.* The situation may here be formulated as follows: The prefix *ab,* before initial *p* and *c*[49], took the form *abs* to preserve distinction of form from *ad;* the form *abs-* was extended to the position before the other voiceless stop, *t.* While the *b* of *abs* would normally be lost before a consonant, it was restored by analogy before *c* and *t,* but not before *p,* since the group *-bs-p-,* pronounced *-psp-,* would have stops of the same position at beginning and at end, a combination which is avoided in Greek also.[50]

A special case may be made of the prefixes before *sc- sp- st-.* For the only examples of *ab* in these combinations are *ab-scindō a-spernor ab-stō,* with products exactly like those of *abs* + *c- p- t-,* and for the same reasons. With these combinations *ad* stands unchanged, or is reduced to *a-: adscendō ascendō, adspectō aspectō, adspīrō aspīrō.* The only ambiguity is in *aspernor,* where the meaning of the root forbids an interpretation as **ad-spernor. Abstō* occurs but once[51]; *astō* or *adstō* is frequent, but distinct in form.

We return again to the form *abs,* as used before certain other consonants. After the loss of the *b* before *s* + a consonant, the *s* also will be lost with lengthening of a preceding vowel if the next consonant is *b d l m n v:* thus we have *ā-mittō āmoveō, ā-vehō ā-vertō ā-vocō,* etc., in contrast to *ad-mittō ad-moveō*[52],

---

[49] Theoretically also before *qu-,* but there are no occurrences.

[50] Cf. βλάσφημος from *βλαπσ-φημος, to βλάβη; other examples in H. Hirt, *Hdb. d. gr. Laut- u. Formenl.* §244.

[51] Hor. *AP.* 362. A second possibility is the ASTED in the second line of the Duenos inscription, *C.I.L.* I², 3; cf. *Lang.* II, 217–220.

[52] While *d-m* normally became *-mm-,* the group is in these compounds remade after the analogy of the component parts.

ad-vehō ad-vertō ad-vocō, etc. The form *ā* is not used before *d l n,* where, as we have already seen, the simpler form *ab* is employed.

There remain the sounds *b g f;* the prefixes, when in the position before these, have not yet been discussed here. Before *b, ab* seems not to be used in any form; even *abbreviāre* is a derivative of the phrase *ad breve. Ad* retains its identity before *b: adbibō,* and the very rare *adbītō adblaterō adbellō.*

Before *g, ab* is found only in one rare word, *abgregāre*[53], where it retains its identity by analogy instead of being merged in with *ad-* in the assimilated form *ag-,* phonetically correct for both combinations. As for *ad,* it appears in *agger aggravō aggredior* and other words, which may mostly be written *adg-* by the influence of the separate word.

The position before *f* was the most troublesome of all. *Ad* made *afficiō afferō affinis,* etc., which may be written *adf-.* But *ab* in any form is likely to result in collision with *aff-: ab-f-* became *aff-,* and *abs-f-* would normally become first *asf-* and then *aff-.* For the use of *ā-* before a voiceless sound there was no model.[54] But there were only three words in which the combination was met: those with *ferō fugiō fuī.* These were likely to trespass on the *ad* compounds, *adferō afferō, adfuī affuī,* and the **adfugiō *affugiō* "to flee to (for refuge)", which very probably existed at one time before its meaning was taken over by *perfugiō.* For distinction, therefore, **ab-ferō* and **ab-fugiō* suffered a special change, in which the prior *f* in *-ff-* became voiced and then easily assumed the value of the second element of the diphthong.[55] That the *au-* in *auferō aufugiō* is not a

[53] Paul. ex Fest. 23 M = 17 ThdP: *abgregare* est a (*or* ab) grege ducere.

[54] Although *ē-* develops from *ex-* in precisely the same manner as does *ā-* from *abs-,* and is much more widely extended in its use (before *b d l m n v* by regular phonetic development, and before *g j r* by analogical extension) than *ā-* for *ab-,* there is no support here for *ā-* before *f-.* The form taken by *ex-* before *f-* is seen in old *ecferō ecfātus,* early replaced by *efferō effātus,* etc.; cf. Sommer, *Hdb.*[2] 259, Neue-Wagener, *Formenlehre d. lat. Spr.*[3] 2.870–873.

[55] Cf. Muller, *Altital. Wrtb.* 51, with references; also my interpretation of Umb. *uou.se* in its relation to **vufetes,** "Studies in the Iguvine Tables", in *Class. Phil.,* XV (1920), 364–365.

prefix unrelated to *ab,* is rendered the more probable that the perfect and participle of *auferō* are *abs-tulī ab-lātus,* with unmistakable forms of *ab-.*

With the compounds of *fuī* the situation was somewhat different. The presents are respectively *ab-sum* and *ad-sum* or *as-sum.*[56] The latter must give perfect *adfuī* or *affuī,* future infinitive *adfore* or *affore.* The former, despite lack of similar forms, took the *ā* form of *ab: ā-fuī ā-fore.* But that there was a feeling of the awkwardness of the two similar words in opposite meanings, seems to be shown by the participles: *absēns* means "absent", while its opposite is not **adsēns,* but *prae-sēns.* By meaning, though not by form, *praesēns* belongs to *adsum* and not to *praesum.*

The more we study the compounds of *ab* and *ad,* the more we become impressed with the fact that *ad* was crowding *ab* to the wall. As Latin developed into its later form, the *ab* compounds became more and more restricted, and comparatively few of them were productive in Romanic dialects, as compared with the *ad* compounds. This is true also in English, where the *ab* derivatives are limited to a few common word-groups, while the *ad* derivatives are very numerous and are present in many disguised forms.

It so happens that there is in Greek also a similar competition between two adverbs, there in both values, preposition and prefix. Primitive Greek had two inherited adverbs, ἐξ "from" and ἐν "in, into", the former governing the ablative-genitive and the latter the locative-dative and the accusative; even as in Latin *ex* governed the ablative and *in* the locative-ablative and the accusative. Now in primitive Greek, ἐξ before a consonant lost its σ and became ἐκ, except before κ γ χ, where it was the κ of ἐξ which was lost on account of the second palatal stop which closed the group. Thus ἐξ has by right three forms: ἐξ before

---

[56] The form with assimilated consonants has been identified in Praen. ASOM, *C.I.L.* I², 560, by P. Turnbull, *Lang.* V, 15–17.

vowels, ἐκ before most consonants, ἐς before κ γ χ. Attic and Ionic, and certain other dialects, generalized the ἐκ form of ἐξ for use before all consonants, and then added to ἐν a σ, after the model of its semantic opposite ἐξ; this ἐνς gave regularly various forms, including Attic εἰς. But in other dialects, notably Thessalian, Boeotian, Arcadian, and Cyprian, the ἐς was generalized as antevocalic form of ἐξ, and in these dialects no remade ἐνς was possible, for before consonants ἐνς at once became ἐς by regular phonetic development and was identical with its semantic opposite ἐς "from". In those dialects, therefore, ἐν remained as preposition governing the accusative as well as the dative, and likewise was the only prefix corresponding to (Attic) ἐν- and εἰσ-.[57]

§6: CONCLUSION.

There are naturally some homonyms remaining in Latin: *vēnit* "(he, it) came" and "(he, it) is sold"; *īs* "thou goest" and dat.-abl. plural of the pronoun *is; arcēs* "citadels" and "thou wardest off"; etc. The most striking instance is the preposition *in* and the negative prefix *in-*, which in a few instances unite with the same element: *īn-fectus* "stained, dyed" as participle of *īnficere,* and *īn-fectus* "not done". Despite these scattered examples, the avoidance of homonymity, or, as I have termed it in the title, the principle of "no trespass", appears to be a factor to be considered in the history of the Latin language, and presumably of most languages[58], along with other more generally recognized processes, often operating in conjunction with one another. To emphasize this principle of

[57] I have disregarded here the details of the phonetic processes and the dialectal assimilations of the consonants. Cf. C. D. Buck, *Greek Dialects,* §78, §100, §135.4, for details.

[58] For a general view of homonymy in the Indo-European languages, but without special application to Latin, see A. Meillet, "Sur les Effets de l'Homonymie dans les anciennes Langues indo-européennes", in *Bibl. de l'École des Hautes Études,* CCXXX, part 2 (1921), 169–180; and for a detailed treatment of a special case of this sort in French, see J. Gilliéron, "Les Conséquences d'une Collision lexicale et la Latinisation des Mots français", *ib.,* 54–74.

"NO TRESPASS" IN LATIN LINGUISTICS

"no trespass" and to present its claims, is the purpose of this paper which I present to my honored teacher, John Carew Rolfe, who introduced me to the joys of linguistic science as exemplified by the history of the Latin language, and thereby indirectly to those of comparative linguistics.

UNIVERSITY OF PENNSYLVANIA

LEONARDO BRUNI'S TRANSLATION OF ACT I OF THE *PLUTUS* OF ARISTOPHANES

Dean Putnam Lockwood

A NUMBER of years ago I called attention to the translation of Act I of the *Plutus* of Aristophanes, ascribed to Leonardo Bruni, in codex Latinus 6714 of the Bibliothèque Nationale of Paris.* In spite of the increased interest in humanistic literature in the past few years, this translation has remained unnoticed, and it was overlooked by Dr. Hans Baron in his recent treatise.† No other manuscript of this translation has come to light. It has seemed worth while, therefore, to publish a critical edition of this brief text.

So far as I know, there is only the evidence of the manuscript itself that this translation comes from the pen of Leonardo Bruni. The index neither of Mehus' edition of Bruni's *Epistles* nor of Dr. Baron's treatise contains any reference to Aristophanes. There is, however, no reason to doubt the possibility of Bruni's acquaintance with Aristophanes or of his undertaking to render a portion of the easiest of Aristophanes' comedies into Latin. Guarino's library contained an Aristophanes, presumably as early as 1408, and Aurispa brought a manuscript of the comedies to Italy in 1423.‡ On the basis of internal evidence there is nothing in the Preface of this translation which is contrary to Bruni's habits of scholarship. The Preface is clearly not a dedication to anyone; it is merely an historical introduction. The only possible echo of a phrase occurring elsewhere in Bruni's works, so far as I have been able to discover, is in the last sentence of the Preface, namely, the fixing of the period

* Cf. "Aristophanes in the XVth Century," in *T.A.P.A.*, XL (1909), lvi.
† *Leonardo Bruni Aretino, Humanistisch-philosophische Schriften* etc., Berlin-Leipzig, Teubner, 1928.
‡ Cf. R. Sabbadini, *Le Scoperte dei Codici*, Firenze, 1905, pp. 44, 45, 47.

when Aristophanes lived by reference to Socrates: "Fuit autem Aristophanes per tempora Socratis philosophi," with which may be compared a sentence in Bruni's *De Studiis et Litteris:* "Aspasia quoque per Socratis tempora fuit" (Baron, *op. cit.,* p. 6, line 7). I have not now available the data (which I hope ultimately to collect for all of the Graeco-Latin translations of the fifteenth century) for comparing the actual rendering of the Greek with other known translations of Bruni's. I also regret that I have not at hand a summary of the contents of Parisinus Lat. 6714. Bruni's translation of the *Plutus* occupies folios 69 recto to 71 recto, which are hastily and carelessly written. I have transcribed the text from a photographic copy. I have preserved the spelling of the manuscript; only the punctuation and the capitalization have been modernized. The text presented by the Paris manuscript is poor; in the case of all emended passages the manuscript reading will be found in the footnotes.

*　*　*　*　*　*　*

(BRUNI'S PREFACE AND ARGUMENT)

Leonardi Aretini super commediam Aristophanis prefatio foeliciter incipit. ARISTOPHANES poeta comediam scripsit non quo modo Plautus et[1] Terentius sed quomodo Cratinus et Eupolis. Hoc autem genus comediarum tandem lege prohibitum fuit propter maledicentiam et nimiam libertatem, unde inquit Oratius: Eupolis atque Cratinus Aristophanesque poete atque alii quorum comedia prisca virorum est, siquis erat dignus describi[2] quod malus ac[3] fur, quod mechus foret aut sicarius aut alioqui[4] famosus multa cum libertate notabant.[5] Ego igitur volens latinis ostendere quale[6] genus erat illarum comediarum, primum actum huius comedie Aristophanis in latinum contuli. Fuit autem Aristophanes per tempora Socratis philosophi, in quem etiam scripsit commediam ridiculis notationibus plenam.

---

[1] Following "et" the word "Ennius" is deleted.　[2] rescribi.　[3] aut.　[4] alioquin.　[5] Horace *Serm.* 1.4.1–5.　[6] quare.

BRUNI'S TRANSLATION OF THE *PLUTUS*

Argumentum

CREMES[7] vir bonus, ceterum inops, cum paupertate offenderetur, ad oraculum Appollinis quesivit utrum[8] prestaret mutare mores et aliter vivere. Respondit Apollo, qui primum obvius fieret de templo exiens, eum sequeretur et domum suam adduceret. Ille autem accepto responso cęcum sequebatur, nam is primum obvius fuerat. Carinus[9] autem servus, qui cum Cremete venerat, ignarus huius responsi mirabatur domini factum et insanisse illum existimabat. Itaque pluries eum revocaverat ab illius ceci insequtione. Cremes vero nihil penitus respondebat sed omni studio cecum sequebatur. Cum igitur frequenter(?)[10] ita faceret nec responderet, insaniam domini ac fortunam suam conqueritur elatis(?)[11] servus.

(THE TRANSLATION)

[In the text which follows, asterisks denote mistranslations; italics indicate approximate translations or free paraphrases; square brackets denote additions by the translator; dots mark omissions. I have not, however, been unduly critical of Bruni's abilities as a translator nor have I censured his Latinity. I have drawn attention only to obvious departures from the Greek original. At times the line of demarcation between mistranslation and paraphrase is hard to draw. In his use of free paraphrase Bruni rarely expands or embroiders his original; for the most part his paraphrases are efforts to gloss over difficulties by abbreviating the original passage and giving its substance only, e.g., page 167, note 27. In the case of omissions we cannot too rashly accuse Bruni of ignorance. There is always the possibility that the copyist, not the translator, may have made the omission. Where the Greek text is without difficulty and the Latin shows an awkward lacuna, we must surely ascribe the omission to the carelessness of the scribe, e.g., page 168, note 47, and page 170, note 79. In the case of insignificant phrases and formulas, such as τί φῄς, page 168, note 44, it is impossible to assign the blame, but the more probable assumption is that the translator himself occasionally discarded these tags. But there remain

[7] Bruni's Greek ms. must have contained only the abbreviations of the speakers' names, Chremylus and Carion; from Χρ he deduced "Chremes," from Κα "Carinus." [8] unum: see "an," p. 167, line 7. [9] See note 7. [10] fr(?). [11] Blurred and unintelligible.

certain omissions which can only be taken as evidence of Bruni's inability to understand and to render the original, e.g., page 169, note 55, where the Greek text is corrupt and difficult, and page 172, note 118.

The most interesting case of free handling of the original is the expurgation of lines 149–159 on moral grounds—the same lines which are omitted for the same reason in modern school editions. This is perhaps an argument in favor of Bruni's authorship of the translation, for such modesty was not characteristic of other and later humanistic circles.

The few corrections which I have made in the text of the manuscript are obvious emendations, easily deduced from the Greek original.]

CREMES. CARINUS. CECUS. INCIPIT CARINUS.

UT[12] permolesta res est, o Iuppiter[13] o dei, servum fieri desipientis domini. Si recta sunt enim illa que servus monet, placeat tamen domino nequaquam sic agere, necessum habet servus eisdem esse in malis, corporis enim fortuna non ipsum sui sinit esse compotem sed eum qui possidet. Et ita quidem ista. Nempe ego obliquo[14] deo,[15] responsa qui dat ex tripode *volvens*[16] aureo, iustam querelam conqueror, succensens quod cum augur sit et medicus ut aiunt optimus, herum tamen remisit insanum meum, qui nunc sequatur cecum hominem, contra faciens quam oporteat facere. Videns enim solet dux esse ceco, at iste post cecum vadit, meque una trahit ac nil respondet[17] dum peto. Ego igitur nil est cur sileam nunc iam amplius, ni mihi respondeas, here, cur istum[18] sequaris. Tibi molestus esse non desistam ego; non hercle me pulsabis coronatum quidem. Cremes: Nequaquam, at enim dempta tibi corona prius, . . .[19] quo tu magis doleas. Carinus: Nuge! Equidem non desinam priusquam mihi dicas quis[20] est,[21] namque hoc fides erga te mea facit ut adeo de te petam. Cremes: Non te latebo, namque

---

[12] "U" omitted; space left for rubricator. [13] terram (probably a careless mistake of the scribe in expanding an abbreviation). [14] oblico (corrected to "obliquo"). [15] i.e. τῷ Λοξίᾳ, line 8 of the Greek original, Oxford text (in the margin of the Latin ms. is "Apollo"). [16] τρίποδος ἐκ χρυσηλάτου, line 9. [17] A translation of the vulgate reading ἀποκρινομένου, line 17. [18] ista. [19] om. ἢν λυπῇς τί με, line 22. [20] quid. [21] End of folio 69 recto.

meorum omnium fidelissimum te unum puto ac *sagacissi-mum*.²² Ego *pietatis iustitieque servator in vita ac honestatem colens,*²³ pauper quidem eram multisque premebar malis. . . .²⁴ Alii ditabantur sacrilegi,²⁵ . . .²⁶ sicophante, improbi. Carinus: Credo equidem. Cremes: [Apollinem] ego petiturus adivi deum non de me equidem, nam *rem meam iam actam*²⁷ puto, sed de meo gnato qui unicus adest mihi, an prestet hos mutare mores ut nequam iniustus [impius sacrilegus mendax] sit nec *sani habens quicquam, ut pote ad vitam utile. Ca: Quid re-spondit ad hec deus?*²⁸ Cr: . . .²⁹ Aperte sic ait. Cui obvius essem primum [de templo] exiens, hunc ne dimitterem sed domum adducerem meam. Ca: Cui tu ergo obvius factus es primo? Cr: Huic. Ca: O rudis, an non intelligis mentem dei dicentis aperte, debere gnatum tuum sectari civium suorum mores? Cr: *Ne*³⁰ tu ista ita existimas? Ca: Videlicet, siqui-dem ceco etiam palam esse *putat*,³¹ quod vehementer expedit nihil sani agere istis moribus qui nunc sunt. Cr: Non *istuc profecto vult*³² sed aliud quiddam maius. Si nobis hic dicat quis ipse sit et quoius³³ gratia et quo indigens huc et ipse venit,³⁴ oraculum nosceremus quid tandem velit. Ca: Age ergo tu prius³⁵ nobis expedi quisnam sis, *deinde reliqua pergas*,³⁶ dicendum enim tibi est occissime.³⁷ Cecus: Ego tibi merorem dico. Ca: Intelligis quem se dicat esse? Cr: Tibi hoc dicit non mihi. Dure sane ipsum acerbeque rogasti. At si leteris viri persancti moribus, mihi dicas. Ce: Erumnam tibi. Ca: Accipe virum et augurium dei. Cr: Non mehercle posthac . . .³⁸ Nisi dicas enim te male perdam malum. Ce: O sodalis,³⁹ *ne tibi mecum quicquam negotii sit*⁴⁰ [si sapis]. Cr: *Etiam cessas*?⁴¹ Ca: *At quid dicam potissimum*,⁴² here? Perdam enim hunc

---

²² κλεπτίστατον, line 27.   ²³ = line 28.   ²⁴ om. Κα. οἶδά τοι, line 29.   ²⁵ sac-rilegii.   ²⁶ om. ῥήτορες, line 30.   ²⁷ = lines 33–34.   ²⁸ = lines 37–39.   ²⁹ om. πεύσει, line 40.   ³⁰ τῷ (= cur), line 48.   ³¹ τυφλῷ . . . δοκεῖ (= caeco videtur *or* caecus putat), lines 48–49.   ³² = line 51.   ³³ quovis.   ³⁴ veni.   ³⁵ A transla-tion of the vulgate reading πρότερον, line 56.   ³⁶ ἢ τἀπὶ τούτοις δρῶ, line 57. ³⁷ "Occississ" is deleted before "occissime."   ³⁸ om. χαιρήσεις, line 64. ³⁹ sodes.   ⁴⁰ = line 66.   ⁴¹ πώμαλα.   ⁴² καὶ μὴν ὃ λέγω βέλτιστόν ἐστ' (not a question).

hominem pessime, deductum siquidem in sublimi loco ipsum dimittam abiens ut preceps cadat. Cr: Rape ipsum cito. Ce: Ne facias. Ca: Dicas ergo. Ce: At si noveritis quis ego sim, scio quod malo aliquo afficietis nec dimittetis. Cr: Per deos ita quidem, si tu voles. . . .[43] Ce: Audite igitur, quando quidem oportet me dicere que oculere statueram. Ego sum Plutus. Cr: O scelestissime, tune hoc silebas? Ca: An tu, Divitie, sic miserabiliter habes? O Phebe, O Apollo, et dei et demones et Iuppiter, . . .[44] *tune Divitie?* Plutus: Ita. Ca: Divitie tu? Pl: Ipse profecto. Ca: Unde ergo tam sordidus venis? Pl: Ex Patroclis[45] sedibus, qui numquam *lavi postquam senex fui.*[46] . . .[47] Iuppiter me sic affecit hominibus invidens, nam ego puer cum essem, *illi suspectus fui*[48] quod vadebam ad iustos sapientes et honestos solum. Quare me cecum fecit, ut discernerem illorum neminem. Cr: *An*[49] sic ille bonis invidet? Atque per bonos colitur solos ac per iustos. Pl: Fateor. Cr: Age quid si oculos[50] recipias ut habebas prius; fugeresne improbos? Pl: Ita. Cr: Et ad iustos vaderes? Pl: Nimium certe, nam diu est quod[51] nullum illorum vidi. Cr: Non est mirabile, nam nec ipse vidi qui oculos. Pl: Sinite me nunc iam; scitis omnia. Cr: Nolo medius fidius, at multo magis tenebimus te. Pl: Nonne ego dixi vos fore mihi molestos? Cr: Consulo tibi ne abeas, non enim reperies alium hominem qui sit probior. . . .[52] Pl: Hoc aiunt omnes, at postquam nacti sunt me ac dites facti, haud simulata superexcedunt nequitia. Cr: Est ita. Verumtamen non omnes sunt improbi. Pl: Immo plane omnes. Ca: *Deplorat iam*.[53] Cr: Tu vero senties quod apud nos bona, si permaneas, fiant, attende enim ut intelligas. Reor, equidem reor, cum deo tamen sit, te ab ista liberare cecitate

---

[43] om. line 75. [44] om. τί φῄς, line 82. [45] Patrocli. [46] ἐλούσατ' ἐξ ὅτουπερ ἐγένετο (= lavit postquam natus fuit), line 85: it is difficult to believe that Bruni had our Greek text before him. [47] om. line 86. [48] ἐγὼ . . . ἠπείλησ', line 88. [49] Not a question; belongs to the preceding speech; Chremylus speaks only the next sentence in the Greek. [50] End of folio 69 verso. [51] The ms. has ·H· (= enim), which must be emended to "quod" or "cum." This abbreviation is not used elsewhere; "enim" ordinarily is "ȇ." [52] om. line 106. [53] οἰμώξει μακρά, line 111.

facereque ut videas. Pl: Nequaquam hoc ages, nolo[54] enim rursus videre. Cr: Quid ais? Ca: Homo hic natura miser est. Pl: Iuppiter . . .,[55] si rescierit,[56] *morti me traderet.* Cr: An nunc non id agit, qui quidem te offendentem ambulare facit? Pl: Nescio quidem istuc. Sed illum[57] formido magis. Cr: O *stulte et*[58] ignavissime demonum omnium, puta[59] Iovis potentiam . . .[60] vix dignam[61] trinummi, si videas modo vel brevi tempore. Pl: Ne dicas, sceleste. Cr: . . .[62] Equidem ostendam te multo plus posse quam Iovem. Pl: Mene? Cr: Per celum ita. . . .[63] Ca: Propter pecunias videlicet, plurimas namque hic habet. Cr: Age quis est qui pecunias *hominibus*[64] tradit? Ca: Iste. Cr: Sacra Iovi fiunt an non per *illas?* Ca:[65] Et precantur hercle ditari *omnes*.[66] Cr:[67] Itaque hic est causa, at facile potest cessare modo velit. Ca: Quid? Cr: Ut nemo sacra faciat posthac, non bovem mactans, non *ovem*,[68] non quicquam aliud . . .[69] Pl: Quomodo? Cr: Quod nil est quod quisquis emerit, nisi tu presens ei tradas pecuniam, quare Iovis potentiam, si te offendat,[70] tu evertes solus. Pl: Quid ais tu? Per me illi sacrificatur? Cr: Nempe ego dico, ac medius fidius siquid est in hominibus splendidum pulcrum gratum, per te id fit, cuncta enim divitiis obedientia sunt. Ca: Equidem propter modicum argenti sum factus servus . . .,[71] et mulieres perhibent corinthyas, si pauper quis eas roget,[72] nequaquam concedere, at si dives sit qui rogat, continuo *obsequi,*[73] non amatoris sed pecunie[74] gratia. Cr: *Meretrices forsan,* nam *improbe*[75] pecunias non petunt. Ca: [Quid refert id si alie palam flagitant,

---

[54] volo. [55] om. εἰδὼς τὰ τούτων etc., line 119. [56] resicierit. [57] illud. [58] ἄληθες, line 123. [59] A question in the Greek. [60] om. καὶ τοὺς κεραυνούς, line 125. [61] digna. [62] om. ἔχ' ἥσυχος, line 127. [63] om. line 130. [64] αὐτῷ, line 132. [65] om. [66] ἄντικρυς, line 134. [67] om. [68] ψαιστόν, line 138. [69] om. μὴ βουλομένου σοῦ, line 139. [70] offendāt. [71] om. διὰ τὸ μὴ πλουτεῖν ἴσως, line 148. In the Greek the next four lines are given to Chremylus, but Bruni gives them to "Carinus" and expurgates the whole passage through line 159. [72] roget] om. [73] Line 152 is thus expurgated, and line 153, with its reference to παιδεραστία, is omitted. The omission of the speaker's name at this point is indicated by a colon (:) in the ms., perhaps added by a corrector. For another occurrence of this colon see below, note 94. [74] pecunia. [75] οἱ χρηστοί, line 156. In the ms. "valde" is written above "improbe."

alie sapienter[76] verite(?)[77]],[78] siquidem . . .[79] pecuniam petere, aliis verbis tegunt verecundiam. Cr:[80] Artes vero cuncte ac sophismata, quecumque sunt in hominibus, propter te *fiunt*.[81] Hic quidem sutoriam exercet sedens, alter ferrum cudit, alter fabricatur, alter inaurat auro a te suscepto, alter predatur rapinis, alter furatur, alter est fullo, alter *linit pallia*,[82] alter *decorat*,[83] alter venundat cepas, alter deprehensus meccus per te *evadit*.[84] Pl: O me miserum, hec me latebant prius.[85] Cr:[86] Quid? Persarum rex nonne per te *comatur*?[87] . . . [88] Quid? Triremes nonne tu solus imples? Ca: Militem conductum nonne in Corintho nutrit? Pamphilus vero nonne per hunc *lugetur*?[89] *Velopola*[90] non una cum Pamphilo? Attirius vero nonne per hunc est[91] *prodigus*?[92] Phylesius nonne[93] per te fabulas docet? Federa belli nonne per te sunt egyptiis? Cr: Amat vero Thays nonne propter te Philonidem. Ca: Timothei turris— Cr: Super te cadat. Ca: Negotia vero omnia nonne propter te fiunt? Solissima enim omnium tu es causa[94] bonorumque et malorum. Cr: Superant certe inimicos ubique illi *quibus tu ades solus*.[95] Pl: Ego tanta possum? Cr: Et medius fidius plura quam hec. . . .[96] Itaque aliarum rerum omnium satietas est hominibus; amoris. Ca: Pulmenti. Cr: Musice. Ca: *Dapum*. Cr: Honoris. Ca: Placentarum. Cr: Virtutis. Ca: *Cibariorum*. Cr: Glorie. Ca: Muscatiorum.[97] Cr: Rerum gestarum. Ca: *Esus*. Cr: At vero tui nulla umquam satietas est, sed siquis talenta possideat *decem*,[98] concupiscat sedecim; ac si hec perficiet, *qui dragmata*[99] volet; ac nisi habeant, sibi

---

[76] Blurred in the ms. [77] verīte, blurred. [78] This sentence is substituted for line 157. [79] om. αἰσχυνόμενοι, line 158. [80] The following speech of "Cremes" is distributed between Chremylus and Carinus in the Greek, lines 160–168. [81] ἐσθ᾽ ηὑρημένα, line 161. [82] πλύνει κᾠδια, line 166. [83] βυρσοδεψεῖ. [84] παρατίλλεται, line 168. [85] End of folio 70 recto. [86] Again the speakers are confused, lines 170–185. [87] κομᾷ. [88] om. line 171. [89] κλαύσεται, line 174. [90] βελονοπώλης. [91] est] om., see note 93. [92] πέρδεται, line 176. Is the indecency of the original intentionally avoided? [93] After "nonne" the words "per hunc est prodigus" are deleted. [94] cā Cr Bonorumque et malorum: superant. (See above, note 73). [95] = line 185. [96] om. line 188. [97] I do not know the meaning of this word. [98] τριακαίδεκα, line 194. [99] τετταράκοντα.

vivendum non putent.[100] Pl: Bene vos quidem mihi dicere videmini. Sed unum vereor. Cr: Dic quid. Pl. *Nec*[101] ipse huius potentie quam dicitis fiam compos. Cr: *Fies tu pol quidem, ne timeas.* Aiunt vero omnes timidum esse Plutum.[102] Pl: Non est ita, sed fur quidam me calumpniatus est, nam domi repens omnia clausa et obserrata reperit, nec quicquam auferre valens, providentiam ille meam nuncupavit timiditatem. Cr: Non tibi nunc sit cure quicquam, si fies[103] efficax enim ipse ad agendum vir, te[104] perspicacius *linceis*[105] videntem reddam. Pl: Quomodo id facere poteris cum sis mortalis? Cr: Habeo spem quandam optimam ex quibus dixit mihi Phebus ipse fiticam[106] laurum quatiens. Pl: Et ille[107] ergo conscius est horum? Cr: Ita. Pl: Videte. Cr: Noli suspicari in me quicquam, nam etsi oporteat me mori, ista perficiam. Ca: Et ego si vis. Cr:[108] Multique erunt alii adiutores nobis, quicumque iusti farina carent. Pl: Pape, laboriosos mihi narras sotios. Cr: Non si[109] ditescant. Sed heus tu cito curre. Ca: Quid[110] ago? Dic. Cr: Agricolas voca, reperies forsan in agro facientes opus, ut partem equam quisque eorum veniens istius capiat. Ca: Equidem vado, sed hoc carnis aliquis capiens intro auferat. Cr: Mihi cure erit. Curras. Tu vero, Plute, optime demonum, introeas una mecum, hec est enim domus quam hodie implere te divitiis oportet[111] iuste et iniuste. Pl: Invitus mehercle intro alienam domum, nec mihi umquam profuit, nam si parcus sit hic cuius domum intro ipse statim me abscondit sub terram fodiens, petentique vel modicum argenti bono viro, qui ad eum rogatum veniat, vidisse me unquam inficiatur, sin vero prodigi hominis intro domum, libidine et alea dissipatus foras deturbor[112] nudus . . .[113] Numquam mediocrem hominem nactus *sum*.[114] Cr: Ego medio-

---

[100] Blurred in the ms. [101] ὅπως (= quomodo), line 200. "Nec" is perhaps an error of the scribe for "ne." [102] Plutum] om. [103] quicquam, si fies] quemadmodum(?) fiet. [104] vir, te] iuste. [105] τοῦ Λυγκέως, line 210. The ms. has "lanceis." [106] i.e. Πυθικήν, line 213. [107] Above "ille" is written "Apollo." [108] om. [109] sic. [110] Quicquid. [111] oportet te ditiis. [112] Above "deturbor" is written "deicior." [113] om. ἐν ἀκαρεῖ χρόνου, line 244. [114] This line (245) is spoken by Chremylus in the original, and the verb is in the second person.

cris quidam sum, nam amo parsimoniam ut nemo alter,[115] rursusque ego[116] expendo[117] cum opus est. Sed introeamus, nam videre te volo et uxorem et filium unicum meum, quem ego post te amo maxime. Pl: Audio. Cr: Cur enim quis verum non fateatur tibi? Ca: . . .[118] O populares *agricolae* laboriosi, . . .[119] *cessate iam ab opere ac leti vivite si iubet herus.*[120] Agricole: Est autem quid et unde, quod ita iubet? Ca: Venit secum adducens senem quendam sordidum, . . .,[121] miserum, *obsitum*,[122] calvum, sine dentibus, puto quoque *testiculis eum carere*.[123] Agricole: O *aurum verbis*[124] significas . . .,[125] videtur enim venisse nummorum acervum habens. Finis.

[115] End of folio 70 verso. [116] rursusque ego] rursus quidem(?) egoque.
[117] Written above "exego." [118] om. line 253. [119] om. lines 255–261.
[120] = lines 262–263. [121] om. κυφόν, line 266. [122] ῥυσόν. [123] ψωλὸν αὐτὸν εἶναι, line 267. [124] χρυσὸν ... ἐπῶν. [125] om. πῶς φῄς; πάλιν φράσον μοι, line 268.

HAVERFORD COLLEGE

FROM MONTE GIANICOLO[1]

Louis E. Lord

THE best approach to Monte Gianicolo is from the north and the best method of approach is on foot. The casual traveler who is whisked through the lovely Passeggiata Margherita by automobile in approved Roman style will see little but a blur of trees, ilex and pine, a vision of a fair city lying below him, and a noble horseman silhouetted against the sky. He will, however, get one real Roman touch—the delight in noise for noise's sake which leads the chauffeur to drive his machine with the muffler open on the slightest provocation. It does no good to assure him that he gains neither in power nor "gas." He loves to hear the machine go.

The environs of St. Peter's beyond the colonnade are not attractive and are best passed in silence with head bowed, or in any position that will most impede the functioning of the olfactory nerve. Beyond Sangallo's Porta di Santo Spirito carriages must turn to the right by the broad Via del Gianicolo but the pedestrian may go straight up the steep Via di Sant' Onofrio till he reaches the church and monastery of that name. Here the melancholy poet Tasso died in 1595 and here he lies buried. Just above the monastery is the oak beneath which he used to sit and look out over the wonderful panorama of the Borgo and the Seven Hills.

Tasso's life was one long series of disappointments. His genius was early recognized and he was given a place of honor

[1] This chapter is in no way a contribution—welcome or unwelcome—to the sum of human knowledge. It is an effort to recall a few of the memories that will always be associated in my mind with the Janiculum Hill and with Professor Rolfe. For it was here in the American Academy that it was my privilege to spend with him the year 1923–1924. It was a year of rare pleasure—a pleasure in a large degree due to the delightful companionship of the urbane scholar in whose honor this book has been prepared.

173

at the Este court in Ferrara. Here he wrote the work by which he is still most favorably remembered, the *Aminta,* the most happily conceived and most poetic of pastoral dramas. Arcady is far removed from our modern world. Its shepherds and shepherdesses, its groves and its streams all seem to us what they really are—most artificial creations. But in the *Aminta,* unreal as it is, Tasso has succeeded in catching something of the charm of Theocritus. Its tender simplicity and studied direct-ness make us for a moment forget its artificiality. Its dreamy atmosphere is "soft as sleep."

Tasso was recognized as the leading Italian poet of the day and the Pope decided to make the recognition public. He pro-posed to crown him with laurel on the Capitol, the Poet Laure-ate of Rome. It was while awaiting in the Vatican the bestowal of this decoration that Tasso fell fatally ill. At his own request he was taken to the monastery of St. Onofrio where he died, and the wreath that was to have encircled his brow was placed in tribute to his memory on his tomb.

The oak beneath which Tasso was wont to sit arrests the visitor just before he reaches in his climb the level summit of the hill. It was blasted by lightning in 1842 but another shoot has taken up the tale and will probably last out the century. A third slip of an ilex just below is ready, in case of emergencies, to perpetuate the tradition and to be cherished in due course of time as "la quercia del Tasso."

From Tasso's favorite seat the panorama of Rome begins to unfold. To the left rises the dome of St. Peter's—the last mighty work of the mighty Angelo. Tradition says that for his work on the dome he refused all compensation, saying that he was rearing it for his soul's salvation. He did not live to see it completed, but after the drum was finished he built a model which later architects closely followed. The vagaries of for-tune, his enemies' spite, and the vacillating will of a sick Pope prevented him from finishing the noble monument he had de-signed for the tomb of Julius II, but in the august dome that crowns St. Peter's church, dominating the whole landscape as its designer dominated the art of the Renaissance, Michelangelo has found his own appropriate memorial.

Much that Tasso saw has passed, much has been added since his time. The Castle of St. Angelo—refuge of the Pope in the awful sack of Rome in 1527, and prison of the delightful bravo, Benvenuto Cellini—remains almost unchanged. Before it still stretches the bridge which Hadrian built about 1800 years ago to form the approach to his mausoleum. Just beyond the tomb rise the Law Courts—the Palace of Justice—a vast building testifying to the desire of modern Rome to equal the dignity of her past.

Below us, across the river, is the circular glass roof that covers the most unique music hall in the world. In the Campus Martius, between the Via Lata (the modern Corso Umberto Primo —anything but a "wide street" today) and the Tiber, Augustus built a circular mausoleum, a tomb for the remains of his family. He lived to see all that were dear to him, except his noble wife Livia, buried here, and here too the founder of the Roman Empire lay till his empire dissolved and Alaric, the barbarian, rifled his tomb. Later the Colonnas made it one of their fortresses. It has been entirely cleared of interior partitions; seats, boxes (tier above tier), a stage, and an organ have been installed and now, each Sunday, Rome listens to the finest of concerts in the imperial tomb. Its circular shape and great height make it an ideal audience room. Since Augustus was by a pious court almost immediately transferred to the Heaven of the gods, he cannot mind his eviction. One wonders if he looks down from his isolation, with that well-known wintry smile on his cold countenance, in approbation of the use to which his successors have put his formal monument.

Nearer us, as we gaze from our Janicular height, and further to the right, the flat dome of the Pantheon just shows above the roofs of the adjacent buildings. Though the building is now known to be almost entirely the work of its reconstructor, Ha-

175

drian, Tasso must have looked on it as the work of its original builder—Agrippa—Secretary of War under Augustus—responsible for most of the emperor's victories and rewarded for his services with the doubtful boon of his daughter Julia's hand. The Pantheon still stands essentially unharmed. Spared by Goth and Vandal, it was robbed of its bronze adornments by the Christian Pope of the Barberini family to make pillars for the baldachino in St. Peter's Church and cannons for St. Angelo.

> Quod non fecerunt barbari, fecerunt Barberini
> "What the barbarians spared, the Barberini spoiled."

From the oak of Tasso a few steps lead up to the summit of the Janiculum—a level space half a mile long. Through this runs the broad Passeggiata Margherita—a lovely avenue flanked by pines and ilex, named in honor of the mother of Victor Emanuel III. At the left one passes by a "faro," a marble lighthouse presented to the city by the Italians of South America, who have chosen their gift with more patriotism than taste. Perched on this commanding eminence above a bend in the Tiber it can be seen from all parts of Rome flashing at intervals of twenty seconds the national colors, red, green, white. It might be a benefit to the storm-tossed mariner if there were any such. Since navigation on the Tiber has ceased, the statement that there have been no wrecks subsequent to the erection of the beacon is probably true.

Just beyond the parapet that bounds the Passeggiata on the city side, one looks down into the Botanical Gardens. They are not astonishingly well kept but in their wild and decadent beauty they remind the wanderer, through their moss-green, shady avenues, of the failing fortunes of the old Roman nobility. They are the old gardens of the Corsini Palace, which lies immediately between them and the Farnese Villa. The Farnese Villa, shorn of all its beautiful grounds, is still private property where for a few cents the visitor may see the glorious Psyche frescoes designed by Raphael, and his own masterpiece in fresco, "the Triumph of Galatea." But the Corsini Palace has passed, like so many of its fellows, into the hands of the State. The palace, where the nephew of Clement XII held his cardinal's court and where the daughter of Gustavus Adolphus died after renouncing the protestant religion—the cause her father so mightily defended—this palace now affords a home for the Royal Academy of Sciences and the National Gallery of Painting.

It is altogether fitting that the crown of the Janiculum Hill should be surmounted by the noble equestrian statue of Garibaldi. No statue in the world has a more superb location. The horse stands firmly at rest on all four feet. It does not rear into the contortions which threaten to unseat even such capable riders as Peter the Great and General Jackson. Below, on each side of the pedestal, are writhing groups of bronze figures which the beholder would gladly forget as he looks upward at the quiet dignity of Garibaldi himself. Clad in his historic pancho, the hero sits surveying with eternal calm the fair prospect of his beloved city. The tumult of the struggling groups below does not reach him, the rumble of the city's traffic does not disturb him. Impatient and unjudicial as he was in peace, the tumult of war was a kind of music to him. It stilled his restlessness, and when his quiet voice, vibrant with its noble magnetism, was heard uttering the simple "coraggio," the wavering ranks would stiffen and men forget their panic in the inspiration of his quiet fearlessness. So he sits, forever at peace, looking out over the city he once so mightily defended, over Roma Capitale, which he was permitted to enter but not to capture. And so he may be seen even from the Pincian Hill across the city, where the careless traveler sits and sips his tea at sunset. As the sun sinks behind the Janiculum, on its summit just above the trees—as if it were suspended in air—there appears the silhouette of a great man on a noble horse.

The Passeggiata sweeps on from the Garibaldi statue between lines of busts of eminent and forgotten Romans and terminates at the bronze gates that stand on the line of the old Aurelian Wall.

Just below is one of those magnificent fountains for which Rome is so uniquely famous. From an ornamental façade the water bursts forth in five great streams. The two, one at each side, are smaller but each is quite the size of a considerable brook. The three great central cascades might each come from a large water-main spouting under pressure. This great mass of water leaps down with the noise of a cataract into a wide semicircular pool whence it passes underground to other fountains by the Ponte Sisto and into the Tiber. The water is used only for irrigating the gardens below and for these fountains. It is not pure enough to be potable. The lavish abundance with which the fountain pours forth its water is a pleasant contrast to the niggardly jets that are often called fountains in America. Many a traveler coming suddenly upon these roaring waterfalls on a hot summer afternoon has been cooled by their grateful spray and refreshed by their music, and has blessed the memory of Paul V whose munificence restored this aqueduct. The inscription above on the façade records that the Pope restored and enlarged the Alsietina aqueduct of Augustus. It is a regrettable inaccuracy. The aqueduct of Augustus reached Rome where the emperor had built his naumachia, near the Villa Corsini, but only slight traces of it have been found. The aqueduct which the Pope did restore was that built by Trajan a hundred years later. Its course may be followed for a long way beside the ancient Via Aurelia that leads out from the Porta San Pancrazio, and passes beneath the walls of the Villa Doria Pamphili.

A few steps below the Fontana Paola, stands the church of San Pietro in Montorio. Beside it is the Spanish Academy and between the two buildings, in a small court, stands Bramante's "Tempietto." Although this structure is only about twenty feet high, its finely adjusted proportions and its delicately executed details give it a graceful dignity that is rare in Roman monuments. It marks the spot, or (as the scoffer may well say) one of the spots where St. Peter suffered martyrdom.

The church of Saint Peter on the Mount of Gold (the sand of the Janiculum Hill at this spot is a bright yellow) contains a few paintings of moderate interest. The altarpiece, Raphael's "Transfiguration," received Napoleon's "imprimatur" and was taken to Paris. When Metternich and his ilk tried to set the clock of history back from 1815 to 1315, it was returned to Rome but not to its place in this church. It may be seen in the Vatican Picture Gallery. In the floor beneath the place where the Transfiguration stood, lies Beatrice Cenci. The slab above her coffin used to bear the simple inscription "orate." Now even that has been removed and one must beg the sacristan to identify the place and put a somewhat doubting trust in his knowledge and veracity.

Rome is still divided on the question of the justice of her execution. To the charge of murdering her father both she and her mother confessed under torture. They had paid assassins to commit the murder. When suspicion was aroused they hired other assassins to kill the first pair and were only deterred by lack of time from employing a third set to dispose of number two in the series. At the last moment the Pope was about to pardon Beatrice but he was shocked by the commission of another family murder and determined to make an example of her and her mother. These facts in the dispute, which has become warm to the point of acrimony in the last few years, appear clear: first, Beatrice either committed the murder herself or hired brigands to do it; second, the old man richly deserved to be killed by somebody. The point at issue seems to be—Was he bad enough to deserve to be killed by a wife and daughter or only by a more remote relative.

From the platform before the church another fine panorama of Rome is disclosed. Beyond the Pantheon and to the right is the great Quirinal Palace—so long the home of the Popes. Here Papal consistories were formerly held and from the balcony overlooking the square, where the "horse-tamers" stand, the newly elected Pope pronounced his blessing on his subjects. Here Pius IX was elected, the last Pope to occupy the palace. Driven out of the city in 1849 by an outraged people, he was replaced by the French and protected by them for a weary twenty years, till Victor Emanuel II forced him to take refuge in the Vatican, a prisoner for the rest of his days. In fact so deep was the hatred inspired by Pio Nono that for years after his death his body could not be taken to the tomb awaiting it in "San Lorenzo without the Walls." When the attempt was first made the crowd attacked the *cortège* and nearly succeeded in projecting the venerable corpse into the Tiber.

Still to the right, the white mass of the monument to Victor Emanuel II rises, and mingled with its white sheen comes the gleam of gilded bronze. Unsatisfactory in its details, over-wrought and over-elaborated, ill seen down the stretch of the narrow Corso, it is still impressive by virtue of its mere size and dignified proportion. It is notable as the effort of a people, just reunited after centuries of enforced separation and mis-government, to express its devotion to the firm and just king who had made that union possible. By tradition a Roman monument must be colossal. Could a people whose ancestors reared the Augusteum and the Castle of St. Angelo be content to express their gratitude in a pointed shaft or sculptured arch? This pile of polished marble with its golden adornments in its vastness is the measure of Italy's thanks for her deliverance. In its boldness it is a proof of her courage, of her determination undaunted to match a glorious past with a vivid present.

Beyond, rises the truncated shaft of a medieval tower—one of the very few still standing in Rome, called "Nero's Tower" because from its top Nero would have watched the burning of Rome if the tower had been built some twelve hundred years earlier.

Only a glimpse can be had of the Capitol where stands the church of "St. Mary on Heaven's Altar." It was here Gibbon conceived the idea of writing his *Decline and Fall of the Roman Empire,* and it was on the steps of Ara Coeli that Henry Adams, as he revolved in his orbit of Boston, London, Paris, Rome, used periodically to sit and wonder why an inscrutable providence had not made him, as well as his grandfather and great grandfather, a president of the United States but merely the author of a "best-seller."

Then on the Esquiline Santa Maria Maggiore lifts her two domes and pointed shaft. Beyond, to the south, is the Lateran "Sacrosancta Lateranensis ecclesia omnium urbis et orbis ecclesiarum Mater et Caput." Above the bulk of the Lateran Palace and Basilica appear the colossal saints that crown the battlements outlined against the sky.

All over the city, domes and square brick towers flecked with graceful marble shafts appear, but nowhere a Gothic spire. As St. Paul's dome is almost isolated among the spires of the capital of that other-world empire in the north, so Santa Maria Sopra Minerva alone in Rome shows the Gothic tradition. Even here Gothic architecture may be seen only in the interior—the church has no carved façade nor spire.

In the center of the picture is the Rome of the Republic and the Caesars. At the far end of the Forum area are the sweeping arches of the Basilica of Constantine. The lofty arches of the nave have fallen but those which span the aisles rise eighty feet in the clear, great masses of cement, once richly decorated, but no less impressive now in their majestic despoliation. The Palatine is a bit to the right—a mass of green verdure that partly hides and partly adorns the ruins of the Palaces of the Caesars. Here Rome began—*Roma quadrata,* Rome four-square,—fit symbol of a city that was to hold her walls unbreached for one thousand years. Horatius as he turned his back on the Janiculum, when the bridge he had so stoutly held fell in ruins behind him, gazed across the yellow Tiber to the city he had saved and "saw on Palatinus the white porch of his home." Here later only the wealthy could afford to live, Cicero and Clodius, Catiline and Crassus (to take only a few names from the C's in the telephone book of 63 B.C.). Later still it was set apart for the Emperor, his family, and the other gods, and now excavations show one palace built over another as each successive family found their inherited or captured home too cramped.

To the right lies the Aventine, all trees and towers. Three churches, one fashionable tea room, and a few truck gardens have about covered its crest. The largest church is the center of a Benedictine international seminary only recently completed. Here on the Aventine the few survivors of the once powerful Order of the Knights of the Hospital of St. John in Jerusalem still dwell. Retreating before the victorious Turks from Jerusalem they resided successively in Acre, Cyprus, Rhodes, and Malta. When they were compelled during the Napoleonic war to leave Malta they were hospitably received by the Pope at Rome. At first they were given sanctuary in a small villa on the Pincian Hill just behind the Villa Medici. This villa is still called the Villa Malta. It later became the property of the former German Imperial Chancellor von Buelow, and the Knights of Malta, as they are now universally called, have been moved to the Villa Maltese on the Aventine. Here the few Knights, who can still proudly display on their shields the four quarterings of nobility, look down the long vistas of their avenue to the dome of St. Peter's, tend their roses, and worship in their chapel. Their priory contains the portraits of all their Grand Masters since the foundation of the order in the twelfth century.

Though the Janiculum did not play a large part in Rome's ancient history, there are a few scenes which come vividly to mind. It was here that Lars Porsena of Clusium made his headquarters when he tried to restore the hated Tarquin the Proud to his kingdom. Up the slope of the hill, perhaps beneath San Pietro, Caius Gracchus fled from the mob which a hostile Senate had set to pursue him. As he ran through the streets and up the hill, followed by one faithful slave, he begged the bystanders to give him a horse that he might escape, but, says Plutarch (*C. Gracchus* 17.2), they merely looked on, urging him on to greater speed, like the audience that watches a race in the games. When he fell in the "Grove of the Furies" and his spirit had joined that of his murdered brother, the smug Senate doubtless thought it was the last act of the drama on which the curtain had fallen. It was but the close of the first act. The tragedy of the Republic was not to end till their grandchildren brought the weary drama to a close in the *curia* of Pompey's theater, when Caesar fell at the foot of his rival's statue.

Of Caesar, too, the Janiculum Hill has memories. Here lay those famous gardens which he bequeathed to the Roman people. And in them, perhaps toward the southern end of the hill, was the villa where Cleopatra and their son Caesarion were living when Caesar was murdered. The presence and the memories of "the foremost man of all this world," and of her for whom "a man might well have lost the world" and of whom it could be said

> Age cannot wither her, nor custom stale
> Her infinite variety

would alone make any region famous. Who can walk unmoved through the lovely gardens of the Janiculan Villas, when he thinks he may be treading the very paths down which Caesar and Egypt's queen once loitered?

In one of his kindlier moods, that literary chameleon, Martial, who could, equally well, be a pale imitation of Horace or a sooty replica of Juvenal, described the estate of Julius Martialis on the Janiculum:

The few fields of Julius Martialis, more favoured than the gardens of the Hesperides, rest on the long ridge of Janiculum; wide sheltered reaches look down on the hills, and the flat summit, gently swelling, enjoys to the full a clearer sky, and, when mist shrouds the winding vales, alone shines with its own brightness; the dainty roof of the tall villa gently rises up to the unclouded stars. On this side may you see the seven sovereign hills and take the measure of all Rome, the Alban hills and Tusculan too, and every cool retreat nestling near the city, old Fidenae and tiny Rubrae, and Anna Perenna's fruitful grove that joys in maiden blood. On that side the traveller shows on the Flaminian or Salarian way, though his carriage makes no sound, that wheels should not disturb the soothing sleep which neither boatswain's call nor barge-men's shout is loud enough to break, though the Mulvian Bridge is so near, and the keels that swiftly glide along the sacred Tiber (Martial 4.64.1–24, *Loeb* Translation).

Truly Rome is Immortal. Nothing vital has changed in the 1800 years since Martial from this villa beheld the imperishable beauty of the Campagna and the Roman hills. Well may he, in a burst of rarely genuine enthusiasm, prefer a few acres on Jani-culum "to cool Tivoli, or Palestrina or all the eyrie of Setia."

But before he leaves the Janiculum there is one more place that the traveler should visit, as a pleasure if he be not an American, as both a duty and a pleasure if he be—The Ameri-can Academy in Rome. The American School of Architecture was founded in 1894 largely through the efforts of Charles F. McKim and Daniel Burnham. Its scope was enlarged in 1897, when painting and sculpture were added and the name changed to "The American Academy in Rome." Its home was first in the Villa Aurora, later in the Villa Mirafiore. In 1909, the Villa Aurelia on the Janiculum was given to the Academy which was moved to that site in 1914. Meanwhile, in 1912, the American School of Classical Studies in Rome—founded in 1895—had been incorporated in the Academy, largely through the efforts of Dean Andrew F. West of Princeton. In 1921 the School of Music was added, so that now the arts are united at the American Academy in a manner which cannot be matched in the academies of France, Spain, or England. The respon-sible head of the Academy is the Director. Each of the schools, Fine Arts, Classics, Music, has its own director and faculty. The Board of Trustees who govern the Academy was created by act of Congress.

The grounds of the Academy cover the highest point of the

THE AMERICAN ACADEMY IN ROME

Janiculum, just inside the Porta San Pancrazio. In addition to the Villa Aurelia, there is the main building, a dignified edifice erected by the generosity of far-sighted Americans who believed in the value of training to the highest point of perfection of a few talented artists and scholars. Here are the offices of the Academy, the studios of the painters and sculptors, a lecture room, a common room for the men and dining rooms for the men and women fellows, studios and rooms for the men, and one of the most beautiful libraries in Europe, a suite of rooms for the Director of the School of Classical Studies and another for the Professor of Latin, annually appointed to Rome from one of our American colleges. The Director of the School of Music occupies the adjacent Villa Chiaraviglio. In these delightful and stimulating surroundings the men and women who have won the "Prize of Rome" in the fine arts, the classics, or music do not work under meticulous supervision, for they are all students tried and tested, graduates of recognized colleges or art students of long training and approved performance. With all of Rome about them and literally at their feet, well cared for, with funds sufficient to enable them to visit the famous sites and museums of Greece and Italy and Africa, or the concerts of Munich and Paris, or the galleries of Venice and Florence, with the sympathetic advice and guidance of experts, this fortunate group of young men and women are preparing themselves to become the leading artists and classical teachers of America.

The Villa Aurelia, the residence of the Director of the Academy, crowns the Janiculum Hill. It may be seen against the western skyline from any part of Rome. Its terraced walls, its palms and ilexes, its lovely flower gardens, and fair prospects are among the most cherished possessions of the Academy. Their beauty is unsurpassed in Rome. Its terrace affords the finest views in Rome. To the north rises St. Peter's dome with its lovely lantern. Midway, between it and the terrace, Garibaldi is seen, mounted on his horse, outlined against a background of green trees. Far beyond St. Peter's rises Monte Mario with its dominating fortress; here appear, too, the International College (a Methodist fortress), and the Villa Madama to remind one of old Rome. Here lived Margaret of Parma, the natural daughter of the Emperor Charles V. Her villa was erected after designs of Raphael and still shows some of the finest stucco decoration in Rome.

All Rome lies below, unfolded as the landscape unrolls beneath the aviator. North past Monte Mario the Tiber circles down in many a gleaming fold. Soracte rears its great detached bulk out of the valley. "Vides ut alta stet nive candidum Soracte." So Horace saw it, but in most weathers it is white not with snow but with its own barren, limestone rocks. The Apennines take up the tale and range all along the eastern horizon, gray in the dawn, purple at noon, and pink in the evening light, with here and there in early fall a snow-capped pyramid, cloud-white against the sky. There is Gennaro, Horace's "fair Lucretelis," and just beyond it the "Digentia downward flowing" ran past his sequestered Sabine farm: "Satis superque me benignitas tua ditavit." On the edge where the Anio "makes one leap of it from the Sabine Hills to the plain below" hangs Tivoli—Horace's Tibur, where the orchards are still bedewed with "the spray from the swift river." The Volscian Hills rise a bit to the south where perches Praeneste—she who suffered Sulla's wrath and gave to the world the inventor of modern music.

To the south lie the Alban Hills, the glory of the Campagna: Rocca Priora, the pass of "cool Algidus," and Monte Cavo, the Alban Mount, home of the Latin Confederacy before Rome was its chief city and the chief sanctuary of the Confederacy till Christianity stilled the babel of heathen worship and quenched the fires on its altars. Even at this distance the stately grove of beech trees that encircles its summit like a crown may be seen. The white villas that shone on the "lofty walls of Circe's Tusculum" have gone but not the memories of that town where

Cato the Censor was born and where Cicero so often found rest from the annoyances of an ungrateful people who refused to reflect continuously on the superlative merits of his consulship. Tusculum is gone but the priceless *Disputations* remain, and Frascati remains, by day a white gleam in the dark woods of the hillside, by night a twinkling jewel in its darker silhouette.

The circle of Aurelian's mighty walls is clearly marked. Mighty walls indeed they were, with their double gates, their battlements, and their towers, but none the less a confession of weakness. For six centuries Rome had needed no walls. Her walls were her legions, her guards their eagles. When Hadrian built a wall for Rome he built it in Britain, or on the Danube, or the Euphrates. One hundred years later, the trumpets were sounding the retreat in the streets of "sleepy Chester," and the legions were marching home. Rome was glad to shelter herself behind imperial mortar and brick which for still another century and a half served the dying state instead of stout hearts and hands.

From one of its gates runs the Harbor Road past four tombs known to all the world. Cestius is known only for his tomb, a tall pyramid which a Pope has tried to appropriate as a memorial for his "munificence." Beside it grow the cypresses that mark the grave of that young English poet who thought his "name was writ in water," and the tomb that enshrines the heart of Shelley, "cor cordium." Only a little way beyond is the great basilica church that stands over the spot where Paul the Apostle is buried. This short stretch of road and its memorials are an epitome of the varied spell that Rome casts on men, of the way in which she still holds sway over the nations. Archaeologists from France and Russia and Denmark and Germany study the Pyramid of Cestius, lovers of poetry from America and England bow in reverence before the simple slabs of Keats and Shelley. Pilgrims come from every land and the islands of the seven seas to worship in the church of Saint Paul without the Walls. Ave Roma Immortalis!

From the next gate, near where St. Sebastian is buried, the Via Appia, Rome's first great road, runs south to Anxur and Capua. We can follow its course, a white line straight as an arrow past the circle of Caecilia Metella's tomb on and on till it rises to the shoulder of Monte Cavo, passes, and drops out of sight toward the sea.

The picture is complete. History and art and literature, Etruscan culture, Republican legend and history, Imperial builders, Christian martyrs, Barbarian destroyers, Popes and Painters and Architects of the Renaissance, the Founders of Modern Italy, call to you from every side as your eyes swing around the panorama, from Angelo's dome to where the Alban mount flows down in crested ridges to the waves of the Tuscan sea.

But before the visitor leaves the grounds of the Villa Aurelia there is still one more tribute to pay. For it was here that Garibaldi fought so stubbornly for Mazzini's Roman Republic. This is not the place to tell the story of his life. It may be read, and no story but the *Odyssey* is so interesting, in the books of Trevelyan. Since Odysseus listened to the voice of the Sirens, fought the Cyclops, made love to Circe, was loved by Calypso and Nausicaa, and returned to his own land—even far seen Ithaca—and his steadfast Penelope—since that time so long ago, the world has known no career so romantic and adventuresome as that of Garibaldi and his Penelope, the gracious and beloved Anita. A common sailor on the Mediterranean, thrice captured by pirates, conspirator and soldier, an exile in South America, admiral of a navy and commander of an army, a defender of Mazzini's Roman Republic, once more an exile, a candle maker in New York, a common sailor, and later captain of a merchantman in the China trade, in command of a corps in Victor Emanuel's army, a shepherd on the rocky isle of Caprera, dictator of the kingdom of Sicily and Naples, and once again by his own choice, a simple peasant. Where in the annals of history or the imagination of the novelist can such a career be found? Historians are wont to regard as a myth the story

that Manius Curius after thrice triumphing on the Capitol re-
tired to a life of simple frugality. Garibaldi bestowed two
kingdoms on Victor Emanuel, refused a general's commission
and a patent of nobility, and asked for his reward a bag of seed-
beans for his little farm and transportation to his island.

The Villa Aurelia stands on the spot where legend has it that
Servius Tullius built the fort which was the outpost of Rome.
The ruins of the wall of Aurelian are its foundation. It was
Garibaldi's headquarters during his brave defence of Rome.
From its roof he watched the battle. On the floor of the salon
below, his officer slept. His own room may still be seen. It is
one of the smallest in the Villa, for, as his granddaughter said,
"he always chose a small room with a wide view."

Just below the Villa, outside the Porta San Pancrazio, is the
terrible "death angle" where so many Italian boys and young
men fell that June—Enrico Dandolo of Milan, Masina, the
young noble of Bologna, Mameli, the poet of the Risorgimento
battle hymn "Fratelli d'Italia," names that are today dear to the
heart of a united Italy, and with them Manara, commander of
the little band of Bersaglieri Volontari, who was killed in the
Villa Spada that stands within the gate just below the Academy
buildings.

Outside the gate, are the ruins of the Vascello where Medici
and the Red Shirts held out to the end of the siege. Just beyond is the cool, shaded Villa Doria Pamphili where, a hundred yards from the gate, stands the triumphal arch of the four
winds that marks the spot where the Villa Corsini stood. Up
that path the fiery Bixio rode his horse, while behind him the
Garibaldini fell beneath the guns of the French—up the path,
up the outer staircase of the Villa, through its drawing room,
and out on to the balcony beyond, till he fell wounded but
victorious.

And when treachery and superior numbers had given victory
to the enemy, the Pope graciously permitted the walls that had
been breached by the French and bathed in Italian blood to be

repaired, and on the wall beneath the central bastion he placed a tablet which in decadent Latin records the act.

An. Sal. Rep. $\overline{\text{MDCCCL}}$
AVCTORITATE. PII. $\overline{\text{IX}}$. PONT. MAX.
S.P.Q.R.
MOENIA IANICVLENSIA
IN PERDVELLIBVS. EX. VRBE
FRANCORVM VIRTVTE PROFLIGANDIS
QVA PATISCENTIA QVA DIRVTA
INSTAVRAVIT REFECIT

Twenty years later a reunited Italy matched the tablet with a second, placed beside it, where in the language of a living state a free people honors those who fell in a hopeless cause, giving gladly their lives that the ideal of an Italian state might not die but living in the minds of their followers might one day be realized in *Italia liberata e Roma Capitale.*

$\overline{\text{IV}}$ GIUGNO $\overline{\text{MDCCCLXXI}}$
S.P.Q.R.
DOPO VENTI ANNI
DA CHE L'ESERCITO FRANCESE
ENTRATO PER QUESTE LACERE MURA
TORNO I ROMANI
SOTTO IL GOVERNO SACERDOTALE
ROMA LIBERA E RICONGIUNTA ALL'ITALIA
ONORA LA MEMORIA DI COLORO
CHE COMBATTENDO STRENUAMENTE
CADDERO IN DIFESA DELLA PATRIA

And the broad road that winds up the steep hill beneath the palms and ilexes—past the platform of San Pietro in Montorio and the fountain of Paul the Pope, past the lovely Villa Aurelia to the Porta San Pancrazio is called the Via Garibaldi.

OBERLIN COLLEGE

ANCIENT WIT AND HUMOR

Eugene S. McCartney

"Now inasmuch as, when men have become illustrious, not only what they said in earnest but also what they said in jest is worthy of record, I will write down Polemo's witticisms also, so that I may not seem to have neglected even them." These are the words of Philostratus,[1] but many ancient writers show that they entertain similar views about other famous men. Perhaps a little light may be thrown on the character of nations as well as of individuals by a collection of the things they laughed at. After the lapse of two millennia we are prone to forget that, though the ancients did not use the expression "funny bone," they had in abundant measure the thing signified by it.

In the acquisition of a foreign language the appreciation of its wit and humor is one of the last conquests. The first witticism that the Latin student meets *in situ* is the one on *ad equum rescribere,* which a certain soldier of Caesar's Tenth Legion uttered *non irridicule.*[2] The joke is sprung so unexpectedly that the student feels aggrieved. He looks dubiously at the teacher who confirms the statement in the notes that it is a witticism. His own experience in Latin equestrianism does not permit him to see how a Roman could be an *eques* without having an *equus.*

It is the purpose of this paper to render readily available a cross-section of the everyday wit and humor of the ancients. I shall quote only occasionally authors whose chief interest is fun, such as Aristophanes,[3] Lucian, Plautus,[4] and Martial.[5] Cicero,

[1] *Vit. Sophist.* 2.9 (p. 540) (W. C. Wright's translation).
[2] Caes. *Bell. Gall.* 1.42.6.
[3] See K. Holzinger, *De Verborum Lusu apud Aristophanem,* Vienna, 1876; J. W. Hewitt, "Elements of Humor in the Satire of Aristophanes," in *The Class. Journ.,* VIII (1913), 293–300.
[4] See C. J. Mendelsohn, *Studies in the Word-Play of Plautus,* Phila., 1907; V. Brugnola, "Le Facezie di Plauto," in *Atene e Roma,* VI (1903), 291–302.
[5] See the bibliography in Paul Nixon, *Martial and the Modern Epigram,* pp. 203–204 (in the series "Our Debt to Greece and Rome").

however, one of the prolific wits of antiquity, will be quoted several times. His jokes were passed along and collections of them were made.[6] In addition to many witticisms he uttered and recorded, the paternity of numerous others was ascribed to him,[7] a thing which happened to Lincoln also.

Although the ancients were much addicted to the pun, "where a word, like the tongue of a jack-daw, speaks twice as much by being split," and though they thought it—

> Quite legitimate fun
> To be blazing away at every one
> With a regular double-loaded gun,[8]

I desire to give a broader idea of the things that appealed to them as amusing and to show that they had the same types as we do.[9] They too poked fun at the doctor, the lawyer, the musician, and in fact at the general run of human foibles and frailties. They had some Irish "bulls" and a few prohibition jokes, though none on golf and Scotch parsimony. There are indications that even in antiquity jokes had begun to run in grooves and to become standardized.

There is a traditional joke about too great attainments in the

---

[6] Cic. *Ad Fam.* 15.21.2; Quint. *Inst.* 6.3.5; Macrob. *Sat.* 2.1.12; Plut. *Cicero* 38; *Ciceronis Facete Dicta* (C. F. W. Mueller's edition of Cicero, Part 4, III, 341–350). Modern collections have been made by V. Brugnola, *Le Facezie di Cicerone*, Città di Castello, 1896; L. Gurlitt, "Facetiae Tullianae," in *Rheinisches Museum*, LVII (1902), 337–362; Herwig, *Das Wortspiel in Ciceros Reden*, Attendorn, 1889; Hans Holst, *Die Wortspiele in Ciceros Reden* (in "Symbolae Osloenses," 1925). See also F. W. Kelsey, "Cicero as a Wit," in *The Class. Journ.*, III (1907), 3–10; F. W. Kelsey, "Cicero's Jokes on the Consulship of Caninius Rebilus," *ibid.*, IV (1909), 129–131; Mary A. Grant, *The Ancient Rhetorical Theories of the Laughable: The Greek Rhetoricians and Cicero*, University of Wisconsin Studies in Language and Literature, No. 21, Madison, 1924.

[7] Cic. *Ad Fam.* 7.32.1.

[8] On humor in names see two of my own papers: "Puns and Plays on Proper Names," in *The Class. Journ.*, XIV (1919), 343–358; "Canting Puns on Ancient Monuments," in *Am. Journ. Arch.*, XXIII (1919), 59–64. See also J. C. Austin, *The Significant Name in Terence* (Illinois Studies in Language and Literature, Vol. 7, No. 4).

[9] See also Irene Nye, "Humor Repeats Itself," in *The Class. Journ.*, IX (1914), 154–164.

minor things of life. At the conclusion of a billiard match with a youth who beat him badly, Herbert Spencer remarked: "Young man, such proficiency in games of skill argues a misspent youth."[10] When Antisthenes heard that Ismenias was a capital flute-player, he remarked: "But he must be a worthless man, for if he were not, he would not be so capital a flute-player."[11] King Philip, on hearing his son playing brilliantly on a harp, said to him: "Are you not ashamed to play so well?"[12] Sallust says of Sempronia: *Psallere, saltare elegantius quam necesse est probae.*[13] The following lines making fun of useless skill are based on Plutarch, *Moralia* 233B:

> The stranger long stood on one leg
> Just like a deftly balanced peg;
> The genius lacking in his head
> Had gone to that one leg instead.

> "You can't do that," he proudly said,
> A boast that spake an empty head.
> The Spartan coiled a verbal noose.
> "That stunt is done by every goose."

One of the most obvious characteristics of American humor is exaggeration. In this respect, however, it would be hard for us to excel some of the Greek epigrams. According to one of them, a certain man had a nose so long that he did not say Ζεῦ σῶσον, "Zeus save us," when he sneezed, for the simple reason that the nose was too far off for him to hear.[14] Fondness for exaggeration and ridicule is well illustrated by another epigram: "A small mouse finding little Macron asleep one summer's day dragged him into its hole by his foot. But he in the hole, though unarmed, strangled the mouse and said: 'Father Zeus, thou hast a second Heracles.' "[15]

---

[10] This is the way the quotation is given in *The Outlook,* October 10, 1928, p. 949. It is quoted with some variations in other places.

[11] Plut. *Per.* 1.5.

[12] *Ibid.* See also Diog. Laert., *Diogenes* 2.6.46, 65; Plut. *Mor.* 220A.

[13] *De Coniuratione Catilinae* 25.2. Cf. Macrob. *Sat.* 3.14.5.

[14] *Anthol. Graec.* 11.268.   [15] *Ibid.* 11.95 (W. R. Paton's translation).

Under humor of exaggeration falls the fish story. When one Galba was informed that in Sicily eels five feet long had been bought for half a denarius, he replied: "That's not strange, since they are born there so long that fishermen tie them around their waists instead of ropes."[16] In the Ganges eels grew to a length of thirty feet.[17] In the same river there was a species of fish, called *vermis* from its general appearance, which seized elephants by the trunk as they came to drink and pulled them in.[18] There are stories of fish so large that anglers had to attach their hooks to chains and use a yoke of oxen to draw their prey from the rivers.[19] A prayer of a modern fisherman runs as follows: "Lord grant that I may catch a fish so large that even I when speaking of it afterwards may have no cause to lie."

Jokes about third-rate doctors are very ancient. When a physician said to Pausanias, the son of Pleistoanax, "Sir, you are an old man," the retort came: "That happens because you never were my doctor."[20] We say that there is safety in numbers, but there was an ancient inscription which read: "I perished through a multitude of doctors."[21] Another jest runs as follows: "Marcus the doctor called yesterday on the marble Zeus; though marble and though Zeus, he is to be buried today."[22]

A certain Nicocles used to declare that physicians were fortunate because the sun beheld their successes while the earth covered their mistakes,[23] a joke which has modern parallels. Pliny,[24] after discussing some instances of medical quackery,

---

[16] Quint. *Inst.* 6.3.80. Fishermen may still be seen in Italy using ropes as belts.

[17] Pliny *Nat. Hist.* 9.4.   [18] *Ibid.* 9.46.

[19] *Ibid.* 9.44. For other fish stories see Ael. *De Nat. Anim.* 14.25; 16.12; 17.6; Plut. *Ant.* 29.3–4.

[20] Plut. *Mor.* 231A.

[21] Pliny *Nat. Hist.* 29.11. See also Dio 69.22.4. It is supposed that this jest is borrowed from a line of Menander's (Frag. 1112, Kock, *Comicorum Atticorum Fragmenta,* vol. III, 269).

[22] *Anthol. Graec.* 11.113.   [23] Antonius Melissa 1, chap. 56.

[24] *Nat. Hist.* 29.18.

bemoaned the fact that there was no law to punish the ignorance of physicians, and that there was no instance of capital
punishment having been inflicted upon them.

If one of my former students is to be trusted, there were
numerous animal doctors in antiquity. He informed me that
Caesar's army was composed of many "veterinary" legions. A
typesetter is responsible for the statement that the doctor felt
the patient's purse and said there was no hope.

The lawyer was a close second to the doctor as a butt of
jokes. On one occasion a certain Granius tried to persuade his
advocate, whose voice had become husky, to take a mixture of
cold wine and honey. The advocate said it would ruin his
voice if he did so. "Better to ruin your voice than the defendant," Granius retorted.[25]

A Sicilian too poor to hire an attorney was assigned one by a
praetor. On seeing the selection he asked the praetor to transfer the man to his opponent, feeling sure that with such a
handicap imposed upon his adversary he himself needed no
attorney.[26]

A stock character in our funny columns is the tyro musician
next door or in the flat above. He had his ancient counterpart:
e.g., "The night-raven's song bodes death, but when Demophus
sings the night-raven itself dies."[27] The instrumental musician
was subject to the same sort of criticism: "Simylus the lyre-
player killed all his neighbours by playing the whole night,
except only Origines, whom Nature had made deaf, and therefore gave him longer life in the place of hearing."[28-29]

The versifier too is a traditional laughingstock. For criticising the poetry of the tyrant, Dionysius of Syracuse, Philoxenus

---

[25] Cic. De Orat. 2.282.
[26] Ibid. 2.280. For legal humor see R. J. Bonner, "Wit and Humor in
Athenian Courts," in Class. Phil., XVII (1922), 97–103; A. H. Becker, De
Facetiis Iuridicis apud Scriptores Latinos (a German dissertation, 1896).
[27] Anthol. Graec. 11.186 (W. R. Paton's translation).
[28] Ibid. 11.187 (W. R. Paton's translation). For other jests on musicians
see Ael. Var. Hist. 14.8; Plut. Mor. 174F; 220A, F.
[29] For other jests on deaf persons see Strabo 14.2.21; Anthol. Graec. 11.251.

was imprisoned in the stone quarries. On being summoned to another recital he endured it as long as possible and then arose. "Where are you going?" asked the tyrant. "To the quarries," he replied.[30] When a versifier handed Sulla an epigram whose sole merit was its structural resemblance to the elegiac distich, he gave orders that the man be rewarded, but on condition that he should not versify thereafter.[31]

The best ancient joke which I have found on the lazy man is contained in an epigram: "Lazy Marcus, having once run in his sleep, never went to sleep again, lest he should chance to run once more."[32] The same type of jest is seen in a modern Negro story: "Rastus, your dog seems to be in pain." "No, suh, he ain't in pain—he's just lazy." "But surely he must be suffering, or he wouldn't howl like that." "Jes' plumb laziness, jes' laziness; he's sittin' on a thistle."[33]

In antiquity too there were typical jokes about certain nations. Cretans were liars and Boeotians symbolized stupidity. When a certain Caecilius, who was suspected of Judaism, wished to undertake the prosecution of Verres ("Mr. Pig"), Cicero asked: "What has a Jew to do with a pig?"[34] A lady in New Orleans improved upon Cicero's joke. As she was waiting to buy a ticket, a stranger selfishly edged his way in front of her. She glared at him coldly. "Well," he growled, "don't eat me up." "You are in no danger, sir," she said, "I am a Jewess."

A collection of witticisms which, in my opinion, is superior to any issue of *Life* or *Punch* with which I am familiar was made in the sixth (?) century after Christ by a Greek named Hierocles.[35] It consists of twenty-nine *facetiae* at the expense

---

[30] Stob. *Flor.* 13.16. Cf. Philostr. *Vit. Sophist.* 2.9 (p. 541).

[31] Cic. *Arch.* 10.25. For other jests on poets see Lucian *Demon. Vit.* 44 (p. 389); Athen. 351F; Martial 2.88.

[32] *Anthol. Graec.* 11.277 (W. R. Paton's translation).

[33] *The Outlook*, April 13, 1927, p. 449.   [34] Plut. *Cic.* 7.5.

[35] The only copies I have ever seen are of the 1873 London edition, "Ex Officina Johannis Redmayne." Smith's *Dictionary of Greek and Roman Biog-*

of the *scholasticus* ("pedant"), a word which one is tempted to translate by "Herr Professor." The collection does in fact furnish some models for German gibes at the absent-minded professor. Some of these jokes are anachronistic Irish bulls.

A pedant heard that ravens live two hundred years. Not satisfied with traditional lore, he went and bought a raven in order to make a test. When Josh Billings was informed that a toad would live four hundred years, he said that he was going to catch one and see for himself.

A pedant, wishing to train his horse to live without eating, withheld his feed. On the death of the horse the man said: "I have sustained a great loss. When I had just about taught him to go without eating, he up and died."[36] In Scott's *Waverley*[37] the same story is told of Duncan Mac-Girdie's mare. "He wanted to use her by degrees to live without meat, and just as he had put her on a straw a-day, the poor thing died." The story is well known in Germany and the United States. In the Hibernian version it is a cow whose hunger is thus subjugated.

A pedant who almost choked in his first efforts to swim vowed he would never again enter the water until he had learned to swim. To a novice whose first attempt at skiing ended with his nose furrowing the snow a companion shouted: "You jumped too late, Joe!" "Naw"—from the smother below —"I jumped too soon. Should have learned more about the game first."[38]

An absent-minded pedant tarrying in Greece was asked by a friend to take advantage of the opportunity to buy him some books. He neglected to do so and when he met his friend he explained: "I failed to receive the letter which you sent to me

raphy and Mythology thinks Hierocles must have been "a very insignificant person."

[36] Cf. *Fabulae Aesopicae Collectae,* 176 (ed. Halm).

[37] Chap. 54. See also *The Argosy,* vol. V, 143.

[38] *Everybody's,* June, 1922, p. 186.

about the books." According to *Life*,[39] a firm which had sent a dunning letter received this reply:

Dear Sirs,—In answer to your letter, I have not received same, as I do not live here now.—Yours,

NANCY WOTO.

A pedant met a pedant. "I understood that you had died." "But you see that I am even now alive." "Yes, but the man who told me is more trustworthy than you." This reminds one of the delicious humor of the well-known story of the visit of Ennius to Nasica,[40] and also of Mark Twain's comment on one occasion that the reports of his death were greatly exaggerated.

The person who plumes and peacocks himself has always been a subject for gibes. During my own college days it was the fashion for men to pad their shoulders and to wear very baggy trousers. We used to say of one of our classmates: "When X goes in to swim, he leaves his physique in the locker." A Roman epigram records the same sort of jest: "When Sertoria puts on her chalk, she puts on her face. When she has lost her chalk, she has lost her face."[41] The *ne plus ultra* of vanity is, however, manifested in a man. A pedant who had purchased a house stood at the window and asked passers-by whether the house became him.[42]

Sparta was one place where a lack of sincerity was not tolerated—at least in others. An aged Chian on a mission to this city had dyed his hair gray. During an assembly King Archidamus rose and said that the Chian was carrying a falsehood not only in his heart, but on his head.[43] To Agesilaus the Great sham was so distasteful that, when he was invited to hear a man who gave wonderful imitations of nightingales, he exclaimed: "I have often heard nightingales themselves."[44]

[39] March 23, 1922, p. 28.   [40] Cic. *De Orat.* 2.276.
[41] Baehrens, *Poetae Latini Minores*, Vol. IV, No. 46. Very similar is epigram 11.310 in the *Greek Anthology*. See also Martial 5.43; 12.23.
[42] Hierocles 11.
[43] Ael. *Var. Hist.* 7.20. Quite similar is Plut. *Mor.* 178F. See also Martial 6.57.
[44] Plut. *Mor.* 212F.

Exaggerated ego due to success was likewise an ancient afflic-
tion. Archidamus, the son of Agesilaus, thus replied to a
haughty letter of Philip after the battle of Chaeronea: "If you
measure your shadow, you will find it is no greater than before
the victory."[45] When one garland after another broke as it was
being adjusted to the head of Scipio Africanus Maior, Publius
Licinius Varus remarked: "No wonder it doesn't fit, *caput enim
magnum est*,"[46] which, being interpreted, means, "You've got a
swelled head." *Bis vincit qui se vincit in victoria* (Syrus).

Recently acquired culture is likely to lead to affectation, as in
the case of the girl who laughed and laughed till she couldn't
laff any longer. A Roman who had been to Athens returned
with his pronunciation "hatticized," saying *hinsidiae* for *in-
sidiae, Hionii* for *Ionii, chommoda* for *commoda* ("hadvan-
tages"[47] for "advantages").[48] On one occasion Mestrius Florus
told Vespasian that *plaustra*, not *plostra*, was correct. The next
day the Emperor squared accounts by saluting him as Flaurus.[49]

Nations ever find humor in long words. Mark Twain was
much amused by telescopic German word formations, which he
called not words, but alphabetical processions. During the war
the Germans built a humorous compound of thirty-six letters for
"tank," "Schützengrabenvernichtungsautomobile." This word
looks like a pigmy in comparison with one in the *Ecclesiazusae*[50]
of Aristophanes: "lopadotemachoselachogaleokranioleipsanodri-
mypotrimmatosilphioparaomelitokatakechymenokichlepikossy-
phophattoperisteralektryonoptekephalliokinklopeleiolagoosirai-
obaphetraganopterygon." This example of hyperpolysyllabic-
sesquipedalianism,[51] consisting of one hundred and seventy
Greek letters, may be translated by the simple word "hash."

No people ever took greater delight than the Greeks in mere
verbal cleverness. They were much given to *sophismata*, a

---

[45] *Ibid.* 218E-F.   [46] Cic. *De Orat.* 2.250.
[47] So Professor G. M. Lane translates *chommoda* in his *Latin Grammar*, 2071.
[48] Catullus 84.   [49] Suet. *Vesp.* 22.   [50] 1169–1175.
[51] For this word I am indebted to *The Literary Digest*, May 12, 1928, p. 83.

word which Aulus Gellius translates by *captiones,* "catches." He tells[52] how during a festival season at Athens a group of men of kindred spirits amused themselves by playing sophisms as people played dice. A coin was the reward for solving one or the penalty for failure. If a guest failed to tell in what part of the syllogism or in what word the dialectic noose lay and what premise ought not to be granted, he was fined.

Perhaps the best known of these sophisms is the following: "If you have not lost something, you have it. You have not lost horns. Therefore you have horns."[53] According to another one, "Mouse is a syllable; mouse, however, nibbles cheese; therefore syllable nibbles cheese." Seneca[54] gets a different conclusion from the same premise: "Mouse is a syllable; syllable, however, does not nibble cheese; therefore mouse does not nibble cheese."[55]

"All Cilicians are bad men," says Demodocus, "but among the Cilicians is one good man, Cinyras, yet Cinyras is a Cilician."[56] There is a modern version of this type of humor at the expense of the Germans:

> The Germans in Greek
> Are sadly to seek,
> Except only Hermann,
> And Hermann's a German.

At repartee with teeth in it the ancients were exceedingly clever. Iphicrates, a shoemaker's son, was once reviled for his mean birth by a descendant of the famous Harmodius. He retorted: "My nobility begins in me, but yours ends in you."[57] On one occasion the orator Demades cried out to Phocion: "The

---

[52] *Noct. Att.* 18.13.
[53] Diog. Laert. *Chrysippus* 7.11.187; *idem, Diogenes* 2.6.38; Sen. *Ep.* 5.49.8. Cf. Aul. Gell 18.2.9; Mart. Capella 4.327.
[54] Sen. *Ep.* 5.48.6.
[55] For other nonsensical syllogisms see Cic. *De Nat. Deor.* 3.23, 25; Aul. Gell. 18.5.10; 18.13; Lucian *Vitarum Auctio* 24.
[56] *Anthol. Graec.* 11.236. Of the same type are epigrams on the Chians by Demodocus (*ibid.* 11.235) and on the Lerians by Phocylides (Strabo 10.5.12).
[57] Plut. *Mor.* 187B.

Athenians will kill you if they become mad." Phocion answered: "And you, if they regain their senses."[58] When Salinator boasted to Quintus Fabius Maximus, "Thanks to me, you have regained Tarentum," he paved the way for the retort: "By all means, for unless you had lost it I should never have regained it."[59]

Considerable droll and whimsical humor is extant. Vatinius, who had been stoned while giving a gladiatorial exhibition, influenced the aediles to proclaim that nothing should be thrown into the arena except fruit (*pomum*). When Cascellius, who was quite a wag, was asked whether a pine cone was fruit, he replied: "It is if you are going to throw it at Vatinius."[60]

Today the warning "Look out! Look out!" sometimes follows instead of preceding the danger. A man who accidentally struck Cato yelled *"Cave!"* Cato asked: "Are you carrying anything besides the box?"[61]

Aristides was once sent on an embassy with Themistocles, with whom he was not on good terms. He proposed that, on reaching the border of their country, they should leave their enmity there, explaining that they could resume it on their return.[62]

Was any debtor ever more cheerful than Caesar? He is quoted as saying that he needed 25,000,000 sesterces in order to have nothing at all.[63]

On coming to a town with pale-faced inhabitants Stratonicus asked whether the water was drinkable. "We drink it," said the water-drawers. "Then," replied he, "it is not drinkable."[64] Another wag visiting his farm asked whether the water from a certain well was potable. When assured that his parents had

[58] *Ibid.* 811A.
[59] Cic. *Cato* 11. For another retort see "Themistocles and the Seriphian," in *The Class. Journ.,* XVII (1922), 225–226.
[60] Macrob. 2.6.1.
[61] Cic. *De Orat.* 2.279. Cf. Diog. Laert. *Diogenes* 2.6.41, 66.
[62] Plut. *Mor.* 186B.   [63] Appian *Bell. Civ.* 2.2.8.   [64] Athen. 352A.

drunk from that very well, he asked: "And how long necks did they have that they were able to drink at such a depth?"[65]

The punning directions of the *magister bibendi*, ἢ πῖθι ἢ ἄπιθι, or, as the Latin puts it, *aut bibat aut abeat*,[66] would seem to indicate that at banquets the ancients were as much opposed to dry humor as we are. The ancient vintage of drinking humor must have been rather large. A Greek lady, who, on being presented with a diminutive vessel of wine, was told that it was sixteen years old, responded: "And small indeed for its age."[67] This reminds one of Cicero's comment[68] when he was invited to sample some Falernian wine forty years old: *Bene aetatem fert*.

When dishes that were served to King Ptolemy first were emptied before reaching Phyromachus, the latter asked: "Ptolemy, am I drunk, or do I just fancy that these things are going round?"[69] In this connection one thinks of a joke attributed to a great Italian archaeologist. A portion of the floor of the palace of Augustus upon the Palatine Hill has been pretty severely twisted by earthquakes, so that it gives an up-hill-and-down-dale effect. The archaeologist informed some inquisitive Italian guides that the floor was a product of the ingenuity of Augustus and was designed so that guests losing their equilibrium might be able to find some place in which they could stand upright. This information is said to have been passed on to tourists.

There is a better authenticated story of the Emperor Augustus. As he was engaged in dismissing an officer with dishonor, the soldier kept interrupting him with the question: "What shall I say to my father?" Augustus replied: "Tell him that I incurred your displeasure."[70]

A good example of grim humor is to be found in Herodotus's account of the battle of Thermopylae. The Spartan Dieneces, informed that the Medes shot arrows in such numbers that they

---

[65] Hierocles *Facetiae* 18.
[66] Cic. *Tusc.* 5.118.
[67] Athen. 584B.
[68] Macrob. *Sat.* 2.3.2.
[69] Athen. 245F. For another story see Plut. *Pyrrh.* 8.5.
[70] Quint. *Inst.* 6.3.64.

darkened the sun, replied: "If the Medes conceal the sun from us, we shall fight in the shade and not in the sun."[71]

Perhaps no jest ever had a greater military value than one uttered by Hannibal. Just before the battle of Cannae he and a few followers rode to an eminence to get a view of the Romans forming in ranks. When Gisco remarked that the number of the enemy was amazing, Hannibal replied with a serious air: "Another circumstance much more wonderful than this has escaped your notice, Gisco." Upon being asked what it was, Hannibal replied: "It is that among all those men before you there is not one named Gisco." This started all the auditors to laughing. The jest spread among the soldiers and created great assurance in them, since they regarded their commander's levity in the face of danger as due to his confidence of success.[72]

Soldiers' slang is picturesque. It is largely the humor of miscalling things and transferring familiar names to things unfamiliar. Servius[73] says that soldiers derived names for their military devices from names of animals. One thinks of such names as *caput porci, corvus, corax, equus, ericius, lupus, muli Mariani, musculus, onager, porculus, scorpio, sucula,* and *testudo.* During the World War we read of "elephants" (balloons), "flying pigs," "whippets," "penguins," and many other machines with similar names not only in English, but also in French, German, and Italian.

To certain kinds of defences at Alesia the legionaries gave the nicknames *lilia, cippi,* and *stimuli,*[74] words which were familiar in far different senses to the soldiers who had been country boys in Italy. The English Tommy called Missouri mules "Shetland ponies," the same type of humor that caused the Romans to call the elephants in Pyrrhus's army "Lucanian cows."[75]

---

[71] Herod. 7.226. See John A. Scott, "The Spartan Repartee in Herodotus vii. 226," in *The Class. Journ.,* X (1915), 178.
[72] Plut. *Fab. Max.* 15.2–3.   [73] On *Aeneid* 9.503.
[74] Caes. *Bell. Gall.* 7.73.5–9.
[75] See, for example, Pliny *Nat. Hist.* 8.16. For ancient military slang see W. Heraeus, "Die Römische Soldatensprache," in *Archiv für Lateinische Lexi-*

Had all ancient literature come down to us without evidence of authorship, the greater frequency of the jokes upon women would enable us to conclude that men dominated the literary profession. The triteness of such jests never limits their repetition.

A man who heard a bereaved husband lament that his wife had hanged herself on a fig tree remarked: "Please give me a shoot from that tree to plant."[76] This reminds one of a jest made by Diogenes.[77] As he looked at an olive tree on which some women had been hanged, he exclaimed: "I wish all trees bore such fruit!"

A fragment of Hipponax[78] runs somewhat as follows:

> Two days there are in woman's life
> That she makes man the happiest,
> The day that she becomes his bride,
> And when a corpse she's laid to rest.

Someone asked Democritus why, since he was a large man, he had married a small wife. He explained that in picking out an evil he had chosen the smallest.[79] When the question whether it was better to marry or not was put to Socrates he replied: "Whichever you do, you will repent it."[80] As regards the proper age for men to marry, Diogenes said: "For young men, not yet; for older men, never."[81]

---

cographie, XII (1902), 255–280; I. G. Kempf, "Romanorum Sermonis Castrensis Reliquiae Collectae et Illustratae," in *Jahrbücher für Classische Philologie,* Suppl. XXVI (1901), 337–400. For slang in general see W. W. Baker, "Slang, Ancient and Modern," in *The Class. Weekly,* II (1909), 210–213.

[76] Cic. *De Orat.* 2.278; Quint. *Inst.* 6.3.88.

[77] Diog. Laert. *Diogenes* 2.6.52. Compare Plut. *Ant.* 70.3.

[78] Bergk, *Poetae Lyrici Graeci*⁴, vol. II, 472, Frag. 29. See also *Anthol. Graec.* 11.381, which is rendered by Professor Shorey in *Classical Philology,* XXIV (1929), 108, as follows:

> "A woman's two best days are when she's mated,
> And secondly the day she's cremated."

[79] Antonius Melissa 2, chap. 34.   [80] Diog. Laert. *Socrates* 5.16.33.

[81] Diog. Laert. *Diogenes* 2.6.54. For other jests on marriage see Antiphanes, Frag. 221, 292 (Kock); Anaxandrides, Frag. 52 (Kock); Plut. *Mor.* 804B; *Anthol. Graec.* 11.375; Antonius Melissa 2, chap. 34.

Metellus Numidicus came to the conclusion that we can't get along with women and that we can't get along without them.[82] A modern novel makes Menelaus say of Helen: "I can't do without her, and I don't know what to do with her."[83]

A modern story tells how a widow confided to her children that she was going to marry the family doctor. "Bully for you, ma!" exclaimed one of them. "Does Dr. Jones know it?" There is also the well-known case of a girl who married a struggling young man. Doubtless many a Greek man did not marry, but was married (οὐκ ἔγημεν, ἀλλ' ἐγήματο).[84] An article called "Wooing and the Wooed"[85] shows that the ancient woman did not always wait supinely for something to turn up.

We do not find much evidence of dissatisfaction of Greek women with their lot. Like Lot's wife, they had to submit to their lot. It has been said that present-day intellectual, college-bred women do not marry. There is some classical precedent for this. Minerva, too, who was the goddess of wisdom, failed to marry. *Amare et sapere vix deo conceditur* (Syrus).

A standard type of joke is that on the mother-in-law. It may be as old as the world, although I can find no reference to it in the accounts of Creation.[86] One example from the classics will suffice. In Leptis, a city in Libya, it was the custom for the bride on the day after the wedding to send someone to ask her mother-in-law to loan her a boiler. This her new relative would refuse to do, and, what is more, would say that she did not have any. All this was done with the idea that the bride, having seen at the outset the bad side of her mother-in-law's charac-

---

[82] Aul. Gell. 1.6.2. See Menander Frag. 651 (Kock, vol. III, 192); Aristoph. *Lysist.* 1039 and Rogers's note *ad loc.*

[83] John Erskine, *The Private Life of Helen of Troy*, p. 280.

[84] Anacreon, Frag. 86 (Bergk, vol. III, 278). Cf. Antiphanes in Meineke, *Fragmenta Comicorum Graecorum*, vol. III, 24. See also Livy, 1.46.6; Tac. *Ann.* 12.1.

[85] By K. P. Harrington, in *The Class. Journ.*, XVII (1921), 132–140. See also Phaedrus 2.2.

[86] Plut. *Comparison of Lycurgus and Numa* 3.7, says that the first woman to quarrel with her mother-in-law was Thalaea, wife of Pinarius, in the reign of Tarquinius Superbus.

ter, might take any subsequent harsh treatment as a matter of course.[87] I know of no mother-in-law joke superior to the following: One morning a judge who was about to open court received a note from his court-crier. It read: "Dear Judge, My wife's mother died last evening. Hence I shall be unable to cry today."

If mothers-in-law are so terrible,[88] one wonders why the Law feels it necessary to take action against bigamists, not to mention polygamists, while the mothers-in-law are still alive.

Step-mothers, however, were a much more frequent target than mothers-in-law. Their cruelty is a commonplace in ancient literature[89] and in fact almost every reference to them in Greek and Latin dictionaries contains something uncomplimentary. "To complain to one's step-mother" was proverbial in Latin for futility.[90]

By one of the laws of Charondas it was ordained that those who cared so little for the happiness of their children as to place a step-mother over them should be excluded from the councils of the state.[91] In one of Seneca's *Controversiae* (4.5) the question is raised whether a physician who cured his father is justified in refusing to treat his step-mother. Plutarch[92] preserves the story of a man who threw a stone at a dog. When it hit his step-mother instead, he exclaimed: "Not so bad."

Although references to domineering wives are not infrequent,[93] Socrates is the proverbial hen-pecked husband. After roundly upbraiding Socrates on one occasion, Xanthippe poured water on him. Socrates remarked: "Did I not tell you that Xanthippe thundering would cause rain, too?"[94] When Alcibiades in wonder asked Socrates why he did not drive his terma-

---

[87] Plut. *Mor.* 143A.
[88] See Juvenal 6.231–241.
[89] See Jerram on Eurip. *Alc.* 305.
[90] Plaut. *Pseud.* 314.
[91] Diod. Sic. 12.12.1–2.
[92] *Mor.* 467C. See also *De Fluviis* 8.4.
[93] Plut. *Them.* 18.5, and *Cato Maior* 8.2. See also *Anthol. Graec.* 9.167; Hesiod *Opera et Dies* 54–82; Serv. on Virg. *Buc.* 6.42.
[94] Diog. Laert. *Socrates* 5.17.36. Compare Plut. *Mor.* 461E.

gant wife from the house, he replied in effect: "The nagging I get at home keeps me in training to endure petulance and wrong outside."[95] In a Menippean satire Varro says that the short-comings of a wife should be removed or endured. "Whoever removes them makes his wife easier to live with; whoever endures them makes himself better."[96]

Reluctance of women to reveal their age is nothing new. When Fabia, the daughter of Dolabella, insisted that her age was thirty, Cicero[97] agreed: "I believe it; for I've been hearing that for twenty years." A modern jest allows women to age a little in an equal period: "What will the modern girl be twenty years from now?" "Oh, about three years older."

The ancients regarded loquacity as one of the "strongest weaknesses" of the female sex. Aelian[98] tells us that it is only the male cicada that knows how to sing, that the female is mute, and that, as is the case with the modest bride, silence is becoming to her. Xenarchus[99] envies the male cicada because its wife has no voice.

> Of harvest flies, the ancients say,
> The male alone knows how to screech.
> O happy Mister Harvest Fly,
> Whose wife doth lack the gift of speech.

Among the groups of portents so often mentioned by Livy[100] there occurs very frequently the one of the speaking ox, almost always in the feminine. It seems to me that *bos locuta est* should have been less portentous than *bos locutus est*.

In the story of Echo and Narcissus, as told by Ovid,[101] Echo always has the last say, *verba novissima*.[102] A recent jest runs as follows: "What were your father's last words?" "Father had no last words. Mother was with him to the end."

Phidias's statue of Venus at Elis showed the goddess resting

---

[95] Aul. Gell. 1.17. [96] *Ibid.* [97] Quint. *Inst.* 6.3.73.
[98] *De Nat. Anim.* 1.20. [99] As quoted by Athen. 559A.
[100] 3.10.6; 27.11.4; 28.11.4; 35.21.5; 41.13.1; 41.21.13; 43.13.3.
[101] *Met.* 3.380–392. [102] *Ibid.* 3.361.

one foot on a tortoise, an animal that was a symbol of silence and domesticity,[103] never even going out of the house. Κόσμος ὀλιγομυθίη γυναικί, says Democritus.[104]

Loquacity is not confined to women, however. When a barber asked King Archelaus how he should trim his Majesty, the king replied: "In silence."[105] A male chatterbox who told a woman that he had just visited the Hellespont was asked why he did not go to the chief city, Sigeum[106] (cf. σιγή, "silence"). The loquacious sophist Polemo gave orders that his tomb be closed while he was still alive, so that the sun should never see him reduced to silence.[107] Petronius[108] called Cerberus a forensic attorney, "apparently because of his three jaws or the cumulative glibness of three tongues."[109] *Miserum est tacere cogi quod cupis loqui* (Syrus).[110]

The anecdotal humor of antiquity is good. The story goes that in his youth Virgil was a groom in the imperial stables of Augustus. With each new evidence of his skill in appraising animals, the Emperor would increase his allowance of bread. Finally, Augustus, who was in doubt whether he was really the son of Octavius, consulted Virgil about the matter. "Thou art the son of a baker," said Virgil. In amazement Augustus asked how he knew that. Virgil replied: "When I proclaimed and predicted certain things which could not have been understood or known except by the wisest and greatest of men, thou, the

---

[103] Plut. *Mor.* 142D.

[104] Apud Stob. *Flor.* 74.38. Compare *tacita bonast mulier semper quam loquens* (Plaut. *Rud.* 1114). See also Democritus, Frag. 110 and 274 (Diels, *Die Fragmente der Vorsokratiker*, 1903).

[105] Plut. *Mor.* 509A.

[106] Athen. 584D. The play is upon the fanciful derivation from σιγή, "silence."

[107] Philostr. *Vit. Sophist.* 2.11 (p. 544).

[108] Fulgentius, p. 99 (Teubner edition).

[109] M. Bloomfield, *Cerberus, the Dog of Hades*, The Open Court Publishing Co., Chicago, 1905, p. 7.

[110] On feminine inability to keep a secret see Plut. *Mor.* 507B–F; *idem, Cato Maior* 9.6; Antiphanes, Frag. 253 (Kock, vol. II, 120); Tac. *Ann.* 1.5.

prince of the world, again and again bade me be rewarded with loaves of bread, a thing which was the act of a baker or a baker's son." "Well," said Augustus, "from now on you will be rewarded not by a baker, but by a generous prince."[111]

The talking bird has long been a source of funny stories. When Augustus was returning exultant from his victory at Actium, he was greeted by a raven which had been taught to say: *Ave Caesar victor imperator!* He bought it for 20,000 sesterces. An employee of the tradesman, feeling aggrieved because his master had not shared the imperial generosity with him, told Caesar that there was still another raven and asked the Emperor to have it brought. Its greeting was: *Ave victor imperator Antoni!* In the land of Janus, the double-faced, the resourceful dealer could not consistently be punished. In spite of his duplicity Augustus thought that such forehandedness should not go entirely unrewarded, and so merely ordered him to share the largess with his employee.[112]

After this incident Augustus bought a parrot[113] and a magpie which had been taught to greet him. Subsequently a shoemaker tried to teach a raven to utter a greeting, but, finding the bird unresponsive, he would say in disgust: "Work and money wasted." Finally he did manage to teach the bird the imperial greeting, but when Augustus heard it, he said he had enough of such birds at home. At this juncture the bird exclaimed: "Work and money wasted." Thereupon Augustus laughed, and, according to the quaint phraseology of the Latin, "bade the bird be bought for as large a sum as he had bought none previously."[114]

Among the Romans even death became a subject for levity. As Vespasian felt his end approaching, he said: "I think I am

---

[111] This story was interpolated in the life of Virgil by Suetonius. See A. Reifferscheid, *C. Suetoni Tranquilli praeter Caesarum Libros Reliquiae,* pp. 55–56, apparatus criticus.

[112] Macrob. *Sat.* 2.4.29.

[113] With regard to the parrot see *Anthol. Graec.* 9.562.

[114] Macrob. *Sat.* 2.4.30. For another raven story see Pliny *Nat. Hist.* 10.121.

becoming a god."[115] Nero declared that mushrooms were the food of the gods, since his father Claudius had become a god by eating them.[116] In the *Apocolocyntosis*[117] ("Pumpkinification") Claudius is represented as realizing that he was dead only when he saw his own funeral. The dying words of Nero, the musician and actor, were *Qualis artifex pereo!*[118]

A gruesome practical joke was perpetrated by Tiberius. A man whispered into the ears of a corpse a message for Augustus. Tiberius had the man executed in order that he might carry the message himself.[119]

In spite of several aspects of wit and humor upon which this paper does not touch,[120] I believe that it is fairly representative of the mirth-making side of the ancient character. The Greeks seem to have been more inclined to combine wisdom with wit.

It does seem that the number of types of jokes is fairly limited, but that their garb is as fickle as fancy. A quotation

---

[115] Suet. *Vesp.* 23.
[116] Suet. *Nero* 33; Xiphilinus 146.30–32 (R. Stephanus).
[117] 12.3.   [118] Suet. *Nero* 49.   [119] Dio 57.14.1–2.
[120] Groups of witticisms and humorous incidents may be found in many ancient authors, e.g.: Athen. 245D–246C; 337D–338D; 583F–585F; Cic. *De Orat.* 2.216–287; Macrob. *Sat.* 2.3.1—2.6.6; Plut. *Apophthegms;* Plut. *Cic.* 38; Quint. *Inst.* 6.3.1–102; Stob. *Flor.;* Suet. *Vesp.* 22–25. Witticisms are scattered here and there in the works of Diogenes Laertius, Plutarch, Suetonius, and other writers. The *Cena Trimalchionis* and the *Apocolocyntosis* should not be omitted. See also E. Wölfflin, *Archiv für Lat. Lex. und Gram.,* I (1884), 381–389; *Harper's Dictionary of Classical Literature and Antiquities* s.vv. *Epigramma, Jests, Puns;* J. W. Hewitt, "The Humor of the Greek Anthology," in *The Class. Journ.,* XVII, 66–76; J. W. Hewitt, "Homeric Laughter," *ibid.,* XXIII, 436–447; J. W. Hewitt, "Humor in Homer and in Vergil," in *The Class. Weekly,* XXII (1929), 169–172, 177–181; W. I. Hunt, "Homeric Wit and Humor," in *Trans. Am. Phil. Assn.,* XXI (1890), 48–58; T. Oesterlen, *Komik und Humor bei Horaz,* Stuttgart, Metzler, 1885; L. Lersch, *Die Sprachphilosophie der Alten,* Bonn, König, 1838–41, III, 11–17; J. O. Lofberg, "Quotiens Revocatum," in *The Class. Weekly,* XII (1919), 164; J. O. Lofberg, " 'Unmixed Milk' Again," in *Class. Phil.,* XVI (1921), 389–391; Stephanus, *Apophthegmata Graeca Regum . . .* (1868). More extensive than any of these references is F. A. Paley, *Greek Wit, A Collection of Smart Sayings and Anecdotes Translated from Greek Prose Writers,* London, 1881. A recent addition to this list is H. E. Wedeck, *Humor in Varro, and Other Essays,* Oxford, B. H. Blackwell, 1929; cf., too, W. N. Bates, *Euripides: A Student of Human Nature,* Philadelphia, Univ. of Penna. Press, 1930, pp. 51–56.

from *Life* (March 23, 1922) echoes my own feeling about many of our own witticisms:

"What do you think of the modern jokes?"

"Oh, they are about the same as the old ones."

"Yes, and a little older, eh?"

Perhaps, in a way, our own jokes are a form of ancestor worship.

UNIVERSITY OF MICHIGAN

SOME PHASES OF ROMAN SOCIAL USAGES

Walton Brooks McDaniel

WHILE various books too well known to scholars to be listed here discuss and describe the chief social functions of the Romans, such as the morning call, a wedding, and a dinner party, and incidentally mention some of the traditional conventions that controlled the deportment of the participant, there seems to be no work in any of the languages familiar to the present writer that deals with Roman society from the specific point of view of a modern book on etiquette and good manners.[1] For this reason he has been gathering during the many years that he has been specializing in the field of Greek and Roman private life passages in the ancient authors which concern the social usages of those times. It must inevitably be a rather imperfect picture that will eventually result, but it should be more instructive to the scholar and general reader than the incoherent impressions which he is otherwise likely to retain from so many scattered references. But the completion of this undertaking belongs to an uncertain future.

Perhaps the reason why antiquarians have engaged in this field of research in only sporadic fashion is because, while good manners are of eternal concern to man—and of more mayhap to woman—their usual associate, etiquette, is something that many persons possessed too abundantly, shall I say, of either a sense of humor or of feelings of pride mention with a smile of derision or with apologies. Social conventions have often included so much that seems artificial, arbitrary, and absurd that any set code is likely to be slurred as constituting a sorry substitute for true and natural politeness. To investigate a system

---

[1] A doctoral thesis covering a limited field, *Roman Etiquette of the Late Republic as Revealed by the Correspondence of Cicero* by A. Bertha Miller, University of Pennsylvania, 1914, proved to be of such interest that the edition was long ago exhausted.

two thousand years dead does not make an immediate appeal. So far, indeed, does the disrepute of etiquette extend that a modern didactic treatise on manners and the rules of social intercourse in the world of fashion is a work that many of our contemporaries would refuse to own, and if they do own one, they resort to it as surreptitiously as respectable people used to read a pornographic novel, and they will disclaim possessing it as they might a dream-book, a manual on how to play the races, or, until recently, a book of receipts for the making of non-poisonous alcoholic beverages. In other words, the latest edition of Emily Post's book of instructions for the "would-be" never nestles on the drawing-room table within the same book-ends with the family genealogy, presentation copies from authors of enviable acquaintance, and the Bible or Book of Common Prayer. One must look for it in the boot box or the cedar chest.

From the Romans we have no manual of manners, no cyclo-paedia of social usage, although they seem to have had certain books of that type.[2] If Pliny the Elder had only shown a little less interest in the deportment of wild animals, the conduct of insects and the behavior of minerals, and used the space to give us the formula of introduction that Dido ought to have used in presenting Aeneas to Anna—or was it Anna to Aeneas?—to tell us whether Tullia ever could have taken a walk with a young *eques* without the company of a supernumerary Terentia, or even whether women gave dinner parties of their own and paid formal calls on one another leaving their papyrus cards, we should have been grateful; for Pliny belonged to the élite of his age. But even his most catholic and unnatural *Natural History* has no chapter on etiquette, and we can thank him here and there for only the illumination of a flickering candle where we need the concentration of a searchlight.

It has seemed to me that it might appeal to general scholarly interest to which, to some extent at least, a memorial volume in

[2] Cf. *e.g.* Ovid *Trist.* 2.488.

honor of a man eminent in far-reaching studies, may properly cater, to present a few of the minutiae of etiquette as they appear among the Romans, indicate some of their interest in style and in the life of fashion, and note some of their ideas about good and bad manners. It is the character of the minute points upon which Mrs. Grundy was even then insisting which shows how powerful she was in an age which readers may have imagined was spared most of her vexations. To realize how complex and exacting a social life those Romans lived, whom the untutored often suppose to have been but barely removed from barbarism, seems to the writer as important as to visualize their bloody battlefields and follow their politics from consulship to consulship.

Besides its merely human interest a study of the polite usages of different countries and different ages is conducive to the spirit of tolerance. We find the widest divergence in practice between foreigners and our compatriots of an equal degree of breeding. Men will still quarrel over which is the least indelicate way to eat an egg or a succulent fruit, and the respective merits of the concave and convex sides of a fork can set guests of different nationalities at hectic variance. One of the most delightful men socially whom I have ever met showed the supreme skill of a master mason in erecting on the back of his fork a leaning tower of food that never collapsed unseasonably thanks to the knife that he had used as a constructing tool. He once explained to me that such dexterity and necessarily also sinisterity were normal in good society in his land, and, as a matter of fact, this was about the truth of the matter.

The Roman had a disposition that would take kindly, it would seem, to a code of etiquette. Various formative factors were at work. Militarism in the early days taught him the value of discipline and habituated him to self-control. He was a ritualist in his religion. The performance of its ceremonies made him conscious daily of the importance of precision, and of the virtue of doing things exactly right in accordance with traditions which were hallowed by the subscription of the whole community to them. He was conservative to a proverbial degree. His instinct for preserving what had been tried and tested made him the lawmaker and lawgiver. A custom once established was likely to be continued. If it became incompatible with the requirements of life in a later age, it would be modified rather than abolished. Again, the Roman was no individualist: he liked to "follow the crowd." Moreover, even in the range of art, he could not escape his tendency to formalism. Not to speak of painting or sculpture, a reading of Quintilian's *Manual on Oratory* alone makes one uncomfortably aware of it for the field of public speaking. Again, now as anciently, if one would enjoy fully the landscape gardening of a typical Italian villa, one ought to be a geometrician: it is so formal. On the other hand, the Roman was so utilitarian in his habit of mind and action that he was ready to assimilate the offerings of other nations in lines in which he was weak.[3] He felt a profound respect for his own traditional conventions, but just as soon as he recognized Hellenic superiority in the art of social living as in the other arts, he registered his protests of national pride and then succumbed.

We may carry the thought further. The Romans loved show. *Far figura* is no new heart-desire of an Italian breast. Life at Rome was externalized. A passion for pageantry and parade possessed all ranks. Italians have always been a processional people. Of old, it was now a triumph that glorified the streets with its pomp and pride, now a funeral that filled them with din and gloom. Weddings meant a merry march from the home of the bride to that of her new husband. Religious rites were constantly claiming the thoroughfares for processions of priests and worshippers. Troops must have been tramping to the music of their horn-blowers and trumpeters at all seasons, outward or inward bound. The ceremonial of a splendid social life was, therefore, sure of welcome when there was an increase

[3] Cf. Athen. 6.106 = 273 E–F.

of wealth and luxury. While, however, pomp and ceremony were dear to them, these had to be well-ordered and conform to the different levels of social and political position. Roman society was graded. Each stratum carried its own social obligations as well as privileges. If you belonged to the senatorial order, certain things were expected of you that were pretty onerous, and there were certain things that you could not do. Moreover, there was no homogeneity of democracy, no chance to hide. The orders were set apart for all to see by uniforms as well as by financial rating and by eligibility to certain offices of state.

With the influx of riches and luxury, the upper classes developed a deep interest in style and fashion. Mrs. Grundy came into her own, as she always does, and "keeping up with the Joneses" became a gruelling, impoverishing, and demoralizing occupation of wealthy and aristocratic rivals and, of course, of the aspiring newly rich. The climbers were always liable to break themselves, even as the frog burst in imitation of the ox— the fable[4] that points this very moral in one of Martial's cleverest epigrams.[5]

Although the Romans were by race so suited to develop a punctilious system of etiquette under the instruction of peoples who were more advanced in the social arts, the Greeks and Etruscans, yet there was nothing in their native traditions or in their own natures that would lead us to expect any special aptitude for the development of the finer amenities of human intercourse. Upon the whole, they are not overly interested in good manners. These, we may add, are only loosely connected with etiquette, anyway, being based primarily, of course, not on conventions at all, but upon qualities of the heart. In the early centuries of their history, in particular, the Romans appear admirable for many qualities, but none the less, a stern, graceless, utilitarian people. We cannot say that they were naturally

[4] Phaedr. 1.24: inops potentem dum vult imitari, perit.
[5] Mart. 10.79.

considerate of the rights and feelings of others or innately sensitive, refined, and delicate. The instincts of a Pliny or a Seneca were exceptional.

When an investigator takes a comprehensive view of polite society during, let us say, the first century of our era, he must recognize at once the most important characteristic that differentiates it from our own, it was man-made and, like every other phase of ancient life, run by man. The exacting nature of either a business or a professional career of prominence in our country and the greater leisure of American women, added to the superior grace that Aglaia conferred on the sex for the management of society—and men, has led the latter to relinquish to their expert partners a major share in the gratifications of social functions and to allow them the mastery of the etiquette that is to be imposed. Not so, two millennia ago. In the Rome of that time, it is not Gaia who holds the sunrise reception—she, we trust, was still in bed—it is not Gaia who sends out invitations for an author's reading—it might have been much less a bore— it isn't Gaia who plays her game of ball, bathes herself into an appetite and then presides at the top of the lowest couch at a dinner party with the guest of honor next above her—not Gaia but Gaius. Think of the far-reaching drastic consequences of the Roman social attitude. No male of that race who had graduated from his gown of boyhood was ever "taken" to an afternoon tea, and it wasn't because Rome knew no such beverage but because he was *dux* and *duxit* from the day he wed until the day he died.

And yet, although man was the protagonist at every gathering and in all the relationships of human intercourse, the number of social functions already in existence was impressive. We may fairly conclude that a Roman of eminence who satisfied all the obligations of his position led a life comparable in its social duties to the career of a queen of fashion in a modern metropolis. Morning receptions and dinner parties came with some regularity. His family or families of friends were always having such sporadic events as birthdays, betrothals, marriages, and funerals. Ceremonies attendant upon the assumption of the manly gown, the laticlave, or political office, claimed his presence. The signing of a will was a semisocial function, the *recitatio* a compelling one. New Year's brought public as well as private duties. Festivals like the Matronalia and Saturnalia were time-exacting. The law courts imposed social duties quite unknown to ours. Farewell parties and coming-home parties were expected among the élite. To fill in the interstices, we have those calls of condolence and of congratulation that disease, calamity, and death, and births, promotions, and enrichments respectively occasion. Nor does even this summary exhaust the possibilities of the social calendar of a mere man. His wife would be present at many of these functions but she was—"taken."

Since marriage began social life for the Roman woman and all but began it for most men, we may well consider that topic first, although in only a few selected particulars. It is well known that a Roman union did not postulate love before its consummation nor even necessarily thereafter. This had some effect upon the etiquette of marital behavior. We wonder whether it was a factor in the rather puzzling conduct of Cato who ejected from the senate a man who kissed his wife in the presence of his daughter. Had he been a bit too amative for the Roman *mariage de raison?* Was it such an unusual sight as to shock the daughter and make her inform against an uxorious father? But Plutarch,[6] who chronicles this scandal in wedlock, has perhaps the right of the matter in his interpretation that conjugal endearments as well as family bickerings should be private.

We do find, however, one unsolvable enigma in the ceremony of marrying. As all students of the subject know, there was a sort of anticipation of our bridal custom of having the new wife toss her bouquet among the bridesmaids or even among the

---

[6] Plut. *Coniug. Praec.* 13 = 139E.

women of the company at large in order to secure for the girl who gets it (elderly spinsters usually forbear to scramble) the omen of an early marriage. All this a Roman would find entirely in accord with his conception of the way signs work, but why does he tell us—it is Festus[7] this time—that his contemporaries staged a similar contest at their weddings without allowing us to understand the psychology of it? The torch of white thorn wood which had lighted the bride in the marriage procession to her new home was thrown among the guests. They, thereupon, constituting themselves two parties representing respectively the bride and groom fought to secure it from each other, because, if the wife was able to put it under her husband's bed on the wedding night or he on his part could have it burned in some tomb, it foretokened an early death for the unsuccessful. But why should the couple be so indelicate as to resort to magic before they could even guess which ought to die first for the felicity or the relief of the other?

Incidentally, we may note how contrary in spirit this life and death scramble was to the conduct of Tiberius Gracchus when confronted with a similar prognostic omen.[8] He found a pair of snakes upon his bed. Although these animals were domesticated as ratters, their appearance in such a place together was obviously a prodigy. Diviners advised neither to kill them both nor to spare them both. The death of the male as representing his genius would mean his own passing, that of the female, as his wife's Juno, hers. He, therefore, slew the male, because Cornelia was younger and very dear to him, and not long after, he died. The tale, however, may seem to be somewhat marred from the point of view of modern cynicism as an illustration of conjugal devotion by the fact that he left her with one dozen children to bring up.

Etiquette is never so imperious as at weddings. It even dictates a different scale of joy and ceremony for the widow or divorcée who is marrying again. The latter are thought to

[7] Fest. 289M (Linds. 364).   [8] Plut. *Tib. Gracch.* 1.

show good taste, if they attenuate somewhat the splendor and publicity of their wedding on a second or higher venture, but not, fortunately, according to the number. Otherwise for some there might come a vanishing point. In any case, the woman who has been separated from her mate by either law or death may not remarry in the perfume of orange blossoms and the white of maidenhood, nor wear the white veil of virginal modesty. A matron of honor is all the feminine attendance that her major experience is estimated to need. But she may have her father give her away a second time. To that sort of generosity modern etiquette seems to set no limit. How much this appears to accord with ancient spirit and with the conventions of two millennia ago! Maidens then avoided a holiday for their wedding as they do now, but the widow deliberately picked one for hers. The polymath Varro,[9] who knew everything, or at any rate, wrote on everything, said that virgins were married weeping but the others rejoicing and that nothing should be done on a holiday in heaviness of heart or by compulsion. Plutarch,[9] on the other hand, queries whether the reason was not because maidens ought to be married in the presence of a large company and numbers are difficult to assemble on a holiday: there are so many conflicting diversions. Women, he continues, are ashamed to marry a second husband while their first is still alive—the good man is writing eighteen centuries ago—and they grieve to do it, even when he is dead, and so it is that they prefer for weddings subsequent to the first the social solitude of a holiday.

From ancient sources we can recover a few special points of etiquette concerned with the treatment to be accorded woman. Thus, Plutarch in his *Quaestiones Romanae* takes up various puzzling questions of Roman social usage and tries to solve them. Sometimes, it must be admitted, he theorizes in a rather fatuous fashion. Of considerable human interest is his inquiry[10]

[9] Plut. *Quaest. Rom.* 105 = 289 A–B; cf. Macrob. 1.15.21.
[10] Plut. *Quaest. Rom.* 9 = 266B.

why a man who has gone into the country or on a long journey
and left his wife at home sends a messenger ahead of his return
to apprize his mate of his near arrival. His first explanation of
this rule of etiquette bases it on a feeling of delicacy. The husband trusts his wife not to misbehave and so wishes to avoid
coming upon her unannounced, as if to catch her in a possible
failing. Another conjecture offered is that he hopes by sending her the glad news of his coming to heighten the joyousness
of his actual reception. Or he desires to have news of her to
learn whether he is to find her at home in good condition and
eager to greet him when he arrives. Finally, there may be another motive. The absence of the man of the house sometimes
upsets the morale of the home and over-busies the mistress of it.
She needs time to restore the discipline of the fussing slaves and
the quiet that insures her husband a calm and agreeable restoration to his family.

Marriage may bring us, properly enough, to children as our
next topic, and again for scattered comment. We begin with
their birth. First and last, etiquette has always used a good
deal of symbolism. It is a familiar fact that the practice of
hanging crêpe or flowers on the door to announce a death in the
house had its antecedent in Rome in the display of branches of
pine[11] or cypress[12] there. Some may not know, however, that
in modern Sicily the poverty of some homes has been so extreme
that the arrival in life of a girl infant is declared by the black
of mourning at the entrance. What a contrast with the ancient
custom of publishing the birth of babies of either sex by hanging garlands of flowers on the door,[13] a practice that might well
be adopted in our own prosperous country. In the region where
Virgil, one of the most promising (although they did not know
it!) of all infants, was born some two millennia ago, the inhabitants cherished the pretty custom of planting a poplar for

[11] Pliny *N.H.* 16.40.
[12] Pliny *N.H.* 16.139; Serv. on *Aen.* 2.714; 3.64; cf. Hor. *Od.* 2.14.23.
[13] Juv. 9.85.

the occasion. That which stood for the future bard grew, we are told,[14] with miraculous speed, and the tree gathered such a reputation for sanctity that pregnant and newly delivered women made and paid vows beneath it. But alas! no amount of "honing" petition beneath that exuberant poplar could produce another Virgil.

While a short paper cannot include all references to the conventions which controlled the rearing of children to maturity, there is one topic which it may not ignore and that is the relations of the sexes. Until youth recently became so sophisticated as to need no tutelage and mothers themselves achieved such rejuvenation as to attain at least adolescence, some sort of chaperonage still survived to safeguard the traditions of mid-Victorian daughterhood, and our self-appointed directors of manners laid down the rules for its exercise. Those ladies whose reluctant profiting by these in the "gay nineties" now enables them to estimate the losses of their granddaughters in the "flaming thirties" may be interested to learn something of Roman prophylactics. If our girls of fourteen or thereabouts were living under the Caesars, they would commonly be entering matrimony[15] rather than a high-school, and in spite of the notable freedom that was accorded married women in Rome, maidens of good family seem to have had but little extramural social life even in those generations around the beginning of our Christian era when bonds were loosening. We know, indeed, that women went to the shows[16]—like bees or a long line of ants, says Ovid[17] picturesquely. We know, too, that at the circus men and women were privileged to sit together.[18] But

---

[14] Suet. *Vita Verg.* 5.

[15] The youthfulness of the bride called for the chaperonage that Caesar's wife got from her inseparable mother-in-law when Clodius was assaying her virtue, Plut. *Caes.* 9.2; she had to be *adservanda nigerrimis diligentius uvis,* to use the expression of *doctus Catullus* 17.16.

[16] Ovid *A.A.* 1.89; 1.164; 1.171–174. Augustus, however, would not let them see even the gladiators except from the upper seats. Suet. *Aug.* 44.2.

[17] Ovid *A.A.* 1.93–97.

[18] Ovid *Trist.* 2.284; *A.A.* 1.139; *Am.* 3.2.19.

it is obvious that in almost our only pictures[19] of such propinquity the girl was not of the sort that at any age of either her own life or of the world needs a chaperon. We learn from Ovid that her escort is free to fan her, to hold her parasol, to adjust a cushion for her, to put a stool under her delicate feet, to brush off dust from her clothes—even if it isn't there—to lift her trailing garment from the dirt and to show all the other attentions of an active flirtation. He must furthermore watch the man on the other side of her to see that he doesn't sit too close and the spectator behind her to keep him from pressing his knees into her tender back. If at the shows he had any time left from courting to spend on betting on the contestants, our author would have him do it:[20] it might be a better gamble. But whoever that inamorata of his might be, she wore no fillet of Roman maidenhood, and, as we have seen, there was no duenna at flank or back to matronize her, and a frontal position would have been no post of vigilance for anybody who had to protect innocence or its remnants.

We do have, however, some few references to the proprieties to be observed by young people not only in high society but in any. Thus, Augustus, according to a statement of Suetonius, would not allow beardless youths to run in the Lupercalia, nor young folks of either sex to go to any of the night celebrations during the Secular Games, unless they were chaperoned by adult relatives.[21] But even more interesting is the way in which that emperor supervised the lives of his daughter and granddaughters. He had them taught to spin and weave, as girls would be in any ordinary family, and forbade them to do or say anything that might not be recorded in the household diary, whatever that chronicle may have been. He was very strict in keeping them from meeting strangers. A young gentleman of

[19] Ovid *A.A.* 1.135–163; *Am.* 3.2.
[20] Ovid *A.A.* 1.145–146; 168; *Am.* 3.2.73; cf. Juv. 11.201–202. Gaming was an accomplishment essential to Ovid's type of girl. *A.A.* 3.353–354; 3.367–368.
[21] Suet. *Aug.* 31.4.

excellent position and character, Lucius Vinicius, received an unpleasant letter from him: "You have acted presumptuously in visiting Baiae to call on my daughter."[22] But here one is tempted to remark first that Baiae was no place for a good girl anyway, nor, indeed, for any girl at all;[23] secondly that in the light of Julia's subsequent record, she is more likely to have been a menace to Lucius than he to her;[24] and thirdly that Augustus, who himself at any period of his mature life would have borne watching,[25] ought to have known that vigilance never kept daughters safe from anybody—"anybody" includes him—and certainly never kept them virtuous.

Children suggest that other favorite topic of conversation of slightly over one-half the inhabitants of the United States, servants. In the Imperial Period palatial mansions teemed with them, and the etiquette of their maintenance was severe: it had to be. Yet already the barrier of sharp social differentiation which propriety has always required between master and servants at least during the actual performance of their services was subjected to criticism by some of the more humane among the Romans.[26] Nowhere, however, has arrogance reached such heights—or is it depths?—as among some members of that race of whom we hear. One of the most signal instances is given by Tacitus in his *Annals*[27] and concerns Pallas at the time that he was accused of conspiring to raise Cornelius Sulla to the Imperial throne. When his freedmen were arraigned as his accomplices, he told the court that in his own palace he made known his wishes by a mere nod or gesture, or if further information was needed, he resorted to writing in order not to degrade his voice by using it in such company.

If this story is not sufficiently telltale to bring back some of the conditions of the time vividly, we may companion it with Plutarch's anecdote[28] of Pupius Piso, an orator of distinction.

[22] Suet. *Aug.* 64.2. [23] Ovid *A.A.* 1.255–258.
[24] Suet. *Aug.* 65. [25] Suet. *Aug.* 69.
[26] Cf. *e.g.* Sen. *Ep. Mor.* 47.13–19. [27] Tac. *Ann.* 13.23.
[28] Plut. *De Garrulitate* 18 = 511 D–E.

Being annoyed by the loquacity of his domestics, this admirable disciplinarian bade them never open their mouths except in answer to his questions. On a certain occasion, he invited Clodius Pulcher to dinner. All the guests arrived in due time except him. Piso sent the slave who had delivered the invitation, again and again to look for him. At last, when evening came and he had given up all hope, he said to the man: "Didn't you deliver the invitation?" "Certainly," replied the slave. "Then why hasn't he come?" "Because he declined." "Then, why didn't you tell me so in the beginning?" "Because you never asked me." "This was a Roman slave," comments Plutarch; "an Athenian, while digging, will tell his master on what terms peace was made."

We may take up one more matter of service, because of its ubiquitous and timeless character. In Italy an American woman of entirely respectable antecedents can in perfect innocence declass herself socially by carrying her own bundles instead of having her purchases sent by the shop or borne by an attendant. Such self-service was even more disreputable in the Rome of our studies. Not even the smallest object would a citizen transport in his own hands, unless he was so very poor as to have no slave at all.[29] We wonder whether this accounts somewhat for the fact that Roman youths never carried canes, although that was usual among the Greeks, who did not maintain such a huge corps of personal servants.

Martial lampoons the person who enters a shop and has the keeper bring out for inspection most of his merchandise, only to make at the weary end a penny purchase.[30] Now this has, of course, been a popular diversion since the days of Eve—in this case, justice, even if not gallantry, requires the additional name of Adam—but the sting of the epigrammatist is reserved for Adam's final conduct: he carried that worthless article home in his own hands. Similarly Theophrastus in his character-

[29] Mart. 12.70.1; 12.87.　　　　[30] Mart. 9.59.22.

sketches pictures the "mean man"[31] as buying meat and vegetables in the market place and then transporting them personally in the bosom of his cloak.

If we select just one Roman social function in order to discuss
a few of its conventions it must be a dinner party; for it was
from our point of view the most important of all. Invitations
to them must have been passing constantly among citizens of
prominence under the Empire. Although we are prone to think
of them as "stag" dinners, we must remember that there were
many at which the does and hinds were also present.[32] Even
public affairs on a large scale brought together a mixed company. Thus, Caligula[33] gave a lavish banquet to the senate and
the equestrian order. In both cases, the men were accompanied
by their wives and children. Whether or not a husband could
accept an invitation to a party for both sexes in which his spouse
was not included, we have no data to determine.

The books which seek to regulate the manners of our age
discuss at some length the virtue of prompt attendance at a
formal dinner. To arrive on the stroke of the hour is com-
mended as perfection, but the congenital laggard or the victim
of those unavoidable accidents that Fate or Fiction centers on
the dinner hour is granted fifteen minutes' grace. After that
his ignominy is supposed to be deep, no matter how much he
may brazen it, or apologize, or his host outwardly condone it.

But modern punctuality was impossible to a Roman. Lacking all instruments of precision, he could not observe an exact
point of time. Even bright sunshine and a portable sundial
such as the Museo delle Terme possesses among its rarer treas-
ures, could assure no such accuracy as our watches permit.
While a special slave in any home of luxury had the job of
announcing the arrival of the hours as they noted them through

[31] Theophr. 'Ανελευθερίας 25 (22).
[32] Juv. 6.424; Val. Max. 2.1.2; cf. Sen. *Ep. Mor.* 95.21; Plut. *Quaest. Conviv.*
1.3.1 = 619D.
[33] Suet. *Cal.* 17.2; cf. 24.2.

observation of a stationary sundial[34] or eventually perhaps even a water clock would serve as a robot and bellow the time,[35] this could not have established business or social life in general upon any such basis as ours is run. Theirs was no stop-watch age. There actually were gentlemen of leisure in those days. In the hectic rush of American life we can hardly sense much that modern inventions have destroyed. All that a Roman or a Greek social mentor could say about punctuality at a dinner party was that to arrive either first or last was not the best of form.[36] Everybody ought to hit the mean between the extremes, even though mathematically such a coincidence would eliminate them, focussing, it might be, at a point of time, a crushing crowd at the door. Some, however, overdid even their promptness. Of one dinner guest who was more than premature, Martial says[37] sarcastically that he was arriving late for breakfast.

But the same poet, sensing well that remissness in these matters required a good excuse, shows perhaps more wit than manners when he blames his own hour of tardiness in keeping a dinner engagement upon the slowness of the mules which his host had been good enough to send for his transportation,[38] mules being the "Rolls-Royce" of the Roman fashionable world and horses a "Ford." On the other hand, that past-master of social craft, Ovid,[39] gives to the girl who would be *recherchée* the wily advice to arrive after everybody else, to enter the dining-room just as the lamps are brought in: that at once centers every masculine eye and makes a hit. The device has, of course, not lost all its temptation even yet—nor its efficacy.

We may pass to another point and note that taking a recumbent position on a dinner-sofa was not the simple process that sitting down at table is today. A gentleman did not simply throw himself supine like a tired man going to bed. He was

---

[34] Juv. 10.216; Mart. 8.67.1.
[36] Lucian *De Mercede Cond.* 14.
[38] Mart. 11.79.
[35] Lucian *Hippias* 8.
[37] Mart. 8.67.10.
[39] Ovid *A.A.* 3.751–752.

wearing clothes the disclosive character[40] of which required their careful adjustment, if he was not to violate decorum.[41] To the superior sex decency seemed to be so much beyond the capacity of the inferior sex to maintain horizontally that they long denied recumbency at a dinner to women who had any decency to lose.[42] But wives of two millennia ago were no more going to submit permanently to the discomfort of a coercive verticality during a five-hour dinner than they would nowadays to a male monopoly of eating breakfast in bed, and so we find them eventually sharing the male privilege. And, after all, the manipulation of their *stola* and *palla* could have been no more difficult than the management of a court-train, not to speak of the ingenuity only recently displayed in pulling down a short skirt over obtrusive knees at the prompting, every two minutes, of either pudicity or its imitation, when that very skirt was deliberately abbreviated in the first place in obedience to Dame Fashion, whose reputation for modesty has never been notable.

In the allotment of places around the small tables there was much ado about precedence. Guests got their feelings hurt.[43] Plutarch thought that sensitiveness about such matters was contemptible.[44] He recalls aptly the story of the Spartan, who when the director of the chorus put him in the very last place, exclaimed: "Good! you have learned how this may become a post of honor." In other words: "Where MacGregor sits is the head of the table." Among the Romans Seneca put it[45] as wisely as it ever needs be put: "Through excessive idleness," he says, "natures that are weak and womanish and disposed to

[40] Cic. *De Off.* 1.35.126–129; Hor. *Sat.* 1.2.26; cf. Plut. *De Curiositate* 3 = 516F.

[41] Sen. *Ep. Mor.* 71.21.

[42] Cf. *e.g.* Val. Max. 2.1.2; Isid. *Orig.* 20.11.9. Ovid is expert in the seductive possibilities, *Am.* 1.4.15 ff.

[43] Sen. *De Ira* 3.37.4.

[44] Plut. *Sept. Sap. Conv.* 3 = 149A; cf. *Quaest. Conviv.* 1.2.3 = 616 D–E; Theophr. Μικροφιλ. 7. (21).

[45] Sen. *De Const.* 10.3.

fancy injuries in default of suffering real ones are upset by matters of this sort, most of which arise from the misunderstanding of the person who interprets them as slights."

Readers of this article need no review of the rules of recumbency for an appreciation of the one revealing story[46] which we have space to tell. It concerns the post of honor, the so-called *locus consularis*. If a consul was actually present, it would naturally be his without any word from the host or his social secretary, the *nomenclator*. But the strain on etiquette seems to have come on the rare occasion when a state dinner was given a general who was celebrating a triumph. No sister of a vice-president could ever be such a menace to the peace and prosperity of a community where the meek do not inherit the earth. The rules required that a triumpher should be assigned the *locus consularis* and be escorted home with ceremony after the banquet. On the other hand, Roman etiquette was the tightest thing ever invented, and if a consul came, he had to lie where his adjective assigned him. Can we adduce any better evidence of the immutable conservatism of the Roman people than the subterfuge to which they resorted in this dilemma to avoid a national crisis? They despatched special messengers to both the consuls earnestly beseeching them not to come.

In a discussion of ancient manners much may be said about the menu of a dinner. In foods there was already a certain social gradation. Beans[47] and oysters[48] were remote from each other in the scale and in the same relationship that they still bear to each other. Onion and garlic were plebeian vegetables that sometimes figured in superior company. The onion is now, of course, the forbidden fruit of Eve, and Adam also is supposed to eschew it, unless he lives as lonely as his ultimate forebear before his union with the first woman. Modern books of etiquette single it out for infamy, declaring for the instruction

---

[46] Plut. *Quaest. Rom.* 80 = 283A.   [47] The *faba fabrorum,* Mart. 10.48.16.
[48] Cum palma mensarum divitum (not *diu iam,* as some editors) tribuatur, as Pliny *N.H.* 32.59 says.

of those whose appetite gets the better of any sort of sense that they possess that no onion, no garlic shall appear on the menu of a formal dinner. If they are introduced at all, their presence must be as inconspicuous as that of the shyest condiment. That is the only way that one can satisfy at the same time the claims of taste esthetically as well as gastronomically. But, after all, this taboo is not wholly new even in Italy where garlic and onion must run a close race with the grape for agricultural supremacy. Thus, Horace[49] composed a diatribe against the former vegetable, shrewdly suggesting to Maecenas, as a potential offender, the only thing that might cure an Italian garlic-eater of his indulgence, a penalty to be imposed by the lady of his heart:

> manum puella savio opponat tuo
> extrema et in sponda cubet.[50]

But Vespasian whose nature was not notably delicate and sensitive, nor his sense of smell, we judge, over-keen,[51] demoted a young man whom he had just commissioned in the army, because he reeked with perfumery when he came to thank his benefactor. "I would rather you had smelt of garlic,"[52] he said in utter disgust at his effeminacy.[53] In any group of *contadini* today the tourist will find enough of the breath of manliness to content even a Vespasian.

At a formal dinner party there were some of the same opportunities to discover the quality of breeding possessed by host or

---

[49] Hor. *Epod.* 3.21–22.

[50] But the first vendor of onions had already had the anathema of Naevius (Ribbeck, *Scaen. Rom. Poes.*, p. 9): ut illum di perdant qui primus holitor caepam protulit, and Tranio in the *Mostellaria* of Plautus, 38–39 had roundly cursed the eater of garlic: at te Iuppiter dique omnes perdant, fu, oboluisti alium.

[51] We remember that to his nostrils there was no source from which a *vectigal* could come that would make it "tainted money," Suet. *Vesp.* 23.3.

[52] Like the Romans of the good old times; cf. Varro *Bimarchus* in Non. 201. 5: avi et atavi nostri cum alium ac cepe eorum verba olerent, tamen optume animati erant.

[53] Suet. *Vesp.* 8.3.

guest that we have today. He would reveal it while he ate and drank and talked and sang and listened to the entertainment offered by others, and, of course, in the clothes he wore and in the manner in which he wore them. The Curii and Fabricii[54] could have had no complicated code of table etiquette to puzzle them. The consumption of porridge allows of few formalities and small choice of implements. Gellius tells[55] us that even in Cato's day the man who devoted himself to dinner parties or to the study of poetry—a significant bracketing—was called a *grassator* or vagabond, and people paid more for horses than for cooks. The Romans had, indeed, considerably passed the age when they could be picked upon as pulse-eaters, *pultiphagi,* before the teachings and example of the more refined and luxurious Greek had brought the intricacies and minutiae of social conventions into their dinner service along with superior cooking.

But even under the Empire diners escaped some modern pitfalls. For example there was no army of implements halted on either side of the plate to discourage appetite by posing problems of precedence which offer no difficulties to the knowing but to an Arcadian are beyond serene solution. The Roman did most of his eating with no such helps at all. Between thumb and forefinger he could seize almost anything that did not actually flow and so convey it with all the skill of some modern Orientals to the open mouth. He did have, however, one peculiar spoon with a round bowl and a pointed handle, the *cochlear,* which might have puzzled us, had we attended one of his banquets uninstructed. The sharp end enabled him to extract the meat from a snail or shellfish, the spoon-end served for the consumption of an egg[56] when it was not being eaten in a way that may still be heard in Italy, where "uova da bere" command an extra price because of their non-explosive character.

---

[54] Juv. 11.78 and 91.   [55] Gell. 11.2.5; cf. Livy 39.6.
[56] Mart. 14.121.

But the Roman could do some dreadful things with his fingers in the common dish from which all were helping themselves to food in turn. He was not supposed to reach too far and select the tidbit that lay in a neighbor's territory. Horace tells[57] us that; and as one who had lain down at the tables of the mighty, he ought to know. Any exhibition of gluttony was particularly obvious because of the closeness with which the guests reclined, encircling a small table. For instance, you could not take three fistfuls of olives at a time without being noticed,[58] nor sweep into your napkin too many delicacies to take home with you without being asked to replace them on the table and to remember that your invitation did not include tomorrow's dinner, too.[59]

It might make the company laugh to see one of their number swallow whole cakes at a mouthful, but such an exhibition of oral capacity and speed was unmannerly. This particular cake-eater, aptly named Porcius by our informant Horace,[60] might have won the championship in one of our porcine contests in pie-eating or egg-swallowing, but, even as a fictitious character, he died long before this more appreciative age. The way a diner ate with his fingers must have revealed his social background to persons of gentility quite as ruthlessly as use of knife and fork can do it in our own age. A man may have the perfect courtesy of the heart and yet alas! grip and wield his table-implements as his ancestors did a spade and pitchfork. Between Pliny and one of his tenant farmers there must have been a wide divergence in delicacy and neatness.

Of all Latin writers Ovid would perhaps have written a book of etiquette with most zest. Even as it is, the works which he composed, as a knowing man-about-town, are full of the sort of lore and admonition that the modern treatises contain. So, with reference to eating with the fingers, he remarks that it is a matter of some moment how one uses them. One should not smear

---

[57] Hor. *Sat.* 1.3.92–94. [58] Petron. 66.
[59] Mart. 2.37; cf. 3.23; 7.20. [60] Hor. *Sat.* 2.8.23–24.

the entire face with a dirty hand. "Don't eat first at home, before coming to the party,"[61] he advises, "and cease eating before you have satisfied either your desires or your powers."[62]

But there were other digital troubles. Food was often stinging hot.[63] Seneca says[64] of his time that in homes of luxury, the kitchen was now coming in with the dinner, referring to a new custom of having the food brought into the dining-room in some sort of cooker that would keep it at a top temperature. The heat of the dishes was often hard on both fingers and gullet. We read[65] of one gourmand who used to inure his hand to suffering by plunging it into hot water at the baths and to practice himself to swallow anything by gargling his throat with the same. Having prevailed upon those who prepared the dishes to serve everything very hot, he figured at banquets as the only diner, the other guests acting as mere spectators and auditors. He was, indeed, such a famous epicure that certain flat cakes were honored with his name.[66] However, he hardly ranks with a certain Pithyllus,[67] who wore a skin-covering over his tongue and on his digits finger-stalls to protect them as they conveyed food that was too piping hot for anybody else to touch. He then cleansed his precious tongue with the powdered skin of a fish—let us hope, a shark.

But these were Greeks, and we must expect therefore to find among them some hyper-refinements to which the ancient Italians never rose. In Roman society of one sort or another gentlemen had to contend with vulgarians who, instead of trying to acquire an asbestic tongue, would simply blow on the food to reduce its temperature sufficiently for seizure and consumption. This method modern works on etiquette roundly condemn in spite of its appeal to our mania for speed, and of the possibility of reducing the noise of the blasts as experience accumulates.

---

[61] A gluttonous trick, Pliny *Panegyr.* 49.
[62] Ovid *A.A.* 3.755–758; cf. Hor. *Ep.* 1.16.23.
[63] Mart. 5.78.6. [64] Sen. *Ep. Mor.* 78.23.
[65] Athen. 1.9 = 5E. [66] Athen. 1.9 = 5D.
[67] Athen. 1.10 = 6 C–D.

Martial[68] speaks feelingly of a delectable but fiery dish that after receiving its refrigeration from the guest who was fortunate enough to have the first blow, continued on its rounds, refused by everybody.

While, as I have said, there was no extensive service of eating utensils to exploit the ignorance of those for whom a broad-bladed knife has always met most needs, the Romans did have a strict etiquette governing the order in which a guest should partake of the dishes set before him.[69] Belonging ourselves to the academic clan, we may sympathize with the Greek professor of some thousands of years ago who was attending an elaborate dinner party given by some Romans. There was nothing for him to do in his ignorance but watch out of the corner of his eye what the nearest of the βάρβαροι was doing and play a simian rôle. The worst of it was, the servants all had their eyes focussed on him, his table-companions stared at him, even the host kept a worried watch over his conduct to see what his next performance would be. You can never anticipate what a pundit is going to do. The slaves in attendance on the other guests observing his awe and bewilderment cracked jokes on him and concluded that this must be his first dinner party, since his napkin was new.[70]

In the days when Bacchus still presided at some American boards with more éclat and welcome than any of the water nymphs, taste prescribed by a rather severe etiquette a proper succession of his gifts, white wine, sherry, champagne, claret, and port, with post-prandial liqueurs as a last attempt to win the wit and gaiety that alcohol bestows or at least counterfeits. The Romans knew a list of wines that would tire the memory of any victualler to rehearse and connoisseurs rated their merits with some precision from Setine and Falernian to the sort that Oliver Wendell Holmes described as requiring three men to

[68] Mart. 3.17.

[69] Lucian *De Mercede Cond.* 15; cf. *Quaest. Conviv.* 1.2.2 = 616A.

[70] Since each guest had brought his own, this was as revealing as to appear today in a brand-new dinner-coat.

drink, one to hold the victim, another to pour it down, and the third to suffer. But to the drinkers of those days, the association of the right wine with the right food seems to have been of less consequence than the size and shape of the container they chose as a bowl or goblet.[71] Of course, modern usage prescribes a glass of distinctive shape or size for each of the varieties we named for table use. Antiquity, I believe, knew nought of this.

At one of our formal dinners it is well understood that neither dyspepsia nor inner revulsion gives one the privilege of refusing anything except liquids, sweets, and hors d'oeuvres; for one is supposed to be able to nibble deceitfully and to make some gesture of polite conformity in taste. To be odd is to be socially dead. We haven't sufficient data to determine which sort of death the ancients preferred, but we do know that diners were reckoned to have committed somewhat of an affront, if they declined absolutely anything that was served. If a person did refuse, as dieting or mere decency or capacity might require, he was expected to make his excuses in some clever and witty fashion, so as to contribute to the gaiety of the guests rather than arouse their apprehensions or cause the host discomfort.[72] But it was far more laudable to be heroic, as was Julius Caesar both at table and on the battlefield. On one occasion when his host served rancid olive oil and all the other guests shied from using it, he partook of it even more plentifully than usual, in order not to seem to reproach his entertainer with carelessness or discourtesy in his hospitality.[73] Plutarch[74] makes what is probably the same story a little worse by saying that it was a dish of asparagus which had had perfumed ointment poured over it instead of the proper oil for dressing.

But Caesar was a thoroughbred. In an age when men who knew better would serve different grades of wine and food and

---

[71] Cf. *e.g.* Plut. *De Cohib. Ira* 13 = 461E.
[72] Plut. *De Tuend. Sanit.* 5 = 124 B–C.
[73] Suet. *Jul.* 53.   [74] Plut. *Caes.* 17.5.

even water[75] at the same party to accord with the social status of the guest, he put his baker in irons for providing him with superior bread.[76]

As a matter of fact, one seems to have taken some of the same chances with olive oil anciently as one does with butter today. The best quality was used, of course, for the salad dressing. If it were somewhat inferior, it might be the vehicle for perfume and be used to anoint the body. The worst was relegated to the lamps as fuel. Horace says[77] that a certain Natta was so mean that he robbed his lamps to oil himself, while others seem to have done the same to dress their greens.[78]

Even at a respectable banquet of the Romans there might be deportment which we should censure as gross. But we must remember that at their worst they were more refined than the people of many a century between their day and our own. Banqueters even without the excuse of a carelessness due to intoxication appear to have been rather free in discarding inedible or undesirable portions of the food on the pavement.[79] There were no rugs or carpets, but there were sawdust and brooms[80] to use on the marble or lithoidal floor that could be heavily doused with water. Moreover, probably pretty well up in the social grades, they ate in coöperative intimacy with all sorts of pet animals, as one still does in many a delightful rustic inn in Italy.[81]

But a mere illustrative sample of what may be told about the manners and social usages of the Romans must be kept within limits that vex the writer, though they may relieve the reader. If someday the ghosts of us are going to associate with their ghosts in a world of better manners than we have ever had in

[75] Juv. 5.52. [76] Suet. *Julius* 48.
[77] Hor. *Sat.* 1.6.124. [78] Juv. 5.87; cf. Hor. *Sat.* 2.2.59.
[79] Hor. *Sat.* 2.8.12; Sen. *Controv.* 8.2.(25)4. We think of the mosaic of Heraclitus in the Lateran Museum and of the pavements of the artist Sosus, Pliny *N.H.* 36.184.
[80] Hor. *Sat.* 2.4.81–83; Mart. 14.82; Petron. 68; Sen. *Ep. Mor.* 27.7.
[81] Mart. 3.82.19; 7.20.17; Petron. 40.

this, it may be worth our while to learn how men like Cicero and Pliny lived agreeably with the most cultivated people of their time. Moreover, there is always the chance that the goddess of grace and beauty will exercise the rights and powers of a divine ancestress and send into our midst a tall, soldierly man, whose slender build and noble bearing will still recall the athleticism of his youth. The pallor of his cheeks may be no more notable than the un-Roman fairness that characterized them during all his life. His spirit raiment could be no whiter than the immaculate toga that alone would satisfy his fastidious taste in the days when the love of women meant much to him and his to them. In his features we should mark the broad and lofty forehead behind which were once, we may suppose, the best brains of Rome. His poise and quiet courtesy, salient tokens of good breeding in any age, would stamp him unmistakably a gentleman. If the high-pitched voice that thrilled his compatriots into action and glad subjection to his will should gibber as those of ghosts are supposed to do, a Latinist might welcome this fair excuse for a failure to understand.

But if our phantom visitor turns upon the manners and customs of our age those keen black eyes that served so well to make him the greatest Roman of them all, will he find nowadays many gentlemen much finer than the finest that he knew? If he begins to criticize the asininity of our masculine attire, the indecencies of modern androgynous dancing, the grim fashions of our funerals, the rude rush of our life, the—are we prepared to match him into silence? We might require all the unfavorable comparisons that we can draw from the life that his fellow-citizens were living two millennia ago, and such a defense would depend upon a more comprehensive study than has as yet been made.

UNIVERSITY OF PENNSYLVANIA

THE *CLIENS* IN THE TIME OF MARTIAL

S. L. Mohler

IN our study of ancient literature, one of the most difficult tasks we confront is that of freeing ourselves from artificial modern standards of ethics and propriety. For instance, a boy may understand the Latin of an Ode of Horace fairly well, but if it happens to contain a reference to wine he is apt to lose the whole point. The author assumes in his eyes the character of a wild debauchee, thrilling with the joys of forbidden pleasure. His teacher becomes perforce a wet propagandist in trying to explain the ancients' attitude toward intoxicants. But the effort is futile; the student "finishes" Horace with a feeling that a Sabine *diota* was something like a hip flask. In the field of sex relations, the development of sympathetic understanding might be a mental acquisition of doubtful value for impressionable youth. However, the question is purely academic, since few ideals are undermined by the study of the classics, few minds are dangerously "broadened." The natural reaction to expurgated editions of Horace and Catullus is one of utter disgust— a disgust which militates unfairly against any full appreciation of their characters.

In certain other phases of their customary thinking we should, perhaps, admit the superiority of the Roman point of view. One of these is their attitude toward the making of money. Trimalchio, I need hardly suggest, is not an extinct type: he is the self-made man who has risen from the ranks by his own efforts, a recognized leader in the world of finance, a shining example of those who have availed themselves of the unlimited opportunities offered by this land of freedom and plenty, to whom we "point with pride" from rostrum and pulpit. In ancient Italy captains of industry, *of this type,* were the object

239

of ridicule, *such* millionaires were relegated to the "peanut heaven" of the theater.[1]

In the highest, senatorial class, working for a living was not only frowned upon but so closely restricted by law that one might say it was prohibited—as most moralists would insist it should have been, in the case of men whose Babson rating insured them a comfortable income. The two fields left open to them were those of law and agriculture. In the first, the time-honored traditions of the profession were opposed to the receipt of any remuneration whatever; the great structure of Roman Law was reared without a profit motive. To be sure, Claudius legalized gifts to counsel to be made after the completion of a suit, but these must have constituted a very uncertain source of income for the majority of practitioners; and Quintilian lays it down as a self-evident principle that no one in comfortable circumstances should accept even such gratuities.[2] In agriculture a senator's efforts were probably limited to the most gentlemanly type of farming—the only sort practicable with their widely separated estates. We smile when we read Pliny's apologetic account of riding over his Tuscan estate "for the exercise."[3] But should we? Is there not some point in Horace's observations on the "hard working" ant, which stops hoarding when its real needs are supplied?[4]

However, in a society such as that of ancient Rome, based on the economic institutions of slavery and absentee ownership, it was only the favored few who could adopt a philosophic attitude toward the acquisition of money. In its effect on the great

[1] Cf. Mart. 5.8, 14, 27. We take it for granted that characters such as Phasis will occupy the box seats.

[2] *Inst.* 12.7.9: Caecis hoc, ut aiunt, satis clarum est: nec quisquam, qui sufficientia sibi (modica autem haec sunt) possidebit, hunc quaestum sine crimine sordium fecerit. Pliny consistently refused all remuneration for his services; *Epist.* 5.13.8, . . . in causis agendis non modo pactione, dono, munere, verum etiam xeniis semper abstinui.

[3] *Epist.* 9.15.3: Interdum tamen equum conscendo et patrem familiae hactenus ago, quod aliquam partem praediorum, sed pro gestatione percurro.

[4] Hor. *Serm.* 1.1.33–40.

mass of the population, such a system possessed little but evil. The scorn of remunerative work on the part of the socially élite not only reduced the free laborer to a position little above that of the slave, but it created a large class of persons without enough capital to subsist independently, but with too much pride to earn a living. The only alternative to the loss of caste which would result from "entering business" was the acceptance of charity. And, incredible as it seems, a large number turned to this solution of their difficulty. For certainly the *cliens,* as described by Martial and Juvenal, appears to us as a peculiarly shameless mendicant, accepting trifling gifts and the poorest of table fare in return for degrading services as an *anteambulo.* The fatherly *patronus* of the Republic[5] has become a *rex superbus,* stingy and haughtily disdainful of his humble followers, only tolerating them to keep up appearances by insuring himself a numerous following. The old intimacy, the old *pietas* has disappeared; nothing but a sordid opportunism unites the receiver of the dole with its donor. The picture is certainly repulsive: is it true to life?

To begin with, no Roman could forget the grim truth of the saying, "the poor you have always with you." At the bottom of the scale we find the tribesman, *tribulis,* ready to receive a cast-off toga from anyone.[6] Probably it was such individuals as this of whom we hear as the *clientes* of certain tribes, organized primarily to facilitate the distribution of *congiaria.*[7] However even this rabble had their patrons and "fathers"—titles which always carried with them some degree of financial obligation.[8] One of their thinly disguised methods of promiscuous begging is to be seen in Martial's description of the shabby *cliens* carrying gilded dates and paltry coppers on New Year's

---

[5] See Marquardt, *Privatleben der Römer*[2], pp. 202–203.

[6] Cf. Mart. 9.49.7: (of a toga) nunc anus et tremulo vix accipienda tribuli.

[7] See Th. Mommsen, *Römisches Staatsrecht,* vol. III, p. 267, n. 3.

[8] Cf. *C.I.L.* IX. 5823 . . . honoratus in tribu Cl. patrum et liberum clientium et adcensus patroni . . .; XIV. 374 . . . tribuli tribus Claudiae patri et avo decurionum patruum (*sic*) et liberorum clientium.

Day[9]—of course expecting larger donations in return. Whether these gentry commonly enjoyed the personal intimacy of true *clientes* may be subject to grave doubt, though a chance allusion in Horace would seem to indicate that the *tribulis* occasionally "dined out."[10] Freedmen, certainly, were accepted as regular members of their patrons' households: at the dinner table[11] (and frequently as *umbrae* at the tables of their patrons' friends), in the forum, in the family tomb. They might also be regular recipients of the *sportula*.[12] And in spite of Juvenal's picture of the *rex* who habitually dined by himself, I believe that we shall find evidence that there were hosts of unassuming *clientes* in Rome who enjoyed a relation with their patrons closely analogous to that of freedmen—a relation which reflects nothing but credit on their patrons.

The most engaging picture of ancient clientship which has come down to us is found in Horace's account of the relation between Philippus and Maena.[13] The senator is attracted by the appearance of a humble plebeian, inquires as to his name and profession, and invites him to dinner. Maena fails to accept this first overture, and from his later embarrassment we can see the formal implications of such a proffer of hospitality: he apologizes not only for his failure to appear at the meal, but also for his absence from Philippus' *salutatio* and failure to speak first when he saw him on the street. Acceptance of a second invitation led to his becoming "an early morning *cliens* and a regular dinner guest," *mane cliens et iam certus conviva*, as well as his companion on trips to the country—and eventually

[9] Mart. 8.33.11–12:

> hoc linitur sputo Iani caryota Kalendis,
> quam fert cum parco sordidus asse cliens.

Cf. also 13.27.

[10] *Epist.* 1.13.15: (he is giving a messenger instructions as to how *not* to carry his book to Augustus) ut cum pilleolo soleas conviva tribulis.

[11] Plin. *Epist.* 2.6.4; below, p. 250, n. 45.

[12] Cf. Pliny's provision of an annual income of 112,000 sesterces for 100 freedmen, *C.I.L.* V. 5262.

[13] *Epist.* 1.7.46–76. (Philippus was consul in 91 B.C.)

to his being set up as a small farmer. One simple invitation to dinner made Maena a member of Philippus' household! Picture any of our socially élite, living in a "democratic," "Christian" country making such advances to poor tradesmen! And pardon the *rex* of Juvenal's day if he did not feel inclined to enter into such an intimate relationship with any ambitious parasite who took the trouble to say good morning to him. No wonder patrons required a period of probation of prospective *clientes,* as Maecenas did with Horace, in whose case nine months intervened between the first introduction and his final acceptance into the circle.[14]

If there were no Maecenases in the latter part of the first century A.D., there were certainly Maenas. Matho was the name of one of them. He was so constant a guest at Martial's Tiburtine villa that he cheated himself when he bought it,[15] and he had a regular meal-ticket in the city.[16] Another of the same type christened Charopinus, "Drinkwell," became deeply insulted when Martial failed to invite him.[17] Whether these characters are to be considered as true *clientes* or simply as *amici,* what a nuisance they must have been! We hear, furthermore, that the *cliens* was proverbially querulous and gossipy,[18] that is, possessed of characteristics which could hardly be acquired without considerable real intimacy with his patron's

---

[14] Hor. *Serm.* 1.6.61–62. Cf. Juv. 5.15–16 (where the *cliens* is put off two months) ; Lucian *De Merc. Cond.* 10, 11, 14; below, p. 260.

[15] Mart. 4.79:

> Hospes eras nostri semper, Matho, Tiburtini.
> hoc emis. Inposui: rus tibi vendo tuum.

Friedländer lists the name as fictitious, which simply means that the character is typical rather than individual, and that Martial may be addressing him as a typical *cliens.*

[16] Mart. 8.42; below, p. 257.

[17] *Ibid.,* 5.50.1, 2:

> Ceno domi quotiens, nisi te, Charopine, vocavi,
> protinus ingentes sunt inimicitiae.

Cf. the *scurrae* who were cheated out of a meal by Horace's eleventh hour departure, *Serm.* 2.36–37.

[18] Cf. Mart. 1.49.33; 4.88.4; 7.62.4.

household. Juvenal, meanwhile, would have us believe that all the wealthy dined by themselves—and that slop jars fell on the streets of Rome like apple blossoms in a May orchard.

Above these humbler *clientes,* dependent on their patrons for their very existence, we find a large class of Roman society perhaps best typified by the poet Martial. Without sufficient fortune to keep up independently in the social life of the capital, and without the inclination or the ability to make money in the few ways possible to a gentleman, members of this middle class became *amici.* What pride they had was easily swallowed, especially since in accepting the rôle of *clientes* they did not lose the respect of their fellows, but actually found means for bettering their social position. This advantage was due in part to the fact that they were not, as a rule, dependent on a single patron, but divided their attentions between several. In fact it became a question of "the more the merrier" in winning patrons as well as *clientes.* Their duties were arduous, as it appears to us, but so far from "degrading" to ancient eyes that their performance became the style, as well as the recognized means for social and political advancement. Accordingly clientship became a purely relative matter, as is shown in Martial's repeated complaints that his patrons in turn pay court to others: in "hunting" for dinner invitations, in attending the morning levée and the *deductio,* and in giving vociferous, if insincere, support at recitations.[19] Under these conditions definition becomes well-nigh impossible. However, for the period of Martial, perhaps the

[19] 2.18:

> Capto tuam, pudet heu, sed capto, Maxime, cenam,
>   tu captas aliam: iam sumus ergo pares.
> mane salutatum venio, tu diceris isse
>   ante salutatum: iam sumus ergo pares.
> sum comes ipse tuus tumidique anteambulo regis,
>   tu comes alterius: iam sumus ergo pares.
> Esse sat est servum, iam nolo vicarius esse.
>   qui rex est regem, Maxime, non habeat.

10.10:

> Cum tu, laurigeris annum qui fascibus intras,
>   mane salutator limina mille teras,

most convenient criterion of clientship would be that of the receipt of the everyday *sportula*.[20] It is always dangerous to place too much reliance in negative inferences, but we may be justified in assuming that if the patrons who on occasion performed *cliens*-services and "hunted" for dinner-invitations, had also received the dole, the epigrammatist would have mentioned it. Considered relatively, the matter of definition is simple enough, as is illustrated in an amusing poem of Statius. At the Saturnalia his friend Grypus had disappointed him by sending nothing but a paltry book. After enumerating the trifles usually sent as "Christmas" presents—any of which would have been more acceptable to an author than an addition to his library— he addresses him in these words:[21]

> Quid si, cum bene mane semicrudus
> inlatam tibi dixero salutem,
> et tu me vicibus domi salutes?
> aut, cum me dape iuveris opima,
> expectes similes et ipse cenas?

---

[19] (continued)

> hic ego quid faciam? quid nobis, Paule, relinquis,
> qui de plebe Numae densaque turba sumus?
> qui me respiciet dominum regemque vocabo?
> hoc tu—sed quanto blandius!—ipse facis.
> lecticam sellamve sequar? nec ferre recusas,
> per medium pugnas et prior isse lutum.
> saepius adsurgam recitanti carmina? tu stas
> et pariter geminas tendis in ora manus.
> Quid faciet pauper cui non licet esse clienti?
> dimisit nostras purpura vestra togas.

Cf. 12.29(26).1–6 for the politician's use of the *salutatio*. In Juv. 3.127–130, on the other hand, the praetors are racing to call on certain rich and childless ladies. Paulus' free use of "domine" (Mart. 10.10.6), commonly associated with the obsequious *cliens* (cf. Mart. 1.112; 2.68; 6.88), may represent one of the steps by which the word came to be used as a purely formal appellative. (Cf. Symmachus *Epist.* 6.57(58).1 domina filia.) Even before the time of Martial the word was used in addressing strangers (Sen. *Epist.* 3.1): quomodo obvios, si nomen non succurrit, dominos salutamus . . .; cf. Mart. 5.57:

> Cum voco te dominum, noli tibi, Cinna, placere:
> saepe etiam servum sic resaluto tuum.

However, granting that the word kept all its original significance, one might prefer it to the "frater" and "pater" of an earlier generation of vote hunters (Hor. *Epist.* 1.6.54–55).

[20] See below, pp. 251–260.   [21] *Silv.* 4.9.48–52.

A *cliens,* then, is one who pays morning calls and doesn't expect to have them returned; who is entertained at dinner without reciprocating the favor; and who expects to do more than come out even, in the exchange of seasonal presents. In relation to Grypus, Statius was a *cliens;* in relation to his own freedmen, and probably to certain other humble dependents, he was a patron.[22]

The "degradation" of the *cliens* began in the wee small hours at the *salutatio,* a pleasing institution of the old patriarchal *familia,* but corrupted by its adoption in the city. A suggestion of its family origin is contained in a late reference in the correspondence of Fronto,[23] while occasional glimpses of its practice in the country contrast strongly with the formal levée in the city. One that I particularly like is contained in Pliny's familiar letter describing the circumstances of the establishment of his school at Comum.[24] Apparently it was customary for boys to go along with their fathers to make the acquaintance of the big man of the town. Conversation did not flow easily for these gawky, bashful lads, but the sympathetic Pliny succeeded in breaking the ice with that still effective question: "Are you going to school?" On the farm, Martial would have us believe that *salutatores* regularly came with gifts—of honey, cheese, capons, etc.—and that the farmers' wives sent special baskets of dainties by their buxom daughters.[25] Such occasional glimpses of the informal personal relation between different social classes disclose the most pleasing side of ancient life.

In the city, friends might still exchange a cheerful good-morning, but the institution of the *salutatio* necessarily became unduly formal as it grew in size. The political life of the republic had produced this unfortunate result, and it is perhaps the irony of fate that the democratic leaders Gracchus and

[22] As was probably the case with Martial: see above, p. 243, nn. 15, 16, below, p. 257.

[23] *Ad M. Caes.* 4.6: Inde salutato patre meo . . . fauces fovi. Faucibus curatis abii ad patrem meum et immolanti adstiti.

[24] *Epist.* 4.13.3. [25] Mart. 3.58.33–44.

Drusus were credited with first making invidious distinctions between their callers.[26] Hordes of political supporters, largely composed of insincere time-servers, crowded out honest friends and persons with legitimate business to transact.[27] In self-defense patrons were driven to grading their callers, grouping them according to *admissiones,* or marshalling them in order of official rank.[28] The "morning greeting" became a cold, formal reception, made more burdensome to those who had to go, by its unearthly hour, the crowded condition of the streets, the haughtiness of tip-grasping slaves.[29] Add to all this the moisture of kisses[30] and you have a function which any sane man would escape if he could. But I fear the Romans were hardly sane, if this be the criterion; the worst features of the *salutatio* were due to the fact that everybody went: the client for legal advice, the politician for votes and influence,[31] the *cliens* for a dinner-invitation, the will hunter to play his game of flattery.[32] Friends might be there *en masse* to greet someone recently returned to the city,[33] or to pay their respects on such occasions as the assumption of office or the marrying of a daughter;[34] women took up the fashion, and even held receptions of their

[26] Sen. *De Ben.* 6.34.2: Apud nos primi omnium Gracchus et mox Livius Drusus instituerunt segregare turbam suam et alios ,in secretum recipere, alios cum pluribus, alios universos.

[27] Cic. *Ad Fam.* 9.20.3: Mane salutamus domi et bonos viros multos, sed tristes, et hos laetos victores, qui me quidem perofficiose et peramanter observant; *Ad Att.* 1.18.1: Nam illae ambitiosae nostrae fucosaeque amicitiae sunt in quodam splendore forensi, fructum domesticum non habent. Itaque, cum bene completa domus est tempore matutino, cum ad forum stipati gregibus amicorum descendimus, reperire ex magna turba neminem possumus, quocum aut iocari libere aut suspirare familiariter possimus.

[28] Sen. *op. cit.,* 33.4: Non sunt isti amici, qui agmine magno ianuam pulsant, qui in primas et secundas admissiones digeruntur. Juv. 1.101: da praetori, da deinde tribuno. See below, p. 259.

[29] Juv. 3.184–189; Lucian *De Merc. Cond.* 10; below, p. 260.

[30] Mart. 12.29(26).4: et referam lassus basia mille domum; 8.44.4–5:

> sed omne limen conteris salutator
> et mane sudas urbis osculis udus.

[31] Mart. 12.29(26).1–6; 10.10.1, 2; above, p. 244, n. 19; Epictetus *Diss.* 4.10.20.

[32] Juv. 3.126–130. [33] Mart. 9.6(7).

[34] Stat. *Silv.* 1.2.229–235.

own.[35] As a late-sleeping, crowd-hating American I sympathize deeply with Martial's bitterest complaints, but to avoid the *salutatio,* either as host[36] or guest, one would have been constrained to flee the bounds of the Roman Empire or become a country slave.

A similar condition prevailed with reference to the menial services of the *anteambulo.* And again our epigrammatist takes a rational view of the matter in a poem which facetiously offers the services of a freedman to take his place:[37]

> Exigis a nobis operam sine fine togatam:
> non eo, libertum sed tibi mitto meum.
> "Non est" inquis "idem." Multo plus esse probabo:
> vix ego lecticam subsequar, ille feret.
> in turbam incideris, cunctos umbone repellet:
> invalidum est nobis ingenuumque latus.
> quidlibet in causa narraveris, ipse tacebo:
> at tibi tergeminum mugiet ille sophos.
> lis erit, ingenti faciet convicia voce:
> esse pudor vetuit fortia verba mihi.
> "Ergo nihil nobis" inquis "praestabis amicus?"
> Quidquid libertus, Candide, non poterit.

Imagine full-grown, self-respecting men trailing around with a pompous lawyer like the children behind a circus parade! However, that was just the way Romans behaved—all of them. For

---

[35] Juv. 1.121–122. The passage referred to in n. 32 describes two praetors racing to the houses of childless women before daybreak, dudum vigilantibus orbis (that is, the ladies were awake, expecting their callers). For the general participation of women in this phase of social life we may perhaps compare Hor. *Od.* 2.18.7–8:

> nec Laconicas mihi
> trahunt honestae purpuras clientae.

[36] 12.68 (written in Spain):

> Matutine cliens, urbis mihi causa relictae,
> atria, si sapias, ambitiosa colas.
> non sum ego causidicus nec amaris litibus aptus
> sed piger et senior Pieridumque comes;
> otia me somnusque iuvant, quae magna negavit
> Roma mihi: redeo, si vigilatur et hic.

[37] 3.46.

in other poems Martial bewails the fact that senators and patrons are supplanting the indigent *amici.*[38]

The goal of the *deductio* was the forum or the basilica, where instincts of gregariousness and love of display found their freest outlet. An audience, large and enthusiastic, was considered absolutely essential to the transaction of legal business. Apparently it made little difference whether the case concerned some prominent politician involved in sensational charges of grafting or a peasant whose cow had gone astray, by fair means or foul the lawyer had to appear with a formidable array of supporters. The fairest of all fair means was simply to issue invitations to his friends, a practice which Pliny commends in his detested rival.[39] *Clientes,* whether his own or his friends',[40] were his surest source of numerical support; but if these were inadequate a claque might still be hired for the occasion at two or three denarii per head.[41] The bellowing of the barristers and the din of the city could be depended on to keep the mob awake; cheer leaders, assigned the onerous task of listening to the speeches, could call for hisses or hurrahs as occasion seemed to demand. Bona fide *clientes* did indeed lead a hard life—though possibly no harder than those attached to a self-styled poet. At least it is time for us to be looking to their rewards.

The summum bonum of the *cliens'* philosophy was to dine at somebody else's table,[42] while dining at home entailed his worst

---

[38] See above, pp. 244, 245.   [39] *Epist.* 6.2.3 (concerning Regulus).
[40] Cf. Mart. 2.74.6–7:

> Hos illi amicos et greges togatorum
> Fuficulenus praestat et Faventinus.

Cf. Juv. 7.43–44.
[41] Plin. *Epist.* 2.14.4–6; below, p. 252.
[42] Juv. 5.1–2:

> Si te propositi nondum pudet atque eadem est mens,
> ut bona summa putes aliena vivere quadra:

Cf. 1.133–134, Longissima cenae spes homini; Mart. 2.11, 14, 18, 27; 3.14; 7.20; 9.14, 19; 11.24 *et passim.* Entertaining at the *cena* is also the prime duty of the patron, Mart. 10.19(18).1–2, 4:

> Nec vocat ad cenam Marius, nec munera mittit,
> nec spondet, nec volt credere, sed nec habet.
> Eheu! quam fatuae sunt tibi, Roma, togae!

The giving of the *sportula* is not mentioned here because, as I believe, it accom-

disgrace.[43] Yet even when he obtained the object of his desires his lot might be far from enviable: he was treated like a dog, and given the poorest of fare, while the host and a few specially favored friends enjoyed the best which money could buy.[44] Pliny, however, protests most strenuously against this "new alliance of luxury and stinginess" as being out of all harmony with the true spirit of hospitality. Incidentally he speaks of the practice as something new, and his own custom of treating all alike could hardly have been unusual.[45] At that, what would a modern "prominent club-man" do if confronted with the necessity of entertaining a horde of poor relations, college professors, and office clerks almost every day—together with a smaller group of his personal friends and associates? Would he serve Scotch to the whole assembly or to none? that is, would he drink water to avoid the expense of treating half the town? It happens that Pliny tells us very definitely how he managed it: "my freedmen don't drink the same as I; I drink the same as they." Such a spirit does credit to the old-time conceptions of the *familia* and the obligations it imposed, as well as to the finest traditions of hospitality. We can hardly doubt that there were others who preserved the same high ideals; but even if the majority compromised in the direction of economy, we must still give them credit for tolerating the presence of these dependents at all.

panied the dinner; see below, pp. 251–260. For other motives of the *cliens* see Marquardt, *op. cit.,* pp. 206–207.

[43] Cf. Mart. 5.47:

> Numquam se cenasse domi Philo iurat, et hoc est:
> non cenat, quotiens nemo vocavit eum.

11.24.14–15 (the poet's confession for his failure to publish):

> Sic fit
> cum cenare domi poeta non vult.

[44] Cf. Juv. 5 *passim;* Marquardt, *op. cit.,* p. 207, n. 4.

[45] *Epist.* 2.6, especially 3, 4 (in which he is describing his own practice): "Eadem omnibus pono: ad cenam enim, non ad notam invito cunctisque rebus exaequo quos mensa et toro aequavi." "Etiamne libertos?" "Etiam: convictores enim tunc, non libertos puto." . . . liberti mei non idem quod ego bibunt, sed idem ego quod liberti.

To a modern reader, perhaps the worst feature of the *cliens'* lot was the necessity of his accepting the petty alms doled out to him in the form of the *sportula*. Such a pauperizing, pride-destroying institution may never command our respect, but we are bound, in fairness to the ancients, to make an effort to appreciate their point of view.

To begin with, we must recognize a twofold use of the word, as it is applied to large "public" functions and to private entertaining. With reference to the first, I have tried to show that the *sportula* did not simply represent the value of the refreshments served, but was rather in the nature of a gift or favor accompanying a "meal" which was usually light, to say the least.[46] At these functions, referred to in hundreds of inscriptions, it is noteworthy that if any discrimination was made in the distribution of the money it was likely to be in favor of the wealthier classes, the *decuriones* and *Augustales*.[47] From this it is perfectly evident that no stigma was attached to the receipt of such gratuities: they simply constituted a part of the host's obligation, especially important when the number of guests precluded the serving of a satisfactory meal. Viewed in this light the *sportula,* both public and private, is to be considered as a guest present, comparable with *xenia* and *apophoreta*.[48] Abuses there were, but even in the "decadent" society of Martial there was enough of true generosity left to give us pause in our criticism. The humorist himself has put the case of the patrons in its best light, in a poem explaining the failure of an acquaintance to invite him to a birthday dinner—because Martial had neglected to send a present the previous year. The sting of the protest is contained in the words, *non est sportula quae negotiatur,* that which expects a return is not a *sportula* at all. However there never has existed a race of men so unselfish as to

---

[46] "Notes on Public Meals," in *T.A.P.A.*, LIX (1928), xxv.

[47] Cf., e.g., *C.I.L.* IX. 5823; X. 5796, 5853, 5917, 5918; XI. 6014; XIV. 2120; Dessau, 6584.

[48] "Apophoreta," in *C.J.*, XXIII (1928), 248–257.

carry out such an ideal of disinterested generosity fully, and our consideration of the *sportula* can perhaps best be introduced by noticing one of its most flagrant abuses.

In his letter concerning claques, Pliny uses these words to describe the method employed in hiring them:[49] Sequuntur auditores actoribus similes, conducti et redempti: manceps convenitur: in media basilica tam palam sportulae quam in triclinio dantur. The cheapness of oratorical fame purchased in this way can hardly excite serious scorn, and the sordidness of such a *sportula* is beneath contempt; according to Martial's definition it would be no *sportula* at all. However, the chief interest in the passage for us lies in the comment of our shocked informant, who gives a clue as to what would have been "proper": *tam palam sportulae quam in triclinio dantur.* At first glance the distinction would seem to be slight: it is all right to give *sportulae,* but the recipients should follow their employer home and receive their wages in the privacy of his dining-room. Thus would appearances be preserved—and the cheering section remain intact. Such is the common interpretation of this passage. But there is a little more to it if we remember the natural use of the dining-room: the supporters in court should be entertained at dinner.[50] They became their patron's guests, temporary members of his household, to whom he owed a certain measure of support. If the relation between the *sportula* and the dinner was normally as close as Pliny suggests,[51] the *cliens'* position was one of real intimacy with his patron; and his wage was at least thinly disguised as a dinner-gift, or a part of the obligation due to him as a member of the *familia.*

[49] *Epist.* 2.14.4. See above, p. 249, n. 41.
[50] Cf. Mart. 6.48:

> Quod tam grande sophos clamat tibi turba togata,
> non tu, Pomponi, cena diserta tua est.

For the significance of an invitation to dinner cf. above, pp. 242, 243, below, p. 260.

[51] But cf. the view that it was a substitute for the dinner, Marquardt, *op. cit.,* p. 207; W. A. Becker, *Gallus*[3], vol. II, p. 164. It is this view which I hope to correct.

In the poem from which we got our idealistic definition, the *sportula* referred to was probably of the public variety, as is true in the case of another epigram describing the birthday party of a parvenu:[52]

> Natali, Diodore, tuo conviva senatus
>   accubat et rarus non adhibetur eques,
> et tua tricenos largitur sportula nummos.
>   nemo tamen natum te, Diodore, putat.

In this wholesale entertainment of the élite of Rome, the guests were given thirty sesterces apiece as a sort of favor. Why they should condescend to accept such bounty it is hard to see; it is still more difficult to understand why this form of entertainment appealed to the supposedly stingy patrons. The fact remains that it did. Indeed it was carried to such lengths that Domitian made a vain effort to abolish the whole institution "in the interest of public welfare:"[53] Multa etiam in communi rerum usu novavit: sportulas publicas sustulit revocata rectarum cenarum consuetudine. Somewhat later we find the institution flourishing in the distant province of Pontus and Bithynia, where Pliny brought its excesses to the attention of Trajan. On occasions such as the assumption of the *toga virilis,* the celebration of a wedding, entry on office, or the dedication of public buildings, cash was distributed to whole communities in a manner which savored strongly of public largess.[54] The emperor politely agrees that Pliny's fears as to the conduct of *sollemnes sportulae* are well founded—and leaves the solution in his hands. He showed real shrewdness in adopting this noncommittal attitude, since attempts at restriction were remarkably unsuccessful

---

[52] 10.27.　　　　　　　　　　[53] Suet. *Dom.* 7.1.

[54] *Epist.* 10.116(117): Qui virilem togam sumunt vel nuptias faciunt vel ineunt magistratum vel opus publicum dedicant, solent totam bulen atque etiam e plebe non exiguum numerum vocare binosque denarios vel singulos dare. . . . ita vereor, ne ii, qui mille homines, interdum etiam plures vocant, modum excedere et in speciem διανομῆς incidere videantur. As to the occasions here enumerated, it might be noted that the assumption of office and the dedication of public works are mentioned very frequently in inscriptions. Trajan's reply is contained in the following letter, 117 (118).

throughout the empire, if we may judge from the copious evidence of inscriptions.

The relation of the *sportula* of the *cliens* to these large-scale entertainments is evident not only in the fact that both were called by the same name, but also in the circumstance that Domitian's temporary abolition of public *sportulae* also affected the private dole. Indeed it happens that there is no evidence either epigraphical or literary of the effect produced on the public *sportulae,* whereas we do find references to the effect of this decree on private ones in the third book of Martial's epigrams.[55] That it was unpopular with *clientes* appears clearly in all three of the poems we shall consider;[56] if it lightened the financial burden of the patrons, they and their emperor had to yield to the general demand for its abolition. Fortunately for us, this sudden interruption of the even tenor of *cliens*-life made "copy" of an institution which had previously been taken for granted, so that Martial's poems on the subject form a good starting point for the study of the relation of the *sportula* to the dinner. Let us consider them in order:[57]

> Centum miselli iam valete quadrantes,
> anteambulonis congiarium lassi,
> quos dividebat balneator elixus.
> quid cogitatis, o fames amicorum?
> regis superbi sportulae recesserunt.

Here we learn definitely that the *sportula* was a dole or gift, given out at the bath which terminated the escort's weary day;[58]

---

[55] Published in 87 A.D. Since the regular *sportula* is referred to in succeeding books we may infer that the decree was in effect for a year or less.

[56] Cf. also 3.14. [57] 3.7.1–5.

[58] Cf. 10.70.13–14:

> balnea post decumam lasso centumque petuntur
> quadrantes. Fiet quando, Potite, liber?

This poem suggests 11.24, above, p. 250, n. 43, in which the author confesses that his distaste for dining at home interferes seriously with his writing; the *centum quadrantes* and the dinner together constituted the reward of *cliens*-service. In the case of Martial it appears that the social intercourse of the dinner had more of an appeal than trifling *sportulae* (cf. 10.74.4 centum . . .

254

hunger, as usual, is the distinguishing characteristic of the *amici*[59]—hunger for the patron's meal, and greed for the small change which went with it.

The other two confess in unblushing terms to the utter lack of personal pride which permitted Roman gentlemen to welcome invitations which carried with them an offer of charity.

> Sportula nulla datur; gratis conviva recumbis:
> dic mihi, quid Romae, Gargiliane, facis?
> unde tibi togula est et fuscae pensio cellae?[60]

"No *sportula* is given; you recline at dinner without being paid for it. . . ." The dole and the meal were so closely associated that the *cliens* could say he was paid for his trencher service! From 3.60 we learn that the *cliens* was habitually and willingly "venal" (vv. 1–2, 10):

> Cum vocer ad cenam non iam venalis ut ante,
> cur mihi non eadem quae tibi cena datur?
>
> .   .   .   .   .   .
>
> sportula quod non est prosit: edamus idem.

The shabbiness of this form of entertaining was at best an affront to the *amicus*,[61] when unaccompanied by a gift of small change it indicated plain, inexcusable stinginess on the part of the host. Most important for our purpose, however, is the use of the expression, *Cum vocer ad cenam . . . venalis,* "since I am not invited to dinner for a consideration as I used to be." The financial arrangement is perfectly clear; the *cliens* might be paid off immediately before the meal,[62] or in the dining-room.[63]

---

plumbeos). For the close connection between the bath and the *cena,* cf. 10.48.3; 11.52.3 (both dinner-invitations); *C.I.L.* XI. 3811; XIV. 2112 *fin.:* et di(ebus natalibus) Dianae et Antinoi oleum in balinio publico po(nant antequam) epulentur.

[59] See above, pp. 249, 250, nn. 42, 43.   [60] Mart. 3.30.1–3.
[61] Cf. above, p. 250, nn. 44, 45; below, p. 256.
[62] That is, at the bath; above, p. 254, n. 58.
[63] Above, p. 252. Martial is simply saying the same thing in another way

This whole procedure is so inconceivable to the modern mind that scholars have gone to great pains to explain away references to cash in connection with meals. In the expressions *vocer . . . venalis* and *gratis recumbis,* we might see general references to the giving of a *sportula* at some time other than that of the evening meal. In other cases editors have accepted the ingenious explanation that sums of money mentioned in connection with meals refer to the cost per plate—how or why computed, we are not told. With laudable consistency they apply their formula to both literary and epigraphical references —with equally unconvincing results.[64]

The type of expression to which I would call attention is illustrated in Mart. 4.68:

> Invitas centum quadrantibus et bene cenas:
> Ut cenem invitor, Sexte, an ut invideam?

Friedländer and Post, in their notes, assert that this means he was invited to a meal whose preparation cost 100 *quadrantes,* while the host himself enjoyed superior fare. To begin with, this interpretation requires that we accept as a pure coincidence the fact that the sum mentioned corresponds with the common amount of the dole, the *congiarium anteambulonis lassi.* Further, we must forget that these lesser guests were regular recipients of the *sportula,* which was something with which to quiet

when he protests that a patron's dinner-guests, *convivae,* are cheated of their *sportula* by the host's sudden attacks of illness, 9.85:

> Languidior noster si quando est Paulus, Atili,
> non se, convivas abstinet ille suos.
> Tu languore quidem subito fictoque laboras,
> sed mea porrexit sportula, Paule, pedes.

Friedländer here pronounces the *sportula* "eine grosse Bewirthung," *i.e.,* a public *sportula.* But it seems much more simple to understand it as the everyday, private *sportula: si quando* implies a habitual practice of excusing himself, not from the rare special occasions on which hundreds or even thousands might be entertained—and from which it would be difficult to escape on any pretext—but from the daily routine of *salutatio, deductio,* and *cena* (for which see below, p. 261). The patron would offer his apologies through a slave at the time of the *salutatio,* Mart. 9.6(7).

[64] For the evidence of inscriptions, see *T.A.P.A., op. cit.,* and below, pp. 257–259.

an insistent tailor or landlord.[65] In view of all the evidence
that money was distributed to guests at ancient meals, why not
accept here the simple interpretation that our author received
a nice polite dinner-invitation in the form usual to recognized
clientes, and that he was disgusted at the treatment he received
when he accepted it? Martial himself issued invitations in this
form, if we may take his words seriously:[66]

> Si te sportula maior ad beatos
> non corruperit, ut solet, licebit
> de nostro, Matho, centies laveris.

The last line is certainly a whimsical reference to the conventional *sportula* of 100 *quadrantes.*[67] The absence of any mention of *cliens*-service, for which the dole served as a reward,
increases the probability that it was a dinner-invitation; and
from what we know of Matho, it may be that the subtle point
of the poem lies in its needlessness: it would have required an
"act of God"[68] to keep him home.

It is not my purpose here to go into a discussion of the public
sportula and the inscriptional evidence on which our knowledge
depends, but there is one striking case in which we have a fairly
detailed account of a dinner served in a style far surpassing not
only the mass entertainment at public *sportulae,* but even the
most lavish private banquets. I refer to the ceremonial feasts
of the Fratres Arvales. In the records of this priesthood we
find these words:[69] et coronae et un(guenta) et sportul(as)

---

[65] Mart. 3.30.3, above, p. 255.

[66] 8.42. For the name, Matho, see above, p. 243, n. 15.

[67] For the larger *sportula* referred to in v. 1 cf. 9.100.1, Denarîs tribus invitas
. . . ; 12.29(26).13–14, rogat ut secum cenes . . . viginti nummis? Both of
these passages describe dinner-invitations, the first accompanied by a suggestion
that Martial make a complete *cliens'* day of it, the second received at the *salutatio.*
See below, p. 261.

[68] Cf. 12.77.4–6:
> . . . sed ipse divom
> offensus genitor trinoctiali
> adfecit domicenio clientem.

[69] Henzen, *Act. Frat. Arv.,* p. ccvi (218 A.D.). Cf. p. ccv: post epulas

acc(eperunt) sing(uli) ✕ C. Hoc anno cenat(um) est *in* dies sing(ulos) ✕ C VI IIII III Kal(endas) Iun(ias): pueri cenav(erunt) senator(um) fil(ii) n(umero) IIII et sport(ulas) acc(eperunt) in d(ies) ✕ X . . . et felic(ia) dixerunt. In the first clause we are told in the plainest possible language that the *fratres* received three different things at the end of their elaborate and formal banquet: wreaths, ointment, and 100 denarii apiece. The "sons of senators" received less (the numerals have been effaced from the inscription, but if the X is correct, the amount was probably less than 50 denarii): the receipt of their *sportulae* was a pleasant formality at the end of the meal, which undoubtedly lent true fervor to the "benediction" with which it is here coupled. This all sounds strange and sordid, like a footnote for Upton Sinclair's "Profits of Religion," but it is exactly what the Latin words say.[70] In spite of this fact, the expression, *cenatum est* . . . ✕ *C,* "they dined at 100 denarii apiece," has been interpreted to mean the banquet cost 100 denarii per plate.[71] But the hundred denarii was the sum given to each guest—call it tip, favor, or priestly graft —and this expression following the detailed description of the whole function simply summarizes the previous account, laying emphasis on its most important feature, the unusual size of the *sportula.* In the more condensed accounts commonly found, inscriptions mention nothing but the money distributed, leaving the nature of the "refreshments" to our imagination. For the present, I wish simply to call attention to the striking similarity

. . . acceperunt sportulas; p. cxlvii 1.39 (105 A.D.): hoc anno *cenatum est sportulis denaris centenis.*

[70] So accepted by Boissier, "Étude sur Quelques Colléges Funeraires Romains —Les Cultores Deorum," in *Rev. Arch.,* 2d ser., 13.91 n. 1 (1872). For an even larger distribution he compares *Insc. Nap.* 189 (quoted by Mommsen, *De Collegiis et Sodaliciis,* p. 110): dedit ob statuae dedicationem col. dendrophor. et fabr. sing. H. S. millenos et epulum.

[71] Mommsen, *op. cit.;* Henzen, *op. cit.,* p. 16; Marquardt, *Staatsver.* vol. III, p. 434. This interpretation fails to take into account any change in money values between the years 105 and 218, which would have caused difficulties in serving the same type of meal at exactly the same price.

between the expression *cenatum est . . . denarîs centenis* on the one hand, and Martial's *rogat ut . . . cenes . . . viginti nummis, invitas centum quadrantibus,* etc., on the other. All refer to the same peculiar custom of giving money, *sportulae,* to dinner-guests.

Though the private *sportula* was normally associated with the dinner in the period we are considering,[72] a tendency to lose sight of this relation is already observable. We have seen how the old-fashioned Pliny was shocked by the distribution of *"sportulae"* in court rooms.[73] Juvenal, on the other hand, speaks definitely of the distribution of *sportulae* at the *salutatio:*[74]

> nunc sportula primo
> limine parva sedet, turbae rapienda togatae:
> ille tamen faciem prius inspicit et trepidat, ne
> suppositus venias ac falso nomine poscas.
> agnitus accipies. iubet a praecone vocari
> ipsos Troiugenas (nam vexant limen et ipsi
> nobiscum:) "da praetori, da deinde tribuno."
> sed libertinus prior est.
>
> .   .   .   .
>
>   densissima centum
> quadrantes lectica petit, sequiturque maritum
> languida vel praegnas et circumducitur uxor.
>
> .   .   .   .
>
> ipse dies pulchro distinguitur ordine rerum:
> sportula, deinde forum iurisque peritus Apollo.

It might be remarked that the function here described is also unique in its reference to the giving of the *sportula* to women and to men of the highest social rank.[75] From the pains taken

---

[72] The word comes later to have more of the general meaning of "gift" e.g. Saturnalitia sportula, Hieron., *Comm. In Ephes.* 3.6 (Patrologia Latina 26.540) ; Sym. *Epist.* 9.153(134, 124): Sportulam consulatus . . . in solido uno; 3.24, nuptialem sportulam (in this case sent a long distance).

[73] Above, p. 252.

[74] 1.95–102, 120–122, 127–128.

[75] Unless we have here some type of public *sportula.* In that case it is hard to see how it would fit into the day's program described in the last two lines of our quotation.

to exclude possible frauds it would appear that the function was attended on invitation, whereas the patron usually kept "open house" at that time. Further, in the last line of the passage quoted, not only is the *sportula* given first place in the day's program, but both the bath and the dinner are entirely omitted. However, as I suggested, Juvenal's account is unique; and evidence of the informal *salutatio,* as well as of the relation of the *sportula* to the evening meal, is to be found in Lucian's story of the "poor professor."[76] To secure the type of private position he desires, he first becomes a regular attendant at the rich man's *salutatio,* where for some time he receives little notice except from the tribute-exacting slaves. When finally he does attract some attention from the patron, he exerts himself to the utmost to make a favorable impression, "spending sleepless nights . . . not for the sake of Helen or Priam's Troy, but for the hope of five obols." Though the account is quite detailed, there is no mention of his receiving this *sportula,* or any other form of compensation for his efforts, till after he had passed his examination and been invited to his first dinner. Apparently all his previous attentions, burdensome to the professor and to his later employer alike, were in the nature of a probation, looking toward his acceptance—not merely as a *cliens,* in this case, but as a family tutor. And since this final acceptance was signalized by a dinner-invitation, we are justified in the inference that he had been working with that as his goal from the very beginning, and that the five obols were incidental to the meal. Most important for us is the evidence that at this late date the *cena* still retained its significance as a symbol of the closest intimacy and of mutually recognized obligations.[77]

A word remains to be said concerning the relation of the *cliens'* duties to his reward, whether this assumed the form of a dinner-invitation or the *sportula* or both. The original arrange-

[76] *De Merc. Cond.* 10, 11, 14. For the tipping, cf. above, p. 247, n. 29.
[77] Cf. above, pp. 242, 243.

ment is probably reflected in Horace's account of the relations between Philippus and Maena:[78] the patron's invitation to dinner put Maena under obligation to attend his *salutatio* and show proper deference when he met him in the street. In other words, Maena became a member of Philippus' household. A partial survival of this intimate arrangement is perhaps seen in the invitation Martial received from Bassus:[79]

> Denarîs tribus invitas et mane togatum
>   observare iubes atria, Basse, tua,
> deinde haerere tuo lateri, praecedere sellam,
>   ad vetulas tecum plus minus ire decem.
> Trita quidem nobis togula est vilisque vetusque:
>   denarîs tamen hanc non emo, Basse, tribus.

Viewed as a bargain stipulating the payment of three denarii for a day's *cliens*-service it is sordid enough, and Martial's rejection is amply justified. Looked at as an invitation to join Bassus' household for the day—to accompany him on his round of personal calls and join him at dinner—it becomes quite a different matter. Undoubtedly it depended entirely on the personality of the patron as to which way his invitation should be construed.

A brighter prospect for the *amicus* lay in the chance of his winning the patronage of some person without social or political ambitions, who used his early mornings for sleep.[80] There is no suggestion, for instance, that Matho was expected to earn his dinner and *sportula* by paying an early call.[81] In fact if Martial himself had been a wealthy man, it is hard to imagine that he would have issued invitations in the form employed by Bassus. Another possibility was that the patron would recognize his *amici* as veterans after a reasonable period of service, and exempt them from further performance of their arduous duties.[82]

---

[78] Above, pp. 242, 243.   [79] 9.100.
[80] Cf. Mart. 5.22.14: rex, nisi dormieris, non potes esse meus.
[81] See above, p. 257.
[82] Cf. Mart. 3.36.9–10:

> hoc merui, Fabiane, toga tritaque meaque,
>   ut nondum credas me meruisse rudem?

Still others, with a real or pretended interest in the arts, may have been only too glad to accept the "tenth hour" greetings of such persons as Martial.[83]

But the rank and file of *clientes* did not live in such a carefree Utopia as we have been picturing; they had to work for a living—and a precarious living at that. Their task was to overcome the "sales resistance" of possible hosts. They were hunters, "dinner hunters"; the open season was five to eight A.M. every day in the year;[84] any man with a little more money or social position than the sportsman constituted his legal game. In this fact lies the chief defense of the patrons: the great majority of their *salutatores* were social climbers, self-invited guests, greedy for any favors that might be obtained. Through the centuries Maecenas has enjoyed an enviable reputation as the ideal patron, and his taste in choosing Virgil and Horace as protégés constitutes his claim to immortality. But what are we to think of the "bore," the perennial type of the "go-getter" in ancient Rome, who describes his proposed strategy in Horace's familiar satire:[85]

> "Haud mihi deero.
> Muneribus servos corrumpam; non, hodie si
> Exclusus fuero, desistam: tempora quaeram,
> Occurram in triviis, deducam. Nil sine magno
> Vita labore dedit mortalibus."

Are we not made to feel that after he had bribed his way into the *salutatio*[86] and forced himself on Maecenas in his daily parade to the forum, he would still have deserved the coolest of treatment? Should not his hope of a dinner, with the obligation it imposed on the host, have been *longissima?* Such tactics as these undoubtedly had more to do with the corruption

---

[83] 1.108.9–10.

[84] Though the baths and porticoes also offered ample opportunities for pursuit of the quarry later in the day.

[85] *Serm.* 1.9.56–60.

[86] Probably the chief purpose of his "gifts." Cf. Juv. 3.184–189; Lucian, *op. cit.*, 10; above, p. 260.

of *cliens*-life than the "haughtiness" of the rich; the earliest bribers of household slaves were responsible for the development of the annoying tipping system described by Juvenal.

As we started with emphasis on the contrasts between ancient and modern life, we may conclude with mention of what seems to be a strikingly similar characteristic of the Romans and ourselves, namely the possession of an unusual amount of surplus energy. The physical restlessness this produces is well illustrated in Lucretius' vivid picture of the noble driving to his villa as if to a fire—then turning back to the city.[87] One need but multiply the speed to make the description apply to the thousands of holiday motorists who overcrowd our highways. However, in general, the Romans' energy sought different outlets. In the intellectual field, they turned to the writing of epic poetry, we to the reading of novels (or, occasionally, to worthwhile scientific research) ; they "went in for" horse-racing and gladiatorial shows instead of baseball and movies. Furthermore, the Roman-born scorned our chief outlet for energy—or means of escaping from ourselves—which we find in frenzied finance. The bulk of their surplus energy went into maintaining a dizzy social life, featured by early morning calls, the institution of the bath, and protracted dinners. Incidentally they appear to have "muddled through" to a partial solution of the difficulties of the "proud but poor"—a solution which could not command the approval of a jaundiced satirist, but for which we are bound to give due credit to a humane and generous class of capitalists.

[87] 3.1060–1067. Cf. Hor. *Serm.* 2.7.28; *Epist.* 1.8.12; Sen. *Epist.* 28.3.

FRANKLIN AND MARSHALL COLLEGE

PAPYRUS 1804 IN THE MICHIGAN
COLLECTION

Henry A. Sanders

AMONG the papyri bought in Cairo for the University of Michigan by the late Professor Kelsey during the years 1920 to 1925 this fragment has been chosen for a preliminary publication, because it is written in Latin and deals with military matters. Not only is it fragmentary, but some parts are difficult to read. Photographs with copies of my original reading were sent to Professors Wilcken and Hunt, who most kindly made criticisms and suggestions. Also Professor Dittmann of the *Thesaurus Linguae Latinae* gave information on a troublesome word. Suggestions from these scholars will be marked by their names as they occur in the text or discussion. Even with this help the interpretation is still somewhat provisional, and further criticism is invited.

Papyrus 1804 is a ragged discolored piece, 22 by 12 cm. in its largest dimensions. Its entire outer surface is much worn and it must have been badly crumpled up when found. Though a remarkably good job of damping out was done by Mr. Lamacraft of the British Museum, a powerful microscope revealed very many twisted and misplaced fibers. So far as possible these were straightened out during my first attempt to read the text, and not a few readings were made clearer by the process; yet in other cases nothing could be done except to establish that the surface had been so removed or injured, that any reading must remain somewhat tentative. Also for this reason the photograph (Plate I) cannot always be relied upon.

The papyrus contains a list of subordinate officers with brief remarks regarding each. The names of the officers are in large rustic capitals, the descriptions in cursive, as in the Pridianum,

265

CLASSICAL STUDIES

B.G.U. 696; cf. Bell, *Raccolta in Onore di G. Lumbroso,* p. 265.
The date, fixed by the consulships mentioned as just after 242
A.D., makes this an interesting sample of writing.

The document follows as read at present with such additions
in the *lacunae* as seem probable and helpful to the discussion,
and with notes explaining the readings and additions. References are made to the document by line.

1   . . . .
2   . . . .
3   au]FIDIUS VICTORINUS   *Date*
4 probatus ? p]ṛaesente et Ẹxtrica[to] c̣[o]s factus
   dec' ex q' ḷeg[. . . .   217
5 a bas]ị[l]ẹ[o] praẹf Aeg II non[a]ṣ Apriles Attico
   et Prae[textato cos]   242
6   c]ORDIUS PETOSIRIS
7 . . . .] Graṭ[o e]ṭ Seleuco c̣[o]ṣ [fa]ctus dec'
   ex sesq' alae[221
8 et praep]osit. . ạ. iọ et praefẹc̣[tus] aṛcis a Basileo
   p[raef aeg. . . .]   242–5
9   a]NTONIUS AMMONIANUS
10 . . . .] Maximo et Ur[b]an[o] c̣ọs factus dec'
    ex sesq' alae[234
11 a ba]ṣileọ v' p' prae[f ae]g X̣VI Kal' Novembr At-
    tico et Pr[aetextato cos]   242
12   ]ḶỊUS CHIERAX
13 . . . . .cos] factus ḍ[e]c ex dupl' alae
    Gạll Gor[d
14 [a basileo praef aeg . . . . apri]les Aṭtico et Prae-
    texta[to cos]   242
15   ]ỤṢ ORIGIN[E]S
16 . . . .] F[u]ṣco Ị[I et dextr]e coṣ f[actus dec]
    ex sesq[225
17 [ab honoratia]ṇo praẹf Ạ[eg . . . . . n]ovẹ[mbr
    se]veṛ[o et quintiano cos]   235

MICHIGAN PAPYRUS 1804

18   COH III ITURAE[o]RU̧[m]
19   ŌR DD
20   Ç[al]EFOFES HIERAX
21 .... ag]ṛic[o]la et Clementino cos factus dec'
    ex̣[230
22 ab honorat]iano praef Aeg III Kal Sept Agricola et
    Ṃ[aximo II cos]   234
23   a]Ẹ[mi]ḶIUS Ẹ[t]ẸOCRAṬEṢ
24 .... a]gricola et Clementino [cos f]actus orḍ
    [de]ç ex̣[230
25   .....]ạ et .eṣ[

NOTES

1–2. It is an attractive surmise that *Coh. II Ituraeorum equi-tata* stood here, for that cohort was always in Upper Egypt, as was probably *Coh. III Ituraeorum,* which follows. If this document emanated from the camp at Thebes, it would be likely to report on the cohorts in natural order. Against this assumption it must be said, that thus far no title has been read at the top of the papyrus, though there is space for two lines. The slight strokes that one seems to see on the photograph are due to discolorations of the papyrus. Because of the general discoloration we can not assert that the space was blank.

3. The name Aufidius Victorinus is well known. There was a consul of this family in 183 A.D. and another in 200 A.D. That we have here a descendant of that particular family is not likely, though not wholly impossible because of the revolutions of the period. Both names occur often in other combinations. The date added at the right gives the year of the consuls named.

4. *Probatus* is a common term for enlistment in the army, cf. Pliny, *Ep.* 10.30; so also *tirones probati, B.G.U.* 696. *Factus miles* is also used (*C.I.L.* VI.220; XII.2602) and *qui militare coeperunt* is found abbreviated in a *pridianum* (*B.G.U.* 696 and *Racc. G. Lumbroso,* p. 269). In the literature *conscriptus* is

267

often found. We can be quite certain that some expression meaning "enlisted" stood at the beginning of each "cursus honorum," for the space of 25 years before the attainment of the decurionate by this officer precludes any previous promotion being considered. Judging from the names of the officers, where little more than the initial of the *praenomen* is missing in the best-preserved lines, not much of the document is lost on the left-hand side. Also in the beginnings of the descriptions the pairs of consuls' names are almost directly under each other. Not only was there not much more than one word lost at the beginning of each line, but it was the same number of letters for each. The day and month of the date were probably omitted. *dec'* is to be expanded *decurio* and means the commander of a squadron of 30 or more cavalrymen. The abbreviation mark on this word and elsewhere, where visible, looks like an acute accent over or just after the last letter. In some cases there seems to be a slight curve or flourish to the stroke. *q'* is probably to be expanded *q(uaestionario)*, especially if my reading *leg-(ionis)* is right. The only legion in Egypt at this time was "the Second Trajana," cf. Lesquier, *L'Armée Romaine d'Égypte*, pp. 40 ff. The reading *leg(ionis)* is made somewhat doubtful by a discoloration, which precedes the *l*, though it is not sure that this is ink and it looks like no known letter.

5. *praef. Aeg.* has the letters strangely crowded and obscured, yet the reading is made certain by the comparison of the parallel descriptions. Of Bas]i[l]e[o] the bottom of *i* is clearly seen, but the bottom of *e* looks more like *i*. *Basilio* may have been written. Basileus was prefect of Egypt in 242 A.D. The date of the promotion follows and is easily completed to give the consuls for the year 242. Only ten letters have to be supplied. The other lines that can be restored with certainty lack from five to fifteen letters. It is clear that no very wide margin is lost on the right.

6. c]ordius Petosiris; Petosiris was read by both Hunt and Wilcken for my first suggestion, Phosiris. They are undoubt-

edly right. Cordius is a known Roman name of the Republican period (M' Cordius Rufus). Also there was a charioteer Cordius (Gordius in Dio) made *praefectus vigilum* by Elagabalus. To the Greeks of Egypt there was probably little difference in sound between Cordius and Gordius. That may help to explain his double (or triple) promotion in 242 under the Emperor Gordianus III.

7. The beginning of the line, though much injured, is read with certainty as the consuls for 221 A.D. and there are definite traces, though illegible, of two letters before the name of the first consul. Petosiris was made *decurio* from *sesq(uiplicarius)* of an *alae*, of which the name is lost. Originally *sesquiplicarius* was a soldier, who received one and one half times the pay of a common soldier, but here it is the later use of the word meaning a cavalry officer below the *decurio*, though it doubtless marked his pay also.

8. *praep]osit . . a . io et praefec[tus] arcis* is decidedly doubtful. That other promotions are here recorded, parallel to or following that to *decurio*, is made probable by *a Basileo p[raef. Aeg.]*, which follows, but one would expect *turmae, vexillationis,* or *cohortis*[1] to follow *praepositus*. Of the letters recorded as seen in the original, *a* is the nearest certain, yet an *o* with a tall letter following might fit the remnants. There seem to be remains of a larger curved letter before the *a*, so it is just possible that *praeposit. cohort.* was crowded into the space, though it would present some difficulty in interpreting. The first letters following *praeposit* might be reconciled with *equit.* but not the last, unless *equitū* is read, which would crowd the space. *Turmae* and *vexillationis* seem absolutely impossible. The papyrus will have to be examined again, though I doubt if much more can be read. There does not seem to be room at the end of the line for the date. Certainly not more than the consulship could have stood there, and if the different promo-

---

[1] Cf. *C.I.L.* VIII.21560, a *decurio* made *praepositus* of a *cohors quingenaria* (243 A.D.).

tions were not simultaneous, the name of the prefect making them would serve as a date.

9. The name Antonius Ammonianus is found also in *Pap. Hamburg.* 39, as a *decurio alae vet. Gall.* in 179 A.D., and in Dessau, 2304; 3296. It was evidently an old and common name in military circles in Egypt.

10. In this line we need to supply only the word for "enlisted" at the beginning, and at the end the name of the *ala* of which he was *sesquiplicarius*.

11. This line makes certain the restoration of *a Basileo praef(ecto) Aeg(ypti)* for the four promotions made in 242 A.D. Here Basileus is called v(ir) p(erfectissimus), an early but correct use of the title. *XVI Kal'* is a little doubtful, as the numeral looks more like *IVI*. The extra oblique stroke near the top of the first perpendicular is probably the cross stroke of the *x*.

12. The first name probably ended in *lius,* but with Aurelius, Aemilius, Servilius, etc., all so common in Egypt, not even a guess can be attempted. Chierax is a variant of Hierax discussed below. Hunt reads Hierax here, holding that the curve before H is only a part of the cross stroke.

13. The loss of the consuls' names prevents our knowing the length of service of this soldier. He was promoted from *duplicarius* or *duplarius,* a soldier who received double pay and rations as a reward for services. In the form *duplicarius* it later became the title of the cavalry officer next lower than the decurion, which is the meaning here. This time the name of the *ala* is decipherable. It is to be completed *alae Gall(icae) Gor[dianae],* which is probably the same as *ala Antoniniana Gallica,* mentioned in a papyrus of 216–217 A.D. (*B.G.U.* 614). The name was changed with the Emperor, cf. Pauly-Wissowa, I, 1226.

14. The whole line is very fragmentary, but the date of the consuls, 242 A.D., makes it certain that the promotion was made by the prefect Basileus, and we may even restore the day of the

month, [*II Nonas Apri*]*les,* as the prefect would not have been likely to have made promotions in the same cohort more than once in a single month, cf. above l. 5.

15. . . . . . u̦ș Origin[e]s; the *nomen* cannot be restored, though signs of ink are visible on the preceding twisted fibers. The cognomen is known in Egypt; cf. Wilcken, *Ostraka,* 1128a, a centurion. Professor Winter reports another in an unpublished Michigan papyrus, and there is also the famous Christian writer.

16. *F*[*u*]*șco I̦*[*I et Dextr*]*e co̦ș.* The remnants of this date are very scanty, but our choice of consulships is limited to a definite period and the legible letters can be made to accord only with the names of the consuls for 225 A.D. Of *f*[*actus dec*] only the first letter is preserved, but its occurrence in the four previous descriptions and the length of the *lacuna* make it fairly certain. Also again the promotion is made from *sesquiplicarius.*

17. *praef. A̦*[*eg*] must be right, even though the *e* of *praef.* looks more like *i.* However, as in *Basileo* of line 5, only the bottom of it is visible. This is preceded by . . *io* or by . . *no.* Later in the line]*ove̦*[for [*N*]*ove*[*mbr*] is legible and thereafter]*ver̦*[, which must be assigned to the name of the first consul. For]*ver*[one might read]*vei̦*[, which cannot be reconciled with any known consul of this period; also that would leave a mark following the *i,* which resembles no Latin letter. It is better to read]*ver*[and consider the *r* carelessly written. This gives us the consuls for 235 A.D., and Honoratianus was prefect from 231 to 235 or longer, whose name is supported by the doubtful reading]*n̦o* at the beginning of the line.

18. The long blank before the name of the cohort implies a similar blank after it, so *equitata* was not added.

19. O̅R̅ DD; this abbreviation will be discussed below.

20. C̦[al̦]efofes Hierax; *efofes* is read clearly and three letters must have preceded; note the curved top of the C. Καλε is found at the beginning of other Greek-Egyptian names, as is also Κελε. The name as a whole is barbarian, perhaps Egyp-

tian. Hierax is a Greek name meaning the "Hawk." It was very common in Egypt, cf. Preisigke, *Namenbuch*.

21. The general form of the description is the same as for the officers of the preceding cohort. A word meaning "enlisted" stood first, then the consuls' names for 230 A.D. At the end, the previous office and the corps are lost.

22. *ab Honorat]iano praef. Aeg.* seems a certain restoration. That helps to determine the consulship, which I have completed *Agricola et M[aximo II cos.]* = 234 A.D. The *Fasti* give *Maximo II et Urbano cos.* for 234 A.D., and so it is read above in line 10, except that *II* is omitted. However, *Maximo II et Agricola* is already known from *C.I.L.* III.5460, and for that reason the name Urbanus Agricola is usually given to the second consul for the year 234. The change in order of the consuls' names is not particularly rare, and would create no serious difficulty here, were it not for the correct order of the names in line 10 above. Further difficulty is created by any attempt to restore the names of the consuls in line 25. It must also be admitted that the remnants of *M* in *Maximo* are very slight in this line. The identification is by no means certain.

23. A]ẹ[mi]lius Ẹ[t]ẹocrates; the nomen is very doubtful. Caesellius or Servilius would suit the remnants of letters almost as well. For Eteocrates I had at first read, doubtfully, Mocrates or . . ocrates, but the suggestion of Professor Wilcken, A[r]pocrates caused me to consider the possibility of supplying three letters in the space, recognizing, however, that the letters must be narrow. For this reason as well as the shape of the bottom of the letter before *o,* it seems impossible to read Arpocrates. Theocrates is possible, but would require more space, and it is doubtful if an initial T would have been made shorter than the other letters, as would be necessary to conform to the traces of ink preserved.

24. The difficulty in this line is the interpretation of *ord.* [*de*]ς (Wilcken), which will be discussed below.

25. Here only *et* is sure and it must stand between the names

of the two consuls. Before it is seen a bit of an angle, which seems reconcilable only with the letter *a*. It would be easy to supply Agricola, whose name appears more than once in this period, but the letters following *et* cannot be made to harmonize with any known consul's name of the period. Certainly there is no sign of an *m* at the beginning. The second letter, or perhaps the first, is apparently an *e;* after that comes a very doubtful *s* and after a space a letter with a tall shaft. Not only must this consulship remain doubtful, but it casts some doubt on the identification in line 22, unless we read some other name than Agricola for the first consul here. Aviola was consul with Gordianus in 239, but it is inconceivable that the Emperor's name should be put second. There were, however, several consuls in the period, of whom we know but a single name each, so that it is possible that the consuls for a different year are concealed here.

THE ABBREVIATIONS *ord.* AND O̅R̅ DD

We will take up first the abbreviation in line 24, *ord.* [*de*]ç. This was first read *ord* [*d*]*ec* by Wilcken as a query in place of my guess *arç*[*hi*]*ţec*[*tus*] as the nearest approach to the letters, which I thought to read, *orc . . cec . .* In Wilcken's suggestion *ord.* is surely correct; slight remnants of both the bottom and the top of the upright shaft of *d* are visible. [*d*]*ec* hardly conforms to the style of this scribe, for the top of the *d* is too far to the right as well as inclined over the *e,* and it also causes too much blank space to be left between the two words. To be sure the bit of papyrus to the right is almost detached from the rest of the document, and so may be moved to the right or left slightly as the hanging fibers permit. However, the position is well determined by the name above, Eteocrates. In this a bit of the shaft of the T is visible, which should not cut the slanting stroke of A; cf. Chierax and Hierax above. From this it is certain that the fragments cannot be brought nearer together, but should even be drawn apart a little more. For that reason I have read *ord.* [*de*]*ç ex,* yet I do not feel at all sure that the bit of a stroke visible before *ex* is the top of a *c,* and not the abbreviation stroke regularly used after *dec.;* cf. lines 4, 7, and 10. With a very slight moving of the fragment there would be space for *ord.* [*dec*]' *ex.* The only letter presenting difficulty for this modification of Wilcken's reading is *x,* which seems to look more like an *o* or *c.* The papyrus fibers are, however, much disarranged in this frayed edge and the repeated damping out in an attempt to get them straight has not improved the legibility. There are similar illegible spots elsewhere in the document. Therefore as *e* is plain and we cannot read *d* before it, we must read *x* after it, so as to conform to the regular construction of the brief descriptions given in this document. The reading adopted is not to be considered as certain, but rather as possible, or even as probable, if a reasonable interpretation can be found for it. The abbreviation *ord.* is often found in inscriptions and is expanded *ord(inarius)* or *ord(inatus).* If that is adopted here, what will be its meaning? It is premature to discuss the meaning of *ordinarius* and *ordinatus* without access to the large amount of evidence gathered for the *Thesaurus,* but as it is essential to the understanding of this document, I venture to draw some inferences from the evidence at present available.

First: there are numerous cases of both *ordinarius* and *ordinatus* in conjunction with *centurio* and alone. All of these look like technical military terms. *Ordinarius* or *ordinatus* is also found with *magister militum, medicus, architectus, mensor,* and even *miles,* as well as with *consules* and *iudices.* With *miles, ordinarius* means *gregarius* or *manipularis,* as quoted by Isidore, *Orig.* 9.3.33 (Dittmann) and by Festus, p. 182 (M.). Both of these are dictionary references and probably refer to older Latin, as does *ordinarius* = *scurra et improbus* (Festus, l.c.). I know of no inscriptional evidence for such a use of *ordinarius.*

Second: in all inscriptional instances *ordinarius* and *ordinatus* are terms of honor, which the subject of the inscription or his friends have used intentionally.

Third: both words are generally used in brief designations of honors rather than in cases of the full *cursus honorum*. A good example is *C.I.L.* VI.3603: *D.M. Iul. Crescens ex leg. VII Cl. ordinatus centurio in leg. IIII Scyt. vixit ann. XLIII.* From his age we may assume that Crescens served about twenty-five years. He certainly held minor offices at first, but his friends chose to give only his highest. Used thus as a term of honor *ordinatus centurio* should be distinctly higher than *centurio* without designation. We note that he holds it in a named legion so it is a regular command of a century. There is no statement that he held any office in the Seventh Claudian legion.

Fourth: Thirty-three instances of *ordinarius* and *ordinatus* associated with or equivalent to *centurio* have been cited by scholars. In eight cases *ordinarius* stands alone: *C.I.L.* III. 6532; VI.33469; XI.4787; *Pap. Müench.* 105; *Mélange Nicole,* p. 64; Vegetius, 2.7 (*ordinarii dicuntur, qui in proelio, quia primi sunt, ordines ducunt*); *S.H.A. vita Bonosi,* 14; *Notitia Dig. Or.* 37.

Centurio ordinarius (*C.I.L.* V.8275) and *ordinarius centurio* (Capitolinus, *Clodius Albinus,* 11.6) occur once each.

Ordinatus is found alone nine times: *C.I.L.* III.830; 6131; 7454; 7631; 8721; VII.365; 421; VIII.9967; *Mélange Nicole,* p. 60. *Ordinatio mea, C.I.L.* V.7009, seems equivalent.

Centurio ordinatus occurs in two identical inscriptions; *C.I.L.* V.7865–6.

Ordinatus centurio is found once: *C.I.L.* VI.3603.

Ord. or *ordi.* or *ordin.* is found eight times: *C.I.L.* VII.231, 404; 422; VIII.2505; XIII.8208; *Pap. Oxy.* VI.942; *Eph. Epig.* II.781 a; IV.445.

Centurio ord. is noted twice (*C.I.L.* V.942; XI.388), but *ord. centurio* does not appear to occur.

In the above cases *centurio* is sometimes abbreviated, but the expansion is always certain. It may be noted that the evidence is well distributed over the Empire; Rome, Italy, Gaul, Africa, and the Greek-speaking provinces all furnish instances.

No distinction can be drawn between *ordinarius* and *ordinatus* in the cases associated with *centurio*. Both are distinctly honorable terms. Not even *C.I.L.* V.7865 can be classed as different: *Emboudius Montanus leg(ionis) III Italicae centurio ordinatus ex eq(uite) Rom(ano) ab Domino . . .*, for De Ruggiero, II. p. 197, notes two promotions that seem parallel: *C.I.L.* III.750, *primipilaris leg(ionis) I Italicae ex equite Romano,* and IX.951, *pr(imo) p(ilo) ex equite R(omano).* *Adlectus* is the technical expression for the entrance of a Roman knight upon his military career with an appointment as centurion, but it is easily omitted, as here, in the case of the higher ranks of centurions.

The honorable position of the *ordinarius* is shown by the inscription, *C.I.L.* XI.4787: *viro ducenario protectori ex ordinario leg. II Ital. divit. vixit ann. XL, mil. ann. XXV.* The *ducenarii* were of the rank of prefects, even *praefecti legionis* in Egypt, cf. Domaszewski, *Rangord.,* p. 121. In both *ordinarius* and *ordinatus* a definite higher rank of centurions seems indicated. Elsewhere officers of this rank are called *primi ordines* or *centuriones primi ordinis;* cf. Frontinus, *Strat.* 1.11.2; Caesar, *B.G.* 5.44.1; Vell. Paterculus, 2.112.6; Tacitus, *Hist.* 3.22; *Ann.* 1.29; *C.I.L.* VIII.18042; 18065 (so De Ruggiero, II.197; Marquardt, *Röm. Staats.* II, p. 462). The use of *ordinarius* with *centurio* would seem to correspond perfectly with the very common use of *ordinarii* with *consules* and *iudices.*

More generally officers designated as *ordinarii* and *ordinati* seem to have belonged to the legions, or the corps is not stated. Three have been referred to *numeri* and one to an auxiliary cohort. As the interpretation of the words must be determined by the majority of the instances, it is necessary to assume that there was a similar distinction of rank among the centurions in the *numeri* and auxiliary cohorts. For the latter this is shown by Domaszewski, p. 56, under *centurio princeps.* In one case,

C.I.L. III.7631, two are named in the same cohort. As the *numeri* were distributed in centuries after the manner of the legions and auxiliary cohorts, the assumption of a difference of rank among the centurions is a natural one, though I have not found it made elsewhere. At least one centurion, as in the auxiliary cohort, would have outranked the others and so have taken temporary command in case of need.

We have noted above several subordinate offices with which the terms *ordinatus* or *ordinarius* are sometimes associated. These must be briefly discussed. Domaszewski, p. 25, mentions an *ordinatus architectus* from Ravenna (*C.I.L.* XI.20). This is a complete *cursus honorum.* Flavius Rufus starts as *miles* in the *cohortes urbanae,* passes to a praetorian cohort, where he is in succession *ordinatus architectus, tesserarius,* and *beneficiarius praefecti praetorio.* After this he becomes *cornicularius prae-fecti annonae,* and then passes through a succession of centurion-ships in the following legions, XIII, XI, II, and VII. The first part of this *cursus honorum* is unusual. One may suspect that Flavius was originally an architect, who had to be enrolled as a soldier in order to direct military works. *Ordinatus architectus* should mean, not an architect who serves in the ranks, for he is the first stage above *miles,* but rather one who has been re-lieved from the soldiers' duties and is now architect only. He probably continued as architect with each promotion up to the centurionship, if not beyond. With this may be compared *C.I.L.* VI.30715, in which Domaszewski supplies *architectus* in a *lacuna* before *ordinatus.* Perhaps the following are similar: *ord(inatus) custos vivari coh. praet. et urb., C.I.L.* VI.130, and *m(ensor) o(rdinatus), C.I.L.* VI.32520, which has been ex-panded *m(ensor) o(rdinarius).* In all these cases *ordinatus* seems somewhat different from the technical use interchange-able with *ordinarius.* It rather marks the beginning of that use, or a remembrance of it. As the participle from *ordinare,* it means arranged in order, assigned, or appointed, i.e., to some position in a succession or rank, and so it implies promotion.

Medicus ordinarius seems rather a term of honor. Cases cited by Domaszewski, pp. 45 and 58, are *C.I.L.* III.4279 and VIII. 18314, to which can be added *C.I.L.* III.5959; 14347[5]; VII.690. None of these support the interpretation of *medicus ordinarius* as *medicus, qui in ordine meret,* that is, a common soldier. Further, *C.I.L.* VII.1144: *D.M. C.Acilio Basso medic(o) duplic(ario) collegae eius* does'not seem to me an example of a *collegium medicorum,* but rather that the other *duplicarii* in the corps set up the monument to their colleague, who was also *medicus.* Marquardt, *Röm. Staats.* II, p. 556, cites six cases of *medici duplicarii.* Some of these may be simple designations of double pay, but in the later centuries it was probably the subordinate officer. When a non-soldier was employed as *medicus,* he ranked with the *immunes,* but a soldier or subordinate officer serving as *medicus* retained his military rank. The *medicus ordinarius* was probably the commander of a unit (*ordo*), and may even have had centurion rank. *Medicus ordinatus* does not seem to occur. *Magister militum ordinarius,* reported by Dittmann, is doubtless also an honorable title.

From all this array of evidence it is clear that *ord.* [*dec*]′ *ex* is a possible reading in line 24 of our document, even though that combination is not found in the *Thesaurus* material (Dittmann). We cannot say whether *ord.* should be expanded *ordinarius* or *ordinatus,* for in the case of the centurions, those of the same rank appear designated by either title. It may be that the words were entirely equivalent, and, if not, the difference could hardly lie in the rank of the officer designated.

The dates of the inscriptions do not seem to bear out Domaszewski's idea (p. 97) that *ordinati* and *ordinarii* began as designations for centurions in the *numeri* and later spread to the legions. Also he would make them regular centurions, that is, all those actually commanding a century, rather than equivalent to *primi ordines,* as has been assumed above. In the Byzantine period it may have been a general term for officer, though *Pap.*

Müench. 470, ὀρδινάριοι καὶ οἱ λοιποὶ πρίορες can hardly be considered adequate proof.

Ordinarius seems the more natural term as a designation of rank, so that if there is a difference of meaning between the two words, the variation should be sought in *ordinatus*. With this one is inclined to compare *adlectus, deputatus, revocatus, promotus,* etc., all retaining their participial meaning. If something of this remained in *ordinatus,* it may refer to the rapidity of promotion or to skipping the lower grades of the rank designated; cf. *C.I.L.* VI.3603 discussed above.

As applied to *decurio* in this document *ord.* must be considered a technical term, for it follows *factus,* where stands a title in each of the other descriptions. Both in the cohorts and *alae* there was a *decurio princeps,* who led the cavalry division in case of separation from the higher officers, and he may have had certain administrative duties. This is probably the officer meant by *ord. dec(urio)* and I prefer the expansion *ord(inarius) dec(urio).* *Ord(inatus) dec(urio)* might mean that he was promoted directly from *duplicarius* to *decurio princeps.*

The abbreviation in line 19 was read *ordd. = ordines* by Professor Hunt and *ordd. = ordinati* or *ordinarii* by Professor Wilcken. I have no question that the reading of the letters is correct, though I had not thought of reading the first one *o.* The expansion of the abbreviation is not so easily settled. I feel sure that it contains a characterization of the list of subordinate officers that follows. At the beginning of the document there was probably a similar or the same abbreviation, characterizing the list of five decurions in that cohort.

If we take Hunt's interpretation, *ordines,* it would seem to mean "officers" or "ranks of officers." That would hardly be in point, as there is but one rank given, the decurion. Of course it might be a stock phrase that headed every list of officers, regardless of rank, but we can hardly assume that on the basis of a single example.

Professor Wilcken's expansion, *ordinati* or *ordinarii,* takes us back to the discussion just ended. If we are right in reading and expanding line 24 *ord(inarius) dec(urio)*, it does not seem probable that all the list could be called *ordinarii* or *ordinati*, and thereafter one and only one be specially so characterized. If I have interpreted *ordinarii* and *ordinati* correctly, then not all the decurions could be given either title. The complete evidence gathered for the *Thesaurus* may give different and more exact interpretations, but until that occurs I cannot think that either *ordinati* or *ordinarii* satisfies the conditions of this document.

The statement most nearly certain regarding the document as a whole is that it contains a list of the decurions in two cohorts. As the abbreviation seems to describe the following officers, it should have a meaning consistent with their rank. Further careful examination of the abbreviation reveals two points not as yet considered. First, the letters OR are close together, while DD are less close together and are farther removed from OR. Secondly, there is an abbreviation stroke over $\overline{OR}$, but none over DD. Professor Wilcken thought that the mark over OR was only the bottom curve of C of COH. above, but the curve of that C extended with a pair of compasses strikes about three millimeters above the abbreviation mark and exactly where slight traces of the lower end of the C are seen. The C was made as in Victorinus of line 3 and not as in Eteocrates of line 23.

I have accordingly assumed that this is really an abbreviation mark over $\overline{OR}$ and that, as DD is slightly removed, the failure of the mark to extend over DD was not accidental. This is tantamount to saying that two words were abbreviated. If this be admitted, then DD must mean *decurionum,* as all the officers listed held that rank. $\overline{OR}$ would then stand for *or(do)*, and the unusual abbreviation would explain why the abbreviation stroke was used. We have, however, no other evidence on the use of these words as a military designation, though *ordo decurionum* is a commonplace in civic affairs. Yet this expression is exactly what is needed to characterize the list of officers in this document. It obviates the only fault that I found with Hunt's expansion, and adds a definite description of the rank, which accords with the title given to all of the officers named. Professor Wilcken's expansion must stand or fall with the interpretation of *ordinarii* and *ordinati,* and so must again be considered, when that question is finally settled.

In spite of the doubts and difficulties that surround this little document, it gives positive evidence on several points:

1. The decurions in the auxiliary cohorts were appointed in Egypt by the prefect of Egypt. We know that higher officers had their appointment from the Emperor. Domaszewski, p. 82, assigns the appointment of the centurions to the Emperor, and on p. 5 states that the subordinate officers in charge of military units were named by the legate, prefect, or tribune. The only evidence cited is *C.I.L.* VI.33038[a], which is by no means clear because of the fragmentary condition of the inscription. Therefore the definite evidence that five promotions to the decurionship in auxiliary cohorts were made by the prefect of Egypt is a welcome addition to our knowledge. Probably decurions in other corps were named by the same official.

2. In the case of decurions of an auxiliary cohort three were promoted from subordinate offices in *alae* and one after being *quaestionarius* in a legion. Accordingly it seems necessary to revise Domaszewski's statement, p. 57, that centurions and decurions of the auxiliary forces were regularly advanced from lower offices in the same troops. They seem here to have been drawn as freely from other corps as legionary centurions were from other legions. The promotion of a *quaestionarius legionis* to *decurio cohortis* was doubtless exceptional.

3. There is information on the length of service, which preceded the decurionship. It varies from four up to twenty-five years. There is doubtless more evidence on this question in the inscriptions and it would be interesting to have it collected.

4. The *duplicarius* and *sesquiplicarius* are definite subordinate officers and promotion to decurion is made as naturally

from one as from the other. They may have been of the same or similar rank but with different pay, determined by some other circumstance. Domaszewski, p. 53, refers to them as colleagues.

5. The Third Ituraean Cohort was a mixed cavalry and foot cohort, though it did not add the designation *equitata* to the name. Decurions were not known from it previously, but a century is recorded in two inscriptions, Cagnat-Jouguet, 1339–1340. Our document once contained the complete list of the decurions for the cohort, but only two are preserved. As the sheet of papyrus is now 22 cm. long, it is not likely that much has been lost from the end. One or two more names may have stood there, but the cohort was almost certainly one of five hundred men. The other cohort of our document was a *cohors miliaria,* which according to Pauly-Wissowa, s.v., normally had six decurions. Here but five are given. We are probably justified in assuming one vacancy, but hardly in assuming three. Bell, *Racc. Lumbroso,* p. 268, shows four decurions in a *cohors quingenaria;* cf. also *B.G.U.* 696. From this, eight decurions are inferred for a *cohors miliaria,* which would imply three vacancies here. The evidence of this document is not definite, but I think it can be counted against the assumption that every *cohors miliaria* had eight decurions.

6. The *ala Gallica Gordiana,* mentioned in line 13, has been identified above with the *ala Antoniniana Gallica,* cited from a document of 216–217 A.D. Lesquier, *L'Arm. Rom. d'Ég.,* pp. 77–78 decides with some hesitation, that the latter is identical with the *ala veterana Gallica,* known from 130 A.D. on. *Notit. Dignit. Or.* 28, 28 (Seeck) gives the name *ala vet. Gallorum.* We now see that this identification was correct and that the *ala* again accommodated its name to the reigning Emperor in 242 A.D. From 218 to 238 the name remains doubtful. As pointed out above the few *alae* and cohorts, which adopt imperial designations, seem to change with successive Emperors. This was obligatory in the case of a *damnatio memoriae,* and perhaps considered advisable in any case. Therefore it is likely that the

ala veterana Gallica had a succession of imperial names after 211 A.D., but it eventually recovered its original name.

It is not certain for what purpose this document was written, nor is the exact date determinable, though it must have been soon after 242 A.D. It seems, however, a record of the existing condition of the decurions in two cohorts, and not an order nor a promotion. It was perhaps made out to be sent to some higher official or to be kept at the main camp for use in making further promotions.

AMERICAN ACADEMY IN ROME

AUTHORS' LIVES AS REVEALED IN THEIR WORKS: A CRITICAL RÉSUMÉ

Duane Reed Stuart

"Now the Lord had prepared a great fish to swallow up Jonah. And Jonah was in the belly of the fish three days and three nights." This quotation is not designed to serve as a trumpet blast for initiating polemic. Without ruffling anybody's sensibilities one may remark that good citizens have held and still hold different views as to the credibility of the Scriptural assertion. There will be the type of mind that will insist upon the literal truth of the statement because it is contained in Holy Writ. Into another category will fall many excellent persons on whose credulity unmodified acceptance of the story will put some strain. This class of intellects will entertain an uneasy feeling that the tradition does not square with the normal possibilities of zoölogy and natural law. They hope always to hear of or seem to remember that they have heard of some specimen of marine fauna endowed with a guttural capacity adequate for swallowing a man of average girth.

The out-and-out skeptic is easy to classify, difficult to argue with. He and the literal believer have at least a point in common, annoying though the suggestion may be to each of these extremists, that is, downrightness of attitude. Such persons are blunt in either negation or affirmation and leave no room for debate. Dogmatism encourages neither discursiveness nor the critical imagination.

For a display of these two qualities we shall do better to look to the modified skeptic who invokes the subtleties of allegorical interpretation to extricate himself from a tight place. Both resourcefulness and prolixity have marked the progress of the allegorists since the epoch at which Greek thinkers began to

285

rehabilitate the lewd gods and shrewish goddesses of Homer by reading symbolical intent into the stories told about these deities. Resort to this method of criticism can be traced back to the work of Theagenes in the sixth century B.C., perhaps, as a British scholar has recently contended,[1] to an earlier exponent, Pherecydes of Syros. Through the pagan and on into the Christian world the ingenious possibilities of the method continued to appeal. The poet Ennius, following the lead of the Greeks, especially of Euhemerus of Messana, thus glozed over the fantastic elements of Graeco-Roman mythology. Philo Judaeus so interpreted the Scriptures.

Allegorical exegesis, welcomed as a compromise by minds prejudiced in favor of the sacrosanctity of a body of religious tradition but offended by unworthy elements in the content of this tradition, earned, because of its applicability to the fields of ethics and religion, extension to the realm of literary criticism. Here the original purgative impulse gave way to the belief that some great creative personality in literature had hidden in writings innocuous in content occult truth for the initiated to discover. Interpreters of the Homeric poems approached them in this spirit as well as with the rehabilitative aim. A history of the allegorical exegesis of Virgil's *Eclogues* and his *Aeneid* would extend from antiquity down to the present time.

Appearances to the contrary notwithstanding, Jonah has for the purposes of illustration not yet definitely been left astern. An interpreter, while denying the supernatural elements in the story, may still contend that underlying it there must have been some foundation in fact. By critical analysis he will strive to reconstruct this assumed groundwork of historicity. Of course, the most facile method is to select from the tradition only those features that can stand the test of standards of normal plausibility. The process of rationalization will consider existing

[1] J. Tate, "The Beginnings of Greek Allegory," in *Class. Rev.*, XLI (1927), 214.

variants of the story, will weigh matters of chronology and the like. If archaeology helps, its aid will be invoked. The present writer is not aware that archaeology can throw any light on the Book of Jonah. On the other hand, Noah and the Ark come nearer to landing on an Ararat of fact when a competent explorer reports the discovery of eight feet of silt at a prehistoric level in the valley of the Euphrates.

The rationalizing approach exerts an obvious appeal to the modern scientific spirit. Naturally, therefore, when critical sophistication came to the fore in classical scholarship, this was the principle that began to preside over the efforts of investigators to reconstruct the lives of the worthies of Greece and Rome. As everybody knows, the literary monuments of pagan antiquity often attach to the careers of men celebrated in thought, literature, and affairs extraordinary and prodigious events. This matter is not infrequently analogous in kind to that which confronts the student of the Scriptures. However, the chronicler of classical history and personality is not hampered in his search for the truth by any tabu of sacrosanctity connected with his sources of information. Fortunately for his peace of mind and his standing in the church, the achievements of his critical scrutiny depend merely on such conditions as the intellectual enlightenment of the period in which he lives, his own acumen, and the technical apparatus at his disposal.

During the first half of the nineteenth century rationalization was the method approved generally by those who dealt with classical literary biography. In the most fantastic stories handed down concerning ancient men of letters a germ of historicity was supposed to be present. The task of the critic was to isolate this benevolent germ of reality from its noxious fellowship. Furthermore, the life of every subject was studied as a separate phenomenon. The utmost that could be done was to evaluate the variant accounts of any traditional incident in his career and to distinguish the possible from the legendary elements, by subjective judgment if need be.

The modes by which critics once tried to rationalize something of value into the well-known fable of Arion and the Dolphin furnish apposite illustration. This tale is one of the classical analogues of the story of Jonah. In each narrative a sea animal, acting as the god from the machine, rescues from drowning an eminent personage whom constraint of some sort had precipitated into the ocean and transports him to dry land. In the oldest extant account of the legend of Arion (Herod. 1.23–24), the poet, enriched by a professional sojourn in Magna Graecia, meets the adventure on his return voyage from Tarentum to the court of his patron, Periander of Corinth. The rescuing dolphin puts him ashore at Cape Taenarum, whence he proceeds to Corinth and denounces the murderous crew.

Now, old-time scholarship contrived to filter from this legend an essence of biographical reality. According to F. G. Welcker,[2] Arion on an actual voyage had been delivered by a piece of good fortune from a robbers' plot. K. O. Müller[3] also found a historical stimulus to the development of the myth: the colonizers of Tarentum took ship at Taenarum under the divine sanction of Poseidon who had a cult-center there: this event was figuratively signalized on coins of Tarentum which show Taras, son of Poseidon and the eponymous founder of Tarentum, bestriding a dolphin, one of Poseidon's attendant creatures. Thus arose the story of Arion's voyage on a reversed route and his miraculous ride on the dolphin. The dolphin's proverbial devotion to music and perhaps some other circumstance helped to transfer the fable to the poet.

Müller's views are somewhat obscured in his statement of them. However, analysis of his language shows that this critic as well as Welcker accepted the incident of a voyage as an event truly biographical.[4] Indeed, in localizing the voyage as a jour-

[2] *Kleine Schriften,* I, 89 ff., esp. 95 = *Rhein. Mus.,* I (1833), 392 ff., esp. 398.

[3] *Die Dorier*[2], Breslau, 1844, II, 361, n. 4.

[4] Cf. K. Lehrs, "Ueber Wahrheit und Dichtung in der griechischen Litteraturgeschichte," in *Populäre Aufsätze aus dem Alterthum*[2], Leipzig, 1875, 388.

ney from Tarentum to Cape Taenarum Müller's rationalization is more definite geographically than was Welcker's. It was because Arion actually made this voyage that minds attuned to acceptance of the miraculous saw in the figure of Taras riding on a dolphin Arion doing likewise.

Welcker's formula of voyage + robbers' plot + lucky escape does not mark a long step in advance of the typical methods of allegorical interpretation. Even a Byzantine allegorizer, Doxopatres,[5] has left us the not strikingly acute suggestion that the humane dolphin symbolizes an opportune ship. The pseudo-scientific air of Müller's explanation gave it a vogue that was perpetuated in school editions of Herodotus and in handbooks of Greek literature down into the present century. Unfortunately for the cogency of the theory, however, it depends upon the hypothesis that the incident of the rescue occurred on a voyage made by Arion from Tarentum to Taenarum, the course traversed by Taras in the opposite direction. As was pointed out in the learned literature[6] thirty years ago, there are sound reasons for believing that in versions of the story older than that of Herodotus the marvelous rescue was connected with a voyage entirely different, that is, the poet's return from Corinth to his native Lesbos. The coins of Tarentum thus pass out of the picture.

Modern trends of criticism would hold that, in spite of the apparent superiority of Müller's method over Welcker's, their results lay on the same level of error. The flaw in their reasoning is at root the same, namely the assumption that an historical background must necessarily be sought for the stories of this type that enliven ancient history and biography. Karl Lehrs[7] opened a new era in biographical criticism when in the generation following Welcker and Müller he took vigorous exception to the rationalistic principle applied by them in dealing with the story of Arion and the dolphin. The substance of his con-

[5] *Rhet. Gr.*, II, 331, Walz.   [6] Pauly-Wissowa, *R.-E.*, 2, 1.837, 839.
[7] *Op. cit.*

tention urges the folly of positing every datum in such stories as biographical fact that needs only to be stripped of its vestment of the marvelous in order to emerge an authentic incident. After Lehrs' analysis of the story of Arion, not even some perilous voyage undertaken by the poet was left as a crumb of fact. This conclusion will not seem particularly daring to the modern student of literary history; for Lehrs' time it was impressive, even iconoclastic. His brief essay was destined to exert permanent influence on the technique of workers in the field of classical literary biography.

The new mode, abandoning futile search for any historical basis assumed to lie beneath the wonder-stories of literary biography, turned to the quest of the folk ideas, the proclivities of human inventiveness effective in producing the traditions, as well as of the agencies that shaped these legends. The comparative method became, of course, indispensable. The literary historian was instructed to project upon a given instance analogous examples derived from the whole body of ancient biographical narrative. Thus Lehrs sought to put the story of Arion's rescue in its proper surroundings by pointing out that the formative impulse back of it lay, not in some lucky escape from a danger encountered in some actual voyage, but in the folk belief in the sacrosanctity of bards. Poets, it was held, were the darlings of the gods, who guarded their favorites' comings and goings. Especially was this true of lyric poets. This doctrine was efficient in molding such well-known stories as those that relate how the flock of cranes led to the detection and punishment of the murderers of Ibycus and how Simonides was summoned by supernatural visitants from the banquet-hall of the Scopadae before the falling roof crushed the rest of the company.

That such legends may often have had some foundation in an incident real or commonly credited Lehrs[8] was willing to admit. Some utterance by a lyric poet in his works might give

[8] *Op. cit.*, 393.

rise to the story. But he properly insisted that, without other evidence, it is time wasted to try to establish where myth ends and history begins. In this connection we may recall that the Roman Horace was humorously true to the old folk theory when he portrays himself as the stainless minstrel at sight of whom the monstrous wolf turned tail,[9] and again when he sings how one of those patrons of poesy, Faunus or Bacchus,[10] parried the blow of the falling tree. Certainly in this latter instance and, perhaps, in the former Horace was applying to his life the traditional motive.

The study of folk-lore and ancient religion, prosecuted with increasing profit, has since Lehrs' time greatly enriched our knowledge of the workings of creative fancy among ancient and primitive peoples alike. Understanding of the topos of Arion's ride on the dolphin has been extended far beyond Lehrs' evaluation of it as a typical illustration of the belief in the poet's sacrosanctity. Its contacts have been variously multiplied. The story is but one expression of the motive, widely disseminated in the fairy tales of all nations, of the grateful beast that repays with timely aid a human benefactor.[11] Usener[12] collected copious material showing that the dolphin figured as a symbol as well as an incarnation of Apollo, stood in close association with the cult of Dionysus, and in numerous monuments and legends was represented with divine or human riders. These ideas outlasted pagan lore since there are illuminating parallels to be found in the weird fictions of hagiographical imagination. In saints' legends, tales of how holy men, living or dead, were transported to land by a dolphin or often by a pair of dolphins[13] gained a currency comparable with the fame enjoyed by the flying monks of Italy, Joseph of Copertino and the rest, whose reputed feats

---

[9] *Carm.* 1.22.   [10] *Carm.* 2.17.28–29; 3.8.6–8.

[11] A. Marx, *Griechische Märchen von dankbaren Tieren*, Stuttgart, 1889, 5 ff.

[12] H. Usener, "Die Sintfluthsagen," in *Religionsgeschichtliche Untersuchungen*, Bonn, 1899, pt. 3, 139 ff. Cf. E. B. Stebbins, *The Dolphin in the Literature and Art of Greece and Rome*, Menasha, 1929, esp. pp. 66–69.

[13] Usener, *op. cit.*, 143, 168 ff.

furnish entertainment in the spicy pages of Norman Douglas' *Old Calabria.*

It may well be doubted whether antiquity took its Arions any more seriously than the faithful of the seventeenth century from the Pope down took the levitating Joseph. At all events, Arion in becoming an analogue has in the literary history of the present day almost ceased to have a biography. The name, the fact of the poet's existence, and a refinement of the dithyramb at Corinth at the end of the seventh century and the beginning of the sixth are left as historically reliable data. Events of his life and elements of personality resolve themselves, say our most recent exponents of the history of Greek literature, without residuum[14] into conventional legendary motives.

In laying down the principles that he believed should guide reconstruction of the ancient biographical tradition, Lehrs also discussed at length the part played by the animus, real or assumed, of comic poets, partisan orators, rival philosophers, and rhetoricians in producing distorted portraits of great contemporaries, such as Socrates, and of eminent personages of older times, for example, Sappho. Hence it came that scholarship, put on the road to a keener insight into the sources and modes of biographical invention, was brought to the conviction that in numerous instances reports handed down concerning the careers and the personalities of ancient men of letters were based ultimately, not on separate documentary evidence, but solely on inferences derived from perusal of their writings. Nowadays this point of view controls, as does no other hypothesis, reconstruction of the lives of ancient literary men. Lehrs had suggested that utterances of lyric poets in their works might give rise to legends concerning them; nevertheless, the application of this device for getting behind the returns in our extant ancient biographies remained tentative and was for a considerable period limited to study of the lives of Greek poets and

[14] See, e.g., W. Schmid and O. Stählin, *Gesch. der griech. Lit.,* Munich, 1929, I. pp. 406–407.

prose writers composed by the Peripatetic biographers and the learned Alexandrian critics and grammarians.

In the year 1895, a generation after the appearance of Lehrs' paper, Friedrich Leo[15] gave the new method a wider scope than had been assigned to it by those occasional exponents who had utilized it in their study of the Greek side of ancient literary biography. The novel feature of this scholar's contribution to biographical criticism was his assertion that Roman literary biographers took over the practices of their Greek predecessors, consequently that a principle that had proved fruitful in distinguishing fact from fiction in the personal histories of Greek authors should be invoked also by students of Roman literary biography. All the resources of profound scholarship and critical acuteness were brought into play by Leo with the aim of showing that certain items in the ancient lives of Plautus and Terence which, in spite of their suspicious picturesqueness, had never been seriously questioned, were in reality quite apocryphal, being simply deductions from matter found in the comedies of the two dramatists and transferred by ancient critics to the lives of the men who penned the lines in question.

In outline Leo's findings run as follows: our meager knowledge of the life of Plautus, the man, derives from the biographical and critical studies of the learned Varro, no literary charlatan, as we know, but a scholar capable of applying sound standards to one of the tasks that his work necessitated, namely, the separation of the genuine comedies from a mass of unauthentic productions attributed to the playwright. For certain matters of biographical character Varro could depend upon documentary evidence; the official records of the aediles were consulted by him for information concerning the years and the festivals at which plays of Plautus were produced. When other sources failed, the text of the several plays was called into requisition and circumstances connected with the life of the dramatist were deduced from his works. Varro naturally turned to a *modus*

---

[15] *Plautinische Forschungen*[1], Berlin, 1895, chap. 2.

operandi which he inherited from Greek biographers and literary historians, with whose writings he was, of course, acquainted. Leo made this doctrine peculiarly his own and in the pages of his well-known book on the literary forms of Greek and Roman biography,[16] published six years after the appearance of the first edition of *Plautinische Forschungen,* are to be found constant allusions to this feature of ancient biographical practice and frequent application of the method. Despite some caviling against Leo's skeptical handling of certain details contained in the biographical tradition relating to Plautus, the theory has become canonical and has furnished points of attack that no modern biographer of the literary men of Greece and Rome would dream of neglecting. Typical of the attitude at present assumed by critics are utterances like the following: "His [i.e. Heraclides Ponticus'] biography narrates two stories in the manner of the Peripatetic biography that are designed to show that, as is true of his books, Heraclides' life was not free from marvelous events. . . . One cannot say how far in this connection truth and persiflage from the *Dialogues* of Heraclides are combined."[17] And again: "Much that has been set down in the . . . sources concerning the events of the poet's [Hesiod's] life and his connections was fashioned from allusions of a personal nature contained in the Hesiodic works themselves."[18]

On the Latin side the most profitable application of the hypothesis has been made in the criticism of the Suetonian *Life of Virgil.* Virgilian scholars, inspired by Leo's efforts to disentangle reality and allegory in the *First* and the *Ninth Eclogues,*[19] exhibited through several years so lively an interest in the whole biographical tradition of the poet that a considerable literature concerning this subject grew up. It is in no small measure a result of these studies that twentieth-century scholar-

---

[16] *Die griechisch-römische Biographie,* Leipzig, 1901.
[17] Pauly-Wissowa, *R.-E.,* 8, 1.473–474.   [18] *Ibid.,* 1169.
[19] "Vergils erste und neunte Eklogen," in *Herm.,* XXXVIII (1903), 1–18.

ship has been enabled to draw a far more dependable and clearly outlined portrait of the Mantuan than preceding generations ever contrived to produce. Such ancient lives of Roman men of letters as those of Horace, Tibullus, and Juvenal have also received some critical attention. The principles governing the new rationalism always emphasize the suspicious nature of assertions which may rest on exegesis of the works of the writer in question or which range themselves among the conventional topics favored by ancient life-narrative.

It is a rather curious fact that there has been so little disposition on the part of practitioners of the method to meditate upon the intellectual concepts that tended to turn Greek and Roman literary biographers to building their accounts of personalities and careers by deductive study of their subjects' writings. Convinced, it would seem, by the authority of Leo's name and by the attractive character of his reasoning, most modern students of literary history have been quite content to accept his point of view and to interpret biographical tradition in accordance with it without especially considering the why and wherefore of this feature of ancient biographical technique. Leo's sole explanation of its place in the biographical practice of antiquity was the dearth of other sources of information concerning the lives of literary men. This suggestion is sound so far as it goes; living, in the ordinary instance, apart from the stream of political events, the name of the philosopher, the scholar, or the poetic artist would not figure in historical annals. Epitaphs, *didascaliae,* an occasional memorandum in other official records might furnish some facts of outer life but would give no insight into the private life of the man. Such sources would contribute little or nothing toward that portrayal of ethos which, from its beginnings among the Peripatetics, was a prime object of ancient biography.

However, such assertions do not tell the whole story, by any means. The actual restrictive conditions which confronted the ancient biographer of men great in thought or creativity, in his search for pertinent material did not by themselves drive him to deductive use of his subjects' writings. Behind the method there was a formal philosophy, if it may so be dignified, to commend and justify the practice. It is high time that something should be said about this basic idea to which the ancient literary biographer subscribed, naturally enough, as we shall see, because it was a tenet of literary criticism as a whole. In order to make this matter clear in all its bearings, it will be advisable to return to our historical sketch of the progress of criticism and rehearse the well-known controversy carried on by Leo and Friedrich Marx with respect to the historical reliability of the Varronian biography of Plautus.

It will be recalled that one of the high points in Varro's account[20] of Plautus' life is the assertion that the playwright, having fallen into financial straits, contracted to run a hand mill, *molae trusatiles,* in a milling plant and that he added to the income gained from this menial task by writing and selling in his leisure hours three plays. This, argued Leo, is romance pure and simple, the mill-story being a conventional motive transferred from Greek biography where similar fictions are related of Cleanthes,[21] Menedemus, and Asclepiades.[22] Somewhere in the three plays, the *Addictus,* the *Saturio,* and another the name of which had vanished from the tradition, were contexts into which autobiographical allusions could be read; thus the life of Plautus was garnished with the picaresque motive. Manual labor on the farm or at the mill was the typical destiny of him who was down in luck in the social comedy of Greece and Rome. The loss of money in maritime trade which, according to the biography, had originally reduced Plautus to bankruptcy, matches, suggested Leo, the episodes of mercantile adventure and misadventure that figure in the plots of several Plautine comedies. The vicissitudes of the playwright's real life were thus copies of the lives pictured in his stage-world.

[20] Preserved in outline by Gellius 3.3.14.
[21] Diog. Laert. 7.168. [22] Athen. 4.168a.

In his rebuttal of these philological heresies, Marx[23] expressed pained surprise that the learned Varro should be impeached for literary fraud. However, this was an irrelevant accusation to which Leo afterward[24] properly took exception, since he had made Varro the open manipulator of an inherited method, not the conscious perpetrator of deceit. Marx urged that the incidents related of Plautus might well have actually occurred, that the tradition concerning them reverted to testimony contemporary with the dramatist. In planting himself thus on fundamentalist ground, Marx especially stressed the precision with which the Varronian account specifies the type of mill at which the playwright toiled. The hand mill was an archaic machine and *trusatilis* is an archaic word used once by the Elder Cato, younger contemporary of Plautus. *Trusatilis,* therefore, locates the origin of the story in Plautus' time and may well echo the Latinity of some prologue in which the playwright took the audience into his confidence concerning the miseries and the makeshifts of his poverty. So far the gist of the contentions of Marx. Now Leo knew as well as his opponent did that *molae trusatiles* smacked of the age of Plautus. In the first edition of *Plautinische Forschungen*[25] he had already penned the conjecture, repeated in the second edition,[26] that *molae trusatiles* had emerged from some passage in one of the three plays assigned by the biographical tradition to the period of Plautus' manual labor. Allusion to personal experience of Plautus was read into the passage, occurring, be it especially noted, in the action of the play itself, not in an autobiographically couched prologue, as Marx had conjectured.

Just here lies the real point at issue between the two disputants, although neither one seems to have been conscious of the fact. Bandying words about stock anecdotes, linguistic evi-

[23] Fr. Marx, "Die neueren Forschungen über die bürgerliche Stellung und die Lebensschicksale des Dichters Plautus," in *Zeitschr. f. d. öst. Gym.,* XLIX (1898), 385 ff.; see esp. 393–398.
[24] *Griech.-röm. Biogr.,* p. 137, n. 1; *Plaut. Forsch.*[2], p. 74, n. 1.
[25] P. 64.   [26] P. 73.

dence, literary chicanery on Varro's part, and the like was not the sole resource for settling the debate. Especially is it true that Leo was either unfair or obtuse when he essayed to bring about a lull in the polemic by venting the lofty but trite declaration that anyone has a right to his own opinion.[27] Marx and I, he remarks in substance, are at one in admitting that the incidents of Plautus' life were deduced from passages in plays now lost. For me this knowledge destroys the credibility of the tradition; Marx and his adherents deem it enjoined upon them to accept the biographical dependability of these incidents: "Das ist dann seine Sache."[28] But the Marxites chose to accept statements *attributed by them to some prologue* in which the poet would be openly writing about himself in the first person; the Leonians refused to accept statements which they regarded as the products of inference and combination based upon lines put into the mouths of characters *in the action of the play* itself.

Rightly estimated, therefore, the matter cannot be reduced to a simple case of "Katy did" or "Katy didn't." The vital question involved is whether ancient biographical critics were wont to attach a subjective validity so completely to the content of ostensibly objective literature that they would not hesitate to transfer to the life of an epic poet or a dramatist the sayings, doings in general, the atmosphere of the writer's fictional world. This is the postulate of Leo's method that Marx should have tested, since it is obvious that the ancient biographer would utilize material drawn from comic prologue and parabasis, from the choral songs of tragedy, where, as the tragic art developed or, if one will, declined, the dramatist made the chorus the vehicle of self-expression, from the subjective utterance of lyrist, didactic poet, satirist, and elegist. This is a perennial mode of

[27] *Griech.-röm. Biogr., loc. cit.*
[28] In his article entitled "Naevius," in *Bericht. der Abh. d. sächs. Geschft. d. Wiss. zu Leipzig, phil.-hist. Kl.,* LXIII (1911), 39 ff. Marx retorted that Leo's irritable rejoinder had not promoted solution of the problem; see p. 40, n. 1. In this later article Marx, after the manner of his paper on Plautus, defends the authenticity of the ancient tradition concerning the life of Naevius.

biographical reconstruction. On the other hand, Leo, when his illustrations of the deductive process fell short of entire persuasiveness, instead of standing by his guns, *id est,* his examples, would better have sought to strengthen his defences, not by increasing his list of illustrative instances, but by appealing to the ancient point of view with respect to that inveterate problem, to what extent does a literary creation body forth the experience and individuality of the creating intelligence.

The critical attitude of antiquity takes shape most sharply if one studies its doctrines in contrast with modern ways of thinking. Making allowance for occasional vagaries, we may safely maintain that we are sensitive to the distinction between the life lived by a writer in his pages and his nature as a man and a householder. We admit that "the true poem is the poet's mind," and insist that he need not actually experience the life he portrays. A literary creator, we are aware, may be swept by the flux of his imagination into the scenes he pictures, may so merge himself in his characters as to feel identity with them; as, we are told, Flaubert felt that Madame Bovary was really himself, or as Maupassant wrote himself into *Bel Ami.*[29]

By and large consciousness of the integral difference between imaged life and reality is now so axiomatic in our calculations that we read with a smile how in the eighteenth century, Young's biographer, Croft,[30] deemed it sound criticism to point out that the author of *Night Thoughts* was not a gloomy recluse, but that his parish was indebted to his mellow complaisance for those indispensable adjuncts of county gaiety in those times, an assembly and a bowling-green. Neither do we share Boswell's[31] astonishment that Milton, " 'an acrimonious and surly republican, in his domestick relations so severe and arbitrary,' [a man] whose head was so filled with the dismal tenets

[29] J. G. Palache, *Gautier and the Romantics,* New York, 1926, p. 95.

[30] J. Boswell, *Life of Samuel Johnson,* Everyman's Library edition, II, 356–357.

[31] *Ibid.,* 344. The words inclosed in single quotes are Johnson's.

of Calvinism . . . should have written . . . with beauty and even gaiety, . . . imaged delicate raptures of connubial love; nay, seemed to be animated with all the spirit of revelry." "Liberation of inhibited desires," "compensating," and the rest of the Freudian concepts and terminology not having been invented in Boswell's day, he had to content himself with the comment that in the human mind departments of judgment and imagination, perception and temper are sometimes divided with strong partitions, as he says. If this observation is a somewhat hesitant step toward modern doctrines, it marks, as we shall see, an advance over the ancient tenets.

Before we proceed to these ancient theories, it remains to recall one or two other sufficiently obvious trends of present-day biographical reconstruction of literary men. The normal mode in our time is to seek first to establish by recourse to external sources of information, written, verbal, or both, as the case may be, the facts of a subject's personality and career; in the light of the knowledge thus gained his works are levied upon for repercussions of his life and reflections of the vicissitudes encountered by the man and his soul. His writings are thus utilized for corroboration and illumination, not as primary sources of knowledge. Thus it was not until after birth records and family archives had shown that Wordsworth became a father on the Continent without benefit of clergy that Wordsworthians began to find in the poems traces of an emotional intensity appropriate to common clay. Miss Lowell pieces together from objective sources the poignant moments of the unhappy Keats, his grief for his brother, his frustrated love, his struggles with disease, and then proceeds to link his poetry to these respective intervals. Finally, we know that self-revelation of an author in his work inevitably varies with respect to literary form and is affected by his temperament and his individual manner as an artist. A Goethe, a Burns, a Byron will inject more of his life into his writings than will other craftsmen less outspokenly autobiographical.

These distinctions, obvious enough to us, were mostly foreign to the principles of biographical criticism formulated by the Greeks and passed on by them to the Romans. Fundamental in the ancient doctrine was the assumption that the writings of an author were in no transcendental but in a literal sense expressive of his individuality and his personal experience. A certain character was bound to produce a certain type of work and would be incapable of producing any but this type. How deeply rooted in classical literary theory this concept is, many kinds of literature of varying degrees of seriousness attest. We may smile at the Roman elegist when he insists that in order to write elegy one must be actually in love and that *vice versa,* the lover can write only elegy, since the graver forms, epic and tragedy, are for the pens of those whose austerity has never been mitigated by the soft emotion.[32] However, it is a mistake to dismiss such utterances as merely dictated by playful posing. Behind them, it must not be forgotten, was the long-standing belief that a man's writings were his *alter ego,* as it were. That other favorite conceit, scattered throughout Augustan poetry, which represents the poet as acting as he makes his characters act,[33] is a whimsical but logical application of the same notion. Horace was by no means merely jesting when he wrote that Homer's praises of wine prove that Homer himself was "vinosus."[34] At all events the comment is quite in keeping with a point of view that regarded an author's works as furnishing a true negative from which a photograph of his life and character could be developed. This was held to be as true of the epic and dramatic poet as of the lyric and elegiac.

"As are his characters, so is the man."[35] This sardonic comment penned by Aristophanes in one of his several attacks upon

[32] Prop. 1.7; 1.9; Ovid *Amor.* 1.1.
[33] Prop. 2.34.63: qui (Vergilius) nunc Aeneae Troiani suscitat arma may serve to illustrate this common conceit; see also Hor. *Epist.* 1.19.7–8 and Rothstein's note on Prop. 1.9.9 for other instances.
[34] *Epist.* 1.19.6.
[35] Satyrus *Vit. Eur.* 39.ix.25–28, a quotation not otherwise known.

Euripides was destined to be influential in shaping the ancient biographical tradition concerning the tragedian. Elsewhere in a similar vein Aristophanes makes his Agathon say:[36]

> A poet, sir, must needs adapt his ways
> To the high thoughts which animate his soul.
> And when he sings of women, he assumes
> A woman's garb and dons a woman's habits. . . .
> Anacreon, Alcaeus, Ibycus . . .
> When they filtered and diluted song,
> Wore soft Ionian manners and attire.

Again, in the *Frogs*,[37] the same point of view is illustrated when Euripides, twitted by Aeschylus for introducing harlot women on the stage, retorts that Aeschylus did not portray such women because there was no love in his life.

Now, this is not all comic persiflage; the satirist's arrows are more keenly barbed because his assumption that a poet's life is faithfully reflected in the fictional world of the drama rests on postulates accepted by such serious literary theorists as Plato and Aristotle. Both these thinkers held that the nature of the poet's work was directly affected by his temperament and his mode of life. Thus in the *Laws*[38] it is provided that the praises of those who have distinguished themselves by valor shall be sung, not by any chance poet but by a bard who is himself the doer of noble deeds. Here again is the implication that only actual personal experience can equip the poet to do full justice to a given theme. Imagination cannot serve for participation. Aristotle, notwithstanding his partial consciousness of the aesthetic aim of poetry which imparts to the criteria of the *Poetics* so much of the modern spirit, asserted after Plato the close relationship between the character of the poet and the stamp of his work. At its very birth, he says, "poetry diverged in two directions according to the individual character of the writers. The graver spirits (σεμνότεροι) imitated noble

---

[36] Thesmoph. 149 ff. Rogers' translation.
[37] 1043 ff.   [38] 829 C–D.

actions, and the actions of good men. The more trivial sort imitated the action of meaner persons, at first composing satires, as the former did hymns to the gods and the praises of famous men."[39]

Manifestly, it does not fall within the province of this paper to enter upon discussion of the vexed question, on the threshold of which we now find ourselves, the relation of art to morality. Nor need we dwell but incidentally upon the profound influence exerted by the theories of Plato and Aristotle on subsequent literary criticism. It is well known that their tenets were reiterated by Strabo[40] in his famous maxim that none but a good man can be a good poet, a view authoritative in the Renaissance and down to modern times.[41] It is enunciated by Quintilian in his formula *bonus vir, bonus orator.* Throughout all antiquity there was no more eloquent advocate of the principle than the author of the treatise *De Sublimitate* who would have it that "sublimity is the echo of a great soul," the monopoly of the proudest spirits.[42]

It would thus appear that the deductive method of the ancient literary biographer was not the product of intellectual naïveté or utilized merely because of a dearth of external evidence dealing with the career of the literary artist. Its exponents cannot but have been conscious that they were following ratiocinative modes sanctioned in the higher reaches of literary criticism and hence approved generally throughout the Graeco-Roman literary world. Once the admission is made that there is a direct affinity between the character of the literary creator and that of his work, that, as Plato asserts,[43] the right sort of poet will tend to present the deeds of a virtuous man, being himself of that category, and that a poet will represent best and most easily his own experience—οἶς ἂν ἐντραφῇ—[44] it

---

[39] *Poet.* 4.7.1448b. Butcher's translation.   [40] *Geog.* 1.2.5 (Meineke).

[41] J. E. Spingarn, *Literary Criticism in the Renaissance*[5], New York, 1925, 53–54.

[42] 9.2.   [43] *Res Publ.* 396 C.   [44] *Tim.* 19 D.

follows that individuality and τὰ βεβιωμένα can be justifiably disengaged from an author's works. That which has been involved can be evolved. "Times change and we change in them"; so we may regard as a fantasy of deductive criticism Samuel Butler's celebrated attribution of the *Odyssey* to a fair Sicilian authoress, young, ardent, brilliant, who portrayed her own parents in Alcinous and Arete. It was distinctly otherwise when the author of *De Sublimitate* found in the subject-matter and the literary manner of the *Odyssey* proof that Homer wrote the poem in his old age,[45] or when an ancient biographer of Thucydides,[46] after describing some of the historian's physical characteristics, goes on to say that in other respects his bodily habit conformed to his writing. Measured by the standards of antiquity, these were not vagaries but sound methods of biographical reconstruction. It is only when we set against such a background the Varronian tradition concerning Plautus, or the many other analogous instances forthcoming from ancient literary history that we see them in their proper light. For Varro the principle "As are his characters, so is the man" was undoubtedly as valid as it had been for three centuries in Greek literary criticism before him.

[45] 9.11–15.
[46] See A. Westermann, *Biogr. vitarum script. Gr. min.*, Braunschweig, 1845, p. 193.76 ("Vita Marcellini").

PRINCETON UNIVERSITY

ANICONIC WORSHIP AMONG THE EARLY ROMANS

Lily Ross Taylor

THERE is a persistent tradition that for more than a hundred and seventy years after the founding of the Roman state, the Romans worshiped their gods without images. The earliest source for the tradition is Varro, most fully quoted in the following passage of Augustine's *De Civitate Dei* (4.31): Dicit <Varro> etiam antiquos Romanos plus annos centum et septuaginta deos sine simulacro coluisse. "Quod si adhuc," inquit, "mansisset, castius dii observarentur." Cui sententiae suae testem adhibet inter cetera etiam gentem Iudaeam; nec dubitat eum locum ita concludere, ut dicat qui primi simulacra deorum populis posuerunt, eos civitatibus suis et metum dempsisse et errorem addidisse, prudenter existimans deos facile posse in simulacrorum stoliditate contemni . . . cum solos dicit animadvertisse quid esset deus qui eum crederent animam mundum gubernantem, castiusque existimat sine simulacris observari religionem, quis non videat quantum propinquaverit veritati?

Varro's point of view as we see it in this passage and in two others also quoted by Augustine[1] is that the absence of images made the worship of the gods purer among the early Romans than it later was when the gods were regularly represented in human form. In the fragmentary passages preserved Varro does not tell how the absence of images was secured, but from the parallel which he draws with the Hebrews we may surmise that he assumes that the Romans like the Hebrews were forbidden to make likenesses of their gods. Other writers are more explicit in recording a prohibition against images. They attribute it to the second king of Rome, the great religious re-

[1] Varro ap. Aug. *C.D.* 4.9; 7.5.

former Numa. The prohibition is first found in Plutarch's *Life of Numa:* "Numa forbade the Romans to revere an image of God which had the form of man or beast. Nor was there among them at this early time any painted or graven likeness of Deity, but, while for the first hundred and seventy years they were continually building temples (ναούς) and establishing sacred shrines, they made no statues in bodily form for them, convinced that it was impious to liken higher things to lower, and that it was impossible to apprehend Deity except by the intellect."[2] Plutarch goes on to associate the prohibition of images with the legend that Numa was the friend of Pythagoras, and notes that Pythagoras too held that God could only be apprehended by the intellect. Clement of Alexandria suggests that the king was familiar with the law of Moses and took the regulation from him.[3]

Although most students of Roman religion have been inclined to adopt a sceptical attitude toward ancient statements about Roman religious origins,[4] there has been general agreement that Varro and his successors are right in their declaration that the Romans originally had no images of the gods. Even the approximate period of time—one hundred and seventy years— from Varro's date for the founding of Rome to the beginning of

[2] Plutarch *Numa* 8.8. The passage is quoted from Perrin's Translation, Loeb text. It is perhaps Plutarch that Cyrillus is quoting when he makes Dionysius of Halicarnassus responsible for a statement of Numa's prohibition of images. No such statement is found in Dionysius's account of Numa. See Cyrillus, *contra Jul.*, p. 193 (E. Spanh.): γέγραφε τοίνυν περὶ αὐτοῦ Διονύσιος ὁ Ἁλικαρνασεὺς . . . ὅτι τεμένη μὲν καὶ ναοὺς ἱδρύσατο, βρέτας δὲ ἦν ἐν αὐτοῖς οὐδέν.

[3] *Strom.* 1.15.17, p. 358 Potter. The phrasing of the prohibition is so close to Plutarch's as to suggest a common source. It is also quoted from Clement by Eusebius, *Praep. Evan.* 410c.

[4] See for instance Wissowa, *R.K.*, pp. 23 ff. and Warde Fowler, *Religious Experience of the Roman People*, p. 14, where in praising Wissowa's work he says: "He declined to accept as evidence what in nine cases out of ten is no true evidence at all—the statements of ancient authors influenced by Greek ideas and Greek fancy." In opposition to these scholars whom most students of Roman religion have followed, Sir James Frazer has gone far in accepting ancient testimony. See his most recent statement on the subject, *The Fasti of Ovid*, vol. III, p. 125.

the use of images corresponds with certain traditions in the history of Roman temples. The earliest temples with which cult images can be associated are the Capitolium and the temple of Diana on the Aventine, the former begun under the first Tarquin and completed under the second, the latter established by Servius Tullius in the intervening reign. Both shrines with their cult images are associated with the Etruscan kings who, through their contacts with Etruria and the Greek world, brought a new wealth to Rome and a new splendor to its institutions. A hundred and seventy years reckoned according to Varro's chronology from the founding of Rome brings us into the reign of Tarquinius Priscus, and it was to him that tradition assigned the beginning of the Capitolium and that Varro attributed the summoning of Vulca from Veii to make the cult statue of Jupiter.[5] From that time the representation of gods in the form of men had official sanction, though the terracotta statue of Jupiter could not have been dedicated until after the image of Diana had been set up in the temple built by Servius Tullius on the Aventine.

In explaining the absence of images in early cult scholars have not been disposed to accept the tradition that likenesses of the gods were forbidden. A prohibition of images is only understandable if idolatry had actually sprung up and had had to be suppressed, and that possibility is not in accord with the accepted theory of Roman religious development. The prevailing view is that in the period before the Etruscan kings the Romans with their early animistic conceptions of the gods had not yet progressed to the anthropomorphic idea of divine beings, and that they did not conceive of their gods in the form of men until

[5] Quoted by Pliny N.H. 35.157. Vulcam Veiis accitum cui locaret Tarquinius Priscus Iovis effigiem in Capitolio dicandam. According to Varro's chronology Tarquinius Priscus died in the 174th year of the city. See Mommsen, Röm. Chron., p. 134. Varro's report of the summoning of Vulca indicates that his statement of the lack of images in early shrines was made after careful investigation. See the valuable discussion of early statues at Rome in Detlefsen, De Arte Antiquissima Romanorum, I, 3 f. Compare also Valentin Müller, s.v. "Kultbild," in Pauly-Wissowa, Supplement V, 506 ff.

outside influences led to the introduction of Greek and Etruscan images. A statement like Tertullian's (*Apol.* 25) seems to support such an interpretation: Nam etsi a Numa concepta est curiositas superstitiosa, nondum tamen aut simulacris aut templis res divina apud Romanos constabat. Frugi religio et pauperes ritus et nulla Capitolia certantia ad caelum, sed temeraria de caespite altaria et vasa adhuc Samia et nidor ex illis et deus ipse nusquam. Nondum enim tunc ingenia Graecorum atque Tuscorum fingendis simulacris urbem inundaverunt.

But the tradition that there was a prohibition of images deserves more consideration than it has had. As a matter of fact aniconic worship is characteristic not only of certain very primitive religions. It also belongs to some highly developed systems[6] which are under a strong priestly control. In these religions, the character of the people, perhaps also their lack of artistic impulse, may have been responsible originally for the lack of images. Later, when contacts with other peoples brought knowledge of their idols, imageless worship was often abandoned; sometimes it was maintained by a prohibition of the priests who were determined to keep the conception of the god undefiled by contamination with human frailties. The most familiar case of such a prohibition is that of the Hebrews who, when they were tempted to idolatry, were restrained by sacred law from making "any graven image or any likeness of anything that is in heaven above or that is in the earth beneath or that is in the water under the earth." Another example is provided by the Persians whose early habit of worshiping their gods without images was maintained by the commands of the magi.[7] Both among the Jews and among the Parsees, the modern exponents of Persian Zoroastrianism, the prohibition still holds.

[6] See Lehmann in *Lehrbuch der Religionsgeschichte*[4], 1, 1925, p. 89; compare the articles on "Religion" and "Kultus," in the *Reallexikon der Vorgeschichte*. For full treatment see the various articles on "Images" and "Idols" in Hastings, *Dictionary of Religion and Ethics*.

[7] Herod. 1.131; Deinon ap. Clem. Alex. *Protrept.* 5. For the attitude of the magi see Diog. Laert. Proem. to *Vita Phil.* 6.

Throughout the wide extent of the Mohammedan church a similar prohibition has been maintained with extraordinary success. Among other peoples aniconic worship has given way under the influence of a strong tendency toward idolatry usually coming from some outside source. Such was the case in China, among the Shintoists of Japan, among the Vedic Indians, among the Germans, and in the Roman Catholic church. The contests between idolaters and the foes of images are usually shrouded in darkness, but occasionally we can follow the details. Thus although there seem to have been no restrictions on the use of images in early Greek cult, the philosophers had something to say of the meaninglessness of prayer to images. Pythagoras, Heraclitus, and Xenophanes were all quoted by later iconoclasts as supporters for their position;[8] the Pythagoreans who were much like a religious sect—though never an orthodox sect—were said to have been forbidden to have an image of the god even on their signet ring.[9] In the early Christian centuries the contest over images raged fiercely, and pagan writers like Maximus of Tyre were aroused by the attacks of the churchmen to defend the use of images. Images crept into the churches, and the contest was continued. It finally resulted after the excesses of the Byzantine iconoclasts in a compromise which permitted the use of painted icons and of bas-reliefs, but abolished all images sculptured in the round —an adjustment that is still effective today in the Greek Orthodox church. The struggle broke out anew in the West during the Reformation, the opposition to images being carried to great lengths by the Calvinists. Imageless worship, it may be noted, has been successfully maintained only where the ideal of religion has been monotheism. Images crept into the polytheistic systems of the Chinese, Japanese, Indians, and

[8] For a collection of the material see C. Clerc, *Les Theories relatifs au culte des images chez les auteurs grecs du IIme siècle après J.C.*, Paris, 1915; cf. also Geffcken, in *Arch. Rel. Wiss.*, XIX (1916–19), 286 ff.

[9] Diog. Laert. 8, 17; Suidas, s.v. Pythagoras; Julian *Or.* 7, p. 236d.

Teutons; in the Roman Catholic church they gained their strongest hold in the cult not of the Trinity but of the Virgin and the saints. In every case where the prohibition has been successful in keeping idolatry away, there has been a strong priestly control.

Now Roman religion, viewed in relation to the religion of other peoples, is just the sort of worship in which both the original prohibition and its subsequent abandonment are understandable. The early "Italic" peoples of Italy, like other Indo-Europeans, notably the Teutonic and the Iranian groups, seem to have been slow to develop the representation of the human form, and it is probable that they did worship their gods without images. But when they came into contact with other peoples—and their use of bronze and iron is enough to prove the contacts from the earliest period of Rome's history—they must inevitably have come into the knowledge of other men's idols. It is doubtful whether the contacts at first were strong enough to produce much effect, but it is probable that idolatry gradually crept in.

Since it was at variance with native customs, it would naturally have been checked for a time. Rome had in the early period a very strong priestly control which was responsible for giving her an elaborate religious organization and more sacred law, a Greek observer said, than any Greek or barbarian city.[10] Such a religion would naturally be ready to place restrictions and prohibitions on the worshipers. At the same time the polytheistic character of Roman religion, with its hospitality toward gods of other peoples, made it particularly difficult to maintain such a prohibition. When the ruler of Rome, who was the chief priest of the city, was himself an Etruscan immigrant, the restriction would naturally have been abandoned.

The reported prohibition of images is not the only indication of an effort to keep the native religion free from foreign ideas. There is also a tradition that myths which attributed unworthy

[10] Dion. Hal. 2.63.

deeds to the gods were forbidden. This restriction is assigned, curiously enough, to the shadowy Romulus instead of to the religious reformer Numa to whom the prohibition of images is attributed.[11] The regulation is explained as having the same purpose of keeping the worship pure which is assigned to the law against images. If we accept such a prohibition, the lack of an accepted mythology among the Romans cannot be attributed simply to deficiency of imagination; it must be explained in part by the effectiveness of a priestly ordinance which was designed to control what men thought about their gods.

Similarly the vagueness of the early *numina* and the prominence of abstract divinities, so often commented on as characteristic features of Roman religion, may have been maintained by a control of religious ideas such as is familiar in other sects— notably the Jews and the Mohammedans. The curious uncertainty which we find about the gender of a god like Pales and the use in early prayers of formulae like *sive deus sive dea* or *sive mas sive femina* seem to arise not from the naïveté of a people who had not yet reached the point where they thought of their gods as human beings but from a conscious effort to prevent men from attributing sex to the gods. In the same way we see the Persians and the early Christians restrained from assigning sex to God.

With the restrictions on images and myths and the avoidance of the assignment of sex to the gods went a further provision for purity of worship in early Roman times—the insistence on simplicity in all the equipment of cult. Before the Capitolium and the temple of Diana were built, there were of course no temples of the form that was suited to house cult statues. The earlier shrines of the gods were either open to the sky, or, if they were covered, were small structures fitted to hold the simple objects of cult. The shrine of Jupiter Feretrius, attributed to Romulus and described by Livy (1.10) as the earliest Roman

---

[11] Dion. Hal. 2.18–20. The passage is very confused. See the statement in ch. 18 to the effect that Romulus instituted shrines and images of the gods.

templum, measured only fifteen feet in its longest dimension;[12] it was a repository not for a cult image but for the scepter and flint that were used in taking oath on treaties. Numa's shrine of Vesta, which never had a cult statue and could not properly be called a *templum,* was built in the form of the early Italic house to hold the sacred fire. There was great simplicity also in the objects of cult. The vessels used were not of gold and silver but of earthenware or, if metal was used, of bronze. Even iron, as a new material, was forbidden in some cult rites. We can see the early provisions persisting most especially in the rites of the Arval Brethren as they were celebrated in imperial times.

If we accept the tradition of the prohibition of images, we get a new view of the character of early Roman religious organization. The laws belong not to a people still on "the threshold of religion" but rather to those who are tending to abandon some of their ancestral customs and are being pulled back to their old religious forms by a strong directing force. We should expect as leader in such a movement an outstanding law-giver such as the Numa of the legendary kingship. It is noteworthy that in the tradition he comes from the Sabine element in the population, the group which, as archaeological investigation indicates,[13] combined with the Latins to make the population of the city to which the early religious calendar belongs. In the Sabine mountains there were fewer contacts than in the plain below, and the men who came from there down into Latium must have had in them something of the conservative character that has always belonged to the region. Perhaps the laws

[12] Dion. Hal. 2.34. See the discussion of the passage in Platner and Ashby, *A Topographical Dictionary of Ancient Rome,* s.v. "Juppiter Feretrius." The shrine was of course a *templum* in the original sense of the word as a *locus per augurem constitutus.* See Gell. 14.7.7.

[13] See the excellent study of Professor Inez Scott, "Early Roman Traditions in the Light of Archaeology," in *Memoirs of the American Academy in Rome,* VII (1929). For full material on the archaeological evidence for the early peoples of Italy see von Duhn, *Italische Gräberkunde,* and the same author's article "Italien" in the *Reallexikon der Vorgeschichte.*

represent an effort of a Sabine king to maintain in his Sabine subjects and to instill in the Latins something of the *disciplina tetrica ac tristis veterum Sabinorum* which Livy (1.18) describes as the basis of Numa's own training. We can imagine that the prohibition of images was called forth by some unrecorded episode like that of the Golden Calf, for which perhaps the Latins were responsible.

As Rome's contacts grew, the prohibition of images must have been harder to maintain. The Etruscans who came to Rome to live must inevitably have brought with them their own idols and their own worship of them, and doubtless many a private shrine had its images before the first public temple was built to house one. Examples of splendid cult images could be seen by anyone who took the trouble to go as far as the great Etruscan city of Veii, only twelve miles away. Not only were there images in the public shrines there; the city was also the seat of a great school of artists in terracotta who made images for the surrounding peoples. The recent discovery of a terracotta votive group from a shrine at Veii has given us an idea of the finished technique which the Veientine artists mastered.[14] It was from there that an Etruscan, having secured the Roman throne, ordered the cult statue, in disregard of ancient restrictions, for the new temple which he was building: the image probably had about it nothing of the crudity of early attempts to represent the human form. Unlike the *xoanon* that was used as the cult image of Diana on the Aventine, it belonged to a developed art, and it was the first example of the Greek and Etruscan images which, as Tertullian said, flooded the city. Soon it was only ancient shrines like that of Jupiter Feretrius and Numa's sanctuary of Vesta that could still remind men like Varro of the time when "there was a purer worship of the gods."

[14] See G. Q. Giglioli, in *Notizie degli Scavi*, (1919), p. 31. Cf. also *Antike Denkmäler*, III, 1926, Pl. 45 ff., with Giglioli's accompanying discussion.

CLASSICAL STUDIES

It has been my object in this paper to show that there is reason to accept the statements of ancient authors that images of the gods were forbidden in early Roman cult. The prohibition of images was the result of suppression from above. If we accept this tradition, we must alter our conception of the religion of early Rome. We must view the elaborate religious organization of the pre-Etruscan city not as the expression of a people who were as yet too naïve to think of their gods under the form of men, but as a system imposed from above to check tendencies that were already at work at the time when Sabines and Latins united to form a single city. We must go back beyond that time—perhaps to the shadowy period when the "Italic" peoples first came down into the peninsula—to find anything like the naïve state of mind that is usually attributed to the early Romans. The development from aniconic to iconic and anthropomorphic worship was a gradual one, resulting from outside influences, and the prohibition of images, issued in the vain effort to keep the native worship in its ancient form, marked a stage in the development.

BRYN MAWR COLLEGE

EPIGRAPHICA

A. W. Van Buren

I.

FOUR UNPUBLISHED ROMAN INSCRIPTIONS

The following four inscriptions were copied by me four years ago with the kind consent of W. S. Richardson, Esq., in his villa on the Janiculum, at no. 11, Via Giacomo Medici. In the meantime, nos. 2–4 have been returned to the antiquarian, Signor Armando Pacifici, no. 68, Via Foro Romano, from whom they had been provisionally obtained; he too has kindly consented to their publication. *C.I.L.* VI.8068 is also now at Mr. Richardson's villa.

1.

The upper right part of a stele of white marble; h. m. 0.425; w. m. 0.227; th. m. 0.056; border of fascia and cymatium.

> . . . .*Ep* APHRA
> . . . . .*si* BI · ET
> . . . .*con* IVGI · SVAE
> . . . . .IS · BENE
> . . . . .*He* RMEROTI
>   *poster* ISQVE · EÓRVM
>   THR

2.

Stele of white marble; h. m. 0.47; w. m. 0.36; th. m. 0.15; floral acroteria; in tympanum, filleted wreath supported by two Cupids.

315

D . M . S
APONIAE · LOCHIADI
V · A · XXVI
FRVCTVS · FRATER · ET
NICEPHOR · CONIVGI
OPTIMAE · ET
PIISSIMAE

Signor Pacifici had obtained this stone from another Roman dealer, who stated that it was found in Rome. Since ten other stones of the Aponii were discovered about the year 1910 during extensive building operations near the Via Po (*Not. Scav.*, 1910, pp. 426 f.), and another one about 1915 near the corner of the Via Po and the Via Tevere (*Bull. Com.*, XLIII, 1916, p. 310), it is probable that the present stone comes from the same sepulchral monument or monuments.

3.

Stele of white marble; h. m. 0.75; w. m. 0.38; th. m. 0.04; in curved tympanum, rose between flowers; to left, floral acroterium; upper right corner broken. Good letters. Obtained by Signor Pacifici from near the *Velodromo* on the Via Appia Nuova.

D hedera M
FELICI · BENE
MERENTI ATHI
CTVS · FRATER
CVMCONIVGE
SVA · FECIT

In line 5, the preposition is grouped with its noun.

316

4.

Stele of white marble; h. m. 0.75; w. m. 0.40; th. m. 0.08. Obtained by Signor Pacifici from near the *Velodromo* on the Via Appia Nuova.

caput

rosa   in   rosa

corona

D   M

palma   PEDVCAEAE   palma

GRAPTVSAE

FILIAE · DVLCISS

VIX · ANNIS · II

M · VIIID · XV ·

II.

A GREEK *GRAFFITO* AT OSTIA

THE interests of the distinguished scholar in whose honor these pages are published extend to several fields with which the modest epigraphical monument which forms the subject of the present paragraph may claim to have contact.

The *graffiti* from the *Casa di Giove e Ganimede* at Ostia have attracted to a certain degree the attention of scholars ever since their welcome publication by Dr. G. Calza in *Mon. Ant.*, XXVI, 1920, cols. 368–374. It appeared justified several years ago (*Class. Rev.*, XXXVII, 1923, pp. 163 f.) to propose new or modified interpretations of three of those that were expressed in Latin; and while there has been no doubt in my mind for some time as to the manner in which a Greek *graffito* (*Mon. Ant., loc. cit.,* col. 368) should be deciphered, I have only recently had sufficient confidence in its interpretation to warrant appearing in print.

317

CLASSICAL STUDIES

The *graffito* in question is to be found on the northeast wall of the large room marked 9 in *Casa III* on the plan, *Mon. Ant.*, XXVI, 1920, tav. i; it is at a height of m. 1.53 from the floor; it begins at a distance of m. 1.24 from the north corner of the room; the letters measure from m. 0.01 to m. 0.015 in height; and the inscription runs as follows:

Η
ΜΑΤΡѠΝΑΠΕΡΙΨΗ
ΗΑϹΟΥ

The vertical stroke of the first Ρ has been obliterated by a recent vertical scratch.

Transcribed, we must read Ἡ ματρῶνα περίψημά σου and render: "The lady of the house is your scape-goat." The precise circumstances of the situation thus described are not known to us; we lack the elements for a further comprehension of the import of the words, whether serious or ironical; but they indicate that in some way the lady of the house had taken upon herself the burden, material or moral, borne by another, thus relieving him of it as the κάθαρμα of the Athenians and the "scape-goat" of the Hebrews had done for those two communities; an interpretation in an opprobrious or scurrilous sense, though possible, does not appear required.

For us, the interest of the *graffito* lies in the word περίψημα, which is unusual and of picturesque associations. It is not necessary to repeat the discussion in Stephanus, *Thesaurus Graecae Linguae,* edd. Dindorff-Hase, 1831–65, *s.v.* But to the passages there cited may now be added the following: *C.I.G.* 9282, Christian inscription near Smyrna: Ἐγὼ περίψημα πάντων (reminiscent of St. Paul, and having the sense "abomination"); Eusebius *Hist. Eccl.* VII.xxii. 7; *C.I.L.* V.4500 (= *Dessau, I.L.S.* 5725).

These two last passages require further treatment, since Dessau's note 2 appears unacceptable. The PERIPSVMA SV of *C.I.L.* he interprets as Περίψημά σου—a reading which would be identical with that of the inscription at Ostia—and adds: *"Hac acclamatione usos esse Alexandriae salutantes vel discedentes videtur colligi posse ex Euseb."* etc. This statement, however, is not borne out by the text itself of Eusebius, which runs as follows: . . . καὶ τὴν νόσον ἐφ' ἑαυτοὺς ἕλκοντες ἀπὸ τῶν πλησίον, καὶ ἑκόντες ἀναμασσόμενοι τὰς ἀλγηδόνας. καὶ πολλοὶ νοσοκομήσαντες καὶ ῥώσαντες ἑτέρους ἐτελεύτησαν αὐτοί, τὸν ἐκείνων θάνατον εἰς ἑαυτοὺς μεταστησάμενοι, καὶ τὸ δημῶδες ῥῆμα, μόνης ἀεὶ δοκεῖν φιλοφροσύνης ἔχεσθαι, ἔργῳ δὴ τότε πληροῦντες, ἀπιόντες αὐτῶν περίψημα· and which appears to mean: ". . . and taking upon themselves the disease from those nearby, and willingly assuming their woes. And many who had served as nurses and had strengthened others themselves met their end, transferring the death of those others to themselves, and on that occasion in very truth fulfilling the popular saying, 'to seem to cleave to benevolence alone,' departing as their scape-goat."

"The popular saying," τὸ δημῶδες ῥῆμα, therefore, cited by Eusebius, does not consist in the words αὐτῶν περίψημα (a figure foreshadowed by ἀναμασσόμενοι), but in μόνης ἀεὶ δοκεῖν φιλοφροσύνης ἔχεσθαι.

Hence it appears preferable, in interpreting *C.I.L.* V.4500, to follow Haupt and Mommsen in reading *Perips<e>ma su(me)*, in the sense of "Take the towel," i.e. "Dry yourself off," an expression comparable to the *Bene lava* and *Salvu lotu* which precede.

AMERICAN ACADEMY IN ROME

THE AGE OF ROMAN SACRIFICIAL VICTIMS

Horace Wetherill Wright

IT is a well-known fact that Roman pontifical law laid down rules of almost painful exactness concerning the color, sex, and other qualities of the victims offered to each individual deity in the state worship.[1] In order to be chosen for sacrifice, a victim must be what was technically known as *purus,* that is, unblemished,[2] and, according to two eminent German authorities,[3] never yet used in the service of man. The Romans were a thrifty and practical people, however, and it would have been remarkable had they allowed animals to live for many years without making any return in labor for their keep. Moreover, young and tender victims would naturally have been preferred by the priests,[4] for it was these worthies who consumed the flesh of the animal at the banquet which followed the ceremony, the god having received only the *exta,* or inner organs, such as the heart, liver, and lungs. In the earlier period, the period when pontifical law was developing, this sacerdotal preference for tender meat would have been all the greater, due to the fact that the flesh of cattle and sheep was not, until the age of luxury set in, a common article of diet in the home,[5] and the priests were thus procuring an unusual delicacy, which they may be expected to have preferred tender. It is the more remarkable, therefore, that Wissowa in his great handbook on Roman religion, *Religion und Kultus der Römer,* although stating other

---

[1] Wissowa, *Rel. u. Kult. d. Röm.*[2], pp. 412–416; Marquardt, *Röm. Staatsverwalt.*[2], III, pp. 170 ff.; C. Krause, *De Romanorum Hostiis Quaestiones Selectae,* (diss.), Marburg, 1894.

[2] Paul. (Lindsay), p. 13; Varro *Res Rust.* 2.4.16.

[3] Wissowa, *Rel. u. Kult. d. Röm.*[2], p. 416; H. Meyer, article "hostia" in *Paul.-Wiss.,* VIII.

[4] This has been pointed out by Olck in *Paul.-Wiss.,* III, under "bidens."

[5] Cic. *De Nat. Deor.* 2.63.158, 159; Varro *Res Rust.* 2.5.4; Blümner, *Röm. Privataltert.,* p. 173; Daubeny, *Lectures on Rom. Husbandry,* pp. 172–173.

prescriptions of Roman ritual concerning animal sacrifices, is most unsatisfying in his discussion of the age of the victim, merely mentioning the general division into *hostiae maiores* and *lactentes,* and, more particularly, *bos, iuvencus, vitulus, ovis,* and *agnus,*[6] ignoring the word *bidens* and the whole question of whether there was any rule in Roman ritual restricting the age of victims in certain cases to the yearling period, as we find in the case of burnt and sin offerings among the Hebrews.[7] This leads me to believe that Wissowa did not feel sure that there was any such rule, although Olck in his article "bidens" in the Pauly-Wissowa encyclopedia, with which Wissowa must have been acquainted, refers to the rule as an accepted fact. Krause, too, in his dissertation on Roman sacrificial victims, much cited by Wissowa, makes no allusion to the rule in his discussion of the age of victims.[8]

A minute examination, therefore, of the evidence should be of service to our larger knowledge of Roman religion. Owing to the extent of the material involved, however, this study will be confined for the most part to cattle and sheep offered Jupiter and Mars in the state sacrifices.

First of all, Roman sacrificial animals were divided according to age into the two broad classes above mentioned, of *hostiae lactentes,* or sucking victims, and *hostiae maiores,* or those which had been weaned.[9] According to Varro,[10] lambs were weaned when about four months old and pigs when about two, while Columella is our authority[11] that under certain conditions of pasturage, calves were not deprived of the mother's milk until a year after birth. The age when these animals became

---

[6] Pp. 412–416, 2nd edition.

[7] *The Jewish Encyclopedia,* under "sacrifice," X. 617.

[8] He devotes over a page, however, to the word *bidens.* His thesis (see note 1) is still a most useful handbook on the subject of Roman victims, but needs revision in a number of details.

[9] Cic. *De Leg.* 2.29; Wiss., *Rel. u. Kult.*[2], p. 412; *Paul.-Wiss.,* VIII, under "hostia."

[10] *Res Rust.* 2.1.20.

[11] *De Re Rust.* 6.24.4. Varro (*Res Rust.* 2.5.16) says: *cum creverunt.*

puri for sacrifice, as *hostiae lactentes,* is stated by Pliny[12] to have been thirty days after birth for calves, seven for lambs, and five for pigs. In other words, calves, lambs, and pigs were classed as *hostiae lactentes* from thirty, seven, and five days after birth respectively until they reached the ages of one year, four months, and two months, after which they became *hostiae maiores.* There is reason, however, which will be discussed later, to question whether *hostiae lactentes* were offered to the great deities in the worship of the state, for, while Latin literature distinctly mentions this class of victims in *sacra privata,*[13] the expression almost never occurs in reference to the great public sacrifices. It is found twice in Livy,[14] but in accounts of *piacula,* or expiatory offerings, made in the declining days of Roman religion under direction of the *Quindecemviri Sacris Faciundis,* who had charge of the *ritus Graecus* rather than of the *ritus Romanus.* Moreover, these sacrifices, were to a number of divinities, who are not specified or only vaguely so. A third reference to *hostiae lactentes* appears in a *senatus consultum* quoted by Gellius,[15] which reads as follows:

Quod C. Iulius L. filius pontifex nuntiavit in sacrario (in) regia hastas Martias movisse, de ea re ita censuerunt, uti M. Antonius consul hostiis maioribus Iovi et Marti procuraret et ceteris dis, quibus videretur, lactantibus.

Because the pontifex, Caius Julius, son of Lucius, announced that the lances of Mars in the chapel in the Regia had moved, the following vote was taken in the matter: that the consul, Marcus Antonius, should perform expiatory sacrifice to Jupiter and Mars with older victims and to such other deities as seemed best with sucking victims.

Here it should be noted, that, although *hostiae lactentes* are offered in the *sacra publica* under the *ritus Romanus,* they are

---

[12] *Nat. Hist.* 8.51. Varro (*Res Rust.* 2.4.16) says ten days for pigs. The Hebrew custom was closely analogous; cf. *Levit.* 22.27: "When a bullock or a sheep, or a goat, is brought forth, then it shall be seven days under the dam, and from the eighth day and thenceforth it shall be accepted for an offering made by fire unto the Lord."

[13] *Suovetaurilia lactentia* to Mars, Cato *De Agricult.* 141.

[14] 22.1; 37.3.   [15] 4.6.2.

to *ceteris dis quibus videretur,* while the great gods, Jupiter and Mars, are distinctly specified as receiving *hostiae maiores.* This is significant in view of the fact that the records of the great Arval priesthood under the entry for 38 A.D.[16] are likewise definite in specifying the immolation of *hostiae maiores* to Jupiter, Juno, and Minerva at the great Capitoline temple. These *hostiae* were oxen, as is proved by other passages from the same source and by Ovid.[17]

Again under the year 224 the *acta* of the Arval Brethren record the sacrifice of *suovetaurilia maiora,*[18] which according to Wissowa[19] could only have been offered to Mars. This great lustration sacrifice of bull, ram, and hog, can be seen on many sculptured bas-reliefs, and on none of them do the animals appear sufficiently young to be *lactentes.* Numerous references might be given of the sacrifice of *hostiae maiores,*[20] while, as stated before, *hostiae lactentes* are conspicuous by their absence. Varro,[21] to be sure, mentions the sacrifice of an *agna* to Jupiter, but on the basis of two passages of Ovid concerning the victim of the Ides, it is a natural inference that this lamb was over four months old, the age of weaning. In the first of these passages Ovid says:

> Idibus alba Iovi grandior agna cadit;[22]

in the second,

> Idibus in magni castus Iovis aede sacerdos
> Semimaris flammis viscera libat ovis.[23]

---

[16] Henzen, *Acta Fratrum Arvalium,* p. XLIII: (Tau)rus Statilius Corvinus promagister collegii fratrum Arvaliu(m nomine) . . . (in) Capitolio Iovi, Iunoni, Minervae *hostias maiores* III inmola(vit).

[17] *Act. Fr. Arv.* (Henzen), pp. XLII ff.; Ovid *Fast.* 1.79–84; *Ex Pont.* 4.9. 29–32.

[18] *Act. Fr. Arv.* (Henzen), p. CCXIV.

[19] *Rel. u. Kult.*[2], p. 415, n. 1, supporting H. Oldenberg, *De Sacris Fratr. Arval. Quaestiones,* pp. 42 ff.

[20] Liv. 24.10; 28.11; 40.2; 43.13; 30.21.

[21] *De Ling. Lat.* 6.16. Cf. Macrob. *Sat.* 1.15.18, 19 on the sacrifice of an *agna* to Juno. Macrobius may here be quoting Varro.

[22] *Fast.* 1.56.   [23] *Fast.* 1.587-588.

Now generally speaking the poets are unreliable guides in matters of pontifical law, but Ovid would not have gone out of his way to specify *semimas ovis* in the second passage, had he not read *vervex* in his source.[24] His *agna,* therefore, could not have been less than five months old, the age at which we know it to have been customary to castrate lambs,[25] and, so, too old to be a *hostia lactens,* as lambs were weaned at four months. Moreover, Ovid has distinctly said *grandior agna.* To turn from sheep to cattle, I can find in our sources but one mention of the sacrifice of a *vitulus* in the state ritual, and that is to Vulcan.[26] There is no indication that this was a sucking calf. The existing evidence, then, seems to show that *hostiae lactentes* were not offered to Jupiter and Mars in the state ritual. Obviously, however, they could be offered to certain other divinities, as seen from the passage of Gellius and the two passages of Livy above cited.[27]

But it is time to take account of a significant sentence in Pliny. It follows immediately on that already noted regarding the age at which cattle, sheep, and pigs become *puri* for sacrifice.[28] His words are:

Coruncanius ruminales hostias donec bidentes fierent puras negavit.
Coruncanius denied that ruminant victims were clean for sacrifice until they should become *bidentes.*

It will presently be necessary to enter upon a minute examination of the word *bidentes,* but here it should be observed that the quotation contradicts Pliny's own statement in the previous sentence, to the effect that calves and lambs became *puri* at thirty and seven days after birth respectively. There is no disagreement in the matter of pigs. These we know to have

---

[24] H. W. Wright, *The Sacra Idulia in Ovid's Fasti* (doctoral thesis, University of Pennsylvania), 1917, pp. 36, 54.

[25] Varro *Res Rust.* 2.2.18: Castrare oportet agnum non minore(m) quinque mensum.

[26] *C.I.L.* VI. 826: Ut praetor . . . sacrum faciat . . . Volcanalibus . . . vitulo robeo et verre.

[27] Notes 14 and 15.   [28] *Nat. Hist.* 8.51; see note 12.

been *au fait, lactentes* as well as *maiores* in the state ritual.[29] Either the *hostiae lactentes* mentioned by Gellius and Livy were young pigs or Coruncanius' rule did not apply to all deities or admitted of exceptions. If he is correctly reported by Pliny, it seems impossible to avoid giving great weight to his testimony, as this great pontifex maximus was, according to Cicero,[30] highly esteemed for his learning in matters both secular and religious. Any statement of his concerning a matter of pontifical law, if not accepted immediately, requires at least careful investigation. His conflict with Pliny may well be explained on the ground that the one is referring to state ritual and the other to *sacra privata*, in which we know that even Mars received *hostiae lactentes*.[31]

If, then, ruminant victims, i.e., cattle and sheep, were not *puri* for sacrifice until they became *bidentes*, what is meant by

[29] *Porciliae piaculares* in the grove of the Dea Dia in *Act. Fratr. Arv.* (Henzen, pp. CLXXXVII, CXCVI, CCIII). Henzen's comment on these passages (p. 22) is: Porcilias, ut in actis a. 183 213 218 scriptum est, Marinius (p. 306, cf. not. *Tironis*, p. 167 ed. Grut.) docuit esse porcas lactentes, quibus saepe diis sacrificatum esse constat.

[30] *De Orat.* 3.33.134: Haec fuit P. Crassi illius veteris, haec Ti. Coruncanii, haec proavi generi mei, Scipionis prudentissimi hominis, sapientia, qui omnes pontifices maximi fuerunt, ut ad eos de omnibus divinis atque humanis rebus referretur; eidemque in senatu et apud populum . . . et domi et militiae consilium suum fidemque praestabant. *Brut.* 14: Ti. Coruncanium, quod ex pontificum commentariis longe plurimum ingenio valuisse videatur. See article "Coruncanius" in Smith's *Dict. of Biography and Myth.;* also Fowler, *Rel. Exper. of the Rom. People*, pp. 281–282.

[31] Cat. *De Agricult.* 141. In the case of Jupiter, if it be true that pontifical law prescribed the sacrifice to him of castrated animals only, this rule would of itself preclude the possibility of his receiving *porci* or *agni lactentes*, at least in the state ritual, as pigs were weaned at two months old (see note 10) and not castrated before the sixth (Varro *Res Rust.* 2.4.21. Col. 7.9) and lambs were weaned at four months (see note 10) and castrated at five (see note 25). Varro says that young oxen should not be castrated before two years old (*Res Rust.* 2.5.17), but Columella (6.26) and Palladius (6.7) cite Mago as advising the castration of cattle at a very tender age, though Columella asserts that, if the operation is deferred, it is better to wait until the animal is two years old rather than one. In the *Acta Fratrum Arvalium* it is always the castrated animal that is offered to Jupiter, and Macrobius (*Sat.* 3.10) quotes from Ateius Capito's *De Iure Sacrificiorum* the words: Iovi tauro, uerre, ariete immolari non licet. There is, to be sure, evidence on the other side, but to my thinking, it is weak. A reinvestigation of the subject would be timely.

326

the term *bidentes?* It is usually employed in reference to sheep, but there are extant passages, as well as that of Coruncanius, in which it is applied to cattle and even to swine.[32] Much confusion has existed in both ancient and modern times regarding its true significance. The following definition of Hyginus, however, supported in Latin literature by Isidor[33] and two Pseudo-Acron scholia on Horace,[34] has been shown by modern research to be correct:

> Quae bidens est . . . hostia, oportet habeat dentes octo, sed ex his duo ceteris altiores, per quos appareat ex minore aetate in maiorem transcendisse.[35]

A victim which is a bidens ought to have eight teeth, but of these two should be taller than the rest, by which it is evident that the animal has passed from a younger to an older period of life.

Among modern writers who have substantiated this definition are C. Krause in his thesis,[36] J. Henry in *Aeneidea,*[37] Professor Charles Knapp in *The Classical Weekly,* Olck the writer of the article "bidens" in Pauly-Wissowa's *Real-Encyclopädie,* and A. Nehring in an article "Über Bidens Hostia" in Volume CXLVII of the *Jahrbücher für Philologie.*[38] The phenomenon of the teeth is found in ruminants only, the eight teeth mentioned are the incisors, and they are found only in the lower jaw, as ruminants have no incisors in the upper. As the two noticeable incisors, larger than the other six, indicate that the animal has passed from a tender to a more mature age, it is easy to understand how the term *bidens* could have been transferred in general usage to animals of the age at which this phenomenon of the teeth was known to be observable. It is in this looser, secondary sense of an animal of the *bidens* age, that the word is applied to swine, whose dentition differs from that of ruminants. Professor Knapp's discussion of the word in its

---

[32] Gell. 16.6.12; Paul. (Lindsay), p. 31; Pompon. *ap.* Gell. 16.6.7.
[33] *Etym.* 12.1.8–9. [34] *C.* 3.23.14; *De Art. Poet.* 471.
[35] *ap.* Gell. 16.6.15. [36] See notes 1 and 8.
[37] II, 595. [38] 1 Hft., pp. 64–68.

relation to sheep, which appeared in *The Classical Weekly* for January 9, 1928, as part of an article entitled "Scholarship,"[39] is so recent and so good, that I feel apologetic for bringing the subject forward again. He and the late Dr. Henry are correct in all essentials, and for a general understanding of the word as used by the Latin poets, no further discussion would seem to me necessary, but in view of the fact that they have not treated it in its application to cattle, and that a serious discrepancy in detail occurs between their description of the animal and that given by Olck in Pauly-Wissowa, a lengthy and minute examination of the evidence is necessary here, for the question is essential to a really adequate understanding of the age of sacrificial victims.

Olck thus describes the development of teeth in young oxen:[40]

Beim Rinde erscheinen die Milchzangen mit oder bald nach Geburt; im 15–20. Monat werden sie durch sehr breite schaufelförmige dauernde Zangen ersetzt; mit 25–27 Monaten wechseln dann die beiden benachbarten Schneidezähne u.s.w.

The following description is taken from Bailey's *Cyclopedia of American Agriculture,* Volume III:

The ox has eight or four pairs (of incisors) and on the lower jaw only. There are two sets, temporary or milk-teeth, and permanent teeth. The calf is born with the two central pairs of milk-teeth fully up. . . . When the animal reaches the age of about eighteen months, the middle pair of milk-teeth is replaced by permanent ones that are fully twice as broad as the milk-teeth. The interval between the appearance of the succeeding pairs is rather variable, depending on the precocity or early maturity of the individual, and also on the breed and the way in which the animal has been kept. . . . If there is any variation from the above, the animal is likely to be older, rather than younger, than the teeth indicate.

It will be well to bear these last two statements in mind as we turn to the question of sheep.

[39] Vol. XXI, No. 11, Whole No. 568.   [40] *Paul.-Wiss.,* III, 426–427.

The latter mature slightly earlier than cattle. Professor Knapp[41] tells us that he has himself verified all of Dr. Henry's statements by actual examination of the mouths of sheep at various ages. This, I confess, I have not done, but I have consulted a large number of scientific writers on animal husbandry, American, English, and German. To my regret, Italian works on the subject were not available at the time when this investigation was occupying my attention.

Now Dr. Henry, supported by Professor Knapp, makes the general statement that a sheep's first two permanent incisors replace the corresponding milk-teeth at the age of one year, that this condition continues during the whole of the second year, and "when the sheep is two years old complete, two more of the milk teeth drop out, and are replaced by two large permanent teeth, exactly similar to, and one on each side of, the two first." Olck,[42] on the contrary, states that the first pair of permanent incisors appears when the sheep is one to one and a half years old, and that the second pair appears between the ages of one and a half and two years, in other words a difference of six months from the age as given by Henry and Knapp. This discrepancy has driven me to a careful re-reading of Nehring's article,[43] which appeared in 1893, and a search through various volumes published by authorities on animal husbandry. I find that G. Kraff, Professor der Land-u.-Forstwirtschaft an der k. k. technischen Hochschule in Wien,[44] assigns the same age as Olck to the appearance of the first two permanent incisors, namely one to one and a half years. He is astonishingly vague in his assignment of age for the arrival of the second pair, naming one to two years. His average length of time for the appearance of the second, third, and fourth pairs, however, is from one half to three quarters of a year. Nehring carries

[41] See n. 39.   [42] See n. 40.   [43] See n. 38.

[44] *Die Tierzuchtlehre*[7], Berlin, 1900, p. 157. He says that proper feeding brings on the change of teeth earlier, and poor feeding later.

greater conviction for me than any of the other Germans. He says:[45]

Bei den frühreifen, modernen culturrassen des schafes erfolgt der wechsel der betr. zähne meistens bald nach follendung des ersten lebensjahres, bei den spätreifen, primitiven rassen erst mit 1¼—1½ jahren.

He adds that the change of the second pair of incisors generally takes place at an age of from one and a half to two and a quarter years.

With this should be compared the statements of American and English publications. The *Farmer's Cyclopedia* says of American sheep:[46]

At from 12 to 14 months of age lambs pass into the yearling and ewes classes. But it is the degree of maturity the young animal has attained rather than a set, definite age, which determines whether or not it belongs to the lamb class.

Bailey's *Cyclopedia of American Agriculture*[47] says:

The first or middle pair of temporary teeth is replaced by permanent ones when the lamb is thirteen to fifteen months old, and thereafter the succeeding pairs of permanent teeth appear at intervals of a little less than a year.

This corresponds well with the statement of J. Wrightson, Professor of Agriculture, Royal College of Science, London, in the second edition of *Sheep Breeds and Management*,[48] that a sheep "is a two-tooth at fourteen months; a four-tooth at two years old." Compare the following table in Bennet's *Agriculturist's Pocket Book*,[49] quoted in *Sheep, Domestic Breeds and Their Treatment:*[50]

[45] "Über Bidens Hostia," in *Jahrbücher für Philologie*, CXLVII (1893), 1 Hft., note 5 on p. 66.
[46] I, 387.   [47] III, 603.
[48] *Live Stock Handbooks*, ed. J. Sinclair, No. 1, London, 1895, p. 125.
[49] Crosby, Lockwood and Co.
[50] New ed., London, 1896, revised by Sinclair and Archer, p. 105.

Permanent Incisors	Age When Cut
Central	1 year, 3 months
Intermediates	2 years
Lateral	2 years, 9 months
Corner	3 years, 3 months

Henry and Knapp are approximately correct, therefore, only they have given the lower limit of age for the appearance of the first pair of permanent incisors and very nearly the upper limit for the appearance of the second pair.[51] Obviously, however, considerable leeway should be allowed for variation in breeds and in individual sheep. Personally, on the basis of the evidence just presented, my feeling is that nine months must be the average length of time required for the appearance of the second pair of permanent incisors after the first pair has been cut, and the evidence regarding sheep in England and America would place the upper limit of age at which any animal might undergo this change at two years old very little more or less, although Nehring places it at two and a quarter years for some German sheep.[52] A sheep is really, therefore, a *bidens, two-tooth,* or *Zweischaufler* between the ages approximately of thirteen to twenty-two months or fifteen to twenty-four months. Henry and Knapp are approximately right in insisting that sheep actually cease to be *bidentes* as soon as they are two years old and in criticising Servius[53] for deriving *bidens* from *biennis*. It was not unnatural, however, for many of the ancients to look upon *bidentes* as two-year-olds,[54] inasmuch as more slowly maturing sheep today are still *bidentes* as they are ending their second year, and this is the regular rule for cattle. The Pseudo-Acron scholiast, to be sure, makes the statement that the animal is about the age of two when the first pair of permanent incisors are first cut, *nascuntur*,[55] but I would sug-

---

[51] They say one and two years respectively.

[52] *Jahrb. für Phil.*, CXLVII, 1 Hft., p. 66.

[53] *ad Aen.* 4.57.   [54] So Gell. 16.6.12–13.

[55] *C.* 3.23.14: "Bidentes autem proprie dicuntur oves duos annos habentes, sic vocatae ab eminentioribus dentibus, qui circa duos annos nascuntur."

gest that the source of this passage is Servius' comment, *duo eminentiores dentes inter octo qui non nisi circa bimatum apparent*,[56] and that the scholiast has misunderstood Servius' use of *apparent*, which, it seems to me, should be taken in the sense of *are visible* rather than that of *are cut, nascuntur*, for two books further on[57] Servius says:

> Bidentes autem, ut diximus supra, oves sunt circa bimatum, *habentes* duos dentes eminentiores.

Nehring and Olck have understood *apparent* in the same sense as the scholiast, and Nehring[58] has attempted to explain the wide variation which would exist between the development of ancient and modern sheep, if the ancient did not become *bidentes* until they were *biennes* or two years old, by the conjecture that ancient breeds matured more slowly than the modern. This is of itself possible, but it seems unnecessary if we follow another conjecture of Nehring's,[59] namely, that victims were chosen for sacrifice after an *inspection* of their teeth, rather than by any means of keeping track of the precise age of a young sheep from its birth to the day it was led to the altar. Certain Latin passages appear to support Nehring in this, notably that of Servius[60] where, in speaking of the *duo eminentiores dentes inter octo* of a *bidens*, he adds:

> nec in omnibus sed in his quae sunt aptae sacris inveniuntur;

and one from the twelfth book of Isidor's *Etymologiae*:[61]

> Ex his (ovibus) quasdam bidentes vocant, eas quae inter octo dentes duos altiores habent, quas maxime gentiles in sacrificium offerebant.

We know further that the proper officials selected animals for sacrifice after a rigid personal inspection.[62] There is noth-

---

[56] *ad Aen.* 4.57. [57] *ad Aen.* 6.39.
[58] *Jahrb. für Phil.*, CXLVII, 1 Hft., p. 67.
[59] *Jahrb. für Phil.*, CXLVII, 1 Hft., p. 68.
[60] *ad Aen.* 4.57. [61] 12.1.8–9.
[62] Cic. *De Leg. Agr.* 2.34.93: Erant hostiae maiores in foro constitutae, quae

ing in Coruncanius' rule[63] to imply that *bidentes* means a certain age rather than the condition of the teeth, and, as seen above, Hyginus' words merely state that the teeth show the animal to have passed from a tender age to greater maturity.[64]

The word, *bidens,* therefore, must have covered as wide a range, depending on the animal, as the English *yearling* or *two tooth* and the German *Jährling* or *Zweischaufler,* and, while those sheep developing latest might still be *bidentes* on reaching the age of two years, those developing earliest might enter the *bidens* class at twelve or thirteen months. Of such an animal, we at once see how easy it was for Varro[65] or Ovid[66] to use the term *agna* (Ovid says *grandior agna*) where speaking more precisely *bidens* would have been correct, in view of the passage from Bailey[67] above quoted:

The first or middle pair of temporary teeth is replaced by permanent ones when the *lamb* is thirteen to fifteen months old,

and that from *The Farmer's Cyclopedia:*[68]

At from twelve to fourteen months of age lambs pass into the year-

[62] (continued)
ab his praetoribus de tribunali sicut a nobis consulibus de consilii sententia probatae ad praeconem et tibicinem immolabantur. Fest. (Lindsay), p. 202: Optatam hostiam, alii optimam, appellant eam, quam aedilis tribus constitutis hostiis optat, quam immolari velit. The following passage from Pliny *Nat. Hist.* 8.183, illustrates the kind of thing considered in the examination of victims:

Victimarum probatio in vitulo, ut (cauda) articulum suffraginis contingat; breviore non litant.

"In making choice of a calf for a victim, due care is taken that its tail reaches to the pastern joint; if it is shorter than this, the sacrifice is not deemed acceptable to the gods" (Bohn tr.).

This is because calves' tails are very short at birth, but grow rapidly during the first few weeks of life. It will be recalled that Pliny *Nat. Hist.* 8.51 (see n. 12) says that calves were not *puri* for sacrifice until thirty days after birth. I have myself examined a number of calves at the Philadelphia Stock Yards, and found that in those six or seven weeks old the tip of the tail did reach to the pastern joint. It should be remembered that calves of this age would be *hostiae lactentes* and would not be offered Jupiter or Mars in the state sacrifices. Moreover, there is nothing in this passage of Pliny to prove that he is referring to the state sacrifices rather than to *sacra privata.*

[63] See above, p. 325. [64] See above, p. 327. [65] See n. 21.
[66] See n. 22. [67] *Cyclop. of Am. Agric.,* III, 603. [68] I, 387.

ling and ewes classes. But it is the degree of maturity the young animal has attained rather than a set, definite age, which determines whether or not it belongs to the lamb class.

Virgil so employs the word *vitulus* of a two-year-old (i.e. *bidens*) ox:[69]

Tum vitulus bima curvans iam cornua fronte Quaeritur.

But, as pointed out before (p. 325), I have found only one mention of the sacrifice of a *vitulus* not certainly a suckling in bona fide state ritual, and that was to Vulcan.[70]

So far, then, as Jupiter and Mars are concerned in the state sacrifices, we may accept Coruncanius' rule that ruminants were not *puri* for sacrifice until they were *bidentes*.

The above quoted passage from Isidor,[71] however:

Ex his (ovibus) quasdam bidentes vocant . . . quas maxime gentiles in sacrificium offerebant,

as well as that from Servius,[72] where in speaking of the two large, permanent incisors of a *bidens* he adds:

nec in omnibus (ovibus), sed in his quae sunt aptae sacris inveniuntur, nor are they found in all (sheep) but (only) in those which are fit for sacrifice,

might lead to the inference that *bidentes* were *the only* sheep sacrificed, in other words that not only did Coruncanius' rule hold good that a sheep was not fit for the altar *until it was a bidens,* but that it could not be offered *after it had ceased to be a bidens.* Servius, moreover, in the same passage, although supporting the fanciful etymology *bidentes . . . dictae . . . quasi biennes,* may be giving us correct and invaluable information when he continues:

quia neque minores neque *maiores* licebat hostias dare,

[69] *Georg.* 4.299.
[71] *Etym.* 12.1.8–9.
[70] See n. 26.
[72] *ad Aen.* 4.57.

and thus openly asserts that a victim could not lawfully be either younger or older than the *bidens* period of life.

Nehring[73] and Olck[74] appear to accept this statement of Servius, and it has already been suggested that the priests, who banqueted on the flesh after the sacrifice, would have preferred young and tender meat.[75] If the evidence adduced in this article to support Coruncanius be correct, however, they were debarred by pontifical law from selecting victims for Jupiter and Mars *younger* than the *bidens* age. Therefore, it is all the more reasonable to infer that victims offered these two divinities did not *exceed* that age. As a matter of fact, there is evidence that animals destined for the state sacrifices were deliberately fattened for the purpose,[76] and surely it would have impressed the practical Romans as poor business to have prolonged this process over a long period. They may well have understood what is known to the modern Englishman, that "the older a bullock gets, the less will he gain in weight per day as a result of feeding."[77] The tendency in England during the last thirty to thirty-five years has been to bring out beasts ripe for the butcher in a shorter time. The schedule, for example, of the 1905 exhibition of the Smithfield Cattle and Sheep Society assigned the first class for each breed of cattle to steers not exceeding two years old.[78] Likewise the present trend in the American market is toward the consumption of yearling and baby beef.[79] On the basis of extant evidence in the ancient authors, however, I think I can prove the truth of Servius' statement so far as Jupiter and Mars are concerned.

First of all let us examine a Latin name given to young cattle, namely *iuvencus* and *iuvenca*. In official records of sacrifices,

---

[73] *Jahrb. für Phil.*, CXLVII, 1 Hft., pp. 67–68.
[74] *Paul.-Wiss.*, III, 427, under "bidens."
[75] *Ibid.*, and see n. 4.
[76] Varro *Res Rust.* 2.1.20; Horace *C.* 3.23.9–16.
[77] *Encycl. Brit.*[11], I, 408.   [78] *Ibid.*
[79] Whitbeck and Finch, *Economic Geography*[2], ed. McGraw-Hill, New York, 1930, p. 133. *The Trumpeter,* monthly publication of The American Stores Co., Vol. 9, no. 9, p. 15.

such as the *Acta* of the Arval Brethren, one reads only of *boves mares*, male oxen, and *tauri* or bulls, offered Jupiter and Mars respectively,[80] just as in the case of sheep the terms are *verveces* or wethers and *arietes*, rams,[81] instead of *bidentes;* but the word *iuvencus*, like *bidens*, plays an extensive rôle in literature. Virgil constantly uses it, as does Ovid, but one of the most significant passages for our purpose is that from the *Fasti*,[82] where Ovid is describing the oxen sacrificed by the new consuls on their entry into office the first of January:

> Vestibus intactis Tarpeias itur in arces,
> Et populus festo concolor ipse suo est.
> Iamque novi praeeunt fasces, nova purpura fulget,
> Et nova conspicuum pondera sentit ebur.
> Colla rudes operum praebent ferienda iuvenci,
> Quos aluit campis herba Falisca suis.
> Iuppiter arce sua totum cum spectat in orbem,
> Nil nisi Romanum, quod tueatur, habet.

Clearly these animals are offered to Jupiter, doubtless along with *iuvencae* to Juno and Minerva, the two partners in the Capitoline triad.[83]

But a *iuvencus* was a *young* ox. The word is connected etymologically with *iuvenis*.[84] Varro[85] divides cattle into four classes according to age, the second class, i.e., that following *vitulus* and *vitula*, being assigned to *iuvencus* and *iuvenca*. Further, although *bos* is often used as a general term for the ox irrespective of age, he draws a distinction in the following passage between *boves*, oxen broken to the plow, and *iuvenci*, those not yet broken:[86]

Eos cum emimus domitos, stipulamur sic: "illosce boves sanos esse noxisque praestari"; cum emimus indomitos, sic: "illosce iuvencos sanos recte deque pecore sano esse noxisque praestari spondesne?"

[80] *Act. Fr. Arv.* (Henzen), p. CX, and *passim.*
[81] *Act. Fr. Arv.* (Henzen), pp. CLXXXVI and CCXIV.
[82] 1.79–86.
[83] Cf. *Act. Fr. Arv.* (Henzen), p. LXIV, and *passim.*
[84] A. Walde, *Lat. Etym. Wrtb.*[2], p. 400.
[85] *Res Rust.* 2.5.6. [86] *Res Rust.* 2.5.10–11.

Passages of Columella[87] and Pliny[88] strongly support this distinction made by Varro. A *iuvencus*, therefore, was not yet broken to the plow. Columella further says that *iuvenci* should not be broken in before their third year nor after their fifth.[89] This establishes the fifth year as the maximum upper limit of time in which an ox could still be called a *iuvencus*, and it is at once evident that the word is ruled out of court as an exact equivalent in age to *bidens*. Pliny,[90] however, advises the breaking-in of a young ox when three years old, and considers the breaking-in as late if postponed beyond that age. Moreover, the lower limit of time or earliest age at which the term *iuvencus* was applied to young cattle was just after they emerged from the state of being calves. The terms *vitulus* and *iuvencus* are used interchangeably by Columella[91] in discussing castration at the age of two years. The Italians today apply the term *giovenco* to young oxen between the ages of one and a half and two years.[92] This corresponds precisely with the age when the animal can be distinguished by its first two permanent incisors, in other words, when it is a *bidens,* and in my opinion agrees with the use of *iuvencus* in the following lines of Virgil:

> Iuppiter omnipotens, audacibus annue coeptis.
> Ipse tibi ad tua templa feram sollemnia dona,
> Et statuam ante aras aurata fronte iuvencum
> Candentem pariterque caput cum matre ferentem,
> Iam cornu petat et pedibus qui spargat harenam.[93]

Here every detail of the description, except perhaps one, is ritualistically correct: the placing of the victim *before* the altar *at* the temple, rather than *on* the altar *in* the temple;[94] its gilded

---

[87] *De Re Rust.* 6.2: Nam ubi plostro aut aratro iuvencum consuescimus, ex domitis bubus valentissimum eundemque placidissimum cum indomito iungimus.

[88] *Nat. Hist.* 8.45.180.   [89] *De Re Rust.* 6.2.

[90] *Nat. Hist.* 8.45.180.   [91] *De Re Rust.* 6.26.

[92] *Nuova Ciclop. Agric. Ital. a cura di* Alpi e Zecchine.

[93] *Aen.* 9.625–629.

[94] H. W. Wright, *The Sacra Idulia in Ovid's Fasti,* pp. 12–13.

horns,[95] its white color,[96] the fact that it had grown up to its mother in height and so could no longer have been younger than the *bidens* age.[97] If it be true, that only castrated animals were offered to Jupiter,[98] it is possible that our poet errs in the final line, for I take it that scattering the sand with his feet and threatening with his horns, is rather characteristic of the young bull than of the young ox. But inasmuch as Varro[99] and Columella[100] advise the castration of cattle at the age of two years and the latter uses the terms *vitulus* and *iuvencus* interchangeably, I am disposed to believe that Virgil is describing an animal that has reached the age for castration, but not yet passed it. If so, the word *iuvencus* in these lines is used as a precise equivalent to *bidens,* like the Italian *giovenco,* just as *vitulus* is used in the line from the *Georgics* already quoted:

Tum vitulus bima curvans iam cornua fronte.[101]

If, however, *iuvenci* were customarily broken to the plow in their third year[102] and it could be shown that the Roman state ritual *required* sacrificial oxen to be yet unbroken, this would tend to force the age of animals offered to Jupiter down toward the *bidens* or yearling class. Wissowa[103] and Meyer,[104] author of the article, "hostia," in Pauly-Wissowa, make the general assertion that sacrificial victims must not yet have been used in the service of man. The conjecture is reasonable that it would have profaned an animal destined for the god to have first employed it for human purposes. There is also an adjective *iniux* applied to oxen never yet broken to the yoke,[105] and this

---

[95] Wiss., *Rel. u. Kult. d. Röm.*[2], p. 416; *Act. Fr. Arv.* (Henzen), pp. XLII, CXIII–CXIV, and *passim*.

[96] Wiss., *Rel. u. Kult. d. Röm.*[2], p. 413, n. 5.

[97] See Coruncanius' rule and the earlier pages of this article.

[98] See n. 31.   [99] *Res Rust.* 2.5.17.

[100] *De Re Rust.* 6.26.   [101] See n. 69.

[102] See above and n. 90.   [103] *Rel. u. Kult. d. Röm.*[2], p. 416.

[104] *Real-Encycl.,* VIII, 2499.

[105] Goetz, *Corp. Gloss. Lat.,* Scal. V, 602.33: Iniux bos nondum iugo iunctus; *Thesaur. Gloss. Emend.,* V, 629.31: Iniugis bos numquam iunctus. Paul. p. 101 (Lindsay).

is cited by Macrobius[106] as the equivalent of *intactus* and *intacta cervice*, epithets which Virgil[107] bestows on sacrificial *iuvenci* and *iuvencae*. The *iuvenci* offered Jupiter by the new consuls on January 1 in the above quoted passage of Ovid,[108] are *rudes operum*, and in another line of the *Fasti*[109] Ovid is more explicit when he says of the victim:

> quae dederat nulli colla premenda iugo.

The practice of offering oxen not yet broken to the yoke was, doubtless, a very old one in Mediterranean lands, since it appears in Homer[110] and is also found among the Hebrews.[111] Unfortunately, the extant Latin passages do not *prove* that *all* oxen sacrificed to Jupiter *must* be *iniuges*. There are adjectives employed of sheep, however, which exactly correspond to *intactus* and *iniux* in their reference to cattle, and which will be of far more service to us in establishing the age of the animal.

The first of these is *intonsus*, which Virgil employs of a *bidens* offered to Jupiter.[112] This word must here mean *unshorn* in the sense of *never yet shorn*, for we have the analogy of *iniux* in the case of cattle and Virgil so employs *intonsus* of the yet unshaven cheeks[113] of the young Euryalus with the down of youth upon them. Now Columella advises the purchase of sheep unshorn at the age of two years, if I rightly interpret the following passage:[114]

> Eius quadrupedis (ovis) aetas ad progenerandum optima est trima . . . Femina post bimatum maritari debet . . . Igitur . . . mercaberis oves intonsas . . . Maiorem trima dente minacem sterilem repudiabis. Eliges bimam.

This animal's best age for breeding is its three-year-old period. The

---

[106] *Sat.* 3.5.5.
[107] *Aen.* 6.38–39; *Georg.* 4.540.
[108] See n. 82.
[109] 3.375.
[110] *Odys.* 3.382–383; *Il.* 10.292–293.
[111] *The Jewish Encycl.*, article "sacrifice," X. 617; *Numbers* 19.1–3; *Deut.* 21.3–4.
[112] *Aen.* 12.169–170. To Jupiter, at the conclusion of a treaty.
[113] *Aen.* 9.181.
[114] *De Re Rust.* 7.3.

female should be bred after her second year. Therefore you will purchase your sheep unshorn. One older than her three-year-old incisors is in danger of becoming sterile and you will reject her. You will select a two-year-old.

First of all, the word *bimam* in this passage, if correctly used,[115] must mean that the sheep had completed her second year, but it could be employed with the thought in mind that the animal was just crossing the border into the third year.[116] A sheep, therefore, that was *bima* might still have been a *bidens,* though just about to cut its second pair of permanent incisors. This would be all the more true, if Nehring were right in his conjecture that ancient sheep matured more slowly than the modern.[117] We may recall too that he allows an upper limit of two and a quarter years as the age when some German sheep cease to be *bidentes.*[118] Varro, in discussing the purchase of sheep, is less explicit about the age than Columella, and merely says that they should neither be *vetulae* nor *merae agnae,*[119] which I should like to understand as meaning that they should be *bidentes,* but he adds that the animal should be: *corpore amplo, . . . lana multa . . . et molli, villis altis et densis toto corpore,*[120] a description which seems to me to correspond excellently with the type of English wool known as hogget, which, the *Encyclopedia Britannica* says, is fine and tapers into long thin ends. Hogget wool is taken from sheep twelve or fourteen months of age, which have not been shorn before,[121]

---

[115] It will be recalled that many Romans used *bidens* in the secondary sense of two years old (see above and notes 53 and 54). Could it be that *bimus* was also more carelessly employed as an equivalent of *bidens* in its true sense of *yearling?*

[116] Varro *Res Rust.* 2.4.7 (of swine): Quattuor . . . menses est praegnas . . . Neque minores admittendae quam anniculae; melius viginti menses expectare, ut bimae pariant. The noun *bimatus* was applied to the dividing line between the second and third year, e.g. *Lex Sal.* 3.2: Si quis bimum aut anniculum usque ad bimatum furaverit; and Macrob. *Sat.* 2.4.11: pueros, quos in Syria Herodes rex Iudaeorum intra bimatum iussit interfici.

[117] See n. 58.   [118] See n. 52.

[119] *Res Rust.* 2.2.2.   [120] *Res Rust.* 2.2.3.

[121] *Encycl. Brit.*[9], article "Wool," p. 655.

although the usual modern practice is to shear much earlier. These sheep have just become *bidentes*. This brings us back to the above quoted passage of Columella. The sheep whose purchase he advises is *bima* and on the eve of ceasing to be a *bidens,* and it is unshorn. I understand his use of *intonsas* to be in the sense of *never yet shorn*. In the next chapter[122] he says that the wethers of Tarentine sheep were slaughtered when they had completed their second year,[123] and the pelts, because of the beauty of the wool, were sold at a higher price than common fleeces. The analogy of modern hogget wool leads to the inference that these Tarentine wethers had not been shorn before, as the *Encyclopedia Britannica* in discussing hogget wool remarks:[124]

All subsequently cut fleeces . . . possess relatively somewhat less value than the first clip.

To be sure, it would be considered difficult today to keep sheep for two years without relieving them of their first crop of wool, but the Romans would have managed the problem more easily in the case of a breed such as the Tarentine, whose fine, long wool they were accustomed to cover with skins for its protection.[125] And there is always the possibility that Nehring may be right in his conjecture that ancient sheep matured more slowly.[126]

To return to Virgil's line and the sacrifice to Jupiter of an *intonsa bidens,* we find the following explanation of it in the interpolator of Servius:[127]

Nonnulli . . . adserunt . . . poetam . . . intonsam vero bidentem dixisse quam pontifices altilaneam vocant.
Some assert that the poet has in fact called *intonsam bidentem* that which the pontifices term *altilaneam.*

[122] *De Re Rust.* 7.4.
[123] *Cum bimatum expleverint,* in other words were passing out of their *bidens* period.
[124] See n. 121.
[125] Varro *Res Rust.* 2.2.18.
[126] See n. 58.
[127] *ad Aen.* 12.170.

This brings us to the second of the two adjectives applied to sheep which will be useful in determining the age of sacrificial victims, *altilaneus* or *thickwooled*. Its identity with *intonsus* has been accepted by Henzen[128] and Krause.[129] It occurs in the *Acta* of the Arval Brethren for the year 183 A.D., where that document describes sheep offered Jupiter and Mars.[130] Apparently it was the pontifical word rather than *intonsus*. Because it is not attached to the sheep mentioned in the long list of offerings to the lesser deities in the same inscription, Krause[131] believes that these unshorn sheep were a special honor to Jupiter and Mars not accorded the other divinities. However this may be, and I have my doubts, Krause does not appear to consider it necessary that *all* sheep offered these two gods in *all public sacrifices* at all times be *altilanei*.

I venture to believe, however, that the occurrence of the word in this one inscription is sufficient evidence to prove that no sheep could be offered either Jupiter or Mars in the state sacrifices unless it was *altilaneus*. My reason is that the adjective *albus* furnishes a parallel case. In only one entry of the *Acta Fratrum Arvalium,* that for the year 86 A.D.,[132] do we find this adjective among the descriptive epithets of cattle sacrificed to Jupiter, Juno, and Minerva, and even here it occurs part of the time and is part of the time omitted, even in reference to one and the same animal.[133] But I doubt whether anyone would question the widely accepted fact that the Romans *always* offered white victims to Jupiter Optimus Maximus and his two partners in the Capitoline triad.[134]

---

[128] *Act. Fr. Arv.*, p. 144.

[129] *De Rom. Host. Quaest. Sel.*, p. 8.

[130] Henzen, pp. CLXXXVI–CLXXXVII, p. 144.

[131] See n. 129.

[132] Henzen, pp. CXIII–CXIV.

[133] *Ibid.:* Iuno regina, . . . tibi . . . bove femina alba aurata voveo esse futurum. Minerva, quae in verba Iunoni reginae bove femina aurata vovi esse futurum, . . . tibi in eadem verba . . . bove femina alba aurata voveo esse futurum.

[134] Wissowa, *Rel. u. Kult. d. Röm.*², n. 5 on p. 413. Among ancient passages a *locus classicus* is Juvenal 10.65–66.

ROMAN SACRIFICIAL VICTIMS

All sheep offered Jupiter and Mars, therefore, if I am correct, must have been *altilanei,* that is *intonsi,* that is never yet shorn. Hence, if the Romans waited to shear sheep until they were *bimae,* that is two years old and just passing out of their *bidens* period of life,[135] Virgil's words *intonsam bidentem* are no mere vagary of a poet,[136] and we may accept Servius' statement (so far as ruminants offered Jupiter and Mars are concerned) that victims should be neither younger nor older than the *bidens* age.[137]

[135] See above, pp. 339–341.
[136] To be sure, the pig alone seems to have been the regular Roman offering to Jupiter in striking a treaty (Wissowa, *Rel. u. Kult. d. Röm.*², pp. 387–388. Fowler, *The Death of Turnus,* pp. 59–60. Note on *Aen.* 12.170 in Conington's third edition), but that does not destroy the accuracy of Virgil's description of a sacrificial sheep destined for Jupiter.
[137] See pp. 334–335, above.

LEHIGH UNIVERSITY

BIBLIOGRAPHY OF JOHN C. ROLFE

The following abbreviations are used: *A.J.A.*, American Journal of Archaeology; *A.J.P.*, American Journal of Philology; *A.L.L.*, Archiv fur Lateinische Lexicographie und Grammatik; *A.Y.B.*, American Year Book; *B.C.*, Bullettino della Commissione Archeologica di Roma; *C.J.*, Classical Journal; *C.P.*, Classical Philology; *C.R.*, Classical Review; *C.W.*, Classical Weekly; *H.S.C.P.*, Harvard Studies in Classical Philology; *L.C.L.*, Loeb Classical Library; *N.S.*, Notizie degli Scavi di Antichità; *P.A.P.A.*, Proceedings of the American Philological Association; *P.P.N.A.S.*, Proceedings of the Philadelphia Numismatic and Antiquarian Society; *P.A.P.S.*, Proceedings of the American Philosophical Society; *S.P.*, Studies in Philology; *S.R.*, School Review; *T.A.P.A.*, Transactions of the American Philological Association.

1888

Macaulay's Lays of Ancient Rome, edited with notes, pp. 199, New York, Harper and Brothers (With W. J. Rolfe).

1889

The Architectural Inscription Found at Epidaurus in 1885: *A.J.A.*, V, 47 ff. (Abstract).

A New Fragment of the Preamble to Diocletian's Edict *De Pretiis rerum venalium: A.J.A.*, V, 428–439 (With F. B. Tarbell).

Discoveries at Plataea: *A.J.A.*, V, 439–442 (With C. Waldstein and and F. B. Tarbell).

1890

Tests and Topics for Students of Horace, Argus Office, Ann Arbor, Mich. (Privately printed).

The Scientific Knowledge of the Ancient Greeks and Romans: *Pop. Sci. News,* Boston, XXIII and XXIV (Four papers).

Arithmetical Calculations among the Ancient Greeks and Romans: *ibid.,* XXIV.

Discoveries at Anthedon: *A.J.A.*, VI, 96–107.

Discoveries at Thisbe: *ibid.,* pp. 112–120 (With F. B. Tarbell).

An Inscribed Tombstone from Bœotia: *ibid.,* p. 121.

1891

Tests and Topics on the De Senectute of Cicero, Argus Office, Ann Arbor, Mich. (Privately printed).

An Inscribed Kotylos from Bœotia: *H.S.C.P.*, II, 89–101.

CLASSICAL STUDIES

The Essential Uses of the Moods and Tenses in Greek and Latin, set forth in parallel arrangement, pp. 56, Boston, Ginn and Co. (A revision of the pamphlet of R. P. Keep).

Heautontimorumenos of Terence, with stage directions, pp. 61, Boston, Ginn and Co.

The Faith Cure in Ancient Greece: *Pop. Sci. News,* Boston, XXV, 75 ff.

1892

Selections from Viri Romae, pp. xv + 124, Boston, Allyn and Bacon.

Hints to Teachers of Elementary Latin: *Academy,* Boston, March, 1892.

1893

The Tragedy Rhesus: *H.S.C.P.,* LV, 61–97 (Diss. for Ph.D., revised).

Livy, Book I, text with indicated quantities, pp. 76, Boston, Allyn and Bacon.

1894

The Lives of Cornelius Nepos, pp. xvii + 370, Boston, Allyn and Bacon.

1895

The Sources of Our Knowledge of the Pronunciation of Latin: *S.R.,* III, 360–362 (Abstract).

1896

-is in the Perf. Subj. and Fut. Perf. Ind. in Latin: *C.R.,* X, 190 ff.

1897

Die Ellipse von *ars: A.L.L.,* X, 229–246.

A, ab, abs: ibid., pp. 465–505.

An Epoch-Making Lexicon: *Bookman,* New York, XIV, 216–220.

As editor, with Charles E. Bennett: Lindsay's Handbook of Latin Inscriptions, Boston, Allyn and Bacon.

1898

A Junior Latin Book, pp. vi + 492, Boston, Allyn and Bacon (With Walter Dennison).

As editor: Westcott's Selections from Pliny's Letters and Gudeman's Dialogus of Tacitus, Boston, Allyn and Bacon.

BIBLIOGRAPHY

1899

The Construction *sanus ab:* C.R., XIII, 303–305.

As editor: Elmer's Captivi of Plautus and Gudeman's Agricola of Tacitus.

1900

On Horace, Serm. i.4.26 and ii.3.4: *C.R.,* XIV, 126 f.

A or *ab* in Horace, Epod.17.24: *ibid.,* p. 261.

On *a ponte,* Juv.iv.117: *ibid.,* p. 357.

The Formation of Latin Substantives from Geographical Adjectives by Ellipsis: *T.A.P.A.,* XXXI, 5–26.

As editor: Fairclough's Andria of Terence and Gudeman's Agricola and Germania of Tacitus.

1901

Horace, Satires and Epistles, pp. li + 406, Boston, Allyn and Bacon.

The Preposition *ab* in Horace: *H.S.C.P.,* XII, 249–260.

The Wölfflin Jubilee: *Bookman,* New York, XIII, 545 f.

As editor: Bennett's Odes and Epodes of Horace and Granrud's Roman Constitutional History.

1902

The Diction of the Roman Matrons: *C.R.,* XV, 452 f.

Varia: P.A.P.A., XXXIII, 62–64.

The Making and Use of a Latin Lexicon: *S.R.,* X, 375 f. (Abstract).

The Language and Style of Diocletian's Edict *De pretiis rerum venalium: A.J.A.,* VI (New Series), 50 f. (Abstract).

As editor: Fay's Mostellaria of Plautus and Pike's Tiberius, Caligula, Claudius and Nero of Suetonius.

1903

Notes and Afterthoughts: *P.A.P.A.,* XXXIV, 5 f. and 55 f.

Article Vergil: New International Encyclopaedia.

Articles Vergil and Horace: Encyclopedia Americana.

As editor: Platner's Topography and Monuments of Ancient Rome and Westcott's Livy (revised edition).

1904

Some References to Seasickness in the Greek and Roman Writers: *A.J.P.,* XXV, 192–200.

CLASSICAL STUDIES

1905

Extracts from a Teacher's Notebook: *Latin Leaflet*, New York, V, Nos. 112–115.

1906

The Teaching of Latin in Secondary Schools: *ibid.*, pp. 25–37.

Recent Tendencies in Latin Syntax: *S.R.*, XIV, 549–559.

Reports of *A.L.L.: A.J.P.*, XXVII, 90–97, 216–222.

Essential Latin Lessons, pp. xiii + 363, New York, Scribner's (With A. W. Roberts).

1908

Obituary Notice of Edouard v. Wölfflin: *A.J.P.*, XXIX, 503–505.

The Delphin Classics: *Old Penn*, Philadelphia, VII.

Reports of *A.L.L.: A.J.P.*, XXIX, 99–107, 353–359.

As chairman, Comm. on Publication: Supplementary Papers of the American School of Classical Studies in Rome, Vol. II, New York, Macmillan Co.

1909

A Latin Journal: *C.W.*, III, 71.

Two Etruscan Mirrors: *A.J.A.*, XIII, 3–18.

Reports of *A.L.L.: A.J.P.*, XXX, 214–219, 338–344.

As editor: Nutting's Tusculan Disputations of Cicero.

1910

The Mirrors of the Greeks and Etruscans: *P.P.N.A.S.*, XXV, 187–197.

Sicca mors, Juv. x.113: *P.A.P.A.*, XL, 76–78.

Vela cadunt: C.J., VI, 75–77.

Largiter posse, Caes. B.G., i.18.4–6: *ibid.*, pp. 77–78.

Falces praeacutae, Caes. B.G., iii.14.5: *ibid.*, pp. 133–135.

Reports of *A.L.L.: A.J.P.*, XXXI, 96–101, 227–230, 344–352.

Caesar, Gallic War, pp. xcvii + 443, New York, Scribner's (With A. W. Roberts).

1911

Reports of *A.L.L.: A.J.P.*, XXXII, 98–103, 222–227.

Did Liscus Speak Latin? *C.J.*, VII, 126–129.

On Lucan v.424 ff.: *P.A.P.A.*, XLI, 59–65.

BIBLIOGRAPHY

1912

On Vergil, Ecl.vi.34: *C.P.*, VII, 245.

On Horace, Serm.i.4.26: *ibid.*, pp. 246 f.

Teaching and Research in Classical Philology: *P.A.P.A.*, XLII, 41–44 (Abstract).

Research in Classical Philology: *Old Penn*, Philadelphia, XI, 69–75.

Latin Verses: *C.W.*, V, 134.

Origin and History of Dictionaries; Websterian Dictionary, pp. vi–xii, New York, Syndicate Book Co.

1913

Some Temporal Expressions in Suetonius: *C.P.*, VIII, 1–13.

Suetonius and His Biographies: *P.A.P.S.*, LII, 206–225.

Latin Verses: *C.W.*, VI, 87.

1914

Suetonius, *L.C.L.*, Vol. I, pp. xxi + 499; Vol. II, pp. vii + 556, London, Heinemann.

Notes on Suetonius: *P.A.P.A.*, XLIV, 47–50.

1915

On the Meaning of *biduum* in Certain Phrases: *C.P.*, X, 82 f.

Some Sources of Income in Ancient Rome: *Old Penn*, Philadelphia, XIII, 613–621, and Univ. of Penna. Lectures, II, 285–311.

The So-Called *callium provincia: A.J.P.*, XXXV, 323–331.

Notes on Suetonius: *T.A.P.A.*, XIV, 30–42.

Gens and *familia* in Suetonius: *C.P.*, X, 445–449.

The Evolution of English dictionaries; New Universities Dictionary, pp. 971–975, New York, Syndicate Book Co.

The Latin Department's Collection of Antiquities: I. Inscriptions: *Old Penn*, Philadelphia, XIII, 873–877.

Advice to Graduate Students: *Old Penn*, Philadelphia, XIV, 142–144.

1916

The Latin Department's Collection of Antiquities: III. Mirrors: *Old Penn*, XIV, 528–530.

Latin Inscriptions at the University of Pennsylvania: *A.J.A.*, XX, 173 f.

CLASSICAL STUDIES

1917

Cicero, Selected Orations and Letters, pp. lxxiv + 543, New York, Scribner's (With A. W. Roberts).

The "Newest" Education: *Phila. Evening Bulletin,* Feb. 1.

A Reply to Professor Duff: *C.R.,* XXX, 238.

The Aim and Method of a College Teacher of Latin: *Alumni Register,* Univ. of Penna., XIX, 556 ff.

As editor: Pike's Stories from Apuleius.

1918

Brutus and the Ships of the Veneti: *C.W.,* XI, 106 f.

Cicero's Hexameters: *C.J.,* XIII, 668.

A Latin Reader, pp. lii + 809, Boston, Allyn and Bacon (With Walter Dennison).

As editor: Westcott and Rankin's Julius and Augustus of Suetonius.

1919

A Friend of Caesar's: Univ. of Penna. Lectures, VI, 155–187.

The Evolution of Classical Textbooks: *Proc. Penn. State Educ. Assoc.,* pp. 316 ff.

Latin Quotations for the Annual Dinner of the Amer. Philos. Soc. (Printed on the menu).

Claudian: *T.A.P.A.,* L, 135–149.

1920

Latin Verses: *C.W.,* XIII, 216.

Marginalia: S.P., XVII, 402–422.

1921

Sallust, *L.C.L.,* pp. xxii + 535, London, Heinemann.

Latin Verses: *C.W.,* XIV, 128.

1922

Prorsus: T.A.P.A., LI, 30–39.

Prorsus in Gellius: *C.P.,* XVII, 144–146.

Obituary Notice of Charles E. Bennett: *C.P.,* XVII, 279 f.

The Use of Devices To Indicate Vowel Length in Latin: *P.A.P.S.,* LXI, 80–98.

BIBLIOGRAPHY

1923

Cicero and His Influence, pp. 178, New York, Longmans, Green & Co.
On Cicero, *ad. Fam.* vii.10.2: *C.P.*, XVIII, 71.
Reports of *N.S.*: *A.J.A.*, XXVIII, 92–97, 338–341.

1924

Vergil, Aeneid I–VI, pp. 655, New York, Scribner's (With A. W. Roberts).
The *sextariolus*: *C.P.*, XX, 273.
Reports of *N.S.*: *A.J.A.*, XXVIII, 92–97, 338–341.

1925

Ovid, Selections from the Metamorphoses, pp. iii + 116, New York, Scribner's (With A. W. Roberts).
Reports of *N.S.*: *A.J.A.*, XXIX, 337 f. and 346.
As editor: Harrington's Mediaeval Latin.

1926

Latin Literature: *A.Y.B.*, pp. 1012–1015.
Reports of *N.S.*: *A.J.A.*, XXX, 112–114, 218–221.
Reports of *B.C.*: *A.J.A.*, XXX, 219–220.
As editor: *P.A.P.S.*, LXV, 5 suppl.

1927

Gellius, *L.C.L.*, Vol. I, pp. lxiii + 464; Vol. II, pp. xxxvii + 532, London, Heinemann.
Latin Literature: *A.Y.B.*, pp. 1013–1016.
Marks of Quantity in the *Monumentum Antiochenum*: *A.J.P.*, XLVIII, 1–9.
Reports of *N.S.*: *A.J.A.*, XXXI, 108 ff., 369 ff.
Report of *B.C.*: *A.J.A.*, XXXI, 196.

1928

Gellius, *L.C.L.*, Vol. III, pp. xxix + 500, London, Heinemann.
On the Use of *alius* in Jul. Capit., vit. Ant. Pii, v.4: *C.P.*, XXIII, 60–62.
Latin Literature: *A.Y.B.*, pp. 729–731.
A Visit to Hadrian's Wall in Britain: *P.P.N.A.S.*, pp. 87–105.
On Lucilius, 347 Marx: *C.P.*, XXIII, 185.

351

CLASSICAL STUDIES

Reports of *N.S.*: *A.J.A.*, XXXII, 83–87, 366–371.
As editor: Gudeman's Agricola and Germania of Tacitus (revised edition), Boston, Allyn and Bacon.

1929

Cornelius Nepos, *L.C.L.*, pp. 355–743 (bound with Florus), London, Heinemann.
Virum civiliter eruditum, Gell. praef. 13: *C.P.*, XXIV, 89–91.
Latin Literature: *A.Y.B.*, pp. 792–794.

1930

Vergil after Two Thousand Years: *P.A.P.S.*, LXIX, 347–357.
The Latin Department, *Pennsylvania Gazette*, Univ. of Penna., XXIX, 60 ff.
Latin Literature: *A.Y.B.*, pp. 783–785.

Date   Due